Crafting Cooperation

Regional institutions are an increasingly prominent feature of world politics. Their characteristics and performance vary widely: some are highly legalistic and bureaucratic, while others are informal and flexible. They also differ in terms of inclusiveness, decision-making rules, and commitment to the non-interference principle. This is the first book to offer a conceptual framework for comparing the design and effectiveness of regional international institutions, including the EU, NATO, ASEAN, the OAS, the AU and the Arab League. The case studies, by a group of leading scholars of regional institutions, offer a rigorous, historically informed analysis of the differences and similarities in institutions across Europe, Latin America, Asia, the Middle East, and Africa. The chapters provide a more theoretically and empirically diverse analysis of the design and efficacy of regional institutions than heretofore available.

AMITAV ACHARYA is Professor of Global Governance and Director of the Governance Research Centre at the University of Bristol.

ALASTAIR IAIN JOHNSTON is the Laine Professor of China in World Affairs in the Government Department at Harvard University.

Crafting Cooperation

Regional International Institutions in Comparative Perspective

---

Edited by

Amitav Acharya

and

Alastair Iain Johnston

CAMBRIDGE UNIVERSITY PRESS
Cambridge, New York, Melbourne, Madrid, Cape Town, Singapore, São Paulo

Cambridge University Press
The Edinburgh Building, Cambridge CB2 8RU, UK

Published in the United States of America by Cambridge University Press, New York

www.cambridge.org
Information on this title: www.cambridge.org/9780521699426

First published 2007

Printed in the United Kingdom at the University Press, Cambridge

A catalogue record for this publication is available from the British Library

ISBN 978-0-521-87603-2 hardback
ISBN 978-0-521-69942-6 paperback

Contents

Tables

Notes on contributors

Amitav Acharya is Professor of Global Governance and Director of the Governance Research Centre at the University of Bristol. He was Professor of International Relations at the Rajaratnam School of International Studies, Nanyang Technological University, Singapore. Among his publications are *The Quest for Identity: International Relations of Southeast Asia* (2000); *Constructing a Security Community in Southeast Asia* (2001, 2003, 2007) and, as co-editor, *Reassessing Security Cooperation in East Asia* (2007). His articles on Asian security, regionalism (Asian and comparative), multilateralism, international security, and international relations theory have appeared in *International Organization, International Security, Journal of Peace Research, Pacific Affairs, Pacific Review, Third World Quarterly, Asian Survey*, and *Australian Journal of International Affairs*, among others. A past president of the Asian Political and International Studies Association (APISA), he also serves on the editorial boards of *European Journal of International Relations, Pacific Affairs, Pacific Review*, and *Chinese Journal of International Relations.* His current work is about norms, power, and institutional change in Asian regionalism, and the prospects for non-Western international relations theory (with Barry Buzan).

Michael Barnett is the Harold Stassen Professor of International Affairs at the Humphrey Institute and Professor of Political Science at the University of Minnesota. Among his books are *Dialogues in Arab Politics: Negotiations in Regional Order* (1998), and *Eyewitness to a Genocide: The United Nations and Rwanda* (2002). His current work is on humanitarianism and world order.

Jeffrey T. Checkel is Professor of Political Science at the University of Oslo, and Research Associate, Centre for the Study of Civil War, International Peace Research Institute, Oslo. His research and teaching interests are international relations theory, European integration, politics in the former USSR and West Europe, human rights, and civil conflict. He is the author of *Ideas and International Political Change:*

Soviet/Russian Behavior and the End of the Cold War (1997) and, most recently, editor of *International Institutions and Socialization in Europe* (Cambridge University Press, 2007). His current project explores the politics of European identity construction from a variety of disciplinary perspectives.

Jorge I. Domínguez is Antonio Madero Professor of Government, Vice Provost for International Affairs at Harvard University. He is the author or co-author of various books, among them *Between Compliance and Conflict: East Asia, Latin America, and the "New" Pax Americana* (2005); *Mexico's Pivotal Democratic Election: Candidates, Voters, and the Presidential Campaign of 2000* (2004); *The Cuban Economy at the Start of the Twenty-First Century* (2004); *Constructing Democratic Governance in Latin America* (2003); *The United States and Mexico: Between Partnership and Conflict* (2001); *The Future of Inter-American Relations (2000); Democratic Politics in Latin America and the Caribbean* (1998); *International Security and Democracy: Latin America and the Caribbean in the Post-Cold War Era* (1998); *Technopols: Freeing Politics and Markets in Latin America in the 1990s* (1997); *Democratic Transitions in Central America* (1997); *Insurrection or Loyalty: The Breakdown of the Spanish American Empire* (1980); *Cuba: Order and Revolution* (1978), and many articles on domestic and international politics in Latin America and the Caribbean. A past President of the Latin American Studies Association and a past Board Chairman of the Latin American Scholarship Program of American Universities, he currently serves on the Editorial Boards of *Political Science Quarterly*, *Latin American Research Review*, *Foreign Affairs en español*, *Cuban Studies*, and *Foro internacional.* He was Series Editor for the Peabody Award-winning Public Broadcasting System television series, *Crisis in Central America.* His current research focuses on the international relations and domestic politics of Latin American countries. For more information: www.people.fas.harvard.edu/~jidoming.

Jeffrey Herbst is Provost and Executive Vice-President for Academic Affairs at Miami University. His primary research interests are in the politics of sub-Saharan Africa, the politics of political and economic reform, and the politics of boundaries. He is the author of *States and Power in Africa: Comparative Lessons in Authority and Control* (2000) and several other books and articles. He has also taught at the University of Zimbabwe, the University of Ghana, Legon, the University of Cape Town, the University of the Western Cape, and Princeton University. He is a Research Associate of the South African Institute of International Affairs. In 2004–2005, he was a Fellow of the John Simon Guggenheim Memorial Foundation.

Alastair Iain Johnston is the Laine Professor of China in World Affairs in the Government Department at Harvard University. He is the author of *Cultural Realism: Strategic Culture and Grand Strategy in Chinese History* (1995) and *Social States: China in International Institutions, 1980–2000* (2007), and co-editor of *Engaging China: The Management of an Emerging Power* (1999) and *New Directions in the Study of China's Foreign Policy* (2006). He has published articles and book chapters on socialization theory, identity, and strategic culture mostly in reference to East Asian international relations and Chinese foreign policy. He has been a consultant for the Ford Foundation, the Union of Concerned Scientists, and the US government.

Yuen Foong Khong is Professor of International Relations and a Fellow of Nuffield College, Oxford University. He has taught at Harvard University and the Institute of Defense and Strategic Studies, Nanyang Technological University, Singapore, where he also serves as a Senior Research Adviser. His publications include *Analogies at War: Korea, Munich, Dien Bien Phu and the Vietnam Decisions of 1965* (1992), *Unilateralism and U.S. Foreign Policy: International Perspectives* (co-edited with David Malone, 2003), and with Neil MacFarlane, *Human Security and the United Nations: A Critical History* (2006). He is currently working on a book project about the role of identity and power in American foreign policy.

Helen E. S. Nesadurai is Senior Lecturer in the School of Arts and Sciences, Monash University Malaysia. She has held previous appointments as Assistant Professor at the Institute of Defense and Strategic Studies, Nanyang Technological University, Singapore, and as Senior Analyst at the Institute of Strategic and International Studies, Kuala Lumpur, Malaysia. Her research interests center on the link between globalization and regionalism, with a special focus on how this relationship plays out in the broad Asia-Pacific region. She is currently researching the different ways in which elites attempt to build legitimacy for regional economic integration schemes through a case study of ASEAN, while a second project explores the interplay between different forms of economic knowledge in the design of institutions for global/regional governance. She is the author of *Globalisation, Domestic Politics and Regionalism: The ASEAN Free Trade Area* (2003) and the editor of *Globalisation and Economic Security in East Asia: Governance and Institutions* (2006). She is an external associate of the Centre for the Study of Globalization and Regionalization, University of Warwick, UK and a member of the editorial board of the journal *Global Governance*.

Frank Schimmelfennig is Professor of European Politics at ETH Zurich, Switzerland and member of the Center for Comparative and International Studies. His main research interests are in the theory of international institutions and European integration and, more specifically, in the enlargement and democratization of European regional organizations. He has published, *inter alia*, in *Comparative Political Studies, European Journal of International Relations, International Organization, Journal of Common Market Studies*, and *Journal of European Public Policy*. He is the author of *The EU, NATO and the Integration of Europe. Rules and Rhetoric* (Cambridge University Press, 2003), which received the Best Book Award of the European Union Studies Association for 2003 and 2004, and *The International Socialization of Eastern Europe. Regional Organizations, Political Conditionality and Democratic Change* (2006, with Stefan Engert and Heiko Knobel).

Etel Solingen is the author of *Nuclear Logics: Alternative Paths in East Asia and the Middle East* (2007), *Regional Orders at Century's Dawn: Global and Domestic Influences on Grand Strategy* (1998), *Industrial Policy, Technology, and International Bargaining* (1996) and editor of *Scientists and the State* (1994). Her articles on international relations theory, international political economy, comparative regionalism, institutional theory, democratization, and international security have appeared in *International Organization, International Studies Quarterly, Comparative Politics, International Security, Global Governance, Journal of Peace Research, Journal of Theoretical Politics, Journal of Democracy, Asian Survey*, and *International Relations of Asia-Pacific*, among others. She serves as Chair of the Steering Committee of the University of California's system-wide Institute on Global Conflict and Cooperation and is recipient of a MacArthur Foundation Research and Writing Award on Peace and International Cooperation, a Social Science Research Council–MacArthur Foundation Fellowship on Peace and Security in a Changing World, a Japan Foundation/SSRC Abe Fellowship, and a Center for Global Partnership/Japan Foundation fellowship, among others. Her research on regionalism has focused on East Asia, the Middle East, Latin America, and the Euro-Mediterranean region.

Acknowledgments

This book is the outcome of collaboration between the Harvard University Asia Center, the Weatherhead Center for International Affairs at Harvard, and the Institute of Defense and Strategic Studies (IDSS; now the Rajaratnam School of International Studies) at Nanyang Technological University in Singapore. The Asia Center at Harvard offered a fellowship to Acharya during 2000–2001 to facilitate his collaboration with Johnston and generously offered seed funding for the project. The Institute of Defense and Strategic Studies hosted Johnston during 2003 and organized the second project workshop in Singapore during 2004. The Weatherhead Center for International Affairs hosted the first project workshop in Cambridge, Massachusetts in February 2002, and hosted Acharya during 2004 to work on the project. We are especially grateful to directors Ezra Vogel and Bill Kirby at the Asia Center, director Barry Desker at IDSS, and director and contributor Jorge Dominguez at the Weatherhead Center for their enthusiastic and consistent backing for the project. We also acknowledge a grant from the Lee Foundation, a private organization in Singapore, in support of the project. We thank Jeff Checkel, a contributor, in taking the initiative in organizing a panel discussion on the project at the American Political Science Association 2004 annual convention in Philadelphia. The editors would also like to thank Andrew Hurrell of Oxford, Greg Mills of the South African Institute of International Affairs, and Andrew Kydd of Harvard for their comments on the theme of the volume during the Singapore workshop, Tan Bann Seng, Deborah Lin, Karyn Wang, and especially Herbert Lin of IDSS for providing organizational and editorial assistance, and John Haslam and Carrie Cheek of the Cambridge University Press for advice and help in guiding the manuscript review process and its publication as an edited volume.

1 Comparing regional institutions: an introduction

Amitav Acharya and Alastair Iain Johnston

Why study institutional design?

During the past decade regionalism has received increasing attention as a major potential force for global change.[1] While regionalism has been a consistent feature of the global security and economic architecture since World War II, the end of the Cold War and economic regionalization in the context of a rapidly integrating global economy have led to a new emphasis on regionalism. But the make-up and performance of regional organizations around the world is marked by a great deal of diversity. For example, Europe not only exhibits the highest institutional density in terms of the number of overlapping regional mechanisms, but individual European regional groupings also tend to be more heavily institutionalized and intrusive, especially in terms of their approach to issues that affect state sovereignty (such as human rights). Yet, they lag behind many other regions, such as Africa and Asia, in terms of their inclusiveness and flexibility in decision-making. Asian institutions, relatively new on the international stage, have claimed uniqueness in terms of their decision-making norms and approach to socialization, but many have questioned their effectiveness in managing security dilemmas and the economic vulnerabilities of their members.

[1] Some of the recent works on regionalism include: Amitav Acharya, "Regional Approaches to Security in the Third World: Lessons and Prospects," in Larry A. Swatuk and Timothy M. Shaw (eds.), *The South at the End of the Twentieth Century* (London: Macmillan, 1994), pp. 79–94; Louise Fawcett and Andrew Hurrell (eds.), *Regionalism in World Politics: Regional Organization and International Order* (Oxford: Oxford University Press, 1995); Andrew Gamble and Anthony Payne (eds.), *Regionalism and World Order* (Basingstoke: Macmillan, 1996); Jean Grugel and Wil Hout (eds.), *Regionalism Across the North-South Divide* (London: Routledge, 1998); Edward D. Mansfield and Helen D. Milner (eds.), *The Political Economy of Regionalism* (New York: Columbia University Press, 1997); Björn Hettne, András Inotai, and Osvaldo Sunkel (eds.), *Globalism and the New Regionalism* (New York: St. Martin's Press, 1999); Fredrik Söderbaum and Timothy M. Shaw (eds.), *Theories of New Regionalism: A Palgrave Reader* (New York: Palgrave Macmillan, 2003); Shaun Breslin, Christopher W. Hughes, Nicola Phillips and Ben Rosamond (eds.), *New Regionalisms in the Global Political Economy* (London: Routledge, 2002).

Why, then, does it appear that different forms of institutionalization develop in different regions of the world? From a simple functionalist perspective one should not expect too much variation around the world, where states generally face similar kinds of cooperation problems. Thus, the first puzzle in which we are interested is how to describe and then explain any variation in the design of regional security and economic institutions across Asia, Africa, Latin America, the Middle East, and Europe.

The second puzzle, flowing naturally from this first puzzle, is whether variation in institutional design leads to variation in the nature of cooperation, including the efficacy of these institutions for resolving regional cooperation problems. Are the more formalized, bureaucratized, and oftentimes intrusive institutions of European cooperation more effective than the more informal, weakly organized 'talk-shops' of Asia-Pacific in promoting cooperation?

Our interest in this volume stems from two theoretical developments: first, the lack of interest in systematic comparative work on regional institutions from around the world, especially outside of Europe, focusing on variations in their design and efficacy; and second, the shifting emphasis on the theory of international institutions to studying variations in how they work.

Institutional design in the literature on regionalism

With the exception of European institutions, regional institutions have occupied a small and insignificant part of the overall theoretical literature on international institutions. And in this literature, considerations of institutional design have played a minimal part. The literature on regional institutions has evolved through three stages.

The first phase of the literature on regionalism was marked by a debate between regionalism and universalism which accompanied the creation of the United Nations.[2] Advocates of regionalism argued that geographic neighbors would have a better understanding of local disputes, and would be better able to provide assistance to victims of aggression than the universal organization. The regionalist position was recognized in the UN Charter, which listed mediation by regional agencies as one of the

[2] For analyses of the universalist and regionalist positions, see: Francis W. Wilcox, "Regionalism and the United Nations," *International Organization*, 19:3 (1965), pp. 789–811; Ernst B. Haas, "Regionalism, Functionalism and Universal Organization," *World Politics*, 8 (January 1956), pp. 238–63; Inis L. Claude Jr., *Swords into Plowshares* (New York: Random House, 1964), chapter 6; Norman J. Padelford, "Regional Organizations and the United Nations," *International Organization*, 8 (1954), pp. 203–16.

techniques of international conflict control (Article 33/1, Chapter VI), while UN members were encouraged to "make every effort to achieve pacific settlement of local disputes through such regional arrangements" (Article 52/2, Chapter VIII), before taking up the matter with the Security Council. These provisions constituted a framework of regionalism represented by the three "original" macro-regional political groups, the Organization of American States (OAS), the League of Arab States, and the Organization of African Unity (OAU) (created in 1963 and later renamed as the African Union).

But it was with the advent of the European Economic Community (EEC) in 1957 that the second phase in the study of regional institutions came about. This was labeled as regional integration theory. As Nye puts it, "the major developments in the Liberal tradition of international relations theory in the post-1945 period occurred in studies of regional integration."[3] Integration theory represented an attempt by international organization scholars to shift from descriptive discussions of UN and regional political and security groupings to more theoretical pursuits and "to fit legal-formal institutions into a larger context of political community building."[4] Unlike the universalist–regionalist debate, the referent objective of regional integration studies was not just security but also welfare.

A range of approaches to integration emerged, including federalism, neo-functionalism, and transactionalism (communications theory), with neo-functionalism and transactionalism providing the two most influential frameworks.[5] The neo-functionalist approach, led by Ernst Haas, had the following features: (1) recognition of the crucial importance of politics in regional integration; (2) a liberal–pluralist conception of

[3] Joseph S. Nye, "Neorealism and Neoliberalism," *World Politics*, 40:2 (January 1988), p. 239.

[4] J. Martin Rochester, "The Rise and Fall of International Organization as a Field of Study," *International Organization* 40:4 (1986), p. 786.

[5] Donald J. Puchala, "The Integration Theorists and the Study of International Relations," in Charles Kegley and Eugene Wittkopf (eds.), *The Global Agenda: Issues and Perspectives* (New York: Random House, 1984), p. 186. Some of the works on these and other regional integration theories include: Ernst B. Haas, *Beyond the Nation State* (Stanford: Stanford University Press, 1964); Karl Deutsch *et al.*, *Political Community in the North Atlantic Area* (Princeton: Princeton University Press, 1957); Joseph S. Nye, *International Regionalism* (Boston: Little Brown, 1968), Leon N. Lindberg and Stuart A. Scheingold, *Regional Integration: Theory and Research*, (Cambridge, MA: Harvard University Press, 1971); Roger D. Hansen, "Regional Integration: Reflections on a Decade of Theoretical Efforts," *World Politics*, 21 (January 1969), pp. 242–71; Ernst B. Haas, "The Study of Regional Integration: Reflections on the Joys and Anguish of Pretheorising," in Richard A. Falk and Saul H. Mendlovitz (eds.), *Regional Politics and World Order* (San Francisco: Institute of Contemporary Studies, 1972), pp. 103–31.

power; (3) bargaining by regionally-oriented pressure groups; (4) the notions of "task expansion" and "spillover" (the tendency of regional groups to expand the scope of their issue areas and how cooperation over "low-politics" gradually produces cooperation over "high-politics"); and (5) the notion of a political community as an end product of regional integration.

The core aspect of the transactionalist approach, led by Karl Deutsch, was community-building. The most well-known transactionalist notion of community is a "security community," a group of states which have developed long-term expectations of peaceful change and have ruled out the use of force among them.[6] They could either be "amalgamated" through political merger of the participating units, or remain "pluralistic", in which case the members would remain formally independent. The transactionalists developed a socio-psychological understanding of integration, combining both material transactions and ideational dynamics, including the development of collective identity and a "we feeling."[7] As such, less attention was given to the institutional features or designs of formal organizations per se. The neo-functionalist literature placed more emphasis on institutional design features. One was the scope of issue areas, where neo-functionalism took a normative position that security issues should not be brought to the agenda of regional institutions at the early stages of interaction. Another was mandate, where Haas' emphasis was on supranationalism, a concept that "combines intergovernmental negotiation with the participation of independent experts and spokesmen for interest groups, parliaments, and political parties."[8] Supranationalism was indicated by the attainment of a political community which involved a variety of "constitutional and structural factors." A third design feature concerned types of decision-making.[9] Haas identified four types: accommodation on the basis of the lowest common denominator; accommodation by "splitting the difference";[10] accommodation on the basis of deliberately or inadvertently upgrading the common

[6] Karl Deutsch *et al.*, *Political Community*, p. 5. Cited in Ronald J. Yalem, "Regional Security Communities," in George W. Keeton and George Scharzenberger (eds.), *The Year Book of International Affairs 1979* (London: Stevens and Sons, 1979), p. 217.

[7] Karl Deutsch *et al.*, *Political Community*.

[8] Ernst B. Haas, "International Integration: The European and the Universal Process," in Leland M. Goodrich and David A. Kay (eds.), *International Organization: Politics and Process* (Madison: University of Wisconsin Press, 1973), p. 399.

[9] Ibid., pp. 398–99 .

[10] Where conflict is resolved not on the basis of the will of the least cooperative, but somewhere between the final bargaining positions sometimes with the help of an external mediator. Ibid., p. 398.

interests of the parties;[11] and parliamentary diplomacy.[12] Leon Lindberg studied decision-making in European integration with reference to structures and levels of decision-making, participants in the decision-making process, their goals, resources and strategies, and policy outcomes from these processes.[13]

But while neo-functionalism and transactionalism paid attention to institutions, this was not so much to study variations in institutional design per se, especially in the design and efficacy of regional institutions around the world. For the most part, transactionalism and neo-functionalism focused on interactions and processes that helped or hindered integration, rather than on institutional designs and their effects. There was no conscious attempt to link the design features of regional institutions with the dependent variable of integration. This could be attributed to several factors.

First, there was no agreement on the meaning of integration. As Hodges contends, integration theory was controversial because there was no agreement on how integration was to be defined and whether it was a process or a condition.[14] For Haas, as he wrote in his major work, *The Uniting of Europe*, integration was: "a process whereby political actors in several distinct national settings are persuaded to shift their loyalties, expectations, and political activities toward a new center, whose institutions possess or demand jurisdiction over the pre-existing national states."[15] For Karl Deutsch, on the other hand, integration was a terminal condition, meaning: "the attainment, within a territory, of a 'sense of community' and of institutions and practices strong enough and widespread enough to assure, for a 'long' time, dependable expectations of 'peaceful change' among its population."[16] Integration was also conceived as being both a process and a condition.

[11] According to Haas, this occurs where "the parties succeeded in redefining their conflict so as to work out a solution at a higher level, which almost invariably implies the expansion of the mandate or task of an international or national government agency." Ibid., p. 399.

[12] Parliamentary diplomacy "implies the existence of a continuing organization with a broad frame of reference, public debate, rules of procedure governing the debate, and the statement of conclusions in a formal resolution arrived at by some kind of majority vote." Ibid., p. 399.

[13] Leon N. Lindberg, "Decision Making and Integration in the European Community," in *International Political Communities: An Anthology* (Garden City, NY: Anchor Books, 1966), p. 203.

[14] Michael Hodges, "Integration Theory," in Trevor Taylor (ed.), *Approaches and Theory in International Relations* (New York: Longman, 1978), p. 237.

[15] Ernst B. Haas, *The Uniting of Europe: Political, Economic and Social Forces, 1950–1957* (Stanford: Stanford University Press, 2nd ed., 1968), p. 16.

[16] Karl Deutsch *et al.*, *Political Community in the North Atlantic Area*, p. 5.

Second, the place of institutions in regional integration theory was not always clear or salient. Transactionalist approaches studied formal institutions only as one of the variables in the process leading to unification; For the most part, however, their focus was on transactions and processes, rather than institutionalization. Community-building was a precondition for institutional amalgamation. In contrast, for neo-functionalists like Haas, institutions were of central importance in fostering unification; institutional amalgamation preceded community formation.

Third, the literature on regional integration was heavily Eurocentric, with fewer examples of comparative studies that applied the different concepts of regional integration to the Third World.[17] For example, the insights of transactionalist theory about the background conditions that helped or hindered the development of security communities could not be applicable to the Third World, given the focus of Karl Deutsch and his associates on the "political community in the North Atlantic area."[18] Nye found that neither the conflict control role nor the integrative potential of regionalism worked well outside of Europe. In terms of conflict control, regional organizations outside Europe were partially effective in fostering "islands of peace" in the international system by keeping conflicts localized and isolating them from Great Power intervention.[19] But in the most significant later study, Ernst Haas found that the three original regional organizations, although initially somewhat effective in conflict control, became progressively ineffective.[20] In terms of economic integration, although in the Third World several micro-regional groups

[17] Joseph S. Nye, *Peace in Parts: Integration and Conflict in Regional Organization* (Lanham: University Press of America, 1987); Ernst B. Haas, Robert L. Butterworth, and Joseph S. Nye, *Conflict-Management by International Organizations* (Morristown, NJ: General Learning Press, 1972); Ernst B. Haas, "Regime Decay: Conflict Management and International Organizations," *International Organization*, 37 (Spring 1983), pp. 189–256; Ernst B. Haas, *Why We Still Need the United Nations: The Collective Management of International Conflict* (Berkeley: University of California, Institute of International Relations, 1986); Mark W. Zacher, *International Conflicts and Collective Security, 1946–1977: The United Nations, Organization of American States, Organization of African Unity, and Arab League* (New York: Praeger, 1979). A study comparing the OAU and the OAS was Boutros Boutros Ghali, "The League of Arab States and the Organization of African Unity," in Yassin El-Ayouty (ed.), *The Organization of African Unity After Ten Years: Comparative Perspectives* (New York: Praeger, 1975), pp. 47–61.

[18] This has been addressed to some extent in Emanuel Adler and Michael Barnett (eds.), *Security Communities* (Cambridge: Cambridge University Press, 1998).

[19] Nye, *Peace in Parts*, chapter 5.

[20] In general, Haas concluded that the OAS' effectiveness declined sharply after the 1965 Dominican Republic crisis, coinciding with the emergence of the Soviet-Cuban alliance and the declining hegemony of the US within the OAS. The Arab League's decline could be traced to the Camp David Accords in 1979; while for the OAU, a creditable performance during the 1966–1975 period was followed by a poor record during the 1976–1984 period. Ernst B. Haas, *Why We Still Need the United Nations*, pp. 29–34.

sought to emulate the EEC, none could succeed in achieving a level of integration that would create the conditions for a security community, whether of the amalgamated or the pluralistic variety. Neither could the micro-regional groups which proliferated in Africa and Latin America, and which pursued the EEC approach of market centralization and generation of welfare gains, produce the desired "spillover" effect leading to cooperation over security issues.[21]

Attempts to explain the differences between European and "universal" processes were the closest regional integration theory came to addressing the issue of variations in how institutions matter. The core of these explanations, however, was not institutional design per se, but a range of political, economic, social, and cultural variables. Thus, comparing Europe with the Eastern bloc, the Americas, and the Arab Middle East, Haas found that the reason why none of these other areas had a supranational institution could be attributed to the absence of certain "background conditions": social structure (levels of pluralism and interest group activity), levels of economic and industrial development, and ideological patterns (whether political parties are ideologically "homogenous," as in Scandinavia). Here, institutional design could at best be seen as a dependent variable, rather than itself a factor in institutional efficacy. Regions with more pluralism, more advanced economic and industrial development, and more ideological homogeneity are likely to achieve more rapid integration. Haas also identified certain external background conditions, such as common threat, although this did not lead to a consideration of power differentials as the most important determinant of integration.[22]Nye also focused on certain background conditions in explaining variations in the outcome of regional integration. He argued that functionalist approaches are difficult to apply to Third World states, where leadership "tends to be personalistic" and "heroes have trouble cooperating." The gap between the literate elite and the illiterate masses, the scarcity of organized interest groups, and the cultural cleavage between

[21] Lincoln Gordon, "Economic Regionalism Reconsidered," *World Politics*, 13 (1961), p. 245. Charles A. Duffy and Werner J. Feld, "Whither Regional Integration Theory," in Gavin Boyd and Werner Feld (eds.), *Comparative Regional Systems* (New York: Pergamon Press, 1980), p. 497. Haas acknowledged that the "application [of the neo-functionalist model] to the third world . . . sufficed only to accurately predict difficulties and failures of regional integration, while in the European case some successful positive prediction has been achieved." Ernst Haas, "The Study of Regional Integration," p. 117. Julius Emeka Okolo, "Integrative and Cooperative Regionalism: The Economic Community of West African States," *International Organization*, 39:1 (Winter 1985), pp. 121–53.

[22] Ernst B. Haas, "International Integration: The European and the Universal Process," in *International Political Communities: An Anthology* (Garden City, NY: Doubleday, Anchor Books, 1966), pp. 93–129.

city and countryside, which might seem to free the hands of the elites for international integration, have more often resulted in insecurity, isolation, and diversion of attention to internal integration. Scarcity of middle level administrative manpower results in weak governmental and political institutions, which are susceptible to disruption by the relatively organized institutions such as the army. The adaptability of governments under these conditions tends to be low.[23]

Once again, the focus of the explanation of why variations occurred in institutional efficacy between European and other regionalisms was more on a range of political, social, and administrative factors than on how institutions were designed. The so-called background conditions were used to explain the overall efficacy or quality of cooperation of regional institutions. Missing from the picture was a sense of how the way institutions are designed could affect their performance.

Interest in regional institutions peaked in the 1970s, when Haas pronounced regional integration theory as "obsolescent."[24] This was due to the growing disunity within the EEC over the Middle East oil crisis, differing European responses to the American technological challenge, and the rise of trans-regional interdependence which threatened to overshadow regional integration schemes. The lull in the study of regionalism continued until the 1980s, when a new stage in the study of regionalism emerged, helped by a reviving EEC and globalization processes which created new linkages within and between regions. The third stage in the literature on regional organization was marked by the EEC's (which in 1967 became the European Community (EC) and subsequently the European Union (EU)) progress toward a single market and a monetary union serving as the empirical backdrop. It was also marked by growing attention to subregional institutions in the Third World, most notably the Association of Southeast Asian Nations (ASEAN), and the MERCOSUR group in South America. At the same time, the effects of globalization were felt in new and more intrusive kinds of intra-regional linkages which challenged or bypassed state authority, and the emergence of transnational civil society created an alternative framework for regional interactions challenging the state-centric models which had been the dominant theme in the earlier literature on regionalism.

The theoretical response to these developments came in two main forms, which we consider to be the third stage in the literature on

[23] Joseph S. Nye, "Central American Regional Integration," in Nye, *International Regionalism*, pp. 381–82.

[24] Ernst B. Haas, *The Obsolescence of Regional Integration Theory* (Berkeley: Institute of International Studies, 1975).

regionalism. The first was strongly influenced by neo-liberal institutionalism and regime theory. But the application of regime theory was almost entirely confined to international issue areas and Europe.[25] And because of the close association of neo-liberal institutionalism with regime theory, and since regimes were deemed to exist and operate both formally and informally, institutional design was not a core priority of this literature. Instead, regime theory "moved the research agenda [on institutions] away from analyzing specific institutional arrangements."[26]

The second response was called "new regionalism." Hettne and Söderbaum identify several sources of new regionalism: "(1) the move from bipolarity toward a multipolar or perhaps tripolar structure, with a new division of power and new division of labor; (2) the relative decline of American hegemony in combination with a more permissive attitude on the part of the USA toward regionalism; (3) the erosion of the Westphalian nation-state system and the growth of interdependence and 'globalisation'; and (4) the changed attitudes toward (neo-liberal) economic development and political systems in the developing countries, as well as in the post-communist countries."[27] Some analysts of the new regionalism literature accuse it of descriptive accounting of regional organizations to the detriment of "an understanding of the domestic political mainsprings of regional governance."[28] But this would be overstating the case. In reality, the new regionalism literature challenged the rationalist bias of neo-liberal institutionalism. Compared to the earlier regional integration literature, the literature on "new regionalism" viewed

[25] Scholars within the neo-liberal institutionalist tradition who paid attention to Asian regionalism include: Vinod K. Aggarwal, "Building International Institutions in Asia-Pacific" *Asian Survey*, 33:11 (November 1993), pp. 1029–42; Vinod K. Aggarwal, "Comparing Regional Cooperation Efforts in the Asia-Pacific and North America," in Andrew Mack and John Ravenhill (eds.), *Pacific Cooperation: Building Economic and Security Regimes in the Asia-Pacific Region* (St Leonards, NSW: Allen and Unwin, 1994), pp. 40–65; Miles Kahler, "Institution-Building in the Pacific," in Mack and Ravenhill (eds.), *Pacific Cooperation*, pp. 16–39; Stephan Haggard, "Regionalism in Asia and the Americas," in Edward D. Mansfield and Helen V. Milner (eds.), *The Political Economy of Regionalism*; Miles Kahler, "Legalization as Strategy: The Asia-Pacific Case," *International Organization*, 54:3 (2000), pp. 549–71.

[26] Barbara Koremenos, Charles Lipson, and Duncan Snidal, *The Rational Design of International Institutions* (Cambridge: Cambridge University Press, 2004), p. 4. An important exception is: Vinod K. Aggarwal, "Reconciling Multiple Institutions: Bargaining, Linkages, and Nesting," in Vinod K. Aggarwal (ed.), *Institutional Designs for A Complex World: Bargaining, Linkages, and Nesting* (Ithaca, NY: Cornell University Press, 1998), pp. 1–31.

[27] Björn Hettne and Fredrik Söderbaum, "Theorising the Rise of Regionness," in Shaun Breslin *et al.*, *New Regionalisms in the Global Political Economy*, p. 33.

[28] Kanishka Jayasuriya, "Introduction: The Vicissitudes of Asian Regional Governance," in Kanishka Jayasuriya (ed.), *Asian Regional Governance: Crisis and Change* (London: Routledge, 2004), p. 2.

regionalism to be a more multifaceted and comprehensive phenomenon, taking into account the role of both state and non-state actors, as well as the whole range of political, economic, strategic, social, demographic, and ecological interactions within regions.[29] It shifted the focus away from formal institutions toward studying informal sectors, parallel economies, and non-state coalitions. In fact, its focus on informal sectors and non-state actors might have lessened the importance of institutional features of regionalism. Instead, a much broader view of regional interactions emerged, especially a range of transnational processes that seems to operate outside the limits of state sovereignty. The major concern of new regionalism was to show the declining importance of the state and formal intergovernmental cooperation. In this sense, new regionalism is more concerned with regionalization, rather than regional institution-building.

We acknowledge the important contribution made by both neo-liberal institutionalism and the new regionalism literature. We do not underestimate the importance of informal processes and non-state actors in regionalism. But we believe design issues are important and should not be neglected. Moreover, the study of new regionalism does not mean that the formal regionalism among states has become unimportant. Like the overall literature on globalization, the literature on new regionalism might have underestimated the resilience of the state, or have been too quick to predict its demise.

Moreover, the initial comparative perspective on new regionalism was "derived from studying the process of Europeanization, the development of a regional identity in Europe . . . and applied to the case of other regions . . . , under the assumption that despite enormous historical, structural, and contextual differences, there is an underlying logic behind contemporary processes of regionalization."[30] Hence, studying variations in regional institutional design was not an important facet of this literature.

But comparative work is crucial, especially because of the new developments in regionalism in areas outside of Europe. Developments in Asian regionalism are particularly noteworthy here. The emergence of

[29] James H. Mittelman, *The Globalization Syndrome: Transformation and Resistance* (Princeton: Princeton University Press, 2000), p. 113; Björn Hettne, "Globalization and the New Regionalism: The Second Great Transformation," in Bjorn Hettne *et al.* (eds.), *Globalism and the New Regionalism*, pp. 1–24.

[30] Björn Hettne, "The New Regionalism: Implications for Development and Peace," in Björn Hettne and András Inotai (eds.), *The New Regionalism: Implications for Global Development and International Security* (Helsinki: United Nations University/World Institute for Development Economics Research, 1994), p. 2.

regional institutions in East Asia in the 1990s raised major questions about the design and effects of regional institutions. This is because of claims by some Asian leaders that their regionalism was distinctive and more efficacious because of a lack of legalization and institutionalization. For example, what has been called the "ASEAN Way" was presented by some Asian leaders as a culturally-rooted notion, focusing on organizational minimalism, the avoidance of legalism, and an emphasis on consultations and consensus decision-making. For the first time therefore, there emerged a strong claim, backed by impressive growth rates (pre-1997) and relative lack of conflict especially in Southeast Asia, about soft institutionalization being a condition for the success of regional organizations. Because of the longevity of ASEAN and its role in regional conflict management, this claim could not be ignored but would command serious attention.

Moreover, ASEAN also developed institutional mechanisms for the wider Asia-Pacific region. This brought into sharp focus the comparative dimensions of regionalism in Asia and Europe. Are they comparable? How unique is each regionalism? Can we apply European models of regionalism, as represented in the EU or the OSCE (Organization for Security and Cooperation in Europe), to Asia? These questions have become the focus of major and continuous academic and policy debates in Asia.[31] A particular focus of this debate has concerned institutional design, and involves contrasting the bureaucratic and legalistic model of European regionalism with the informal and non-legalistic approach of Asian regional organizations.[32] What causes such variations, and which offers the most appropriate model for Asia and other parts of the

[31] For an overview, see: Amitav Acharya, "Ideas, Identity, and Institution-Building: From the 'ASEAN Way' to the 'Asia Pacific Way'" *Pacific Review*, 10:3 (1997), pp. 319–46. For an earlier study, see: Michael Haas, *The Asian Way to Peace: A Story of Regional Cooperation* (New York: Praeger, 1989).

[32] Peter J. Katzenstein, "Introduction: Asian Regionalism in Comparative Perspective," in Peter J. Katzenstein and Takashi Shiraishi (eds.), *Network Power: Japan and Asia* (Ithaca, NY: Cornell University Press, 1997), pp. 1–46; James Kurth, "The Pacific Basin versus the Atlantic Alliance: Two Paradigms of International Relations," *The Annals of the American Academy of Political and Social Science*, 505 (September 1989), pp. 34–45; Mittelman, *The Globalization Syndrome*; N. D. Palmer, *The New Regionalism in Asia and the Pacific* (Lexington, MA: Lexington Books, 1991); Hans Maull, Gerald Segal, and Josef Wanandi (eds.), *Europe and the Asia Pacific* (London: Routledge, 1998); William D. Coleman and Geoffrey R. D. Underhill (eds.), *Regionalism and Global Economic Integration: Europe, Asia and the Americas* (London: Routledge, 1998); Barry Eichengreen and T. J. Pempel, "Why Has There Been Less Financial Integration in East Asia Than in Europe?," a collaborative project of the Institute of East Asian Studies and the Institute of European Studies, submitted for funding under the umbrella of the "New Geographies, New Pedagogies" initiative of the Institute of International Studies (August 2002) available at: http://globetrotter.berkeley.edu/NewGeog/FinanInteg.pdf. For a policymaker's perspective, see: "How Are Regions Formed: Comparing Asia

developing world in terms of institutional efficacy and normative outcome, have been key questions in these debates.

The claims about Asia's distinctive regional institution-building and the differences between Asian and European regional institutions, which have parallels in other parts of the world, deserve careful scrutiny. This is a major rationale for this volume. Instead of assuming these differences, we hope and believe that a comparative study of regional institutions could both enrich the theory of international institutionalization, especially the question of how they matter, in the regional domain, as well as addressing important policy questions facing leaders in different regions of the world. The timing for such a study is opportune, because of new trends and approaches to the study of international institutions in international relations theory. We now turn to a brief discussion of these trends, and provide our second rationale for the comparative study of regional institutions.

The study of international institutions

The study of international institutions has seen a shift from whether institutions matter to how they matter, or "how they actually work." As part of this, scholars have begun to investigate the design features of international institutions. Foremost among these efforts is the Rational Design of International Institutions project (RDII). The RDII grew out of a concern to study variations in institutions: why "major institutions are organized in radically different ways."[33] These variations include: geographic scope and membership (global versus regional), decision-making (equal voting versus weighted voting or super-majorities), and centralization (strong central authorities with major operating responsibilities versus mainly consultative roles and functions). Unlike realists, RDII theory accepts that institutions matter. But unlike constructivists, it treats them not simply as "outside forces or exogenous actors" but as "self-conscious creation" of states and interest groups and corporations. Hence Conjecture 1: "States and other international actors, acting for self-interested reasons, design institutions purposefully to advance their joint interests."[34]

with Europe," Speech by Bernhard Zepter, Ambassador and Head of Delegation, Asia-Europe Forum 4th Symposium Tokyo International Forum, 22 February 2003. Available at: http://jpn.cec.eu.int/home/speech_en_Speech%2010/03.php [last accessed 8 May 2007].

[33] Koremenos, Lipson, and Snidal, *The Rational Design of International Institutions*, p. 1.

[34] Ibid., p. 21.

The RDII project studied variations along five dependent variables: (1) membership rules; (2) scope of issues; (3) centralization of tasks; (4) rules for controlling the institution; and (5) flexibility of arrangements. It adopts a rationalist methodology, the main part of which is to test a number of conjectures. Examples include "restrictive membership increases with the severity of the enforcement problem,"[35] or "issue scope increases with greater heterogeneity among a larger number of actors."[36]

Despite its contribution, the RDII project suffers from several limitations. First, it does not investigate how institutional design affects the effectiveness of institutions, in terms of their ability to realize the goals they set for themselves. Institutional design is treated only as a dependent variable, not as an independent variable that explains variations in outcomes or the extent and quality of cooperation. In other words, the theory does not ask why different institutions produce different outcomes, why some are better at delivering results than others, and whether this has something to do with design features. It is simply content with investigating why institutions look and act differently. Yet, to study variations in institutional design is not the same as studying their impact.

Second, RDII theory assumes that in designing institutions, actors are mainly concerned with maximizing material gain, rather than legitimacy. Reflecting its basis in rational choice theory, the RDII theory's main concern is what sort of design features would make institutions most efficient and useful, not appealing and morally appropriate. Actors choose specific design features with utility and efficacy in mind, but are they also influenced by moral considerations, or prior beliefs? RDII's neglect of norms has been identified in a chapter by Alexander Wendt appearing in the RDII volume.[37] The effect of this neglect, however, is to leave the task of investigating the impact of ideational variables in the empirical domain to others, including the present volume.

Third, the RDII project neglects the study of non-Western regional institutions. Not a single article in the volume is devoted to the study of Third World regional institutions. This is not surprising, given the longstanding and deeply entrenched Eurocentrism in the study of regional institutions in the theory of international relations. But this leaves crucial questions about the nature of cooperation in a vast area of the world. Are there any differences in institutional designing and building between the developed and developing worlds? Should we judge the effectiveness

[35] Ibid., p. 23. [36] Ibid., p. 25.

[37] Alexander Wendt, "Driving with the Rearview Mirror: On the Rational Science of Institutional Design," in Koremenos, Lipson, and Snidal, *The Rational Design of International Institutions*, pp. 1019–49. See also John S. Duffield, "The Limits of 'Rational Design'," *International Organization*, 57:2 (spring 2003), pp. 418–19.

of Third World regional institutions by employing different yardsticks, given the differences in political, social, and economic conditions in the Third World? "[T]here is a widespread assumption . . . that in order to be 'proper' regionalism, a degree of EU-style institutionalism should be in place."[38] This inevitably leads to the conclusions that weigh heavily in the direction of the failures and limitations of non-Western regionalism. Yet, as Peter Katzenstein notes in relation to Asian regionalism, "It would . . . be a great mistake to compare European 'success' with Asian 'failure'. Such a Eurocentric view invites the unwarranted assumption that the European experience sets the standard by which Asian regionalism should be measured." Katzenstein suggests instead that the "scope, depth, and character" of regionalism should acknowledge variations across "numerous dimensions and among world regions."[39]

This is an important question, given the wealth of available literature pointing to substantial differences in the economic conditions, security predicament, and regional dynamics between the West and the Third World.[40] For example, Westphalian sovereignty concerns and the principle of non-intervention are more acute in the Third World than in the West. This is explained not simply by rationalist factors, but also by normative considerations, including the colonial past of the Third World. Not taking these forces into account leads to only a partial understanding of institutional dynamics in the Third World. For example, RDII theory pays scant attention to domestic political variables, but these emerge as a crucial factor in all the cases of regional institution-building investigated in this volume.

[38] Shaun Breslin, Richard Higgott, and Ben Rosamond, "Regions in Comparative Perspective," in Shaun Breslin *et al.*, *New Regionalisms in the Global Political Economy*, p. 13.

[39] Peter J. Katzenstein, "Introduction: Asian Regionalism in Comparative Perspective," p. 3.

[40] See: Mohammed Ayoob, "Security in the Third World: The Worm About to Turn," *International Affairs*, 60:1 (1984), pp. 41–51; Mohammed Ayoob, "Regional Security and the Third World," in Mohammed Ayoob (ed.), *Regional Security in the Third World* (London: Croom Helm), pp. 3–23; Edward Azar and Chung-in Moon, "Third World National Security: Towards a New Conceptual Framework," *International Interactions*, 11:2 (1984), pp. 103–35; Barry Buzan, "People, States, and Fear: The National Security Problem in the Third World," in Edward Azar and Chung-in Moon (eds.), *National Security in the Third World* (Aldershot: Edward Elgar, 1988), pp. 14–43; Yezid Sayigh, *Confronting the 1990s: Security in the Developing Countries*, Adelphi Papers, no. 251 (London: International Institute for Strategic Studies, 1990); Mohammed Ayoob, "The Security Predicament of the Third World State," in Brian L. Job (ed.), *The (In)Security Dilemma: The National Security of Third World States* (Boulder, CO: Lynne Rienner, 1992); Mohammed Ayoob, "The Security Problematic of the Third World," *World Politics*, 43:2 (January 1991), pp. 257–83; Steven R. David, "Explaining Third World Alignment," *World Politics*, 43:2 (January 1991), pp. 232–56.

These omissions limit the applicability of RDII theory to the study of "how institutions matter" in international politics.[41] In this volume, we go beyond the RDII framework. We believe a comparative study of regional institutions offers one of the best ways to further advance the study of the design of international institutions.

Design and structure of this volume

We asked our authors to treat institutional design first as a dependent variable and then as an independent variable. In treating institutional design as a dependent variable, we asked authors to look at a wide range of plausible independent variables and see which helped them understand the form that regional institutions took. We did not, however, want to impose a matrix of variables which each case study must relate to. We left the decision about the selection and investigation of variables to the contributors, who can use their best judgment as to the relevance of each variable to their respective case studies.

In treating design as an independent variable we asked authors to investigate the degree to which the institution and its design helped explain the nature of cooperation. In addition, in each case we suggested that the authors examine one major cross-regional institution and one minor cross- or subregional institution. In order to make the cross-regional comparisons more valid we wanted to ensure that the sample of institutions did not vary a great deal across regions.

Definition of institutional design

The very term "design" usually implies an act of choice or deliberation. The RDII project refers to institutional design as the "broad characteristics of the institutional outcomes they select," "they" meaning actors.[42] We are more flexible about this, however. Gourevitch makes the distinction between institutions that are created and institutions that are organic.[43] This volume looks at both types of institutions and refers to the formal and informal structures of the institution as design. By institutional design, we mean those formal and informal rules and organizational features that constitute the institution and that function as either the constraints on actor choice or the bare bones of the social environment within

[41] See Duffield, "The Limits of 'Rational Design'," pp. 414–15.
[42] Koremenos, Lipson, and Snidal, *The Rational Design of International Institutions*, p. 21.
[43] Peter A. Gourevitch, "The Governance Problem in International Relations," in David A. Lake and Robert Powell (eds.), *Strategic Choice and International Relations* (Princeton: Princeton University Press, 1999), pp. 137–64.

which agents interact, or both. We will elaborate on the features of institutional design in a moment.

Variables

This volume provides a combination of deductive and inductive hypothesis testing about why regional institutions take on the design features they do and about how these features affect cooperation. Initially we planned to develop a number of deductive hypotheses only about the sources of variation in institutional design, and about the implications of this variation for cooperation. But after two conferences and some intensive discussions with participants and with critics of the project, we decided that one of the strengths of the project was its inductive richness. Put differently, the initial research made it clear that the initial list of independent variables was too limited, and that the data from these regions suggested more variation in explanations for institutional design. We also decided that we did not want the project to assume the superiority of one particular theoretical orientation. After all, this was one of our complaints about the RDII approach – an *a priori* assumption that contractual institutionalist theory and language best captured how and why institutions were formed. Instead, we didn't want to prejudice the search for plausible explanations, explanations that might be associated with only one of the major 'isms'. Thus as the next section shows, we settled on a rich array of possible sources of institutional design which we asked chapter writers to explore. In a sense one could describe our project analogically, using the language of complex adaptive systems: we brought together a range of complex cases, provided the general parameters for the cases, and then watched to see what kind of intellectual 'emergent property' came out of this, this emergent property being some plausible conclusions about the evolution and effect of institutions across regions.

Type of cooperation problem To date most of the work on international institutions has typically fallen within a contractual institutionalist analytical approach. In essence this approach is a functionalist one, positing that, *ceteris paribus*, institutional designs ought to reflect in some rough way, the nature of the cooperation problem facing actors. In other words, assuming rationality and some degree of shared understandings (common knowledge) about the preferences, beliefs, and strategies of other actors, this approach expects that there are optimal institutional designs for the cooperation problem at hand. Thus, for N-person prisoner's dilemma problems (where the issue is how to prevent actors from opportunistically defecting against each other), an institution that can credibly monitor behavior, detect defection, and punish defectors will reduce the incentives to defect. For an assurance game, the cooperation problem is that, while all actors have a dominant cooperation strategy, they can't be sure that the others share this preference for a cooperative outcome. An institution that can provide information about the preferences and actions of all players will ensure that the Pareto-optimal outcome (mutual cooperation) is stable. Basically, it does not need monitoring or sanctioning mechanisms.[44] Thus, as a first cut, one might look at the origins and design features of regional institutions from this functionalist perspective. The institutions' form and function will, in general, reflect the nature of the cooperation problem.

N of actors This argument is derived from the RDII project. As Olson's seminal work on group size and collective action pointed out, the larger the group *ceteris paribus* the less likely that actors will choose to work together for some joint gain.[45] Moreover, when institutions operate on the consensus principle, as opposed to majority voting, a larger group will find it difficult not only to achieve agreement, but also face a greater risk that any agreement be diluted by the "lowest common denominator" problem. On the other hand, social influence theory suggests that when it comes to putting social pressure on actors to cooperate, a larger group might be better since there are greater status rewards and punishments at stake for any particular actor. Thus, does institutional design reflect whether the size of the group is optimal for either collective action based on material incentives or based on social incentives?

Ideology and identity Are institutional designs affected by the dominant ideology of the key entrepreneurs? For example, liberal ideology, it has been claimed, will promote "thick" institutions to regulate interstate affairs. Liberal states, particularly when interacting with other liberal states, will be willing to accept a higher level of intrusiveness (e.g. third-party mediation) because this is an appropriate way of resolving inter-party disputes. Institutions created or led by liberal states are also more supportive of certain types of international collective action even though it might encroach upon traditional notions of state sovereignty, for example, democracy promotion, economic integration, and humanitarian

[44] Lisa L. Martin, "The Rational State Choice of Multilateralism," in John Gerard Ruggie (ed.), *Multilateralism Matters: The Theory and Praxis of an Institutional Form* (New York: Columbia University Press, 1993), pp. 91–121.

[45] Mancur Olson, *The Logic of Collective Action: Public Goods and the Theory of Groups* (Cambridge, MA: Harvard University Press, 1965).

intervention missions. NATO and the European Union provide good examples of such approaches. On the other hand, institutions of authoritarian or semi-authoritarian states will oppose humanitarian intervention and democracy promotion because these will question the legitimacy of their ruling regimes. Asian regional institutions, where a democratic political system is not a requirement for membership, and which were created by coalition of authoritarian or semi-authoritarian regimes (for example ASEAN at its founding) or whose main goal is to socialize authoritarian powers (e.g. China within the ASEAN Regional Forum), have avoided third-party mediation or humanitarian intervention. Similarly, states dominated by post-colonial ideologies (e.g. national liberation, neutralism, and non-alignment during the Cold War) whose key element is to safeguard their new-found independence and sovereignty will be highly suspicious of intrusive institutions. Post-colonial states will be especially sensitive to interference in internal affairs, particularly by former colonizers and other major powers under the guise of institutional effectiveness.

Identity[46] could also play an important role in institutional design, affecting especially membership (who is to be included and who is to be excluded) and the norms of the institution. Identity here is not just a function of common cultural features, such as linguistic, racial, religious, etc., among a group of states, but shared norms, social purposes, cognitive models, and views of outgroups forged through political and economic interactions among culturally diverse units.[47] Sometimes, ideologies and identities may come together, as is the case with pan-nationalist movements in Africa (pan-Africanism) and Latin America (pan-Americanism), which provided a powerful basis for the creation, membership, and norms of regional institutions the OAU and OAS respectively. The absence of such collective identities may explain why Asia could not develop a macro-regional institution in the postwar period,[48] and why its first viable regional institution was a subregional group, ASEAN, which provided a more meaningful venue for socialization among a group of politically more like-minded states. ASEAN's evolving sense of collective identity also helped to shape its decision-making processes such as the "consultations and consensus"

[46] Identity is not the same as ideology although they can be related. Ideologies can embody concepts of appropriate behavior – to be a good communist one should believe in class struggle.

[47] See Rawi Abdelal, Yoshiko Herrera, Alastair Iain Johnston, and Rose McDermott, "Identity as a Variable," *Perspectives on Politics*, 4 (December 2006), pp. 695–711.

[48] Amitav Acharya, "Ideas, Identity and Institution-Building: from the 'ASEAN Way' to the 'Asia-Pacific Way?'".

principles, which its members claim to be a unique feature of Southeast Asian societies.

Systemic and subsystemic power distributions There is every reason to test traditional realist arguments about how institutional designs will reflect the interests of the most powerful states in the system.[49] Depending on the ideology and purposes of the dominant state, the institution could be highly intrusive (designed, for instance, to spread the ideology of the dominant power in order to consolidate a Gramscian hegemony). Post-war international institutions created under US leadership, for example the Bretton Woods institutions, strongly reflected American interests and values. As John Ruggie put it, they were reflections not of American *hegemony*, but *American* hegemony. Regional frameworks created by imperial powers, such as Japan and Germany in the lead-up to World War II, were little more than exclusionary concepts aimed at serving the geopolitical and economic interests of these powers, even though they professed to be based on principles of equality and openness.[50] There are no examples of such blatant "hegemonic regionalism" in the contemporary international system, but regional institutions in several parts of the Third World do reflect the interests and preferences (or at least contestations over such preferences) of regionally powerful actors, such as Nigeria in the Economic Community of West African States (ECOWAS), Saudi Arabia in the Gulf Cooperation Council (GCC), Indonesia in ASEAN, or post-apartheid South Africa in the Southern African Development Community (SADC) and perhaps in the New Partnership for Africa's Development (NEPAD).

Domestic politics Here one could imagine a number of variables having an impact on institutional design. Looking at the contrasting experience of the EU and Asia one might suggest that strong states with regimes enjoying a high degree of legitimacy tend to favor stronger institutions, while weak states with insecure regimes would avoid strong institutions for fear of compromising sovereignty and regime survival. On the other hand, weak regimes might derive some legitimacy from high-profile, but intentionally weakened institutions. Another domestic argument might focus on how "indigenous" modes of socialization have produced a tendency toward different levels of strength and formality of institutions. There is a claim, for example, that Asian "culture" favors

[49] Here we agree with Duffield, "The Limits of 'Rational Design'," pp. 417–18.
[50] John G. Ruggie, "Multilateralism: The Anatomy of an Institution," *Multilateralism Matters* (New York: Columbia University Press, 1993), pp. 3–50.

weakly institutionalized and informal institutions. Another domestic argument might focus on the nature of inter-ethnic relations within and across state borders. If all the states in a region have more or less fragile inter-ethnic relations, with some spillover of ethnic groups across state boundaries, these states have an interest in coordinating around a strong norm against interference in internal affairs. All would be hurt from the collapse of such a norm. This might be one explanation for ASEAN's long-standing norm against interference in the domestic affairs of other states. Finally, states' economic development models might correlate to different institutional designs. Developed states with open industrial economies are likely to avoid participation in supranational regional institutions (especially free trade areas and customs unions) that would restrict their access to the global economy. On the other hand, liberalizing developing states may find regional cooperation highly useful for collective bargaining over market access and other benefits.

Extra-regional institutions and non-state actors How might institutions or non-state actors from outside the region act as "agents" in the development of a regional institution's key features? For example, these agents might provide organizational templates for newer institutions. New institutions may be influenced by the functions, cooperation mechanisms, and decision-making procedures of older and more successful institutions. The role of the Conference (later Organization) for Security and Cooperation in Europe (OSCE) in building trust between the Western and Soviet blocs during the Cold War has been widely discussed as a possible model for regional institutions in the Third World.[51] To be sure, the OSCE's specific agenda of intrusive and sanctions-backed military confidence-building measures (CBMs) to prevent interstate conflicts, and its role in monitoring elections and helping the restoration of order in post-conflict settings, have not found easy acceptance elsewhere, especially in Asia (with the exception of the Shanghai Cooperation Organization, which incorporated an agreement on confidence-building measures that grew out of Sino–Soviet negotiations during the Cold War and which introduced the notion of formal CBMs to the Chinese), due to sovereignty concerns. But the so-called "OSCE model" has been the basis of initial debate and brainstorming about the design features of new institutions in Asia, especially the ARF. At the very least, the OSCE's underlying norm of "common security" or "cooperative security" (the idea that regional organizations should be "inclusive", including both politically

[51] Amitav Acharya, "Ideas, Identity and Institution-Building: From the 'ASEAN Way' to the 'Asia-Pacific Way?'".

like-minded and non-like-minded states of a region, and that members of such organizations should adopt a "security with," as opposed to "security against" approach to their potential or actual adversaries), has been accepted, even if the actual mechanisms supporting this norm have been less intrusive in the case of non-European regional bodies.

History Finally, the project considers how history might affect the extant features of an institution. We refer to history in two senses. The first is history as manifested in historical memory. That is, how has the internalization of appropriate institutional forms across time constrained the design options that current agents believe are available to them? The second is history as path dependence. How have increased returns to historical institutional features and mechanisms for locking in these features affected the current design of regional institutions? Thus normative and institutional path dependence could result from the transference of the institutional features of prior institutions (especially if they are perceived to have been reasonably successful in dealing with challenges at hand) to new ones in a given region, for example, the impact of the "ASEAN Way" (established in 1967) on the ARF (created in 1994). Or it could come into play when the same continuing institution considers revisions to its existing design features, either due to internal demands from some member states or external pressures from new global events and norms, such as the emerging norms of human rights protection and democracy promotion. Many regional institutions in the developing world, created at a time when memories of Western colonialism were still vivid, and economic nationalism was a close complement to state sovereignty, are now finding it difficult to expand their mandate, scope, and decision-making procedures to address new and emerging transnational dangers, such as financial volatility, pandemics, terrorism, and transnational crime, as this would require compromises to the principle of non-interference.

The dependent variable for these independent variables is, of course, institutional design. By this we mean the formal and informal rules and relationships that constitute the institution itself. We identified five major features of institutional design, drawing largely from Rogowski[52] with modifications by Checkel[53] and Johnston.[54] *Membership* refers mainly to

[52] Ronald Rogowski, "Institutions as Constraints on Strategic Choice," in David Lake and Robert Powell (eds.), *Strategic Choice and International Relations* (Princeton: Princeton University Press, 1999), pp. 115–36.

[53] Jeffrey Checkel, "Why Comply? Social Learning and European Identity Change," *International Organization*, 55:3 (Summer 2001), pp. 553–88.

[54] Alastair Iain Johnston, "Treating International Institutions as Social Environments," *International Studies Quarterly*, 45:4 (December 2001), pp. 487–516.

the number of actors allowed to participate. How inclusive or exclusive is the institution? *Scope* refers to the range of issues that the institution is designed to handle. The scope could be narrow, broad, intrusive, or non-intrusive. *Formal rules* refers to the explicit and "legalized" regulations governing how decisions are made. These typically vary from unanimity/consensus to flexible consensus to majority to super-majority rules. *Norms* refers to the formal and informal ideology of the institution. What normative and causal arguments does the institution intend to promote? What normative and causal claims does it actually promote? Finally, *mandate* refers to the overall purpose of the institution. Is it designed to distribute some potentially scarce good (e.g. a treaty deliberation), or is it designed simply to deliberate over some potential conflicts of interest?

To be sure this list includes a fairly wide range of elements of institutional design, including both formal and informal rules as well as norms. But we have a very specific reason to choose these dimensions: we want to combine a standard list of features identified by the rationalist literature with a list of features more common to sociological approaches to institutions. Thus we draw some of the features of design from Ronald Rogowski's work[55] and from the RDII project, as well as from the literature on institutional design and socialization.[56] This, we believe, allows for a fuller test of the different ways in which institutions may affect efficacy and the nature of cooperation, and strikes a balance between conceptual tractability on the one hand and a more complete test of a fuller range of plausible hypotheses.

In the first part of the case study chapters, authors treat these institutional design features as their dependent variables. In the second part of the chapters, the authors were tasked with using institutional design as an independent variable to see to what degree it helped explain actual cooperation among states in the respective regions. We believe these design features are important because one can derive different, sometimes competing, hypotheses about the nature of cooperation from them. According to traditional rationalist collective action theory, large and inclusive memberships, for instance, should be an obstacle to cooperation. However, social influence theory suggests that larger institutions generate a greater amount of status and opprobrium markers which can elicit cooperation from actors who are sensitive to maximizing social image. Different types of formal decision rules can also have different implications for

[55] See Rogowski, "Institutions as Constraints on Strategic Choice."

[56] Checkel, "Why Comply?"; Johnston, "Treating International Institutions as Social Environments".

cooperation. Traditionally, unanimity/consensus rules are seen as conservative decision rules because the purposes or goals of an institution can be diluted or obstructed by holding decision-making hostage to a small number of recalcitrant states. Consensus decision-making, on the other hand, could also help generate social influence effects if an image-sensitive actor is reluctant to be seen as the outlier who obstructs progress in the institution. The normative content of an institution could be important from both a rationalist and a socialization perspective. The normative content, for instance, could mobilize domestic interests to try to capture national policy towards an institution. Alternatively, the normative content might be diffused into national policy processes through the socialization of national representatives in the institution. As for mandate, one could imagine that when the issue is a distributive one, national representatives are going to be more vigilant about defending "national interests," thus less susceptible to social influence or persuasion attempts within the institution. On the other hand, if the mandate is deliberation and if, say, the topic is a highly technical one, they would be more susceptible to the social effects of institutions.[57] Finally, when the autonomy of the national representative (agent) is high, s/he may be more susceptible to social effects to the degree that "national interests" may be less clear.

We asked our authors to use these and other hypotheses in the second part of their chapters to examine a second dependent variable – the nature of cooperation.[58] We disaggregated the cooperation dependent variable

[57] Checkel, "Why Comply?"; Johnston, "Treating International Institutions as Social Environments."

[58] Originally we had thought of developing a metric for the "quality" of cooperation that would allow for cross-regional comparisons in the measures on the dependent variable. Essentially we thought to unpack the Downs, Rocke, and Barsoom definition of the "depth" of cooperation as the extent to which a treaty requires states to "depart from what they would have done in its absence." George W. Downs, David M. Rocke, and Peter N. Barsoom, "Is the Good News about Compliance Good News about Cooperation," *International Organization*, 50:3 (Summer 1996), p. 383. Quality would be measured by at least three dimensions – the degree of change that cooperation required in a state's original policies; the degree to which cooperation affected the relative power of the state; and whether the state's cooperation was elicited through either positive or negative economic and social sanctions, or through normative acceptance. High quality cooperation would entail normative acceptance of cooperative commitments that required large scale costly changes in previous policies and that had an adverse effect on relative capabilities. This initial conceptualization of the dependent variable derived from our concern that a more standard institutionalist definition of cooperation – the adjustment of behavior to the anticipated preferences of others – did not really allow us to understand differences in the reasons why states cooperated or how difficult it might be for them to do so. We wanted to distinguish between adjustments of behavior that were, in some sense, easy and thus likely not to be particularly robust and those that were difficult and likely to reflect a major reconsideration of past calculations of cost and benefit. This reflected

into different components and asked the paper writers to focus on those components most relevant to their respective case studies. We imposed no expectation that each paper writer must assess quality of cooperation in terms of each of the following indicators we provided. This is especially important, since these indicators are drawn eclectically from different streams of research on institutions. From constructivism we borrow the idea of the *degree of normative and preference change.* To what extent does institutional design constitute a social environment within which actors are socialized to internalize new preferences, norms, and roles?[59] From rationalist institutional theory we borrow the notion of the *degree of policy convergence across actors.*[60] At the Singapore Workshop of the project, it was suggested by several participants that the *degree of institutionalization and legalization* ought to be regarded as an indicator of nature of cooperation, since greater institutionalization and legalization suggests a deepening of cooperation. Another possible component concerns the *different routes to the above changes*: persuasion, social influence, and/or material incentives. Are any of these more prevalent depending on variation in institutional design? These forms of change have a bearing on the robustness of cooperation. *Ceteris paribus*, cooperation based on preference change ought to be more robust than that based on material incentive, as the former ought to persist even when material incentives change or dissipate. A fifth component concerns the *degree of adjustment of prior policies* and behaviors that states have to undergo when cooperating inside the institution. Does it require a great deal of change or very little? This speaks to the question of how radical the effect of institutional design

the editors' biases as Asianists: since an explicit claim in the debate about a European versus an Asian way of institutional development was that less institutionalized, more informal Asian institutions might create just as robust and costly cooperation as European institutions did, we needed some kind of characterization of cooperation that could compare the "quality" of cooperation of these different traditions of institutional design.

We were convinced, however, during discussions that such a measure of quality might allow normative bias to seep into measurement of the dependent variable. Why should cooperation that requires major changes in behavior, a high sacrifice of relative power, and is elicited through socialization necessarily be judged as "high quality"? Certainly it is "different" quality, but it doesn't say anything in particular about whether the cooperation solves the "problem" at hand. Moreover, while the metric is clearest at the extremes of the three dimensions, it was unclear how one would characterize the quality of cooperation when the measures along these dimensions were somewhere in the middle. For instance, was cooperation that involved moderate changes in policy, that had moderate constraints on relative power and that was elicited by material incentives necessarily of lower "quality" than cooperation that required the same degree of change in policy, the same level of constraints on relative power, but was elicited by social incentives?

[59] Alastair Iain Johnston, "Treating International Institutions as Social Environments," pp. 487–516.

[60] Liliana Botcheva and Lisa L. Martin, "Institutional Effects on State Behavior: Convergence and Divergence," *International Studies Quarterly*, 45:1 (March 2001), pp. 1–26.

is on actor practices. A sixth possible component concerns the *degree to which the institution (or the agents active in the institution) has achieved set goals*. Does the institution actually produce the cooperative outcomes envisioned by its members or participants? Finally, *to what extent does cooperation elicited by the institution have an impact on the "problem" writ large*? The institution may meet its specific cooperative goals, but these goals may have little overall impact on or relationship to the broader regional or global cooperation problem that nations face.

We recognize that explaining the causal relationship between design and efficacy is fraught with difficulties. Among these is the issue of endogeneity.[61] Endogeneity could take two forms here. One is the theoretical possibility that states will support institutions that balance ease in setting up and preferred outcomes. Institutional designs, therefore, will not have a direct effect on the efficacy of cooperation; rather it will be the level of cooperation preferred by the state at first, not the design, that matters.[62] A second form is that there is a strong interactive effect between design and efficacy – design at time $t + 0$ helps explain efficacy at time $t + 1$ which in turn leads to changes in design at time $t + 2$. Thus separating out the direct causal effect of design on efficacy over time becomes very difficult to do.

We understand the importance of the endogeneity problem; it is a daunting problem for quantitative analysis as well, so we are also unlikely to solve the problem definitively in this book. But we also believe that rather than viewing endogeneity as a process that necessarily confounds causal argument, we should acknowledge that endogeneity is a reality (it is something constructivists have no problem with ontologically, in any event). We do not rule out endogeneity *a priori*, indeed, that is one explanation for the changing nature of the ASEAN Regional Forum (as one of us has argued[63]). So for us, if one accepts the likely reality of endogeneity in both its forms, the issue is how does one deal with it?

In the first form – that states support the type of design which produces the outcomes they prefer – endogeneity can be approached by looking for additional observable implications, where state preferences do not explain features of design over time. Evidence would include: examples where levels of efficacy are higher than states initially wanted;

[61] We thank one of the anonymous reviewers for stressing this point and for provoking our thinking.

[62] This is a point made by Downs, Rocke, and Barsoom, "Good News about Compliance," pp. 382–83.

[63] Alastair Iain Johnston "The Myth of the ASEAN Way? Explaining the Evolution of the ASEAN Regional Forum," in Helga Haftendorn, Robert Keohane, and Celeste Wallander (eds.), *Imperfect Unions: Security Institutions in Time and Space* (London: Oxford University Press, 1999).

instances where institutions were autonomous enough to require levels of cooperation that states initially did not support; instances where states were initially unclear about their preferred levels of cooperation, and where institutional designs help, in a sense, create an outcome that the state then decides to prefer; instances where designs affect preferences (as what Downs *et al.* called the "managerial school" would suggest[64]); instances where micro-behaviors that emerge from participation in a particular institution are not predicted by the prior preferences of the state.

In its second form – that design and efficacy may be interactive across time – there is a theoretical answer and an empirical one to the endogeneity problem. The theoretical answer is to assume, quite plausibly, that institutional designs are sticky (due to sunk costs, organizational inertia, the "taken for granted" elements of institutional behavior, etc). Thus the "success" or "failure" (efficacy) of an institution at time t may not have a large effect on design at time $t + 1$. As for the empirical answer, there are three strategies for dealing with endogeneity. The first is to note that endogeneity is not really an issue when looking at institutions from their birth. Since institutions can't vary in terms of efficacy until they are created, then logically efficacy has no bearing on the initial design of the institution. One can then follow change in design and change in efficacy until a point where it becomes more plausible that efficacy is one possible explanation for a change in design. This allows one to separate out the effects of design from efficacy prior to this point. The second is that one could take a snapshot of the design–efficacy sequence at one particular time well into the history of the institution to see how design influences efficacy within this time period. This does not rule out an efficacy–design sequence, but leaves it bracketed for the purposes of isolating design as an independent variable. The third is an extension of this – once this snapshot has been taken, one can then look to see whether in the next period of time there is evidence that efficacy at some earlier period of institutional development affected later efforts to redesign the institution.

Needless to say we have encouraged the chapter writers to think about all these solutions, while recognizing that endogeneity is a reality that, in a sense, ought to be embraced even if it leads to somewhat messy causal arguments.

[64] See Downs, Rocke, and Barsoom, "Good News about Compliance." They are mainly referring to work by Abram and Antonia Chayes on the role of institutions in changing preferences and/or exacting levels of cooperation that states initially did not prefer. See Abram Chayes and Antonia Chayes, *The New Sovereignty: Compliance with International Regulatory Agreements* (Cambridge, MA: Harvard University Press, 1998).

Summary of findings

Together the chapters provide a very rich array of conclusions about institutional design and cooperation. Below we provide a brief synopsis of each author's findings.

Yuen Foong Khong and Helen Nesadurai examine regional institutional design in Asia. They consider two institutions: the ASEAN Free Trade Area (AFTA), which is the principal economic institution within the multi-purpose ASEAN, and the ASEAN Regional Forum (ARF), which is a larger offshoot of ASEAN dealing primarily in security matters. In the case of AFTA/ASEAN, the need for collective clout to "hang together" plays an important role in maintaining the regional organization. They see AFTA's design as the result of an interplay between "shared external threats and domestic political imperatives." Domestic politics and regime security imperatives ensure the unwillingness of governments to accept institutional rules that intrude into their domestic decision-making, or undermine domestic coalition arrangements. But when external threats seem high and threaten regime security, regional states are willing to accept more intrusive regional institutions. Turning to the ARF, they identity strategic uncertainty as the key factor behind the emergence of this institution. The level of actor independence in the ARF is high; it has no formal rules to constrain members. For the ARF, one of the main sources of institutional design is history, or ASEAN's prior institutional profile. Functional variables are least important, because of high uncertainty over the nature of threat or nature of strategic interaction game being played out at the time of its founding. While the overall quality of cooperation in the ARF is low, they argue that low cooperation is better than no cooperation. The founding of the ARF is itself an important act of regional cooperation.

Jorge Domínguez' chapter on the Americas identifies several key sources of institution-building: (1) ideational legacy; (2) differentiated subsystems within the Americas; and (3) the relative autonomy of the continent from the global international system. An important aspect of his chapter is the discussion of several historical "rules" of Inter-American institutions: such as the rule of *uti possidetis juris* which turned existing administrative boundaries into international frontiers after the departure of colonial powers; the doctrine of non-intervention and defense of state sovereignty; activist intermediation of intra-regional disputes between 1925 and 1942; and finally, laxity in implementation, signifying a gap between formal pledges and behavior. Later in the chapter, he examines how developments in the international system have led to modification of these rules, most notably the doctrine of non-intervention has given way to interest in intervention in defense of democracy. Moreover, laxity gave way to automaticity. Regional institutions in the Americas come across as highly institutionalized, perhaps next only to European institutions, but a higher level of institutionalization (not institutional design per se), does not ensure success. "Organization-poor MERCOSUR performed well. The organization-rich OAS and CACM (Central American Common Market) had varying levels of performance but they were no better performers than MERCOSUR."[65] Despite the long history of regionalism in Latin America (older than Europe's), regional institutions really began to take off in the 1990s, developing new dynamism and roles in trade liberalization, international security cooperation, and democratic defense. Overall, the quality of cooperation is deemed better since the 1990s than before, but quality is both issue-specific and institution-specific. In examining the factors behind this transformation, he dismisses such obvious variables as the end of the Cold War or the shifts in the distribution of power and identifies "prior and independent structural and normative changes in the international system," the role of international non-governmental organizations, domestic changes within countries, and institutional rule innovations as the core factors.

In his chapter on Africa, Jeffrey Herbst argues that facing severe domestic constraints, African states derive their legitimacy from the international system, especially from the norms of sovereignty. Africa has a successful boundary regime. Because of this, leaders do not have to worry about external threats. The preservation of boundaries is an "extraordinary" success, but has led to maintenance of failed states like Somalia. Domestic weakness has led to interest in international agreements, including designing new regional and continental agreements, which augment the domestic power base of leaders. While European states give up sovereignty in developing regional agreements and institutions, African states, like weak and insecure states in other areas, use regional agreements to enhance their sovereignty. Hence, attempts at cooperation that actually seek to challenge sovereignty, such as schemes for federal unions, have invariably failed. Regional integration schemes in Africa have largely failed. Regional institutional design in Africa is not an independent determinant of quality of cooperation but reflects other forces at work, especially domestic politics (mainly regime survival).

Frank Schimmelfennig seeks to explain variation between three NATOs: the Cold War NATO, the enlarged and transformed new NATO, and the NATO partnership in Eastern Europe. He identifies NATO's broad scope of issue areas, process-oriented mandate, and conditional

[65] Domínguez, this volume, p. 121.

membership, as three of the key design features of NATO. The salience of these features is explained by the liberal ideology and identity of NATO, the nature of the cooperation problem, and the distribution of global and regional power. Liberal ideology has restricted membership to an exclusive and trustworthy group. He also notes a lack of functional demand for and hegemonic interest in the pooling and delegation of sovereignty. He concludes that the new NATO has higher flexibility. This is explained by uncertainty about security challenges and diverging threat perceptions.

Michael Barnett and Etel Solingen's chapter on the Middle East points to a case of institutional failure: the Arab League being among the least effective regional organizations in the developing world, although it was the first to emerge after the end of World War II. Dividing their investigation into two periods (1940s to late 1960s and late 1970s to the present), they identify both commonalities and differences. The commonality has to do with the logic of regime survival affecting the creation and design of weak regional institutions. "The domestic survival of ruling coalitions was always a pivotal consideration in the design of the Arab League."[66] But there have been new developments during the second phase with respect to sources of institutional design and the failure to cooperate. The core variable of institutional design in the first phase is the normative force of Arab nationalism. The main obstacles to institutionalization and cooperation were the norms of pan-Arabism and competing domestic political agendas of different Arab states. These have been more important in shaping institutional design and quality of cooperation than the role of extra-regional powers or the Cold War, or intra-regional power differentials. An important lesson of Middle Eastern regionalism is that shared identity can actually hinder collective action, if it's seen as a threat to sovereignty. Overall, cooperation in the League has been subject to the dictates of state sovereignty concerns; no functional cooperation that would circumscribe sovereignty has been undertaken. The authors find support for the argument that regimes enjoying high legitimacy may favor stronger institutions while those with weak legitimacy fear compromising sovereignty and regime survival through the establishment of strongly binding regional institutions. Turning to the second phase, the authors identify the decline of identity and the rise of international market forces, international institutional pressures, new domestic coalitions reflecting among others demand for foreign investment and financial assistance, and a growing interest in regional cooperation outside of the Arab League, as key determinants of regional institutions. While these shifts have led

[66] Barnet and Solingen, this volume, p. 213.

to the further discrediting of the Arab League, the new possibilities of regional cooperation could not be fully exploited because of considerable path dependency created by prior institutional design variables.

Finally, Jeff Checkel's chapter deals with the European Union. While acknowledging that initial strategic, incentive-based cooperation may lead to preference shifts and more durable change, he considers three mechanisms that connect institutions and their design. The first includes mechanisms relying upon incentives and cost-benefit emphasized by rationalist literature, which does not lead to preference change but only to strategic adaptation. The second is cognitive role enhancement, derived from the cognitive/social psychology literature which stresses the impact of organizational or group environments, and leads to some non-calculative behavioral adaptation without internalization. Finally, he considers communication and normative suasion, which is based on a communicative understanding of rationality, rather than instrumental or bounded rationality. Here, actors do not simply calculate costs and benefits, or take their cues from the organizational environment, but present arguments and try to persuade and convince each other. And their interests and preferences remain open for possible redefinition, unlike in rationalist accounts. A distinctive aspect of his chapter is the identification of the social mechanisms or micro-processes that link design features with quality of cooperation. Here, instead of using traditional European research traditions, such as neo-functionalism and intergovernmentalism, he draws from the emerging literature on persuasion. Judged by the intergovernmentalism criteria, cooperation is of high quality. But judged in terms of persuasion, which allows for measuring deeper quality, or thick persuasion, there is less to the EU's quality of cooperation than is commonly believed. Thick persuasion entails "change in the belief, attitude or behavior of another person"[67] leading to deeper levels of cooperation. Checkel's chapter provides a model of data and analysis of micro-processes of cooperation that we hope will inspire future work on other regions.

Overall then, we believe that this project and the book will make a contribution to the comparative study of regionalism and institution-building around the world. Through this project, we hope to advance our understanding of, and stimulate further interest in, the issue of regional institutionalization. We also seek to restore interest in the institutional features of regionalism which has lagged due to the popularity of the "new regionalism" literature which has had little interest in the design features of regional institutions. At the same time, it is especially important that

[67] Checkel, this volume, p. 231.

this renewed interest in institutionalization extends the range of analysis beyond the rationalist approach to institutional design to include constructivist and other approaches. Finally, we hope to illuminate questions, important to both academics and policymakers, about the similarities and differences among regional groups, especially those in the West and those in the developing world. Through a systematic comparison of an exceptionally rich set of empirical studies, we especially hope to throw critical light on whether the claims of uniqueness and exceptionalism, found especially in the case of European and Asian institutions, hold up to scrutiny.

2 Hanging together, institutional design, and cooperation in Southeast Asia: AFTA and the ARF*

Yuen Foong Khong and Helen E. S. Nesadurai

1. Introduction

One of the most fascinating developments in post-Cold War Asia-Pacific is the frenzy of (regional) institution-building that began in the late 1980s. At the intergovernmental level, we witness the founding of the following: Asia-Pacific Economic Cooperation (APEC, 1989), the ASEAN Free Trade Area (AFTA, 1992), the ASEAN Regional Forum (ARF, 1994), and the ASEAN Plus Three forum (APT, 1997). Equally fascinating, the Association of Southeast Asian Nations (ASEAN) – a group of small to middle powers[1] – played a lead role in the creation and maintenance of many of these institutions, in particular the ARF, AFTA, and the APT, while ASEAN's preference for informality and non-binding mechanisms prevailed over American and Australian preferences in the institutional design of APEC. Important too is the enlargement of ASEAN to ten members through the inclusion of Vietnam, Laos, Myanmar, and Cambodia in the 1990s. The reason for ASEAN's leading role in regional institution-building is partly historical, since ASEAN, formed in 1967, was until the 1990s the only regional institution of note in Asia.[2] Hence it seemed natural to build on the strengths and achievements of ASEAN – whether it was the expansion of ASEAN itself, buttressing intra-ASEAN economic cooperation, engaging new partners in financial cooperation through the APT, or reaching out to the great powers in the form of the ARF.[3]

* We would like to thank Paul Evans, the editors, and members of the Crafting Cooperation workshops in Singapore and Cambridge (MA), for their comments on an earlier draft of the paper.

[1] ASEAN comprises ten members – Brunei, Cambodia, Indonesia, Laos, Malaysia, Myanmar, Philippines, Singapore, Thailand, and Vietnam.

[2] Other attempts at regional institution-building such as SEATO (1954), ASA (1962), and MAPHILINDO (1963) were either ineffectual or they petered out quickly.

[3] Non-governmental or Track II regional mechanisms have also become prominent in the region, usually closely associated with one or more of the intergovernmental institutions.

ASEAN has clearly exhibited substantial institutional evolution since the 1990s if we go by one feature of institutional design identified by Acharya and Johnston in this volume (Chapter 1). Institutional scope has expanded as an ever-broadening range of tasks is now addressed by ASEAN, including economic integration, trans-boundary environmental problems, non-traditional security issues (transnational crime, terrorism), and social development issues. In addition, ASEAN has engaged in what may be termed a "functional expansion of membership" through creating ASEAN-plus institutions to deal with new issue areas that involve states outside Southeast Asia or that require capabilities not found amongst ASEAN members. The creation of the ARF and the APT reflect these two dynamics, the former aimed at addressing new security challenges in the wider Asia-Pacific region following the end of the Cold War. While the APT is broadly aimed at creating functional linkages between ASEAN and its three Northeast Asian neighbors, namely China, Japan, and South Korea, its most visible success to date is in financial cooperation, particularly the Chiang Mai Initiative (CMI). A direct response to the trauma of the 1997–98 Asian financial crisis and dissatisfaction with IMF responses to the crisis, the CMI is a regional liquidity facility aimed at providing short-term financing to support currencies in crises. Hence, it was a project that could not have been undertaken by ASEAN alone given its need for large amounts of financial reserves, which only Japan and China were able to contribute when the project was launched in 2000. Together with a second APT project, the Asian Bond Market Initiative (ABMI), the CMI has been lauded as significant to the development of regional capabilities in financial crisis management and prevention.[4]

Notwithstanding the expansion in the scope of ASEAN institutions, institutional design in ASEAN remains wedded to state sovereignty as an initial preference, which results in a high degree of autonomy for national governments in determining domestic policy. The principle of non-interference in the internal affairs of member countries and the search for accommodation and consensus that has traditionally guided decision-making and behavior in the Association – collectively termed the

Among the more prominent of these Track II mechanisms are the ASEAN Institute of Strategic and International Studies (ASEAN-ISIS, formed 1987) and the Council for Security Cooperation in the Asia-Pacific (CSCAP, 1993), not to mention the numerous regional "strategic studies think tanks" with "networking" as one of their primary missions.

[4] Stephen Grenville, "Policy Dialogue in East Asia: Principles for Success," in Gordon de Brouwer and Yunjong Wang (eds.), *Financial Governance in East Asia: Policy Dialogue, Surveillance and Cooperation* (London and New York: Routledge Curzon, 2004), pp. 16–37.

"ASEAN Way" – has remained a constant feature of ASEAN institutions. Yet, institutional adaptation has taken place in some instances as member governments made gradual changes to institutional design in order that cooperative outcomes may be delivered more effectively. Such a process of incremental learning has been especially prominent in economic cooperation, with member governments responding to setbacks in regional liberalization as these arose by devising new rules that raised the costs to members of defecting from commitments they had already made. Nevertheless, flexibility and the search for consensus have remained key design features of all ASEAN institutions, which continue to emphasize intergovernmental decision-making. This combination of flexibility plus rules was evident in the design of the ASEAN Free Trade Area (AFTA) while additional changes to regional economic institutions have been adopted once ASEAN embarked on the ASEAN Economic Community (AEC) project, the successor to AFTA that aims to create a single, integrated regional market by 2020. Member governments have agreed to accord greater authority to the ASEAN Secretariat to monitor compliance in the AEC and adjudicate disputes, including through rule interpretation, while also involving third-party experts in some aspects of dispute resolution, all firsts for ASEAN. Decision-making remains the purview of intergovernmental mechanisms, however, which creates opportunities for intergovernmental bargaining and the search for political accommodation between members. In contrast to the quite substantial institutional changes seen in economic cooperation, the ARF remains closely wedded to the "ASEAN Way." The pattern of institutional design associated with ASEAN is, therefore, a mixed one, and it raises two questions: what accounts for the persistence of the "ASEAN Way," including as an initial or baseline preference, and how do we explain subsequent departures from it?

We account for the persistence of the "ASEAN Way" in terms of historical path dependence coupled with the imperative of domestic regime security. The "ASEAN Way" principles emerged out of a gradual diplomatic process of rapprochement that took place amongst the initial five members of ASEAN since the grouping's formation in 1967. Given the considerable tensions, including overt challenges to sovereignty that existed amongst these founding members, their coming together in ASEAN was unsurprisingly premised on a shared undertaking not to undermine the sovereignty, stability, and territorial integrity of member states, including a commitment to refrain from exploiting domestic divisions to destabilize national governments. Over time, these principles became consolidated in the way ASEAN practiced its internal diplomacy – what has been termed the "diplomacy of accommodation."[5] ASEAN members engaged in regular processes of consultation over key issues of the day, with these processes of searching for accommodation facilitated by the presence of regular forums, committees, and other meetings involving ministers, senior officials, and diplomats from member governments.

Moreover, there were clear gains from approaching cooperation in line with the "ASEAN Way." The "ASEAN Way" had proved to be a valuable blueprint for ASEAN in a number of tasks involving diplomatic coordination, the most notable being ASEAN's role in seeking a resolution to the Cambodian crisis during the 1980s. Adhering to the ASEAN norms of accommodative diplomacy helped ASEAN members develop a consensus position on what they regarded as the most serious challenge to regional security in the 1980s – Vietnam's 1978 invasion and occupation of Cambodia – despite initial internal differences over the nature of the threat and how to address it. By doing so, these principles enabled ASEAN to project and sustain the Cambodian conflict on the international agenda despite the Association's limited material capabilities and the marginal international interest in Southeast Asia at that time.

The "ASEAN Way" also helped prevent ASEAN itself from disunity and policy paralysis stemming from differences on the Cambodian issue. In the early 1990s, following the end of the Cold War, the "ASEAN Way" was found to be a useful *modus vivendi* for engaging with the Western powers now intent on promoting democratization, respect for individual human rights, and comprehensive economic liberalization worldwide, goals to which the ASEAN members gave only qualified support. In addition, subscribing to the "ASEAN Way" shielded national governments from having to commit to addressing joint tasks that governments either found too demanding administratively, politically difficult if these went against dominant domestic interests, or not sufficiently important given a set of national priorities. It is not surprising given these benefits of the "ASEAN Way" that this principle became entrenched as a central institutional feature of ASEAN. While this suggests a functionalist explanation for the persistence of the "ASEAN Way," there is also a pragmatic, perhaps even normative, commitment to a principle that has come to be seen by its members as the most appropriate standard of behavior for a group of very diverse states having to work together on common problems.

[5] Michael Antolik, *ASEAN and the Diplomacy of Accommodation* (New York: M. E. Sharpe, 1990).

Thus, when the ASEAN members began to address new transnational security and economic problems that needed joint action, including through the ARF, their initial preference was for non-intrusive institutional forms based on the "ASEAN Way" that combined a commitment to cooperate with sufficient autonomy for member governments to respond to and safeguard domestic priorities, even if these were not clearly defined at the time cooperation commenced. Over time, ASEAN revealed that it was prepared to adopt new mechanisms of cooperation if the original problem remained intractable, reflecting a process of incremental learning and institutional adaptation. In selected issue areas, member governments even crafted increasingly intrusive regional institutions when these were believed to be necessary for cooperation to succeed. Such institutional departures from the "ASEAN Way" have, however, been confined thus far to problem areas recognized as capable of seriously disrupting economic growth. Economic growth was and remains a central basis of political legitimacy in Southeast Asia and acts as a guarantor of domestic regime security, particularly in the semi-democratic or soft authoritarian political systems found in much of Southeast Asia.[6] In such a context, how economic crises are experienced (severity of domestic impact) and/or how events are construed in terms of their potential to disrupt economic growth provides the political space for members to review the design of regional institutions. A "if we don't hang together, we will hang separately" syndrome operates to prompt the adoption of relatively (for ASEAN) more intrusive institutional mechanisms in order to deliver the *joint* collaboration needed to counter developments construed as threatening to economic growth. Unsurprisingly, it is in regional economic cooperation and integration that we see a significant shift in institutional design away from the "ASEAN Way" toward stronger rules and relatively more centralization.

While the formation of the ARF represents a significant act of institutional innovation on the part of ASEAN, the absence of a shared external threat permitted the "ASEAN Way" – emphasizing non-interference, accommodation, and consensual decision-making – to dominate institutional design, with only a modest degree of institutionalization acceptable. In general, therefore, intrusive mechanisms, formal rules, majority voting, and speedy action have not been part of the ARF's institutional make-up. This might lead us to expect – especially if we rely implicitly or explicitly

[6] R. Stubbs, "Performance Legitimacy and Soft Authoritarianism," in Amitav Acharya, B. Michael Frolic, and Richard Stubbs (eds.), *Democracy, Human Rights, and Civil Society in Southeast Asia* (Toronto: Joint Centre for Asia Pacific Studies, York University, 2001), pp. 37–54.

on European Union and AFTA institutional benchmarks – a much less robust and effective form of cooperation to prevail in the ARF. And the latter seems to be the consensus view of the ARF. We argue, however, that while the ARF has significant failings (in particular its slow movement toward Preventive Diplomacy), it has been able to advance security cooperation in three areas: confidence building, expanding ASEAN's Treaty of Amity and Cooperation (TAC), and counter-terrorism.[7]

Confidence building has been the hallmark activity of the ARF in its first decade. The older ASEAN states extended, writ large to the ARF, a process they had found indispensable in ASEAN's early years, when reconciliation between formerly antagonistic states was imperative. Because the ARF included participants who distrusted one another for historical, ideological, and power political reasons, confidence building was viewed as necessary in its infancy. Most of the activities of the ARF, from the discussion forum itself to the voluntary submission of Defense White Papers to the Inter-sessional Support Group work (ISG), may be seen as Confidence Building Mechanisms (CBMs). These activities were seen by those driving the ARF as essential steps in building trust. Cultivating habits of dialogue and increasing comfort levels among the ARF participants were means to the goal of future security cooperation. Did anything concrete emerge from all these activities? Years of patient confidence building, we suggest, have facilitated the gradual acceptance of the norms of regional conduct espoused by ASEAN's TAC. This can be seen in the accession, in recent years, of China, India, Japan, South Korea, Russia, Pakistan, New Zealand, and Australia to the TAC. France, the European Union, and Timor Leste are on the verge of acceding to the Treaty as this volume goes to print.

The TAC expects its signatories to adhere to norms such as respecting the territorial integrity and political sovereignty of fellow signatories, non-interference in each other's internal affairs, and renunciation of the use of force in settling disputes. Even though the TAC does not specify any sanctions for violating these norms, the latter constitute an important restraint on state behavior. ASEAN's experience convinces it that states do not sign such treaties lightly because of the serious credibility and reputation costs they will incur if they violate norms they have promised to uphold. ASEAN's experience in the 1980s – when it acted in concert to

[7] A fourth important advance in security cooperation is ASEAN's stated aspiration to become a security community by 2020. See Joint Communiqué of the 37th ASEAN Ministerial Meeting, Jakarta, 29–30 June 2004, www.aseansec.org/16192.htm. We omit discussion of this development here because the ASEAN Security Community (ASC) is an ASEAN, not an ARF, project. It may be argued however that there are interactive causal effects between the ASEAN, the ARF, and the ASC.

isolate Vietnam (who had not even signed the TAC!) for violating the TAC norms – suggests that even without strong legal sanction, treaties like the TAC can function as normative focal points around which regional states can organize to marginalize and delegitimize errant states. In that sense, the accession of the major Asian Pacific powers to ASEAN's TAC is an important achievement; it is also a sign of significant security cooperation because ASEAN and the ARF see the TAC as central to creating "a more predictable constructive pattern of relationships for the Asia-Pacific."[8]

The third area of substantive ARF cooperation is in counter-terrorism. Since 9/11, ARF members have also initiated a flurry of counter-terrorism activities, from intelligence sharing, learning about interdicting terrorist finances, devoting high-level attention to people smuggling/trafficking, to upgrading the training of officials in newly created law enforcement and counter-terrorism centers. All in all, the volume and quality of cooperation among ARF participants have been higher than pessimists have allowed.[9]

Our assessment of security cooperation in the ARF suggests that intrusive rules and mechanisms may not be necessary for meaningful cooperation. In fact, "the ASEAN Way," slow and cumbersome as it is, has served the ARF well. Our analysis of the ARF also suggests that the less formal, "weakly organized 'talk-shops' of Asia-Pacific" seem capable of inducing security cooperation, though not to the same extent of robustness seen in "the more formalized, bureaucratized and often times intrusive institutions of European cooperation [and AFTA, we may add]."[10] In recent years, the ARF has taken small steps to formalize and bureaucratize some of its procedures, such as enhancing the role of the ARF Chair and the setting up of an ARF unit within the ASEAN Secretariat.[11] These steps are likely to enhance the ARF's capabilities for robust cooperation. But if our assessment of the ARF's ability to achieve meaningful cooperation via the modalities of the "ASEAN Way" (and in the absence of a consuming threat) is correct, more intrusive rules and greater formality are not the only route to efficacious joint action. The variety of ASEAN experiences in regional institution-building and cooperation detailed in the rest of this

[8] See Chairman's Statement, First ASEAN Regional Forum, Bangkok, 25 July 1994, and The ASEAN Regional Forum: A Concept Paper, in *ASEAN Regional Forum: Documents Series 1994–1998* (Jakarta, 1999), pp. 1–3, and 13–15 respectively.

[9] See for example, Robyn Lim, "The ASEAN Regional Forum: Building on Sand," in *Contemporary Southeast Asia*, 20:2 (1998), pp. 115–36; John Funston, "Challenges Facing ASEAN in a More Complex Age," *Contemporary Southeast Asia*, 21:2 (1999), pp. 205–19.

[10] Quoted phrases are from Acharya and Johnston, Chapter 1, this volume.

[11] ASEAN Secretariat, *Matrix of ASEAN Regional Forum Decisions and Status, 1994–2004*. www.aseansec.org/ARF/MatrixofARFDecisions.doc

chapter illustrates this point: that there is more than one path to quality cooperation.

A brief note on the focus on AFTA and the ARF may be appropriate here. Our choice was based primarily on our interest in exploring the post-Cold War design and features of one important Asian Pacific regional economic, and one important regional security, institution. The two cases may be considered independently, but we have not shied away from comparing them. Their broad similarities as well as important differences seem to invite comparison, insofar as the conclusions of such a comparison are seen as suggestive instead of definitive. Both AFTA and the ARF were post-Cold War creations; they were the regional-institutional responses crafted by Southeast Asia's elites to address the changing environment. AFTA dealt with economic issues while the ARF dealt with security issues. ASEAN would also be in the driver's seat for both. There are indeed issues of scale, scope, and function that make attempts to compare the two challenging. AFTA is composed of the ten members of ASEAN and focuses exclusively on economic integration while the ARF has twenty-four participants – including great, middle, and small powers – addressing a broad range of security issues. We acknowledge these differences, but we maintain that the broad similarities mentioned above provide a basis for meaningful comparisons.

In the next section, we provide a brief history of ASEAN's origins and evolution, with special emphasis on the contributions of the "ASEAN Way" to the organization's early achievements. Section 3 discusses the strategic and economic dilemmas posed by the post-Cold War environment to the "ASEAN Way"; it also analyses the responses of some of ASEAN's key leaders. Sections 4 and 5 examine two regional institutions, AFTA and the ARF, documenting how the former departed from the "ASEAN Way" while the latter continued to adhere to it, and explaining their differences in terms of the presence or absence of a grave external threat. In the conclusion we recapitulate the differences between AFTA and the ARF in institutional design and features and reiterate the salience of external threats (economic in this case) in compelling movement toward a more rule-bound and bureaucratized design. We also argue, however, that the less rule-bound and bureaucratized institution (the ARF) did not languish: it also chalked up important gains in security cooperation.

2. ASEAN: formation and institutional consolidation, 1967–90

ASEAN's 1967 founding members are Indonesia, Malaysia, the Philippines, Singapore, and Thailand. Brunei joined the grouping in 1984 following its independence from Britain, Vietnam in 1995, Laos and Myanmar in 1997, and Cambodia in 1999, bringing ASEAN's current membership to ten. What is remarkable about this grouping is the fact that it could be established at all. Relations among the founding members were highly charged during the 1960s, with interstate rivalries expressed in various forms: (1) irredentism, when neighbors laid claim to the territory of other states; (2) assistance provided by one government to secessionist groups in another state; and (3) non-recognition of another state, thus denying legitimacy to its government. These added to existing vulnerabilities of national governments facing the difficult task of governing domestically divided societies and controlling peripheral parts of the state.[12] By 1967, governments of the day in these five regional states had come to realize that such forms of behavior were decidedly unproductive and costly to national governments.[13] They decided to form ASEAN as a mechanism for regional rapprochement, anticipating that participation in the Association would help moderate the currently unrestrained competitive dynamics between their countries. This, in turn, would enable governments to focus attention and resources on addressing the myriad domestic economic, political, and socio-economic challenges they faced without having to constantly look over their shoulder at what neighbors were getting up to.[14] In common with many developing or "Third World" states, these deeply divided Southeast Asian states were primarily concerned with securing domestic political regimes and ensuring political order.[15] The primary instrument they adopted to deliver on this goal was economic development.[16]

Mandate and scope Neither an alliance nor a mutual defense pact directed against another state, ASEAN was constituted as a diplomatic process of mutual accommodation between its members during this period.[17] Its mandate was decidedly deliberative, stressing regular

[12] On this point, see Arnfinn Jorgensen-Dahl, *Regional Organisation and Order in Southeast Asia* (London: Macmillan, 1982).

[13] The ouster by General (later President) Suharto of Indonesian President Sukarno who had initiated Indonesia's limited guerrilla war against Malaysia was the catalyst for this move.

[14] Michael Antolik, *ASEAN: The Anatomy of a Security Entente*, Ph.D dissertation (unpublished), Columbia University, 1986.

[15] Mohammad Ayoob, *The Third World Security Predicament* (Boulder, CO: Lynne Rienner, 1995).

[16] See Michael Leifer, *ASEAN and the Security of Southeast Asia* (London: Routledge, 1989), pp. 3–4; and Amitav Acharya, "Ideas, Identity, and Institution-Building: From the 'ASEAN Way' to the 'Asia-Pacific Way'," *The Pacific Review*, 10:3 (1997), pp. 319–46.

[17] Antolik, *Anatomy of a Security Entente*, pp. 17–19.

consultations and dialogue among its members on a host of shared intra-regional problems and wider concerns in the political and security arenas. The most notable of these regular consultations was the annual meeting of foreign ministers, termed the ASEAN Ministerial Meeting.[18] These institutionalized consultations and meetings effectively acted as a means of signaling to member governments that each party was committed to continuing cooperation, while intra-mural suspicions were kept at bay by demonstrations of goodwill, including cooperating on specific problems, notably the border disputes between members and the communist insurgency that also spilled across national borders. ASEAN was, in effect, aimed at developing a shared understanding that each member would practice restraint in its relations with fellow members.

Formal rules and norms Given the deliberative or process mandate of the Association during this period and its limited scope, formal rules were unnecessary and therefore not considered, aside from the commitment not to undermine the sovereignty, stability, and territorial integrity of member states. It was only nine years following ASEAN's founding that the Treaty of Amity and Cooperation in Southeast Asia (TAC) was adopted, the first formal agreement of the Association and the first that was signed by heads of state.[19] It was the first time that the principles of interstate engagement in ASEAN were formally articulated. Interstate behavior in ASEAN is guided by two sets of principles – regulative norms, or the "ground rules" on how states should behave to one another, and procedural norms, which guide collective decision-making.[20] The regulative rules of ASEAN are formally expressed in Article 2 of the TAC, and include respect for the sovereignty and territorial integrity of all nations and non-interference in the internal affairs of another state.[21] Apart from these rules, a set of procedural norms also governs the manner in which members engage in collective decision-making – these have been termed the "ASEAN Way."[22] Prescribing means rather than ends, and not formally articulated in the TAC, the "ASEAN Way," which emerged

[18] See *The ASEAN Declaration (Bangkok Declaration)*, Thailand, 8 August 1967. www.aseansec.org/3640.htm

[19] The foreign ministers of ASEAN had signed the ASEAN Declaration (or Bangkok Declaration) that launched ASEAN in August 1967. We define formal agreements as those requiring ratification. See Charles Lipson, "Why Are Some International Agreements Informal?," *International Organisation*, 45:4 (1992), pp. 495–538.

[20] Brian Job, "ASEAN Stalled: Dilemmas and Tensions Over Conflicting Norms." Paper presented to the 1999 Annual Meeting of the American Political Science Association, Atlanta, USA, 2–5 September, 1999, pp. 9–10.

[21] ASEAN, *Treaty of Amity and Cooperation in Southeast Asia*, Indonesia, 24 February 1976, www.aseansec.org/1654.htm

[22] Acharya, "Ideas, Identity and Institution-Building," p. 329.

through a process of elite socialization over time, prescribes informality over formal institutions, flexibility, the practice of consensus, and non-confrontational bargaining styles.[23] Apart from these rules and norms, no formal or centralized mechanism for monitoring and enforcement of collective decisions was proposed in the TAC, apart from the ministerial-level High Council, which has never been invoked to settle disputes in ASEAN.[24]

Actor independence The non-interference principle and the "ASEAN Way" norms help reinforce the domestic autonomy of national governments by reassuring member states that they will not be publicly pressed to undertake actions that run counter to domestic interests.[25] Agent autonomy was, consequently, high in ASEAN during this period. Although these norms were primarily about intra-group behavior, they also helped ASEAN in its international diplomacy over the Cambodian conflict by facilitating the adoption of a concerted group position on the matter.

ASEAN and the Cambodian conflict: a case of successful cooperation

For the ASEAN states, the December 1978 Vietnamese invasion of Cambodia and the subsequent installation of a Vietnamese-backed government in that country was the most serious security threat confronting Southeast Asia during the period in question. This event violated the sovereignty principle of the international system, which was also a fundamental principle of an ASEAN framework of regional order. It exposed Thailand as a frontline state given its shared border with Cambodia and its proximity to Vietnam. This case has been extensively studied and details will not be repeated here save to draw out salient features that illustrate why we regard it as a case of successful cooperation by ASEAN during the 1967–90 period.[26]

Deep divisions within the Association marred ASEAN's initial search for a resolution to the crisis. While Indonesia and Malaysia were prepared to accommodate to Vietnam by recognizing its "legitimate" security interests in Indochina, Singapore and Thailand rejected such a stance. When Vietnamese troops entered Thailand in pursuit of Cambodian guerrillas,

[23] Nikolas Busse, "Constructivism and Southeast Asian Security," *The Pacific Review*, 12:1 (1999), pp. 39–60.
[24] For details, see Antolik, *Anatomy of a Security Entente.*
[25] Busse, "Constructivism," p. 47.
[26] For an extensive treatment of ASEAN and the Cambodian crisis, see Acharya, *Constructing a Security Community in Southeast Asia* (London: Routledge, 2001), pp. 80–101.

Indonesia and Malaysia were prepared to alter their positions in the face of a threat to a fellow ASEAN member. Indonesia now agreed to the holding of an international conference on Cambodia as a means toward seeking a resolution to the conflict, a position long endorsed by Singapore and Thailand but rejected by Indonesia. By adjusting its policy position, Indonesia effectively endorsed internationalizing the crisis, which potentially allowed China considerable clout over the terms of a settlement. This was a significant policy switch by Indonesia given Jakarta's very strong preference for regional autonomy in managing regional conflicts and its perception that China rather than Vietnam posed the greater threat to the region.[27] For Indonesia, this act of policy adjustment was acknowledged to be vital to prevent the collapse of ASEAN, which had become a key plank of Indonesian foreign policy. Policy adjustment was seen as a symbol of Indonesia's aspirations for responsible regional citizenship under the Suharto regime.[28]

Indonesia's and Malaysia's willingness to adjust their policies to the ASEAN "mean" on the Cambodian issue allowed the grouping to project and sustain the issue on the international diplomatic agenda through concerted lobbying despite the relatively low attention accorded to this problem by the great powers. Secondly, ASEAN successfully framed the crisis as a violation by Vietnam of the accepted principles of international order, namely sovereignty and national self-determination. Based on these principles, ASEAN supported the ousted Democratic Kampuchea (DK) government of Pol Pot's Khmer Rouge despite its murderous record. ASEAN also used these principles to successfully prevent a 1979 Vietnamese attempt at the United Nations to deny recognition to the ousted DK government. ASEAN successfully denied Vietnam's claim that the conflict was an internal power struggle between different Cambodian factions, which compelled Hanoi to intervene to stabilize the domestic situation in Cambodia and prevent its spread across the Vietnamese border. ASEAN lobbying helped to isolate Vietnam internationally, reflected in increased majorities supporting ASEAN-sponsored UN resolutions condemning Vietnam.[29] Third, a concerted ASEAN approach on Cambodia also enabled the grouping to push for a resolution of the crisis that required replacing the Vietnamese-installed regime through free and fair elections in which all major Cambodian factions would participate, including the Khmer Rouge, a position that was eventually reflected in the Paris Peace Agreements of 1991 that ended the conflict. Thus, the sovereignty norm held dear by ASEAN as well as its procedural emphasis on consultation, flexibility, and consensus

[27] Acharya, *Constructing a Security Community*, p. 87. [28] Ibid. [29] Ibid., p. 90.

in the end helped the Association function as a coherent international diplomatic lobby group and as a conflict mediator beyond that dictated by its material capabilities.[30]

3. Institutional innovations in a changing environment, 1991–2006: debating the future of the "ASEAN Way"

While the Cambodian crisis constituted the single most important problem facing ASEAN during the 1980s, ASEAN from the 1990s confronted a range of new transnational issues that required joint action. The most pressing included the regional environmental pollution caused by forest fires in Indonesia, the 1997–98 Asian financial crisis, the 1997 coup in Cambodia, the 1999 East Timor crisis, increasing transnational crimes, and more recently terrorism. More generally, ASEAN has had to contend with the strategic implications of the end of the Cold War and the demise of the Soviet Union. Its goal of "One Southeast Asia," to be achieved through the incorporation of Vietnam, Laos, Myanmar, and Cambodia into the Association, also brought new challenges, notably the question of how to deal with continued political repression and human rights abuses in Myanmar and the outflow of refugees from that country, especially into Thailand. Institutional scope expanded as a result of these new pressing problems, with ASEAN now actively engaged in regional cooperation on the environment, regional trade liberalization, and economic integration, among others.[31] ASEAN also formed the ARF and the APT, two new regional institutions that saw an expansion of membership beyond ASEAN.

Task expansion in the face of these new realities was a notable achievement for ASEAN. Yet, there remained the question of whether the Association would be able to devise effective responses to these new challenges. Much would depend on the extent to which ASEAN members were prepared to adjust or alter domestic policies beyond what they had been prepared to do during the 1967–90 period when ASEAN focused largely on diplomatic coordination. The debate that took place in the region on the need for ASEAN to review its cherished non-interference norm and its long-standing emphasis on informality, discreet diplomacy, and the search for consensus revealed how difficult it was for member governments to craft effective joint responses to these new problems whilst retaining core features of ASEAN's original institutional design.

[30] Mely Caballero-Anthony, *Regional Security in Southeast Asia: Beyond the ASEAN Way* (Singapore: Institute of Southeast Asian Studies, 2005), pp. 106–7.

[31] A detailed listing of agenda items addressed by the organization is found in the ASEAN Annual Reports.

The limits to renegotiating the "ASEAN Way"

ASEAN during the 1990s considered a number of institutional modifications that departed from the Association's non-interference norm as a means of dealing with the emerging transnational problems noted above. The ideas of "flexible engagement" and later "enhanced interaction" were attempts to reconsider how ASEAN addressed the growing transnational problems facing its members. This attempt at normative shift was triggered by the Asian financial crisis, the serious transboundary pollution haze caused by Indonesian forest fires, Myanmar's admission into ASEAN, and the coup in Cambodia, all of which took place in 1997. Flexible engagement, it was suggested, could help ASEAN develop more effective common policy responses to address problems such as the haze, financial crises, human rights concerns, refugees, and the pressing problem posed by political repression in Myanmar.[32]

Proposed by Thailand and supported by the Philippines, the other members roundly rejected the notion of "flexible engagement." The incoming new members were especially resistant to any move to review ASEAN's long-standing policy on non-interference. Flexible engagement simply meant that the ASEAN states should be able to freely discuss fellow members' domestic policies, especially those that had regional externalities. The rest of the ASEAN states could not accept this normative shift for the grouping as it had implications for how they conducted their own internal affairs, particularly in relation to democratization and human rights.[33] In fact, the flexible engagement idea had been predated by the more ambitious notion of "constructive intervention." First raised in July 1997 by then Malaysian Deputy Prime Minister Anwar Ibrahim following the coup in Cambodia, Anwar took the view that ASEAN's failure to become involved in Cambodia's reconstruction following the Paris Peace Agreements had contributed to the deterioration in Cambodia's political situation. Anwar then called for a review of the ASEAN non-interference principle to stave off similar crises in other ASEAN states, advocating direct assistance to consolidate electoral processes, legal and administrative reforms, and for the strengthening of civil society in member states, albeit with the consent of the state in question.[34] The idea of constructive intervention was, however, poorly received and short-lived, with little debate on it in ASEAN. Thai Foreign Minister Surin Pitsuwan would later advance the revised notion of flexible engagement, which at

[32] Acharya, *Constructing a Security Community*, p. 153.
[33] Hiro Katsumata, "Why is ASEAN Diplomacy Changing?," *Asian Survey*, 44:2 (2004), pp. 237–54.
[34] Acharya, *Constructing a Security Community*, p. 118.

least elicited rather more debate within the grouping than had the idea of constructive intervention.[35]

While the drive by Thailand and the Philippines to review ASEAN's non-interference principle reflected the normative commitment to liberal values held by leaders and foreign policymakers in these two countries at the time of the debate,[36] there were also instrumental considerations that prompted Thailand especially to advocate reconsideration of non-interference. As Acharya notes, Thailand saw the necessity of shifting away from the non-interference principle if Bangkok was to be able to put pressure on the government in Myanmar over the influx of refugees from that country into Thai territory.[37] At the same time, countries such as Thailand and the Philippines, which at that time had the best record in ASEAN on political rights and civil liberties,[38] were also less concerned about other countries commenting on internal developments in their respective states. They were also the most sympathetic to some form of humanitarian intervention in response to the East Timor crisis in 1999.[39] For the other ASEAN members, adherence to non-interference shielded their domestic policies and practices from external scrutiny. Nevertheless, there was also genuine concern in the rest of ASEAN that abandoning this "time-honored principle" would take ASEAN down the "path towards eventual disintegration."[40] The "ASEAN Way" was seen by most of its members as the bedrock of ASEAN unity, a principle that had well served an Association made up of member states displaying considerable diversity in politics, economics, and society. The balance of preferences in the grouping was firmly against reviewing ASEAN's traditional approach to interstate diplomacy. Thailand and the Philippines as a result deferred to the majority view.

The fragility of these attempts at institutional innovation is reflected in the current Thai position on non-interference. A marked turnaround

[35] Ibid., p. 119.

[36] Katsumata, "ASEAN Diplomacy," pp. 247–9. Incidentally, Anwar too was regarded as a reformist and a champion of such liberal ideals as civil reform. See John Hilley, *Malaysia: Mahathirism, Hegemony, and the New Opposition* (London and New York: Zed Books, 2001), pp. 75–6.

[37] Acharya, *Constructing a Security Community*, p. 153.

[38] See Freedom House's *Freedom in the World, 1998–99: The Annual Survey of Political Rights and Civil Liberties* (Liscataway, NJ: Transaction, 1999). Information recorded in Katsumata, "ASEAN Diplomacy," pp. 243–8.

[39] Derek McDougal, "Regional Institutions and Security: Implications of the 1999 East Timor Crisis," in Andrew Tan and Kenneth Boutin (eds.), *Non-Traditional Security Issues in Southeast Asia* (Singapore: Institute of Defense and Strategic Studies, 2001), pp. 166–89.

[40] The view of the then Malaysian Foreign Minister, Abdullah Badawi, quoted in *Reuters*, "ASEAN debate on democracy, human rights hots up," 26 July 1998.

from previous administrations more committed to liberal principles, then Thai Prime Minister Thaksin Shinawatra (whose normative commitment to liberal democratic principles is doubtful) firmly rejected in 2004 any discussion at the ASEAN level of the growing violence in Southern Thailand, a situation that had implications for Malaysia, which borders the conflict zone.[41] Similarly, and despite much rhetoric, ASEAN has failed to take strong action against the present military government in Myanmar. The latter has been internationally shunned for failing to respect the results of national elections held in 1990 that had been won by the opposition National League for Democracy under Aung San Suu Kyi. Myanmar, in fact, has preoccupied ASEAN since it joined the grouping in 1997. The periodic arrests of opposition members and of Aung San Suu Kyi since then has worsened the pariah status of the military junta, and undermined ASEAN's standing in the international community for its failure to deal harshly with one of its member states.[42]

Western dialogue partners such as the US warned in 2005 that their relations with ASEAN could suffer if Myanmar assumed the rotational chair of ASEAN the following year.[43] There were further concerns that Western governments would also boycott the 2006 ASEAN Post-Ministerial Conference (involving ASEAN and its dialogue partners) and the ARF if Myanmar were in the chair. This prompted considerable debate within ASEAN over how to deal with Myanmar, a discussion that inevitably raised questions about the future of the non-interference principle. The region's lawmakers, through the ASEAN Inter-Parliamentary Organization (AIPO), called for ASEAN to censure the military junta and to expel Myanmar from ASEAN, a position fully endorsed by the region's civil society and human rights organizations.[44] In the end, very little has been achieved by ASEAN to expedite political reform in Myanmar.[45] ASEAN member states did not formally censure Myanmar at the 39th ASEAN Ministerial Meeting (AMM) held in July 2006. The AMM joint communiqué, in fact, acknowledged that "Myanmar needs both time and political space to deal with its many and complex challenges," a considerable let-down after the rhetoric by ASEAN members that Myanmar had to deliver on its commitment to political reform or face the

[41] Human rights groups have accused the Thai government of mishandling the conflict and committing gross violations of human rights when dealing with civilians and suspected insurgents. See *Associated Press*, "Thaksin threatens ASEAN's walkout," 25 November 2004.

[42] Acharya, *Constructing a Security Community*, p. 110.

[43] *New Straits Times*, "US-ASEAN ties at risk because of Myanmar," 5 May 2005.

[44] *New Straits Times*, "Yangon will not be bullied into democracy," 6 December 2006.

[45] Amitav Acharya, "Democracy in Burma: Does Anybody Really Care?," *YaleGlobal Online*, 1 September 2005. www.yaleglobal.yale.edu

consequences.[46] A year earlier, ASEAN had been spared a difficult decision when the ruling military junta in Myanmar "volunteered" to relinquish its turn as ASEAN Chair.[47] That decision not only took the heat off Myanmar, it also avoided a Western boycott of the 2006 ASEAN meetings. The ASEAN Secretariat has noted that expulsion of Myanmar was not an option as there was no procedure for expulsion of any member from the Association.[48]

ASEAN's reluctance to adopt a tougher line on Myanmar reflects partly the close economic links between Myanmar and ASEAN countries, notably but not exclusively Thailand, especially in the natural resource and the oil and gas sectors,[49] which place limits on the extent to which ASEAN governments will intervene in Myanmar's political affairs. Moreover, the courting of a strategically vital Myanmar by regional giants China and India, which refuse to pressure the junta on political reform,[50] leaves ASEAN with very little leverage over Myanmar. However, a major reason why some ASEAN members prefer the institutional status quo has to do with continued authoritarian political practices and the absence of genuine democracies in parts of ASEAN, especially in the new member states (Vietnam, Cambodia, and Laos). These internal political realities explain these states' reluctance to review the non-interference principle for fear of having their own domestic politics potentially open to future scrutiny and censure by ASEAN. In fact, ASEAN's diplomatic options in dealing with Myanmar have been limited by internal differences between the old and new members on the extent to which ASEAN should push for internal reform in Myanmar.[51] Unlike the Cambodian conflict during the 1980s, intractable internal differences on non-interference prevent the Association from forging a strong group position on the issue, which works to Myanmar's advantage. The matter is compounded by the fact that Myanmar is a member of ASEAN, unlike Vietnam and Cambodia during the time of the Cambodian crisis. The "ASEAN Way" thus has strong adherents within ASEAN, even if some of the older members (Malaysia, Philippines, Singapore) are keen to nudge Myanmar toward delivering on political reform.

[46] ASEAN, *Joint Communiqué of the 39th ASEAN Ministerial Meeting (AMM)*, Kuala Lumpur, 25 July 2006.
[47] Acharya, "Democracy in Burma".
[48] Zaid Ibrahim, "ASEAN can do more for change in Myanmar," *New Straits Times*, 31 July 2006.
[49] *Agence France Presse*, "New oil and gas deposits discovered in Myanmar: report," 7 August 2006.
[50] *Associated Press*, "India says it won't pressure Myanmar junta," 27 July 2006.
[51] Acharya, "Democracy in Burma."

The "ASEAN Way" approach to regional institution-building has also been applied to ASEAN's participation in *Pacific-wide* security and economic cooperation initiatives. The ARF, to be discussed in the next section, adheres largely to the "ASEAN Way" while ASEAN insisted on a similar modality for the Asia-Pacific Economic Cooperation (APEC) forum that was established in 1989.[52] When APEC adopted a Pacific-wide regional liberalization agenda in 1994, those ASEAN governments that were also APEC members rejected legally binding trade agreements, insisting instead that APEC liberalization should be unilaterally rather than multilaterally determined, as well as voluntary. This approach, which adheres closely to the "ASEAN Way" has allowed each APEC member government considerable discretion in determining the substantive concessions it is willing to make and its schedule of liberalization.[53] Although most of APEC's Southeast Asian members were relatively open economies, especially with the new round of liberalization undertaken since the mid-1980s recession, these governments were, nevertheless, concerned that any hasty liberalization pushed by APEC's industrial country members would undermine their own industrialization efforts and constrain their use of economic policies for domestic socio-political purposes.

The "ASEAN Way" principles endorsed by ASEAN both in its own grouping as well as in wider Pacific-based institutions served a useful function, helping to ensure that national governments retained sufficient autonomy to determine domestic policy on key issues in line with domestically derived priorities rather than be compelled to follow an externally mandated policy agenda. Retaining national autonomy has been especially salient for the ASEAN governments in both political and economic policymaking. Their ability to control the allocation of civil and political rights in domestic society had long been employed to exercise control over ethnically or linguistically divided societies and deliver domestic order and stability, as well as secure domestic political regimes. Likewise, controlling the domestic allocation and distribution of economic resources has been important in helping governments meet politically important domestic distributive priorities, albeit in the context of overall growth.

[52] For an insightful and theoretically informed analysis of the formation and evolution of APEC, see John Ravenhill, *APEC and the Construction of Pacific Rim Regionalism* (Cambridge: Cambridge University Press, 2001).

[53] Michael Plummer, "ASEAN and Institutional Nesting in the Asia-Pacific: Leading from Behind in APEC," in Vinod K. Aggarwal and Charles E. Morrison (eds.), *Asia-Pacific Crossroads: Regime Creation and the Future of APEC* (London: Macmillan, 1998), pp. 279–314.

4. Institutional innovation in a changing external environment, 1991–2006: economics, crises, and institutional adaptation

Despite the influence of domestic imperatives in the design of regional institutions, the ASEAN member states were, nevertheless, willing to adopt institutional changes to ensure the success of their free trade area project, AFTA. For the ASEAN governments, AFTA had become a vital instrument that helped them better position their respective economies against other sites, especially China, in the global competition for foreign investment, a competition that became increasingly intense in the 1990s. The crucial point to note is that the shift toward relatively (for ASEAN) more intrusive regional institutions to govern regional trade liberalization was triggered by an external event – changing international patterns of investment flows – that the ASEAN member governments considered to be directly threatening to governing regimes, principally by its capacity to disrupt economic growth.

As already noted, economic growth remains a central basis of political legitimacy in the ASEAN states and a key instrument through which governments retain political power and maintain order in domestic society. High rates of economic growth, by raising employment, wages, and incomes for households, also function as an implicit strategy of social protection.[54] Growth, therefore, plays a major role in helping governments build social cohesion and political stability in the divided societies that characterize Southeast Asia. In addition, economic growth allows politically important domestic distributional goals to be achieved with fewer efficiency and socio-political costs.[55] In a context where growth is a vitally important tool of national governance, how economic crises are experienced or how events are construed in terms of their potential to disrupt economic growth generates the political space for considering shifts in institutional design. Thus, we see in the discussion to follow how AFTA's negotiators found it necessary to deviate from the "ASEAN Way" when cooperation stalled. By this time, AFTA had become a vital strategy through which member states hoped to retain and attract foreign investment, especially in competition with China. Any potential disruption to investment inflows was viewed with alarm in member states relying on investment-driven economic growth. A similar driver accounts for the

[54] Stephan Haggard, *The Political Economy of the Asian Financial Crisis* (Washington, DC: Institute for International Economics, 2000), p. 185 (chapter written with Nancy Birdsall).

[55] Helen E. S. Nesadurai, *Globalisation, Domestic Politics, and Regionalism: The ASEAN Free Trade Area* (London and New York: Routledge, 2003), pp. 43–6.

additional changes to institutional design that members were willing to adopt once they embarked on the ASEAN Economic Community (AEC) project, discussed later in this chapter.

The sources of institutional design: AFTA and the "threat" of FDI diversion

Officials preparing for the 1992 Singapore Summit at which the decision to establish AFTA was formally adopted admit that one of the most compelling arguments advanced for the project, and which convinced ASEAN leaders of its necessity, was its capacity to attract FDI to the region.[56] Each of the five original ASEAN members faced declining foreign investor interest in their economies during the early 1990s, seen in the sharp fall in applications for foreign investment approvals.[57] ASEAN's share of global FDI flows declined from a high of 35 percent in 1990 to 24.3 percent by 1992.[58] By the end of 1992, the ASEAN leaders had become anxious that further diversion of FDI from the region would disrupt economic growth.[59] Why they saw AFTA as a means to address this problem can be explained by the way ASEAN officials and leaders construed the FDI crisis facing them.

ASEAN senior officials were, at this time, engaged in extensive consultations with regional scholars and business actors with regard to charting new directions for the Association following the resolution of the Cambodian conflict. They took note of the extensive analyses undertaken by European and North American economists and policy analysts on the implications of the impending North American Free Trade Agreement (NAFTA) and the Single European Market (SEM) for other countries and regions, including ASEAN. While many of these studies reached diverse conclusions, most were agreed that the largest impact would be on FDI inflows to ASEAN rather than on trade diversion.[60] These debates were keenly followed in ASEAN, and helped persuade ASEAN officials that the problem of FDI diversion would be the major fallout

[56] Narongchai Akrasanee and David Stifel, "The Political Economy of the ASEAN Free Trade Area," in Pearl Imada and Seiji Naya (eds.), *AFTA: The Way Ahead* (Singapore: Institute of Southeast Asian Studies (ISEAS), 1992), pp. 27–47.

[57] Nesadurai, *Globalisation*, pp. 82–7. [58] Ibid., p. 81, Table .

[59] On the role played by FDI in national economies, see ASEAN Secretariat, *ASEAN Investment Report 1999: Trends and Developments in Foreign Direct Investment* (Jakarta: The ASEAN Secretariat, 1999), p. 129.

[60] Gordon Means, "ASEAN Policy Responses to North American and European Trading Agreements," in Amitav Acharya and Richard Stubbs (eds.), *New Challenges for ASEAN: Emerging Policy Issues* (Vancouver: University of British Columbia Press, 1995), pp. 146–81.

of the turn to regionalism in North America and Western Europe, and that a similar regional project in ASEAN would be the appropriate policy response. The ASEAN governments also saw the emergence of China in these terms, as a competitor for FDI. Their views can be summed up in the words of Thailand's prime minister in 1993, Chuan Leekpai who cautioned, "the possible diversion of direct foreign investment . . . is a perpetual reminder that smaller countries have to unite."[61] Moreover, ASEAN leaders and policymakers believed that only AFTA could help them meet the FDI challenge from China, particularly as they could not match the extensive investment incentives that a China intent on economic openness was prepared to offer investors. These perceptions were reinforced by growing investor interest in the large, regional markets that were being constructed in North America and Western Europe as well as investors' growing attraction to continental-sized markets like China.[62]

Incremental learning and institutional adaptation: improving the efficacy of cooperation

Despite their keenness to employ AFTA as a regional market creation strategy through which to attract FDI, the ASEAN governments did not put in place supporting institutions that would bind members to implement the reduction of tariffs and non-tariff barriers that was the first step in creating a single regional market. Although some policy targets were initially indicated for the liberalization of goods trade, these were not clearly specified, with individual member governments able to determine when they would begin regional tariff reductions and how they would space out these reductions to reach the end tariff band of 0–5 percent over the fifteen-year time period initially adopted. There were no guidelines on exemptions, and many products soon became excluded from regional liberalization. There were also no guidelines in the event that members wished to alter or withdraw concessions originally offered. The paucity of rules, the inadequate attention paid to monitoring compliance, and the absence of a dispute settlement mechanism were detrimental to the chances of successful regional liberalization.[63]

[61] *Business Times*, "Stepped-up liberalisation of trade can be expected: Chuan," 8 January 1993.

[62] For a full discussion, see Garry Rodan, "Reconstructing Divisions of Labour: Singapore's New Regional Emphasis," in R. Higgott, R. Leaver, and J. Ravenhill (eds.), *Pacific Economic Relations in the 1990s: Cooperation or Conflict?* (Boulder, CO: Lynne Reinner, 1993), pp. 223–49.

[63] John Ravenhill, "Economic Cooperation in Southeast Asia," *Asian Survey*, 35:9 (1995), pp. 850–66.

This changed from the mid-1990s when implementation of the first set of AFTA commitments was due and member governments began backtracking on offers already made, largely due to demands from domestic interest groups wary of regional liberalization.[64] Setbacks in implementation set in motion a process of renegotiation and bargaining between member countries over the terms and conditions of liberalization. Internationally-oriented businesses that would have gained from regional liberalization were partly responsible for pushing national governments to ensure AFTA was implemented as scheduled. By this time, businesses had begun taking AFTA seriously and foreign corporations had begun to factor AFTA into corporate decisions on where to invest.[65] The presence of regularized intergovernmental mechanisms for decision-making in ASEAN – such as the meetings of senior officials, ministers, and leaders – provided an institutionalized arena where renegotiations on implementation could take place. While persuasion was the principal means employed to resolve problems, threats of retaliation were at times also used by one or another ASEAN member government.[66] These processes of bargaining and negotiation over implementation often resulted in the downward revision of original targets. However, they also led to the adoption of a set of clearer rules and procedures for regional trade liberalization.

As a result of these negotiations, ASEAN member governments set a common date for commencing tariff liberalization, brought forward the completion date for the project to 2003, and stipulated rules to govern temporary exclusions from regional liberalization as well as negotiated binding timetables for their eventual termination. Moreover, ASEAN adopted three new sets of procedural rules issued through fairly detailed, binding protocols that required domestic ratification: a dispute settlement mechanism in 1996,[67] a notification protocol in 1998 that obliged members to notify ASEAN before altering or withdrawing concessions already offered,[68] and in 2000 a protocol to govern the modification of liberalization commitments agreed to earlier.[69] The Protocol on Sensitive and Highly Sensitive Agricultural Products[70] adopted in 1999 similarly

[64] For a detailed discussion, see Nesadurai, *Globalisation*, pp. 128–70.

[65] Ibid., p. 185. [66] Ibid, pp. 154–8.

[67] ASEAN, *Protocol on Dispute Settlement Mechanism*, Manila, 26 November 1996. www.aseansec.org/16654.htm

[68] ASEAN, *Protocol on Notification Procedures*, Makati City, Philippines, 7 October 1998. www.aseansec.org/712.htm

[69] ASEAN, *Protocol Regarding the Implementation of the CEPT Scheme Temporary Exclusion List*, Singapore, 23 November 2000. www.aseansec.org/609.htm

[70] ASEAN, *Protocol on the Special Arrangement for Sensitive and Highly Sensitive Products*, Singapore, 30 September 1999. www.aseansec.org/1207.htm

provides rules to govern agricultural trade liberalization, including provisions for its flexible implementation and rules on exempting sensitive agricultural items. Both the agriculture and the notification protocol were negotiated following Indonesian backtracking on its initial liberalization offers on four agricultural commodities (rice, sugar, cloves, and wheat), and in raising duties on selected petrochemical products without informing its ASEAN partners. Malaysia's request to temporarily withdraw automobiles from AFTA disciplines in late 1999 prompted the negotiation of the protocol on excluded products in 2000. This protocol incorporates financial compensation to states damaged by the alteration of original concessions, albeit to be negotiated among the affected parties. Aside from these institutional improvements, consensus decision-making and intergovernmental coordination mechanisms, including in monitoring, enforcement, and adjudication, remained central in AFTA.

The effect of institutional design on cooperation in AFTA

Determining the impact of institutional design on the quality of cooperation in AFTA is complicated by endogeneity effects. As the preceding discussion reveals, implementation failures themselves prompted ASEAN to review AFTA institutions, usually through the adoption of new rules and protocols. While these enhanced transparency and the predictability of regional liberalization, these new rules could not in themselves prevent members from reneging on their AFTA commitments if, for them, short-term domestic gains exceeded the costs of defection and trumped longer-term group benefits. For instance, the Philippines in 2002 was prepared to suffer the costs of opting to temporarily delay regional liberalization of petrochemical products. Compensation may have been required under the new modification protocol, but for the Philippines, there were domestic gains to be had from delaying regional liberalization of an industry accorded the status of a strategic industry.[71]

Renegotiation also meant that there was a failure to realize the original targets of AFTA as these were revised downwards. While not denying its drawbacks, we argue that we need to also consider how renegotiation and the resultant institutional changes it brought about affected the future of AFTA itself. Renegotiation, far from being detrimental to the AFTA project, was critical to its survival despite being a "second-best" outcome.

[71] Hidetaka Yoshimatsu, "Collective Action and Regional Integration in ASEAN," *CSGR Working Paper* No. 198/06 (Centre for the Study of Globalisation and Regionalisation, University of Warwick, March 2006).

Otherwise, officials conceded that the AFTA project was in danger of collapsing.[72] It is for this reason that we characterize AFTA as displaying successful cooperation. Although the revision of original targets downwards was not an ideal arrangement for all parties, it was the best available option that allowed the ASEAN governments to maintain what was for them a valuable project of economic cooperation. Renegotiation permitted costs and benefits to be redistributed between member states (and firms) as original targets were revised downwards.[73] Rule building, the other outcome of renegotiation, performed an informational function by signaling to business investors that regional economic liberalization remained on the cards, though under a revised schedule.[74] Thus, the end of 2002 saw the successful conclusion of AFTA, with tariffs on virtually all products traded within the region set below the targeted 5 percent, involving US$1.4 billion of tariffs,[75] a goal that economists, elements of the media, and even investors themselves had once predicted would never be reached.[76]

Institutional change in the AEC: new mechanisms for monitoring and adjudication

With AFTA completed, ASEAN initiated the ASEAN Economic Community (AEC) project in 2003, which broadened considerably the scope of regional liberalization. The AEC aims to create an integrated regional market with free flow of goods, services, investment, and to a limited extent, skilled labor by 2020.[77] It, thus, builds on the liberalization of goods trade that was the central focus of AFTA. As with the latter, the strategic FDI imperative is a key driver of the AEC.[78] ASEAN policymakers also recognized that completing the AEC project would be a politically more difficult task compared to AFTA given the AEC's

[72] Reported in Nesadurai, *Globalisation*.

[73] Moreover, an extended liberalization schedule permitted for new members kept Vietnam, Laos, Myanmar, and Cambodia on board the project. As transition economies, these states faced even larger hurdles in getting their respective economies ready for regional liberalization.

[74] The views of the US-ASEAN Business Council on this issue were reported in *Special Report Update on AFTA and Regional Economic Integration*, prepared by Pricewaterhouse-Coopers, August 2000.

[75] From the *ASEAN Annual Report 2003–4* (Jakarta: The ASEAN Secretariat, 2004), p. 17.

[76] Nesadurai, *Globalisation*, pp. 1–2. Malaysian automobiles were exempted from liberalization until 2004.

[77] ASEAN, *Declaration of ASEAN Concord II (Bali Concord II)*, Bali, Indonesia, 7 October 2003.

[78] Jose Tongzon, "Role of AFTA in an ASEAN Economic Community," in Denis Hew (ed.), *Roadmap to an ASEAN Economic Community* (Singapore: Institute of Southeast Asian Studies, 2005), pp. 127–47.

ambitious deep integration agenda. This, coupled with pressure from internationally-oriented businesses to hasten regional integration[79] led ASEAN to adopt four institutional innovations for the AEC. First, a legal unit was established in the Secretariat to provide legal advice to member states and firms on disputes arising from the AEC. Second, the ASEAN Consultation to Solve Trade and Investment Issues (ACT) was set up to resolve complaints on AEC-related operational problems within thirty days. Third, the ASEAN Compliance Body (ACB) was established to provide mediation services for resolving disputes. These mechanisms are modeled on existing mechanisms in the WTO and the EU.[80] Fourth, ASEAN also strengthened its dispute settlement mechanism, most notably by providing clear time schedules for the resolution of disputes, establishing panels to decide on disputes, and setting up the Appellate Body that will hear appeals on panel decisions. While the entire dispute settlement process retains a strong role for the ASEAN Senior Economic Officials Meeting (SEOM), the Appellate Body will comprise independent (non-official) professionals of any nationality provided they "demonstrate an expertise in law, international trade or in a field relevant to the dispute."[81]

These institutional changes are noteworthy because they delegate authority to the ASEAN Secretariat to monitor compliance as well as to adjudicate disputes principally by interpreting agreements made by governments under the AEC. Institutional redesign also allows for third-party involvement in adjudicating disputes, through the Appellate Body. These are all "firsts" for ASEAN. ASEAN members not only rejected supranational institutions for the grouping, and still do, they were also hesitant to accord greater responsibility and authority to the ASEAN Secretariat before this. It is too early to tell whether these institutional improvements will be able to ensure that AEC targets are met, since completion of the project is some years away.[82] But, the point to note is that significant changes to institutional design have been adopted by ASEAN to secure members' compliance of AEC commitments. As Yoshimatsu points out, ASEAN governments have demonstrated a willingness to gradually delegate the authority to interpret and apply rules and resolve

[79] See the US-ASEAN Business Council's Special Report on AFTA issued in 2004. See also *Borneo Bulletin*, "Brunei: regional leaders laud ASEAN's BAC efforts," 13 October 2003.

[80] ASEAN, *36th ASEAN Economic Ministers Meeting: Joint Media Statement*, Jakarta, 3 September 2004.

[81] ASEAN, *Protocol on Enhanced Dispute Settlement Mechanism*, Vientiane, 29 November 2004.

[82] Complete liberalization in eleven priority sectors is scheduled for 2010 (2015 for the new members).

disputes to the Secretariat and even to third parties while retaining the authority to make those rules in the first place.[83] Thus, decisions on the scope of the AEC, its schedule of liberalization, and adoption of rules pertaining to regional economic integration remain the purview of national governments.

The discussion so far suggests that ASEAN is prepared to engage in institutional adaptation only in the face of developments that threaten to disrupt economic growth in the region. Otherwise, the baseline preference is for weak institutional forms characterized by the "ASEAN Way." Even in areas displaying clear transboundary effects, such as in the case of haze pollution from forest fires where the gains from joint cooperation are potentially significant, member governments chose to ensure actor autonomy over effectiveness in the way they addressed the issue. The ASEAN Agreement on Transboundary Haze Pollution adopted in June 2002 endorsed national monitoring and enforcement mechanisms over regional ones, while acknowledging in Article 3 the "sovereign right" of member states to "exploit their own resources pursuant to their own environmental and developmental policies." ASEAN members seemed more anxious about the extent to which strict compliance with regional environmental commitments would undermine national competitiveness, governments' ability to pursue rapid economic growth, and vested corporate interests than about the health effects of the haze.[84] Hence, in environmental cooperation, we do not see the kind of institutional innovations found in regional economic cooperation under both AFTA and the AEC.

The point to note is that ASEAN's willingness to turn to relatively more intrusive institutions is conditional on whether regional cooperation is regarded as a necessary response to secure economic survival. This was true in the case of foreign investment diversion. It was also true for regional financial cooperation, which was galvanized by the severity of the Asian financial crisis and the problems associated with the IMF response to it. Anticipating further financial crises in the future that would threaten economic survival, and lacking confidence in the IMF, the ASEAN states together with Japan, China, and South Korea agreed to set up a regional financing facility to help support currencies in crises.[85] This project – the

[83] Yoshimatsu, "Collective Action and Regional Integration in ASEAN."

[84] Lorraine Elliot, "ASEAN and Environmental Cooperation: Norms, Interests, and Identity," *The PacificReview*, 16:1 (2003), pp. 29–52.

[85] Helen E. S. Nesadurai, "Networking their Way to Cooperation: Finance Ministers and Central Bankers in East Asian Financial Cooperation," Project on Developing Country Finance Networks, Global Economic Governance Programme, Oxford University, March 2006.

Chiang Mai Initiative (CMI) – was adopted under the auspices of the APT rather than ASEAN. As mentioned at the beginning of this chapter, the APT rather than ASEAN was the logical institutional location for projects in regional financial cooperation because APT members like Japan and China possessed the much-needed financial resources required for an effective regional liquidity facility.[86]

In the absence of threats to economic survival, therefore, we are likely to see only limited, if any, shifts to more intrusive institutions as an aid to cooperation. In any case, even threats to economic growth did not lead to a fundamental redesign of ASEAN institutions, toward supranational institutions, majority voting, or comprehensive third-party dispute settlement for instance. The incremental changes we saw in AFTA and more recently in the AEC – adopting new rules or delegating authority away from national governments in the performance of certain tasks – co-exist with a commitment to flexibility. This particular feature enables members to retain a degree of domestic policy autonomy while securing their commitment to collective goals. In the next section, we probe whether similar dynamics are found in the ARF.

5. The Sources of the ARF and their impact on institutional design

If FDI diversion and the Asian financial crisis were instrumental in persuading ASEAN to stray from the "ASEAN Way" and adopt more rule-bound procedures (as in AFTA), were there analogous developments in the security sphere that pushed ASEAN in the direction of intrusive security institutions? The short answer is no. This observation helps us understand why the institutional features of the ASEAN Regional Forum remain ASEAN-centric, with all its attendant strengths and weaknesses. The ASEAN states were not living in a security paradise, but when they compared the early post-Cold War period to the previous three decades, the security of their immediate and larger environment seemed more benign. Individual states may have harbored deeper security fears – the Philippines, for example, had to contend with China's claims in the Spratleys – but ASEAN as a corporate entity did not feel besieged. Its main concern was about the strategic uncertainty pervading its larger environment, and it was the need for information and reassurance about an East Asia in transition that led to the creation of the ARF.

[86] APEC, which did have the resources, was unwilling to support a regional financing facility. See Nesadurai, "Networking."

In the discussion that follows, we choose a more methodical than narrative style to examine the purposes and institutional features of the ARF. This is necessary because, unlike AFTA, whose membership and rules are confined to ASEAN, the ARF's membership stretches way beyond the geographic footprint of ASEAN. The ARF, in other words, is a larger, more amorphous, and therefore more complicated creature. Its membership and modalities are still evolving even as they are being contested. There is thus a greater need – for the sake of clarity – to discuss each of the relevant design features (emphasized in this volume) in turn; such a discussion should also provide a comprehensive and in-depth portrait of the institution's features.

The ARF is the only forum that brings together the key actors of the Asia-Pacific to discuss security issues of common concern. It held its inaugural meeting in Bangkok in 1994, in the same week as the ASEAN Annual Ministerial Meeting (AMM). Eighteen "participants" – the ASEAN-6, the United States, Japan, Canada, the European Community, South Korea, Australia, New Zealand, Russia, China, Vietnam, Laos, and Papua New Guinea – met in the inaugural session. Since then eight additional states have become participants or members: Cambodia (1995), India (1996), Myanmar (1996), Mongolia (1998), North Korea (2000), Pakistan (2004), Timor-Leste (2005), and Bangladesh (2006).[87] Analysts of Asian Pacific security affairs at that time hailed the ARF as a multilateral security institution whose time had come. Few expected the ARF to supplant the large number of existing bilateral military agreements permeating the region but most saw the ARF as having the potential to play a vital role in complementing those arrangements in an era of strategic uncertainty.

The notion of strategic uncertainty – and the perceived need to reduce such uncertainty – provides the simplest explanation for the advent of the ARF. With the end of the Cold War and the implosion of the Soviet Union, the security dynamics in the Asia-Pacific became harder to decipher. Theory would suggest that institutions such as the ARF would be in demand by providing information, lowering transaction costs, and preventing cheating.[88] Michael Leifer has written that many in the region

[87] The ARF uses the term "participants" for those who attend the annual forum and perform the inter-sessional work. For the sake of convenience, we shall use the terms participants and members interchangeably in this chapter.

[88] Robert Keohane, *After Hegemony: Cooperation and Discord in the World Political Economy* (Princeton: Princeton University Press, 1984); Celeste A. Wallander and Robert Keohane, "Risk, Threat, and Security Institutions," in Helga Haftendorn, Robert Keohane, and Celeste A. Wallander, *Imperfect Unions: Security Institutions over Time and Space* (Oxford: Oxford University Press, 1999), pp. 21–47.

were concerned about the changing strategic situation, and ASEAN, for example, saw the ARF as a way to keep the United States in, China and Japan down, and ASEAN relevant and safe.[89] Iain Johnston has also focused on the importance of uncertainty as the impetus behind the ARF, but for him, the uncertainty has much to do with China's intentions toward the region as it becomes a great power. Regional actors therefore saw the ARF as a useful venue to observe and socialize China, in addition to giving it a stake in the region.[90] Combining Leifer and Johnston's insights, others have elaborated on the specific uncertainties that worried ASEAN (see below) and argued that the ARF was one strand in ASEAN's strategy in coping with those uncertainties.[91] As this account suggests, international systemic shifts and the uncertainties they generated were certainly important in creating the need for an ARF-like institution, whether focusing on dialogue, the provision of information, or the coordination of policies.[92] But how important were the systemic and functional factors in influencing the ARF's institutional design? Before answering this question, we need to examine the ARF's features.

Membership If membership in ASEAN is based primarily on geography, membership in the ARF has more to do with "history and circumstance" in the first instance. By the latter we mean as the oldest surviving and most successful regional institution in Asia, ASEAN was well poised historically to extend to the Asia-Pacific region the cooperative diplomacy that had served its members well since 1967. When circumstances in the early post-Cold War years suggested the need for an uncertainty reducing mechanism in the Asia-Pacific, ASEAN was quick to respond. ARF members such as Australia, Canada, China, the European Union, Japan, New Zealand, South Korea, and the United States had participated in ASEAN's Post-Ministerial Conferences (PMC) as

[89] Michael Leifer, *The ASEAN Regional Forum: Extending ASEAN's Model of Regional Security*, IISS Adelphi Paper 302 (Oxford: Oxford University Press, 1996). See also Yuen Foong Khong, "Making Bricks Without Straw in the Asia Pacific?," *The Pacific Review*, 10:2 (1997), p. 290.

[90] Alastair Iain Johnston, "The Myth of the ASEAN Way? Explaining the Evolution of the ASEAN Regional Forum," in Haftendorn *et al.* (eds.), *Imperfect Unions*, pp. 287–324.

[91] ASEAN's active role in other regional institutions such as APEC, ASEM, CSCAP, and ASEAN+3 also aids in reducing uncertainty, as does ASEAN's "soft balancing" behavior in providing the United States navy with repair and other facilities. See Yuen Foong Khong, "Coping with Strategic Uncertainty: The Role of Institutions and Soft Balancing in Southeast Asia's Post-Cold War Strategy," in Allen Carlson, Peter J. Katzenstein, and J. J. Suh (eds.), *Rethinking Security in East Asia: Identity, Power, and Efficiency* (Stanford: Stanford University Press, 2004), pp. 172–208.

[92] Cf. Barbara Koremenos, Charles Lipson, and Duncan Snidal, "The Rational Design of International Institutions," *International Organization*, 55:4 (Autumn 2001).

"dialogue partners" since the late 1970s; they have been ASEAN's main (non-Southeast Asian) interlocutors on matters economic and political for more than a decade. Hence for both ASEAN and these dialogue partners, the addition of a security forum to the litany of ASEAN's Annual Ministerial Meetings was an incremental step.[93]

The ARF's inclusive and motley membership – great powers, middle powers, and small powers – is only partly explained by its ASEAN and PMC-related origins. As a "forum" – a venue for discussion and not an organization (say with a Secretariat) – the ARF was broadly inclusive, although as a 1996 document on membership criteria put it, new participants would be "admitted only if it can be demonstrated that it has an impact on the peace and security of the 'geographical footprint' of key ARF activities (i.e. Northeast and Southeast Asia as well as Oceania)."[94] The geographical footprint and impact criteria suggest why Papau New Guinea is a member while Britain and France are not (apart from their representation through the European Union). Perhaps just as important a factor in explaining the ARF participants list is the function ASEAN wanted the ARF to perform: alleviating uncertainty about the post-Cold War environment. Will the United States retrench from East Asia? If so, will China and/or Japan fill the vacuum? Will Japan rearm? Will ASEAN continue to be relevant? The ARF would be a place to learn about, or influence, the intentions of these players. It followed that the United States, China, and Japan had to be key members; and this in turn meant that others in the Asia-Pacific with a stake in the behavior of these countries, from Canada to India to Russia, would have to be included.

Leadership ASEAN has put itself in the driver's seat in the ARF. The ARF meeting is held after ASEAN's AMM, and it is chaired by the host country (always an ASEAN country). ASEAN's decision-making rules and norms for regional conduct (TAC) are the rules/norms governing the ARF. The advantage of this ASEAN-based and ASEAN-led approach is that it puts ASEAN in the role of an "honest broker" between former adversaries; China, for example, feels less anxious about being "ganged up upon" by powerful states such as the United States or Japan if the ARF's agenda is set by ASEAN. The disadvantage of an ASEAN-led ARF, felt by realists like the late Michael Leifer, is that it seems

[93] Yuen Foong Khong, "ASEAN's Post-Ministerial Conference and Regional Forum: A Convergence of Post-Cold War Security Strategies," in Peter Gourevitch, Takashi Inoguchi, and Courtney Purrington (eds.), *United States-Japan Relations and International Institutions After the Cold War* (La Jolla: University of California Graduate School of International Relations and Pacific Studies, 1995), pp. 37–58.

[94] ASEAN Secretariat, www.aseansec.org/3537.htm

incongruous for a group of minor powers (Indonesia being the exception) to play lead roles in a security forum that includes the great powers.[95] The interests of the latter are unlikely to coincide with those of the ASEAN states, and insofar as great powers engage in power politics, ASEAN, with its limited military capabilities, would be left as a bystander who will sooner or later be shunted aside. ASEAN is not unaware of this criticism. All the ISG activities, for example, are co-chaired by one ASEAN and one non-ASEAN state. Recent suggestions by one Track II institution, in the interest of "introducing greater flexibility into the ARF process" include extending this principle of co-chairs to the ARF meeting itself.[96]

Mandate Despite its name, the ARF is more than a forum. The inaugural meeting in Bangkok (1994) may have entailed just one three-hour discussion among eighteen foreign ministers about the South China Sea, the future role of China and Japan, and confidence building measures (CBMs), but even then the ambition was to implement the informal agreements of the discussion. Thus there was a perceived need to set up a regional arms register and the voluntary exchange of defense white papers. The Concept Paper tabled at the second ARF meeting in Brunei (1995) "formalized" the ARF's mandate as a three-stage process, with Stage I being devoted to the promotion of CBMs; Stage II to the development of Preventive Diplomacy (PD); and Stage III, the development of Conflict-Resolution Mechanisms (CRMs). The Concept Paper's understanding of CBMs involved building trust and confidence through regular consultations and exchanges; increasing transparency; and actualizing the principles of good neighborliness as articulated in ASEAN's Treaty of Amity and Cooperation (TAC).

One of the most interesting aspects of the ARF are the inter-sessional support group meetings (ISG-CBMs), co-chaired by an ASEAN state and one other ARF member, that focus on specific issues such as search and rescue and peacekeeping. These ISGs have been occurring since the ARF's inception; the November 2003 ISG-CBM in Beijing noted, for example, the completion of a workshop on Managing Consequences of a Major Terrorist Attack in June, and the convening of the seventh ARF Meeting of the Heads of Defense Colleges in October.[97] As these examples indicate, the first decade of the ARF has emphasized brainstorming, developing habits of dialogue and consensus on threat sources, and has, in the main, avoided more intrusive mechanisms. PD is perceived by

[95] Leifer, *The ASEAN Regional Forum*.
[96] See Seng Tan *et al.*, *A New Agenda for the ASEAN Regional Forum*, Monograph No. 4 (Singapore: Institute of Defense and Strategic Studies, 2002), p. 64.
[97] ASEAN Secretariat, www.aseansec.org/15992.htm

some participants – China, Vietnam, and Myanmar in particular – as being too intrusive. These countries insist that more confidence building activities are required to increase comfort levels before moving to PD. Since the ARF is to proceed at a pace "comfortable to all participants," this means that more than a decade after its inception, the ARF remains largely focused on Stage I of its remit. This is the main reason why some have judged the quality of cooperation within the ARF to be low.

Ideology As indicated in our discussion of ASEAN in the preceding section, the original ASEAN-5 were indeed united in espousing an anti-communist ideology during the Cold War. While the majority of the ARF participants continue to be non- or anti-communist, the inclusion of China, Vietnam, Laos, Cambodia, Myanmar, and more recently North Korea, suggests that the more pragmatic need of tackling the security dilemmas of the region has been given priority over the discomfort of dealing, and even cooperating, with ideological rivals. The ideological divide has also been greatly diluted by the adoption of free-market or capitalist economics by almost all the ARF members except Myanmar and North Korea. Yet tensions stemming from ideological differences are never far below the surface. A major reason why CBMs are necessary is because there remains lingering mistrust among some members (e.g. US–China, China–Japan, EU–Myanmar, ASEAN 5–Vietnam, etc.), and although the sources of this mistrust are not wholly ideological, ideology is certainly partly responsible. For example, the inclusion of Myanmar in ASEAN (and hence the ARF), has created serious friction between the EU, which insists on excluding Myanmar (an illegitimate regime with an atrocious human rights record in EU eyes), and ASEAN.

The impact of 9/11 on the ideological factor is interesting. On the one hand – and this is probably the stronger tendency – it has united virtually all the ARF members in treating religion-based (read Islamic) terrorism as a serious threat. The upturn in US–China relations, despite the Bush administration's identifying China as a "strategic competitor" and the EP-3 incident in March 2001, has much to do with the two countries perceiving a greater threat (for the moment). Judging from the passages devoted to countering terrorism in the Chairman's Statement of ARF meetings since 9/11, counter-terrorism may be the new glue with the potential of binding the ARF participants together. On the other hand, the measures chosen by the United States in prosecuting the war against terrorism, in particular Operation Iraqi Freedom, have the potential of alienating Indonesia and Malaysia, the two ARF members with predominant Muslim populations. Before his retirement, Malaysian Prime Minister Mahatir Mohamad had severely criticized the United States for launching a preventive war against Iraq; in this case, it was probably more Mahatir's personal outrage than playing to a Muslim gallery in Malaysia. Indonesia's criticisms of the war in Iraq have been more muted, but perceptions by Indonesia's Muslims about a United States (and its allies, some of whom are also ARF members) bent on a crusade against Islamic states in order to make itself secure may aggravate religion-based fissures among members of the ARF, making cooperation on other issues more difficult.

Formal rules and norms To the extent that ASEAN's experience was deemed by the ARF to be "a valuable and proven guide," the Forum's rules of procedure were to be based on "prevailing ASEAN norms and practices." As the ARF's Concept Paper put it, "Decisions should be made by consensus after careful and extensive consultations. No voting will take place."[98] These procedural norms reassure those fearful of being ganged up upon by the tyranny of the majority, but they also slow down the progress of the ARF. The refusal of any one participant to move, say, from Stage I to Stage II activities, is enough to keep the ARF stuck in the realm of confidence building. In recent years, the fear among some that the slow progress of the ARF might make it irrelevant has led to recommendations to enhance the role of the ARF Chair. This attempt to loosen the restrictions on the remit of the ARF Chair – including allowing him to convene *ad hoc* meetings or to liaise with international organizations and Track II institutions – is aimed at making the ARF more efficacious and responsive to developments.[99] Other procedural innovations include the setting up of a group of Experts and Eminent Persons (EEP) who could be called upon by the ARF Chair to provide views and analyses relevant to their expertise, and the creation of an ARF Unit with the ASEAN Secretariat to assist the ARF Chair.[100] These recent attempts at tweaking the decision-making contexts and procedures of the ARF (focusing on the role of the Chair) may be seen as efforts to chip away at the stultifying inertia associated with the decision-making by consensus rule.

In addition to these procedural norms, the regulative norms stipulated in the TAC are also relevant. Since the rules and norms of the ARF are similar to those of ASEAN discussed at some length earlier, it is not

[98] ASEAN Secretariat, *ASEAN Regional Forum: Document Series 1994–1998* (Jakarta: 1999) pp. 13–22.

[99] Tan *et al.*, *A New Agenda for the ASEAN Regional Forum*, Appendix 4: Enhanced Role of the ARF Chair.

[100] Co-Chairs' Summary Report of the Meeting of the ARF ISG on CBMs, Yangon, Myanmar, 11–14 April 2004. www.aseansec.org/16097.htm

necessary to elaborate on them here. Perhaps the main point to note about the TAC is the increasing interest that regional (and even non-regional) powers have shown in acceding to the Treaty; this may be read as an indication of how increasing comfort levels made possible by the ARF and other regional processes (such as ASEAN Plus Three) are generating security payoffs (see below for more on accession to the TAC).

Actor independence ARF members retain high autonomy in two senses. First, there are no formal agreements to constrain them. The chief responsibilities of the ARF member are voluntary: for example, members are urged to participate in the United Nations Conventional Arms Register (to enhance military transparency), to provide "voluntary statements of defense policy positions," and to "endorse" the TAC principles. No rules stipulate that they must engage in these CBMs. The major means available to the ARF to nudge members to do these virtuous things are moral suasion and peer pressure. Even those who have signed on to the TAC – states who supposedly have gone beyond "endorsing" the norms to agreeing to adhere to them – have not sacrificed state autonomy in that they can defect without facing policy sanctions. Second, the emphasis on consensual decision-making means that in theory at least, each member state has veto power over the Forum's activities. ARF members who do not want to be bound by findings and decisions that might impinge negatively on their reputation or interests may block such activities (e.g. PD) before inception.

Scope As an outgrowth of ASEAN, the ARF's scope is understandably narrower than its (multi-purpose) parent. The ARF specializes in security issues, broadly construed. More specifically, it is about security dialogue and cooperation in the name of fostering "a regional environment conducive to maintaining the peace and prosperity of the region."[101] The scope of its remit is thus more analogous to that of AFTA (trade) and APEC (economic cooperation) in its specificity.

Dialogue and cooperation in the security realm were made possible by the end of the Cold War, which removed the stark bipolar alignments of the region. They were also necessitated by the strategic uncertainty or flux characterizing the Asia-Pacific in the aftermath of the Cold War. The form that this security dialogue and cooperation would take was confidence building, a concept that encompassed the litany of activities that the original ASEAN-5 have found helpful in their attempts at reconciliation

101 "The ASEAN Regional Forum: A Concept Paper," in *ASEAN Regional Forum: Documents Series 1994–1998* (Jakarta, 1999), p. 14.

and rapprochement with one another. Hence adopting ASEAN's "comprehensive" approach to security, building habits of dialogue, enhanced contacts, and exchanges among ARF members, would all count as CBMs. These and other activities listed in the Concept Paper and successive Chairman Statements are conducive to confidence building because they help establish comfort levels, provide venues for dampening brewing antagonisms, and provide information about policy intentions in an environment of strategic flux.[102] To be sure, CBMs were meant to be the first stage of the ARF process. At some unspecified point in time, Stage II would see the ARF engaged in PD activities, culminating in Stage III, where Conflict Resolution Mechanisms would be explored.

The most important change in scope of the ARF's concerns came in the aftermath of the 9/11 attacks on New York and Washington, DC. Before 9/11, the information, reassurances, and strategies of interest to the ARF were those that revolved around state power and interstate conflicts. Post-9/11, the threat posed by non-state actors or religion-based terrorists has risen to the top of the ARF's security agenda. The seventh ASEAN Heads of State Summit produced an ASEAN Declaration on Joint Action to Counter Terrorism, and this has been followed up with concrete proposals and recommendations in successive ARF meetings and ISGs. This is partly a reflection of the solidarity many in the ARF feel with the United States, al-Qaida's principal target, but "Islamic extremism" has also become a keenly felt threat by countries such as China, Russia, the European Union (especially Spain and Britain), India, Japan, Indonesia, Malaysia, Singapore, Thailand, and the Philippines. Although the terrorist threat does not directly affect the other ARF participants, there is strong consciousness about the negative externalities to all in the event of any serious terrorist attacks on a key ARF member. A terrorist incident in the Straits of Malacca would seriously disrupt trade and energy supplies for many in the region and hence undermine the peace and prosperity the ARF is dedicated to preserving.

The factors influencing institutional design

Anticipated shifts in the distribution of power in the international system in the aftermath of the Cold War is a permissive cause of the ARF. Policymakers in the Asia-Pacific, like those in other regions, were unsure about the implications of the demise of bipolarity for the region. By the

[102] US Secretaries of State Warren Christopher and Madeleine Albright used the ARF gatherings of 1996 (Jakarta) and 1997 (Kuala Lumpur) respectively to hold meetings with Chinese Foreign Minister Qian Qichen to calm US–China relations at a time when those relations were strained. See Khong, "Coping with Strategic Uncertainty," p. 200.

early 1990s, it was clear to Asia-Pacific's strategic planners that Russia, preoccupied with its internal problems and its near abroad, would be less relevant to the strategic equation of the region. It was also clear that China was on the economic and political rise. Beyond that however, uncertainty reigned. Will the United States retrench from the region, as early statements of the George H. W. Bush administration suggest? Will China be a responsible power as it assumes a greater role in the region? Will Japan rearm? And for policymakers in ASEAN, will ASEAN the organization continue to be relevant? It was the need to find answers to these questions about the strategic environment that suggested to the major players that the time was opportune for an information-providing and uncertainty-reducing institution such as the ARF. Perceived shifts in the international distribution of power, in other words, generated an air of uncertainty about the strategic intentions of the key players, and this created the push for an ARF-like institution capable of reducing that uncertainty, and perhaps even socializing the more worrisome (of the key players) to behave in responsible ways. An ARF-like institution would be a venue for the United States, China, and Japan to engage each other, to build confidence; a way to socialize China to play by the "rules of the game," with ASEAN playing the role of the honest broker.[103] The perceptions and intentions of these and other powers could be discerned from their attendance, their statements, as well as the corridor diplomacy or tea sessions.[104]

Yet to understand why the resulting institution took the form the ARF did – inclusive, high agent autonomy, consensual-style, low intrusiveness, and prizing non-interference – it is necessary to go beyond international systemic and functional variables.[105] To be sure, the function the ARF was conceived to perform meant that its membership would be inclusive rather than exclusive. But in our view history, identity, and domestic politics go farthest in elucidating the institutional design and "operative tone" of the ARF.

The most interesting – and we would argue important – feature of the ARF resides in the "A". Why is it the ASEAN Regional Forum, i.e. why is it ASEAN-based and ASEAN-led? After all, the ASEAN-6 (early 1990s) or even ASEAN-10 (late 1990s) are hardly major powers. The

[103] The most significant potential interstate threats to the ARF members stem from within (the group), rather than without. For example, US–China, China–Japan, US–Russia, Myanmar–Thailand, Malaysia–Singapore. This is perhaps one reason why confidence building is so crucial to the ARF.

[104] Khong, "Coping with Strategic Uncertainty."

[105] Cf. Koremenos, Lipson, and Snidal, "The Rational Design of International Institutions."

acknowledged flashpoints of East Asia in the early 1990s – China–Taiwan, North Korea–South Korea, and rival claims in the South China Sea – tended to be in Northeast, not Southeast, Asia; only the South China Sea disputes were within the geographic footprint of ASEAN. Hence in terms of both power capabilities and geographic flashpoints, ASEAN was not the natural nucleus around which a new security forum would be constructed.

But ASEAN was the natural core in a historical sense. It was the only institution of note in the region. It had survived while others such as SEATO and MAPHILINDO had perished. It had also been hailed by many as one of the most successful regional organizations in the developing world: it was successful in preventing conflicts between former adversaries. The resulting peace and stability facilitated the economic growth of Indonesia, Malaysia, Thailand, and Singapore such that by the early 1990s they were considered Newly Industrializing Countries (NICs). It was also the case that ASEAN had progressively engaged the major powers with interests in the region from the 1970s through the 1990s through the PMC (held after ASEAN's Annual Ministerial Meeting), starting with the United States, the European Union, Japan, and Australia in 1978, with China and Russia joining in the early 1990s. Through these yearly ASEAN–"Dialogue Partner" meetings, ASEAN demonstrated its ability to engage, as a corporate entity, the major powers on the economic and political issues of the region. In that sense, the existence and historical track record of ASEAN and the PMC made it easy and natural for a new security forum to be "grafted" onto these existing talk-shops.

History was also important in another sense: as former colonies, most of the ASEAN states would be protective of their political independence and sovereignty. Acharya and Johnston (Chapter 1, this volume) characterize these historical sensibilities as aspects of post-colonial identities. History and identity have always been intimately linked; we need not be too concerned about which is the better characterization of ASEAN's high valuation of its political independence and sovereignty. More interesting are the implications of the latter for institutional design. A concern for sovereignty implies that, under normal circumstances, their approach to regional endeavors (such as the formation and workings of ASEAN) would eschew sovereignty-pooling or integrationist projects. Hence, with the exception of AFTA, one would expect the ASEAN states to favor designs or modalities that are sovereignty-affirming.[106] "The ASEAN

[106] Herbst, and Barnett and Solingen, this volume, also point to the importance of sovereignty concerns in regional institutions in Africa and the Middle East respectively. In contrast, the Domínguez (Latin America), Schimmelfennig (NATO), and Checkel

Way" with its emphasis on non-interference in the internal affairs of others, consultative diplomatic culture, and consensual decision-making, suggests institutional features that are low in intrusiveness, high in agent autonomy, and that prize process over product. In fact, "the ASEAN Way" was a short-hand description of the institutional characteristics and modalities of ASEAN the organization. Insofar as the ARF is "based on prevailing ASEAN norms and practices" it exhibits many of the same features as ASEAN.

Knowing that the ARF would be ASEAN-based and knowing something about ASEAN's security concerns go a long way toward explaining the "design elements" of the ARF. ASEAN would lead the Forum, taking "the driver's seat." Membership would be inclusive (all of ASEAN plus the United States, China, Japan, Russia, India, the European Union, and other relevant actors in the Asia-Pacific), with ASEAN being especially solicitous of the major powers. The decision-making procedures would follow ASEAN's consultative and consensual style, and the mandate is more about process (brainstorming and the cultivation of habits of dialogue) than outcome (solving concrete security problems). Actor independence is high as in most consensual decision-making outfits since any given actor can withhold consent and thereby derail proposed projects. (ASEAN has an x–1 rule which allows a project to proceed despite one or two members opting out; the same rule is difficult to apply in the ARF context because in most cases, the member opting out is likely to be the member that the others want to socialize, persuade, or sanction.) The ARF tolerates a variety of ideologies, again reflecting the heterogeneous regime-type of the ASEAN countries.

Domestic political factors also work to favor the design features described above. Young and weak states still confronted with issues of regime legitimacy and survival can be expected to be extremely protective of their sovereignty. As such they are likely to favor actor independence, consensual decision-making, and toleration of diversity in political systems. The case of AFTA seems to be the exception that confirms this domestic political logic. By adopting an export-led growth strategy that was highly dependent on foreign investment, many of the ASEAN states succeeded in achieving high economic growth in the 1970s right up to the late 1990s. That in turn gave the ruling elites substantial legitimacy. The financial crisis of 1997–99 demonstrated how dependent some

(European Union) chapters do not see sovereignty as a major obstacle to stronger cooperation. The difference may be partly explained by the length of time states in the various regions have enjoyed sovereignty: most in Asia, Africa, and the Middle East are "young" sovereign states compared to the more experienced sovereign states in Europe and Latin America.

ASEAN elites were on high economic growth for their legitimacy and survival. Hence, to the extent that AFTA had the potential to deliver respectable economic growth (by preventing excessive diversion of foreign direct investment to regional competitors), most in ASEAN were willing to live with its (AFTA's) sovereignty-infirming and intrusive aspects. To insist on continuing with "the ASEAN way" in regional economics would have risked economic irrelevance, and with that, the attendant dangers to domestic political legitimacy and survival for many of the ASEAN states.

Interestingly, the functional variable is of least help in understanding the ARF's institutional design – this is in part because as Johnston has argued, the founders of the ARF were uncertain about the kind of strategic interaction or game that was being played; one of the main purposes of the ARF was to clarify the nature of the game.[107] If this characterization of the ARF is correct, it would stand to reason that the functional variable can shed light on the inclusive membership approach as well as the recent broadening of the scope of the ARF to include counter-terrorism, but not much else.

Characterizing ARF cooperation

In the fifth ARF meeting (Manila, 1998), the Chairman's statement praised the ARF process for having "contributed to the achievement of greater transparency and mutual understanding in the region" and "recognized that the ARF had been living up to its potential."[108] The assessments of outside observers are less congratulatory.[109] In particular, the fallout from the Asian financial crisis distracted some of the most proactive ASEAN states – Indonesia, Thailand, and Malaysia – from tending to regional security issues and forced them to focus on domestic economic and political problems. Today, some worry that the ARF may be in a state of malaise, and that if it fails to pick up, it may become irrelevant and perhaps even moribund. In a recent monograph, Singapore's Institute of Defense and Strategic Studies (with which both of the authors were or are connected though neither had a hand in the writing of the monograph) put forth a series of recommendations on how the ARF needs to be revitalized. Among the dozen or so recommendations are: setting up a Secretariat, enhancing the role of the ARF Chair, asking a panel of the Expert Group to review the 1995 Concept Paper, establishing a Risk

[107] Johnston, "The Myth of the ASEAN Way?" p. 290.
[108] ASEAN Secretariat, *ASEAN Regional Forum*, p. 120.
[109] Robyn Lim, "The ASEAN Regional Forum: Building on Sand," pp. 115–136,; John Funston, "Challenges Facing ASEAN in a More Complex Age," pp. 205–19.

Reduction Centre, strengthening Track II forums, and pressing on with the implementation of CBMs in Annex B of the 1995 Concept Paper.[110]

The unstated premise of the IDSS monograph, published just before the 2002 ARF, was that the ARF was stalling and that it needs to be better if it is to remain relevant. If there is one theme that connects its various recommendations, it is the need for greater institutionalization. Here, however, the penchant for greater institutionalization – which means tweaking the institutional design – may run up against the obstacle of the "ASEAN Way" which has hitherto governed the ARF processes, and which is also "enshrined" in the 1995 Concept Paper. Perhaps that is why IDSS wants the Expert Group to rethink the Concept Paper.

The above assessments of the quality of ARF cooperation and its efficacy need to be considered in perspective. The ARF is slightly more than ten years old; at a similar stage in its development, ASEAN the organization was considered to have played a useful role in building confidence among a group of formerly hostile states, and not much more. ASEAN's early efforts in economic cooperation were conspicuous failures. Assessing ASEAN's progress in its first decade, the late Michael Leifer remarked that ASEAN's greatest achievement from 1967–77 was that it survived.[111] ASEAN's finest moment did not present itself until the late 1970s.

One obvious way to measure the progress of the ARF is against its own three-stage conception articulated in its Concept Paper of 1995. If one uses this criterion, like we did in an earlier draft, one is likely to conclude that the ARF has been rather lethargic in moving security cooperation forward. The Concept Paper envisaged the ARF focusing on Confidence Building in its initial years; stage two would involve Preventive Diplomacy (PD), while the final stage would look to establishing mechanisms of Conflict Resolution.[112] The fact that a decade later, the Forum has only taken tentative steps toward stage two, i.e. PD, suggests that the kind of trust required for PD is not yet forthcoming.[113]

Efforts by the ARF to move into areas where there is overlap between CBMs and PD have yet to produce concrete results. At the tenth ARF in Phnom Penh (2003), the participants designated as "advances" in PD their discussion about denuclearizing the Korean Peninsula and their

[110] Tan *et al.*, *A New Agenda for the ASEAN Regional Forum*, p. 13.
[111] Michael Leifer, *ASEAN and the Security of Southeast Asia*, p. 52.
[112] ASEAN Secretariat, *ASEAN Regional Forum: Document Series 1994–1998* (Jakarta: 1999), pp. 13–22.
[113] For the specifics of PD as applied to the ARF, see Annex A and B of Concept Paper, ASEAN Secretariat 1999a: pp. 19–22. For the overlap between CBMs and PD, see pp. 157–60; for a Track II elaboration of the PD concept, see pp. 171–5.

joint efforts in addressing transnational security issues such as terrorism, crime, and piracy. Urging North Korea to cooperate with the International Atomic Energy Agency and rejoin the Non-Proliferation Treaty, as the ARF participants did in Phnom Penh, may be construed as an attempt in PD; cooperation on transnational security problems, however, does not really fit the ARF's own definition of PD, which focuses on preventing disputes "between states" from arising and escalating to the point where they threaten regional peace and security.[114] Yet an examination of the ISG discussion of transnational and non-traditional security issues at the March 2006 meeting on CBMs and PD in Manila suggests that it might be issues like avian flu, pandemics, natural disasters, and HIV/AIDS that are most amenable to PD.[115] Perhaps that is why at the thirteenth ARF meeting in Kuala Lumpur in July 2006, the participating Ministers commended the work on CBMs and PD performed by the ISG in the previous two years in Manila and Honolulu (2005). The Ministers "endorsed their recommendations" and "welcomed the ARF's progress toward Preventive Diplomacy . . . and looked forward to the development of concrete measures in PD."[116] Compared to earlier ARF Chairman's Statements, where remarks about PD tend to be heavily qualified, the 2006 statement indicates that the ARF is inching into PD territory.

When it comes to traditional state-to-state security matters, the notion of PD still appears threatening to some of the ARF participants – especially China, but India and Myanmar too – because it is likely to encroach on their internal and external sovereignty. For instance, PD is likely to involve identifying potential conflicts – whether intra-state or interstate – dispatching fact-finding missions, third-party mediations, and iterated negotiations. This not only contravenes a cherished norm among many ARF members – respect for the sovereignty of member states – but it can be easily construed as "interference" in the domestic affairs of others. PD, in other words, is considered by some to be too intrusive and premature. The changes in mind set, "logics of appropriateness" as well as the policy adjustments (including surrendering complete policy autonomy) required before one feels comfortable with PD are substantial. By these

[114] This discussion of the ARF's progress and Preventive Diplomacy draws from the recent ASEAN Secretariat document, "Matrix of ASEAN Regional Forum Decisions and Status, 1994–2004," esp. pp. 9–10, 20. See www.aseansec.org

[115] Co-Chairs' Summary Report of the Meeting of the ASEAN Regional Forum Inter-sessional Support Group on Confidence Building Measures and Preventive Diplomacy, Manila, Philippines, 1–3 March 2006, www.aseanregionalforum.org/PublicLibrary/ARFChairmansStatementsandReports/tabid/66/Default.aspx

[116] Chairman's Statement of the 13th ASEAN Regional Forum, Kuala Lumpur, 28 July 2006, www.aseansec.org/18600.htm

criteria, the ARF has been inching slowly toward its own cooperative goals.

The slow movement toward PD counts against the ARF. It would be a mistake, however, to judge the achievements of the ARF solely in terms of the PD criterion. Recent developments suggest that ARF security cooperation has moved forward in several anticipated as well as unanticipated avenues. Participants of the ARF, we argue, have used the ARF to facilitate cooperation in at least three important areas: CBMs, accession to the TAC, and counter-terrorism. We would also characterize the agreement to form and institutionalize the ARF as the first important act of cooperation. While some states were enthusiastic about the ARF, others were more wary. Within ASEAN, Indonesia has affection for "(sub)-regional solutions to (sub)-regional problems"; by reaching out beyond ASEAN, Indonesia is restraining its own sense of regional entitlement (by virtue of its size).[117] Inclusion of the US, China, and other major powers to discuss Asian-Pacific issues dilutes Indonesia's influence, though smaller states like Singapore and Brunei would feel more reassured. Outside of ASEAN, the US and China also had initial reservations about such a multilateral forum. The United States preferred its hub and spokes approach, while China feared being ganged up upon. Hence both states had to readjust their policy preferences – an important sign of intent to participate in, and reap gains from, the cooperation game – in order to be among the founding members of the ARF. That is, for actors like Indonesia, the US, and China to agree to the ARF and to participate in it meant a willingness to risk some adjustment of past procedures (e.g. bilateralism) as well as enduring some restraints on their material capabilities. For Acharya and Johnston, these adjustments of prior policies suggest the potential for more robust cooperation.[118]

As to whether these powers acceded to the ARF because they thought it was normatively appropriate or because they feared the loss of status/influence if they opted out, the answer is that both were probably relevant. Moreover, the agreement among the original eighteen participants during the first ARF meeting in Bangkok (1994) to institutionalize the ARF, i.e. to make it into an annual forum following the ASEAN Annual Ministerial Meeting, is noteworthy because there were initial doubts whether there would be a second meeting.[119] The resilience of the ARF in the wake of the Asian financial crisis, and the fact that the highest level officials continue to come (especially in contrast to stillborn attempts to form the ASA and MAPHILINDO in the 1960s) suggest that

[117] Leifer, *ASEAN and the Security of Southeast Asia*.
[118] See Chapter 1, this volume. [119] Leifer, *The ASEAN Regional Forum*.

good quality cooperation was obtained in the lead-up to the formation and institutionalization of the ARF.

Since formation, the ARF activities most indicative of substantive cooperation are those pertaining to CBMs. Much of the work goes on in the Inter-sessional Support Groups (ISGs) and Inter-sessional Meetings. As their names imply, these are intergovernmental sessions and meetings (ISMs) that take place between the yearly ARF meetings. Among the first ISGs and ISMs to be set up were, respectively, those on Confidence Building, Peacekeeping, and Search and Rescue. In an inspired move (in part to anticipate objections that ASEAN was too proprietary about being in the driver's seat), the ARF decided on appointing co-chairs for each of the Groups, with the ISG co-chaired by Indonesia and Japan; the Peacekeeping ISG by Malaysia and Canada; while the Search and Rescue ISG was co-chaired by Singapore and the United States. Formed after the second ARF (1995), these Groups have reported back to the ARF since the third meeting (1996). Moreover, the co-chairs have also been rotated, and new topics such as disaster relief added. In 1996, for example, the Philippines and China replaced Indonesia and Japan as the co-chairs of the ISG on Confidence Building. The wisdom of pairing the two as co-chairs in the aftermath of the Mischief Reef incident can be debated, even though many would have surmised that the two co-chairs were most in need of confidence building among themselves. In the aftermath of September 11, the ARF also established an ISM on Counter-Terrorism and Transnational Crime. More to the point, ISG and ISM work (and their related seminars at the Track II level) now form a prominent part of the ARF agenda. Reports about these activities and their achievements take up about fifty percent of the documentation of the work of the ARF.[120]

Complementing the Ministerial meetings and ISG/ISM work involving government officials (Track I) are the conferences, workshops, and meetings of Track I institutions and players. Track II activities are those conducted by strategic studies institutes (e.g. ASEAN Institute of Strategic and International Studies) and non-governmental organizations in the region (e.g. Committee of Security Cooperation in the Asia-Pacific). At their best, Track II networks bring together academics, policy analysts, and officials in their private capacity, to float and dissect ideas pertinent to security cooperation. ASEAN-ISIS, for example, is believed to have played a major role in pushing the idea of the ARF. Since the advent of the ARF, Track II participants have helped organize seminars,

[120] ASEAN Secretariat, *ASEAN Regional Forum.*

conduct surveys, and elaborate on ideas and practices discussed in Track I forums.[121]

In addition to the proliferation of ARF-sponsored or related Track II seminars and activities, two other recent developments are worth noting. First, there has been a gradual move to include senior defense and military officials of member countries in the ARF deliberations. Until the late 1990s, defense officials were almost conspicuous by their absence in most ASEAN and ASEAN-related activities such as the ARF, in part because these events have been the exclusive preserve of the Foreign Ministries. However, the topics addressed by the ARF tend to have a substantial military content and it was deemed useful to bring in defense officials. A Heads of Defense Colleges and Institutions meeting was convened in 1998 and the eighth such meeting was held in Singapore in September 2004. In 2002, the first formal defense officials' meeting was held as part of the 9th ARF. These meetings have now become a yearly affair, although they are held at a different time from the ARF. In 2004, the senior defense officials asked that their half-day meeting be extended to a full day, so as to give them more time for discussions.[122]

The best indication of how years of dialogue and confidence building have improved regional security cooperation is the recent accession to the TAC by some of the most powerful ARF participants. To be sure, the ARF does not have a monopoly on regional dialogues; the PMC, ASEAN Plus Three, and APEC are parallel regional endeavors that have helped increase comfort levels and confidence building. But it was the ARF that endorsed "the purposes and principles" of the TAC "as a code of conduct governing relations between states" in its inaugural meeting, and it was the ARF Concept Paper that sought to "encourage the ARF participants to associate themselves with the TAC."[123] So when China and India formally acceded to the TAC in October 2003, it was considered a major step forward in regional security cooperation. As one reporter put it: "China and India, both nuclear capable, signed the . . . (TAC), which pledges dialogue, and not force, would be used to settle their disputes with Asean countries." Indonesian Foreign Minister Hassan Wirajuda welcomed the signing as it would bring "almost three billion people . . . under the same rules of good conduct" as well as "help to develop not

[121] For a good discussion of Track II activities in the Asia-Pacific, see Brian Job, "Track 2 Diplomacy: Ideational Contribution to the Evolving Asian Security Order," in Muthiah Alagappa, *Asian Security Order: Instrumental and Normative Features* (Stanford: Stanford University Press, 2003), pp. 241–79.

[122] ASEAN Secretariat, *Matrix of ASEAN Regional Forum Decisions and Status.*

[123] ASEAN Secretariat, *The ASEAN Regional Forum*, pp. 2, 15.

only peace and stability, but also prosperity, in the region."[124] Japan, Pakistan, Russia, and South Korea also signed the TAC in 2004. New Zealand and Australia acceded to the TAC in 2005, while France, the European Union, and Timor Leste have also agreed to sign on.

ASEAN is cheered by the willingness of these major powers to signal their acceptance of TAC norms such as respecting the territorial integrity and sovereignty of all nations, non-interference in the internal affairs of another state, and the renunciation of the threat or use of force. Some in ASEAN see these regulatory norms as weak restraints on state behavior, although they are restraints nonetheless.[125] Nation-states do not sign treaties lightly: they may not suffer significant material sanctions for violating the stipulated norms but they will suffer serious reputation costs. In that sense, the expansion of the TAC is a positive step: an increasing number of Asian-Pacific states seem willing to abide by a code of regional conduct that has been conducive to peace and stability, if ASEAN's experience is anything to go by. It is also possible to view the recent flurry of accessions to the TAC as an instance of ARF-induced confidence building that has spilled over – with positive effects – to "the problem" (of security cooperation) writ large, i.e. maintaining peace and stability in the Asia-Pacific.[126] By contributing to maintaining peace and stability, the ARF thus helps provide the background conditions that facilitate trade and industry in the region, which in turn enhance the political legitimacy of Southeast Asia's successful trading states.

If the TAC's contribution to security cooperation among the ARF participants was to prohibit signatories from violent and destabilizing acts against each other, the counter-terrorism initiatives adopted by the ARF since 9/11 have enabled the participants to move their cooperation a notch up. In addition to initiatives discussed above (in the change of scope section), ARF members pledged to implement United Nations' recommendations on combating terrorist financing, held workshops on "Financial Measures Against Terrorism" (2002) and "Prevention of Terrorism" (2002), and cooperated on border security issues. ASEAN also signed "joint declarations" with India, Australia, and Russia on "Cooperation to Combat International Terrorism."[127] Ministerial meetings have

[124] *The Straits Times*, 9 October 2003.

[125] TAC norms did not prevent Indonesia and Malaysia from dispatching warships to the East Ambalat block in the Sulawesi Sea in March 2005. The naval standoff was occasioned by rival claims to the potentially oil-rich area. See *The Straits Times*, 8 March 2005. The standoff did not result in a military clash, primarily because of intervention by politicians in Kuala Lumpur and Jakarta.

[126] Acharya and Johnston, Chapter 1, this volume.

[127] ASEAN Secretariat, *Matrix of ASEAN Regional Forum Decisions and Status*, pp. 26–9.

been held on counter-terrorism and people trafficking, with *ad hoc* Working Groups formed to follow up on issues raised. The ARF has also commended the advent of regional centers such as the Jakarta Center for Law Enforcement Cooperation, the Southeast Asia Regional Center for Counter Terrorism in Kuala Lumpur, and the International Law Enforcement Academy in Bangkok, all of which are seen by ARF members as playing useful roles in the training of their counter-terrorism and law enforcement officials.[128] In short, in response to the 9/11 attacks and the Bali and Jakarta bombings, the ARF has adopted a multifaceted approach to countering terrorist activities in the Asia-Pacific. While some of these initiatives are declaratory, others are more demanding in requiring senior officials or ministers to discuss and detail steps taken to deal with the terrorist threat. The challenge of terrorism is perhaps the one serious threat that unites a sizable minority of the ARF members. If our hypothesis about how serious threats can engender quality cooperation has merit, we would expect the ARF, in the years ahead, to adopt procedures and policies that are increasingly effective in countering the terrorist threat.

The sluggish movement toward PD notwithstanding, the ARF, by our account, has moved forward in three areas of cooperation: CBMs, extending the reach of the TAC, and counter-terrorism. In contrast to ASEAN's abandonment of the "ASEAN Way" along the path to achieving the robust economic cooperation required by AFTA, participants of the ARF have not jettisoned the "ASEAN Way" in their cooperative endeavors. By and large, the ARF participants have followed the norms associated with the "ASEAN Way." If this description of the ARF institutional design and modalities is correct, it suggests that the ARF has been able to make important cooperative gains in at least three areas without having to adopt the kind of rules and intrusive mechanisms seen in the case of AFTA. To be sure, some ARF members would prefer rules to norms; they would also favor more intrusive mechanisms if these mechanisms are necessary to get the job done. These members tend to be frustrated by the slow pace of the ARF. The "informal, weakly organized, talk-shop" that is the ARF seems capable of engendering significant cooperation.[129] Whether the ARF's achievements to date on CBMs, growing the TAC, and counter-terrorism are as effective as the achievements of AFTA is hard to say. But perhaps the analysis of the ARF permits us to say that we should not assume automatically that "more formalized, bureaucratized, and . . . intrusive institutions" are the only way to achieve meaningful

128 Chairman's Statement, the 11th Meeting of ASEAN Regional Forum, Jakarta, 2 July 2004, www.aseansec.org/16246.htm

129 The words in quotation marks are from Acharya and Johnston, Chapter 1, this volume.

cooperation; the informal and under-bureaucratized processes typified by the ARF produce results too.[130]

6. Conclusion

The preceding discussion suggests that ASEAN is prepared to adopt more intrusive institutions only in the face of developments that threaten economic survival and consequently undermine domestic regime security and political order. Otherwise, the baseline preference is for weak institutional forms characterized by the "ASEAN Way," which results in a high degree of autonomy for national governments in determining domestic policy. The principle of non-interference and the search for accommodation and consensus that has traditionally guided decision-making and behavior in the Association – the "ASEAN Way" – has remained a constant feature of ASEAN institutions.

We explain the persistence of the "ASEAN Way" in terms of path dependence and members' overwhelming concern with domestic regime security. In fact, the two are interrelated. Historical experience has shown that adherence to the "ASEAN Way" provided benefits to ASEAN in a number of ways. One, it aided diplomatic accommodation amidst diverse interests. Two, it helped to deflect external (including ASEAN) scrutiny of domestic policy. Third, subscribing to the "ASEAN Way" shielded national governments from having to address joint tasks that governments either found too demanding, administratively or politically, or that were not deemed to be of national priority. Given these benefits of adhering to the "ASEAN Way," it is not surprising that this principle has become a central institutional feature of ASEAN. Although this points to a functionalist explanation for the persistence of the "ASEAN Way," we also suggest that there is an additional normative commitment to this particular institutional design. The "ASEAN Way" is regarded by its members as the most appropriate standard of behavior for a very diverse group of states compelled to develop collective solutions to an expanding set of transnational problems.

Thus, even when the ASEAN members began to jointly address new transnational security and economic problems, their initial preference was always for non-intrusive institutional forms that combined a commitment to cooperate with sufficient autonomy for member governments to respond to and safeguard domestic priorities and interests. Over time, however, ASEAN was prepared to adopt new mechanisms of cooperation if the original problem remained intractable, reflecting a process

[130] The quotes are from Acharya and Johnston, Chapter 1, this volume.

of incremental learning and institutional adaptation. However, the most marked departures from the "ASEAN Way" have been seen in regional economic cooperation where external developments – the changing pattern of foreign investment flows and the growing intensity of competition for international capital – were perceived to be threatening economic growth. While this prompted ASEAN to adopt regional trade liberalization (AFTA) and later, deeper economic integration (AEC) as strategies to deal with these challenges, it was the failure to deliver on early liberalization commitments under AFTA that first led ASEAN to strengthen the institutions that underpin regional economic cooperation. That experience in AFTA stimulated further efforts at institutional redesign when the AEC was initiated. Despite the shift to binding rules and the gradual establishment of more centralized monitoring and adjudication mechanisms, the long-standing ASEAN commitment to flexibility has remained a constant even in regional economic institutions. This is seen in the still strong preference for intergovernmental processes of dialogue, consultation, and bargaining in decision-making, rule setting, and dispute resolution. Far from undermining cooperation, institutional flexibility, paradoxically, facilitated it, as we see from the experience in AFTA. Institutional flexibility, consequently, is not always an inhibitor of cooperation though it does act to moderate the speed and extent of cooperation attained.

Compared to the problem of economic survival, the security problem confronting ASEAN and its Asian Pacific neighbors in the 1990s was less serious. With the Cold War over, most policymakers in the Asia-Pacific believed that the region would have a respite from the crises and wars (internal and external) that bedeviled the region during the Cold War. The security problem in the early 1990s had more to do with alleviating strategic uncertainty and building confidence among former adversaries. ASEAN realized that in the post-Cold War era, the developments that would impact on its security would not be confined to Southeast Asia. In creating a new security forum – the ARF – to deal with the new issues, ASEAN ensured that the major powers of East and South Asia would be included. Fortunately for ASEAN, major powers such as the United States, China, Japan, Russia, and India were also receptive to the idea of the ARF. ASEAN's founding role and the absence of a grave threat meant that the "ASEAN Way" – with its emphasis on non-interference, informality, and consensual decision-making – basically shaped the institutional features of the ARF.

Our understanding of what makes the European Union work and our analysis of AFTA suggest that institutional features inspired by the "ASEAN Way" are unlikely to be efficacious. The "ASEAN Way" encouraged talk-shops, lowest common denominator agreements, while making defection and cheating costless because there were no sanctions. A systematic examination of the ARF's security cooperation in the last decade, however, revealed a surprising result: the volume and quality of cooperation are higher than what prevailing wisdom might expect. CBMs have been the mainstay of ARF activities in the last decade. While documenting the prevalence and increasing volume of CBMs indicates that some (mild form of) security cooperation is going on, we asked the tougher question, have these CBMs led to anything concrete? The answer seems to be yes: the recent spate of accessions to ASEAN's TAC by powers such as China, India, and Australia may be interpreted as the fruition of years of dialogue and confidence building in the ARF context. The intensification of cooperation among ARF members on the many aspects of counter-terrorism is another indication of the robust security cooperation that is occurring. Formal, intrusive, and sanction-based rules do not seem necessary for meaningful security cooperation in the ARF.

Looking ahead, the ARF is bound for interesting times. It is possible to argue that the ARF is encumbered by one potential design flaw, which might have been essential at inception, but which might prove to be an obstacle to deepening security cooperation in the medium term: the inclusion of potential adversaries or "peer competitors" within the same institution. It was essential to include the US, Russia, China, India, and Japan because it was a way of emphasizing their importance to, and their stakes in, the region; of reading their signals to each other as well as other players in the region; and of allowing them to "balance" one another. By the mid-1990s, some of the uncertainty relating to the intentions and relationships of these great powers had been alleviated: the United States would maintain 100,000 troops in East Asia, Japan would not re-militarize, and China, having raised the ire of ASEAN after the Mischief Reef incident, would act more cautiously.[131] But with the US lurching in the direction of primacy – hinted at by the Pentagon in the early 1990s but "sanctified" as policy in the September 2002 National Security Strategy of the Bush administration – and with powers like China and Russia yearning for some sort of multipolarity, the structural context of the Asia-Pacific's international relations is not only devoid of an "if we don't hang together . . ." syndrome, it may experience one in which the preponderant power and its potential competitors eye each other with suspicion for some time to come.[132] In such a case, confidence building

[131] See Khong, "Coping with Strategic Uncertainty," pp. 180–90, 198–207.

[132] Excerpts of the National Security Strategy of the Bush administration can be found in *New York Times*, 20 September 2002, p. A12.

and PD would remain the ARF's mainstays for a long time, and robust security cooperation might be hard to maintain.

Yet, in a perverse way, the 9/11 attacks and their aftermath may have mitigated this design flaw of potential adversaries eyeing each other in the ARF. Since 9/11, the United States has put worries about peer competitors on hold, since it needs all the cooperation it can muster from allies as well as adversaries. US–China relations, for example, have been on the upswing; the US has also been reticent about criticizing ASEAN states like Malaysia and Singapore for using their Internal Security Acts to detain suspected terrorists. In the past, the latter might have raised human rights violations complaints from the US State Department. 9/11, in other words, may have helped generate a variant of the "if we don't hang together, we will hang separately" security syndrome, even though it directly affects a minority (a very important minority to be sure) of ARF members. Religion-based terrorism – which has reared its head in Indonesia, Philippines, Malaysia, and Singapore, not to mention the United States (and Russia, China, and India who are keen to persuade the international community that they also have to deal with "terrorist" Muslim minorities) – and the need to counter it in a multilateral context might become a rallying point for engendering higher-quality cooperation in the ARF. As suggested above, ARF-sponsored initiatives and activities on counter-terrorism have increased substantially and have become a major feature of ARF discussions.[133]

Despite the expansion of institutional scope in ASEAN since the 1990s, and the institutional modifications to "ASEAN Way" approaches in economic cooperation and even in a limited way in the ARF, we see continuity in ASEAN political institutions over close to four decades. Continued adherence to the "ASEAN Way" as a baseline preference reflects pragmatism on the part of ASEAN, conscious of the diversity of its members in terms of economic development, political regime type, and societal structures that tends to make difficult regional collaboration on issues that are deeply political, such as human rights, democratization, and civil conflict. Yet, this begs the question of the extent to which ASEAN could function as a *driver* of desirable domestic change, particularly in the area of political reform.

Given the intergovernmental nature of ASEAN, conservatism is likely to dominate for some time. The same actors who dominate national governance – officials, ministers, and leaders – also dominate decision-making at the ASEAN level, thereby enabling them to perform a strong gatekeeper function to resist changes they see as threatening to existing

[133] ASEAN Secretariat, *Matrix of ASEAN Regional Forum Decisions and Status*, pp. 26–9.

norms and practices. Consensus decision-making further aids conservatism, especially with the new members of ASEAN – Vietnam, Cambodia, Laos, and Myanmar – continuing to resist changes to the non-interference principle. There are indications, however, that the older members of ASEAN are keen to review the principles and practices under which ASEAN operates. The Association's plan to develop an ASEAN Charter provides it with the opportunity to debate and review the non-interference principle. Although the 2006 AMM did not censure Myanmar, the fact that ASEAN leaders and policymakers have openly discussed the domestic political situation in that country, called for progress on democratic change, and included a section on "Developments in Myanmar" in the 2006 AMM Communiqué suggests that non-interference is already being breached.

Another potential source of change in ASEAN institutions comes from growing civil society activity within ASEAN, which has already begun to consult with this class of regional actors. After all, non-state actors like the Track 2 networks of scholars have long played major roles in prompting new forms of cooperation in ASEAN – and the ARF demonstrates this clearly. Regional social forums such as the ASEAN Peoples' Assembly have begun to challenge official understandings of, and approaches to, domestic and regional governance.[134] Civil society groups and individuals have set up the ASEAN Human Rights Working Group, which has been at the forefront of efforts to develop an ASEAN Human Rights Mechanism.[135] How far its efforts have come is reflected in the June 2006 proposal by the Malaysian foreign minister to establish an ASEAN regional mechanism on human rights, but only among states that are ready to participate in the exercise.[136] Despite the caveat, such calls from official ASEAN reveal that there are shifts in attitudes taking place within the region that have the potential to further alter regional institutions. However, ASEAN is also confronted with an internal divide between the more conservative members and those willing to countenance change. How ASEAN institutions change over the next few years will be a function of how these opposing tendencies play out.

[134] Mely Caballero-Anthony, "Non-state Regional Governance Mechanisms for Economic Security: The Case of the ASEAN Peoples' Assembly," *The Pacific Review*, 17:4 (December 2004).

[135] See the Working Group's website at www.aseanhrmech.org, accessed 9 August 2006.

[136] Syed Hamid Albar, *Keynote Speech at the 5th Workshop on an ASEAN Regional Mechanism on Human Rights*, Kuala Lumpur, 29 June 2006.

3 International cooperation in Latin America: the design of regional institutions by slow accretion[1]

Jorge I. Domínguez

The first regional institutions in the Americas emerged in the 1820s as the successor states of Spain's American empire sought to construct stable, amicable, and productive relations between themselves. A relatively thick array of international institutional rules had emerged by the 1930s, well in advance of the foundation of the first formal international regional organizations in the hemisphere and three decades before the establishment of the first successful international subregional institutions. In the international relations of the Americas, the analysis of the emergence of institutional rules must to some extent be decoupled, therefore, from the analysis of organizations.

Yet not until the 1990s did international regional and subregional institutions in the Americas effectively promote trade, defend democracy, coordinate foreign policies, and contribute to an international milieu that reduced the frequency and intensity of militarized interstate disputes over territory and settled many of those disputes. International regional institutions in the Americas did not, therefore, have a crafting moment or a master architect. They resulted from the long accumulation of failures and occasional successes. The analytical task requires explaining the early establishment, long survival, delayed effectiveness, and eventual implementation of the rules of this array of international regional institutions – long periods of stasis followed by change.

In this essay, I argue, first, that the idea of international regionalism was a response to security problems in the immediate aftermath of Spanish American independence in the 1820s. This ideational legacy lingered well beyond the founding cause, however. Second, the layered subregional texture of international relations stems from a structure of differentiated international subsystems in the Americas created also in the mid

[1] I am grateful to Alastair Iain Johnston, Amitav Acharya, and Andrew Hurrell for many excellent comments. I also benefited greatly from the group discussions at the two conferences held under this project. All mistakes are mine alone.

nineteenth century. These subsystems were reasonably insulated from the global international system in the nineteenth century and, in important respects, retained relative autonomy to our own day, creating the context for the subregional organizations established in, and enduring since, the 1950s. Third, membership has been remarkably constant at the regional and subregional levels and thus unhelpful to explain change. Fourth, the scope of rules and organizations became more intrusive in the 1990s as a result of changes in both the general international system and domestic politics. The regional and subregional organizations were objects, not causes, of the change toward intrusiveness fostered by the governments of the Americas. But, once the organizational design changed, the institutions themselves became instruments of further intrusion in domestic affairs and agents of international cooperation and domestic commitments. The change in scope itself explained little, however, because change expanded uniformly across institutions. Finally, the most effective rules – including those established in the nineteenth century – have been automatic or self-enforcing and thus organizationally thin. Variables regarding 'centralization' or 'flexibility' are much less important than automaticity.[2]

The critical juncture of the 1980s brought together the key independent variables that account for the changes in the international institutions of the Americas and that explain their characteristics at the start of the twenty-first century. They were the region-wide economic depression of that decade, the breakdown of authoritarian regimes, and the effects of the end of the Cold War. Before that time, economic autarchy and sovereignty defense were dominant. Since the early 1990s, more market-oriented democratic regimes strengthened international regional organizations, founded or revitalized international subregional organizations, and made such institutions more intrusive in domestic realms to sustain both democracy and markets. States replaced the non-intervention rule with a collective obligation to defend constitutional democracies.

This essay examines in particular the cases of the Organization of American States (OAS), the Southern Common Market (MERCOSUR, or MERCOSUL in its Portuguese language acronym), and the Central American Common Market (CACM). The role of the United States is made explicit whenever it is pertinent to distinguish its role from that of the Latin American governments with regard to the OAS, MERCOSUR, the CACM, or wider international patterns in the Americas. The focus of the discussion is, however, on the Latin American states.

[2] These concepts draw from the work of this project's leaders, Alastair Iain Johnston and Amitav Acharya. See also Barbara Koremenos, Charles Lipson, and Duncan Snidal, "Rational Design: Looking Back to Move Forward," *International Organization*, 55:4 (Autumn 2001), 1051–82.

The last section assesses several hypotheses. It concludes that several plausible arguments have little or no general and comprehensive utility to explain the change in international regional institutional performance after 1990 (though each may help to explain some particular cases), to wit: domestic political culture and identity, institutional scope or mandate, organizational membership or decision-making rules, organizational centralization and flexibility, choice of economic model, role of countries of varying size and power, and existence of enforcement and uncertainty problems. Three other hypotheses yield mixed results. These are the international effects of domestic political regime, the presence of interstate militarized conflict, and the role of the United States.

Finally, six changes in independent variables have much higher general utility to explain the change in international regional institutional performance after 1990. These are the impact of prior and independent structural and normative international systemic changes, the role of international non-governmental organizations, domestic preferences, choice of automatic rules, relative emphasis on interstate distributional issues, and choice of voluntary and comprehensive institutional strategies. Two other hypotheses bear on understanding important continuities between the pre- and post-1990 periods, namely, the role of Latin Americans as international rule innovators and the importance of ideational and structural legacies. Institutional design variables are important parts of the explanation, but they alone are insufficient to explain either continuity or change.

Founding ideas

The first ideas about the design and construction of regional institutions in Latin America emerged from the ashes of a 'failed state', imperial Spain. In 1815, Simón Bolívar wrote about his hope that 'the Isthmus of Panama could be for us what the Isthmus of Corinth was for the Greeks'. He wished 'to convene [in Panama] an august assembly of representatives of republics, kingdoms, and empires' of Spanish America to address issues of 'peace and war with the nations of the other three-quarters of the globe'.[3] By the end of 1822, Bolívar had created Gran Colombia (today's Venezuela, Colombia, Ecuador, and Panama). And in a glorious example of continental military coordination still celebrated in the patriotic histories that Spanish American youngsters learn, the armies of Argentina, Chile, and Gran Colombia joined to smash the last Spanish

[3] "Bolívar's Jamaica letter," in Helen Delpar (ed.), *The Borzoi Reader in Latin American History* (New York: Knopf, 1972), vol. I, p. 197.

Viceroyalty in South America, forcing Peru to be free.[4] The last Spanish army on the American mainland surrendered at the Port of Callao, Peru, in January 1826.

In June 1826, Bolívar's Gran Colombia convoked a Spanish American international conference at its provincial city on the isthmus, Panama. The newly independent states feared that the concert of European continental powers would support Spain's bid to reconquer its former American territories. Delegates from Mexico, the United Provinces of Central America, Gran Colombia, and Peru met in Panama for three weeks. These four countries covered a span from the northern Mexican provinces of California and Tejas to the southern boundary of Peru. Argentina, Chile, Paraguay, and Bolivia did not attend. The Panama Congress adopted treaties for broad multilateral cooperation, addressing security and other concerns, and called for a second congress to be held in the following year at Tacubaya, Mexico. This first experience of crafting an international regional institution to address security concerns failed, however. Only Gran Colombia ratified the Panama agreements. The Tacubaya Congress never met, perhaps because the threat of a Spanish reconquest was fading.[5] In 1829–1830, Venezuela and Ecuador seceded from Gran Colombia. In 1838, the five constituent units of the United Provinces of Central America split up. Tejas seceded from Mexico in 1836 and the United States seized Mexico's northern half in 1848.

Out of the ashes of these newly failed states and other experiences during the nineteenth century came six long-lasting results:

(1) Political unification of existing states was highly unlikely but attempts at Spanish American interstate coordination were broadly popular.
(2) Spanish Americans thought that they shared some identities, making them supportive of diffuse international regionalist efforts.
(3) Inter-American, Latin American, or Spanish American international regional institutions were difficult to craft, however, and even harder to sustain.
(4) Extra-hemispheric security threats provoked insufficient levels of sustained cooperation but they were likely sources of transient alliance formation.
(5) *Ad hoc* coalitions of willing states were more likely to succeed than grander undertakings. Some governments were aloof from international cooperation.

[4] The expression is Jean-Jacques Rousseau's in *The Social Contract*, trans. G. D. H. Cole (New York: E. P. Dutton, 1950), p. 18, or in any edition in book I, chapter 7.

[5] Arthur P. Whitaker, *The Western Hemisphere Idea: Its Rise and Decline* (Ithaca, NY: Cornell University Press, 1954), pp. 42–3.

(6) The failure to ratify international agreements was an obstacle to coordination.

International subsystem structure

The international subsystems that would be the setting for Latin America's regional institutions date from the nineteenth century, even though the organizations were only founded in the twentieth century. The minimum requirement for an international system is a pattern of bounded interaction; the same holds true for an international subsystem. There must be active communication among subsystem units on an ongoing basis and such activity must be autonomous or weakly affected by units outside the subsystem. International subsystems were created in South, Central, and North America, and the Caribbean; in this essay, I concentrate on the first two of these.

South America

Three nearly concurrent wars involving nine of South America's then ten independent states broke out in the 1860s. Argentina, Brazil, and Uruguay defeated and dismembered Paraguay, hitherto South America's strongest military power. The western South American states fought Spain's last attempt at imperial reconquest. Colombia seized a chunk of Ecuador's territory. Simultaneous wars made South American states keenly aware of their interconnectedness.[6] A relatively stable, interactive South American balance-of-power system developed and lasted relatively unchanged until the early 1990s. There have been only five wars in South America since the 1880s, only one of which was substantial (the Chaco War between Paraguay and Bolivia, 1932–1935).[7]

Central America

In 1850, the United States and Great Britain signed the Clayton-Bulwer Treaty agreeing that neither would construct nor exclusively control a

[6] Robert N. Burr, *By Reason or Force: Chile and the Balancing of Power in South America, 1830–1905* (Berkeley: University of California Press, 1965), p. 106.

[7] For more detail on wars in South America, see Miguel Angel Centeno, *Blood and Debt: War and the Nation-State in Latin America* (University Park, PA: Pennsylvania State University Press, 2002), chapter 2. For more detail on the construction of peace in South America, see Arie M. Kacowicz, *Zones of Peace in the Third World: South America and West Africa in Comparative Perspective* (Albany, NY: State University of New York Press, 1998), chapter 3.

transisthmian canal or 'exercise domain' over any part of Central America.[8] They thus certified the independence of the small states that had emerged from the break-up of the United Provinces of Central America in 1838. The US–British agreement evolved gradually over time and was modified in three ways. Britain exercised dominion over British Honduras, today's Belize. British power otherwise waned in Central America. And in the early twentieth century the United States built and exclusively controlled the Panama Canal. US supremacy was challenged only during the generalized Central American wars in the 1980s.

Boundary setting procedures sustained each subsystem. The behavior of Great Britain and the United States insulated the international subsystems of the Americas from the undifferentiated impact of great power contestation in the international system. Since the 1820s, the boundary setter between Latin America and Europe was the British fleet. Great Britain developed intense economic relations with the Spanish American states and Brazil while also for the most part deterring military operations by other European powers. Britain's boundary setting international role persisted for the South American subsystem until World War I. US influence in South America has been modest, with occasional explosive exceptions at times of military coup or insurgency. In Central America, the boundary setting instrument was the US–British condominium, which US supremacy replaced by the end of the nineteenth century. Only Mexico had also some sporadic, recurrent influence in Central America. Cuban influence in Central America was noteworthy from the 1960s to the early 1990s.

The United States and Great Britain, for the most part, did not look for territorial possession goals.[9] Relative to its immense economic and naval power, British territorial seizures proved modest (British Guiana, British Honduras, and small islands in the South Atlantic). British military interventions throughout the Americas in the nineteenth century were mainly exercises in debt-collecting gunboat diplomacy. Even those were infrequent; British policy was characterized by "carefully limiting its intrusions into local politics."[10] Past the mid nineteenth century, the United States stopped seizing Mexican territory. Its only subsequent permanent acquisitions in the Americas would be the seizure of Puerto Rico

[8] G. Pope Atkins, *Latin America in the International Political System*, 3rd edn. (Boulder, CO: Westview Press, 1995), p. 37.

[9] For the distinction between possession and milieu goals, see Arnold Wolfers, *Discord and Collaboration: Essays on International Politics* (Baltimore: Johns Hopkins University Press, 1962), pp. 72–4 and 91–3.

[10] Charles Lipson, *Standing Guard: Protecting Foreign Capital in the Nineteenth and Twentieth Centuries* (Berkeley: University of California Press, 1985), p. 45.

and the purchases of Alaska and the Danish West Indies. In the first third of the twentieth century, the United States established protectorates over Cuba, the Dominican Republic, Haiti, Nicaragua, and Panama, but in search of milieu, not possession, goals: to prevent state collapse from giving an opportunity for an extra-hemispheric power to establish a foothold in the Caribbean and Central America, and to protect its economic interests.[11]

The units within each subsystem, in contrast, cared intensely about their territorial possession goals. Bolivia, Ecuador, and Paraguay lost significant territory through war or coerced cessions to their neighbors. Militarized interstate disputes long characterized the histories of the South and Central American subsystems; in Central America, such disputes remain worrisome even in the twenty-first century.[12] Brazil greatly expanded its already vast national territory through international negotiation, but without war on a neighboring country after 1870. Between 1816 and 1980, Brazil was the world's third largest gainer of territory, and the top net gainer of territory, but it ranked only twenty-second in its participation in wars.[13] The relative lack of interest of the United States and Great Britain in territorial possession goals and the relatively high interest of other American states in such goals had two systemic effects:

(1) From the perspective of Latin American states, the international system was layered. They engaged in the international system through economic activities and politically through US and British informal intermediation. They had a wide margin of autonomy in relations with their subsystem neighbors. Such layering would in due course make the construction of regional institutions possible.
(2) Relations with neighbors in each international subsystem at times featured conflict over territorial claims or boundary delimitation. Until well into the twentieth century, these conflicts delayed the creation of effective regional international institutions even after war had become rare.

[11] The classic study remains Dana G. Munro, *Intervention and Dollar Diplomacy in the Caribbean, 1900–1921* (Princeton: Princeton University Press, 1964).

[12] David R. Mares, *Violent Peace: Militarized Interstate Bargaining in Latin America* (New York: Columbia University Press, 2001). See also Paul Hensel, "One Thing Leads to Another: Recurrent Militarised Disputes in Latin America, 1816–1986," *Journal of Peace Research* 31:3 (1994), 281–97. Jorge I. Domínguez, *Boundary Disputes in Latin America*, Peaceworks, 50 (Washington, DC: United States Institute of Peace, 2003).

[13] Calculated from Gary Goertz and Paul F. Diehl, *Territorial Changes and International Conflict* (New York: Routledge, 1992), p. 50.

Founding international rules

The Spanish American Republics and Brazil developed four international rules to govern relations between them. The first and fourth of these rules date from the second quarter of the nineteenth century. The second and third developed in the first half of the twentieth century. The legacies of these rules, with a partial exception to the second, still operate today in the context of the OAS. Change over time was remarkably slow:
(1) The inherited boundaries from the empires would be honored.
(2) Sovereignty and non-intervention would be defended.
(3) States would actively seek to mediate disputes throughout the hemisphere.
(4) Implementation of agreements would be lax.

Honoring inherited boundaries

Latin America's first key innovation in international law was *uti possidetis juris* as the rule to govern relations between successor states following imperial collapse: existing administrative boundaries were converted into international frontiers. In the future, this rule would apply to the termination of European empires in Sub-Saharan Africa and the breakdown of the Soviet Union. The Spanish empire's administrative boundaries were sufficiently respected in South America in the 1820s and early 1830s to contribute to securing early on a framework of domestic and international legitimacy in the otherwise bloody passage from the empire to its successor American states.[14] In Central America, *uti possidetis* proved effective after the breakdown of the United Provinces into its constituent units in 1838. Central American states continued to go to war with each other, but not for the most part to alter the territorial configuration of states in major ways, even if still today they differ about where exactly each boundary is.

This rule addressed the security dilemma. It did not require military build-ups, arms races, or heavy taxation. It was facilitated by notions of shared identity but it included both the Spanish American countries and Portuguese-speaking Brazil. It became the dominant post-colonial interstate idea. In time, this rule facilitated international cooperation between states that did not fear for their territorial integrity. Once independent,

[14] Robert H. Jackson, *The Global Covenant: Human Conduct in a World of States* (Oxford: Oxford University Press, 2000), pp. 316–35; Fred Parkinson, "Latin America," in Robert H. Jackson and Alan James (eds.), *States in a Changing World: A Contemporary Analysis* (Oxford: Clarendon Press, 1993), pp. 239–43.

no state has disappeared in South America.[15] Past the travails of independence of the United Provinces of Central America in the nineteenth century,[16] the only successful secession was Panama's (1903) – engineered in large measure by the United States. There has been no significant shift in international boundaries in the Americas since 1942, and remarkably few wars of territorial aggression. This rule of territorial integrity is at the core of the foundation of the OAS. Latin America anticipated the establishment and consolidation of the territorial integrity norm that became widespread worldwide after World War II.[17] Specific boundary delimitation efforts do, of course, shift bits of territories from one country to another by mutual consent. Over nearly two centuries there have been only six significant violations of *uti possidetis juris* through war, to wit:

(1) The creation of Uruguay as a buffer state between Argentina and Brazil through war (1825–1828).
(2) The dismemberment of Paraguay at the hands of Argentina, Brazil, and Uruguay in the aftermath of the War of the Triple Alliance (1864–1870).
(3) Chile's conquest of the territories harboring nitrate natural resources of southern Peru and littoral Bolivia in the War of the Pacific (1879–1883).
(4) Ecuador's loss of territory through cession or wars with Colombia (1863) and Peru (1939–1941).
(5) Bolivia's loss of territory to Paraguay in the wake of the Chaco War (1932–1935).
(6) Great Britain's nineteenth-century seizure of territory from Argentina (south Atlantic islands), Guatemala (today's Belize), and Venezuela (today's Guyana).

Defending sovereignty and non-intervention

The second rule, the defense of state sovereignty and international non-intervention in the domestic affairs of states, developed principally in the late nineteenth century after interstate wars had become much less frequent. This rule became part of a Latin American crusade to contain

[15] Haiti ruled the Dominican Republic during much of the second quarter of the nineteenth century. Bolivia and Peru briefly created a confederation. Central American merger efforts persisted sporadically during the nineteenth century.

[16] Unsuccessful secessionist movements flare up from time to time in certain Anglophone Caribbean islands, such as Nevis or Tobago. See, for example, Ralph Premdas, "Identity and Secession in a Small Island State: Nevis," *Canadian Review of Studies in Nationalism*, 28 (2001), pp. 27–44.

[17] Mark W. Zacher, "The Territorial Integrity Norm: International Boundaries and the Use of Force," *International Organization*, 55:2 (Spring 2001), 215–50.

the United States. Latin American balancing against US power is consistent with neo-realist expectations,[18] but the means chosen by the Latin Americans were the weapons of the weak:[19] international law.

The defense of sovereignty countered the US and European insistence that states have the right to protect their subjects, in their persons and businesses, and thus retain the right to intervene in other states. In the 1880s, instead, the Argentine international jurist Carlos Calvo argued that sovereignty is inviolable and under no circumstances do resident aliens enjoy the right to have their home government interpose on their behalf. The wider Latin American defense of non-intervention – first articulated by Argentine Foreign Minister Luis Drago in 1902 – sought to counter the US and European official view that they had the right to armed intervention to compel states to honor their public debts. The Latin Americans promoted the Calvo Doctrine regarding alleged alien rights from the First International Conference of American States, held in Washington in 1889; the United States voted against the resolution. The Latin Americans introduced the Drago Doctrine regarding public debts at the Third Conference, held in Rio de Janeiro in 1906; the United States opposed it.[20]

In time, the position advocated by the Latin Americans gained support because of changes in the major powers. Armed intervention is no longer used to collect international public debts. Starting in the late 1920s, but associated with the Good Neighbor Doctrine in the 1930s and 1940s, the United States stopped intervening in the domestic affairs of its near-neighbors, ending all military occupations of neighboring countries. Article 1 of the OAS Charter, adopted in 1948 with US support, commits member states to defend sovereignty. Article 18 is the final juridical victory of Calvo and Drago: "No state or group of states has the right to intervene, directly or indirectly, for any reason whatever, in the internal or external affairs of any other state. The foregoing principle prohibits not only armed force but also any other form of interference or attempted threat . . ." The Article 18 rule weakened *de facto* in the 1950s when the United States resumed routine intervention in the domestic affairs of Latin American countries, again in 1991 when the OAS carved a

[18] See the argument in Andrew Hurrell, "Regionalism in Theoretical Perspective," in Louise Fawcett and Andrew Hurrell (eds.), *Regionalism in World Politics: Regional Organisation and International Order* (Oxford: Oxford University Press, 1995), pp. 49–50.

[19] The expression is James Scott's. See his *Weapons of the Weak: Everyday Forms of Peasant Resistance* (New Haven: Yale University Press, 1985).

[20] C. Neale Ronning, *Law and Politics in Inter-American Diplomacy* (New York: Wiley, 1963), chapters 3 and 4; J. Lloyd Mecham, *A Survey of United States–Latin American Relations* (Boston: Houghton Mifflin, 1965), pp. 94–9.

"democratic exception," and once more in 2002–2004 when the United States strayed from unconditional support of constitutional government.

The Latin American defense of non-intervention contributed to international law and became part of the United Nations Charter. African and Asian countries – as the papers on Africa and ASEAN in this project make clear – are the happy latter-day inheritors of this historic Latin American project.

Mediating disputes

The third institutionalist rule was a commitment to activist intermediation, preceding the formal establishment of the OAS. This rule evolved in South America since the 1880s as one means to sustain the peace. By the late 1920s, South America's forty-year absence-of-war owed much to international mediation and arbitration practices as well as more informal means of dispute settlement. In Central America, the long US occupation of Nicaragua interrupted the active contestation of boundaries.

As Table 3.1 shows, intermediary activity across Latin America's subregions surged during the troubled years between 1925 and 1942. At that time, Peru and Colombia went to war over the Leticia territory, Bolivia and Paraguay fought over the Chaco, and Ecuador and Peru battled over the Amazon territories and, after the US withdrawal from Nicaragua, Central American states re-focused on their interstate relations. The chi-square statistic is insignificant, which means that states were not subregional specialists in their intermediary activity. Instead, states volunteered their intermediary activity across subregions, proportionate to the distribution of disputes in each subregion throughout Latin America. Intermediary activity, indeed, contained these conflicts in Central America and would help to end wars between South American states.

From its foundation in 1948, the OAS took up this responsibility for mediation as a key reason for its existence.[21] Its formal institutional machinery performed well in both comparative and absolute terms. For the period from the late 1940s to the 1960s, Joseph Nye assessed the relative efficacy of the OAS, the Organization of African Unity (OAU), and the Arab League in helping to settle serious disputes between member states, most of which entailed some fighting. Nye deemed the OAS twice as effective as the OAU and more than three times as effective as the Arab League. The OAS helped to isolate each clash to prevent

[21] For an excellent history of the OAS as an organisation, see Carolyn M. Shaw, *Cooperation, Conflict, and Consensus in the Organization of American States* (New York: Palgrave MacMillan, 2004).

Table 3.1 *Intermediary activity in south and middle American regions*

	Location of dispute		
Intermediary governments	South America	Middle America	Total
South American	15	3	18
Middle American	3	2	5
United States	5	2	7
Total	28	7	35

$\chi^2 = 1.278$, not significant for two degrees of freedom.
SOURCE: Coded from J. Lloyd Mecham, *The United States and Inter-American Security, 1889–1960* (Austin: University of Texas Press, 1961), 154–76.
NOTE: European governments served as mediators in five South American disputes.

escalation in most cases, abate the dispute in three-quarters of the cases, end the fighting in the majority of instances, and settle the dispute in nearly a third of the cases.[22] For the period from the 1940s to the 1970s, Mark Zacher compared the efficacy of the same three organizations to the United Nations. He found that, in "wars, the frequencies of intervention and success by the OAS are considerably greater than those of the other bodies." The OAS was also the superior performer for crises short of war; the OAS stopped a majority of wars and contained nearly half of the crises between member states. The OAS succeeded in only one out of seven instances of military intervention, however.[23]

These findings may give too rosy an impression about the efficacy of the OAS conflict-resolution machinery, however. The OAS was less effective in securing a permanent settlement of disputes once militarized conflicts broke out or in settling disputes in peacetime to avert future war. Nor did it supplant the old pattern of "coalitions of the willing," which would often be the most effective. Bilateral negotiations between states in conflict, unaided by the OAS, also often yielded effective solutions.

Implementing agreements

The fourth institutionalist 'rule' was laxity in implementation. This may seem an oxymoron, namely, that rule breaking may be a rule. I call it a

[22] Joseph S. Nye, *Peace in Parts: Integration and Conflict in Regional Organization* (Boston: Little, Brown, 1971), chapter 5, especially p. 171.

[23] Mark W. Zacher, *International Conflicts and Collective Security, 1946–77: The United Nations, Organization of American States, Organization of African Unity, and Arab League* (New York: Praeger, 1979), pp. 213–15, quotation from pp. 213 and 215.

rule because it is so pervasive and long-lasting across issue areas and time periods, unpunished by co-signatories, and generally accepted even when its existence hampered the procedures or organizations that participating states sought to create. This behavior differs from formal rules that permit delayed accession to some other rule; for example, the European Union's rules permit some member states to choose to stay outside the *euro* currency. In the inter-American setting, agreements are signed but many states fail to ratify, even though the agreement expects all signatories to ratify.

The 1826 Panama Congress started this pattern. For illustrative purposes, consider the record regarding international security issues. In 1923, at the International Conference of American States held in Santiago, Chile, on Paraguay's initiative the first inter-American treaty on international security issues was signed. A subsequent specialized conference met in Washington in 1929 to produce a more specific general treaty on arbitration and a general convention on conciliation. Ten years later, several major Latin American countries had yet to ratify it, including Paraguay and Bolivia who savaged each other in the interim during the Chaco War. Similarly, in 1940 the American Republics founded the Inter-American Peace Committee as a dispute-settlement instrument; the Committee did not meet until 1948, although it would in the 1950s become effective for conflict resolution between states.[24]

The record is similar with regard to human rights. In 1969, the American Republics signed the American Convention on Human Rights as a binding treaty. Yet not until 1978 had enough states ratified it to bring it into effect. The Convention created the Inter-American Court on Human Rights, which came into being in 1979. In the early 1990s, democratic regimes governed in most countries in the Americas, yet only ten had acceded to the jurisdiction of the Inter-American Court.[25] In 1977, President Jimmy Carter signed the Convention but the United States has not ratified it. The US government does not accept the jurisdiction of this Inter-American Court.

At times, states have ratified treaties but a wide gap remained between text and behavior. At the International Conference of American States held in Buenos Aires in 1936, the Declaration of Principles of Inter-American Solidarity and Cooperation was the first multilateral recognition of the need for "a common democracy throughout America," yet most signatory governments were undemocratic. The key treaty for

[24] Mecham, *A Survey of United States–Latin American Relations*, pp. 102, 107–8, and 178.
[25] Viron P. Vaky and Heraldo Muñoz, *The Future of the Organization of American States* (New York: Twentieth Century Fund, 1993), p. 10.

collective security in the Americas during the Cold War was the Inter-American Treaty for Reciprocal Assistance, commonly known as the Rio Treaty, signed in 1947. Its Preamble commits member states to the "international recognition and protection of human rights and freedoms" and to advance "the effectiveness of democracy for the international realization of justice and security." The Rio Treaty has never been invoked for the defense of democracy, even though democratic regimes toppled frequently in the decades that followed.[26] The gap between the formal norms committing the states to democracy and actual practice was widest in the late 1970s when authoritarian regimes ruled all but three Latin American countries and a torture pandemic spread through the region.

The gap between formal pledges and behavior has been equally evident in the area of economic integration. In 1960, Argentina, Brazil, Chile, Mexico, Paraguay, Peru, and Uruguay signed the Treaty of Montevideo that established the Latin American Free Trade Association (LAFTA). Ecuador, Colombia, Venezuela, and Bolivia joined later in the 1960s. LAFTA established a twelve-year transition period to eliminate most trade barriers through product-by-product negotiations. Twenty years after the Montevideo Treaty, imports subject to LAFTA agreements were no more than 6% of the total imports of the region from the rest of the world. Intra-regional imports not subject to LAFTA agreements grew faster than those imports governed by some LAFTA agreement. In 1980, LAFTA was replaced by the Latin American Integration Association (LAIA), an even looser, less effective, and more limited association.[27]

The 1961 General Treaty of Central American Economic Integration created the Central American Common Market (CACM), freeing more than 90% of Central American trade categories. The CACM had explicit and tighter rules than LAFTA; the CACM mandated a common external tariff as well as intra-regional trade liberalization. During its first decade, intra-regional CACM trade rose from 5 to 26% of total trade. In 1969, however, Honduras and El Salvador went to war, leading to thousands of deaths. That war and other factors stopped CACM's momentum. By 1990, intra-regional trade as a percentage of total trade had fallen to half

[26] Domingo E. Acevedo and Claudio Grossman, "The Organization of American States and the Protection of Democracy," in Tom J. Farer (ed.), *Beyond Sovereignty: Collectively Defending Democracy in the Americas* (Baltimore: Johns Hopkins University Press, 1996), pp. 134–5.

[27] Mario I. Blejer, "Economic Integration: An Analytical Overview," in *Economic and Social Progress in Latin America: 1984 Report* (Washington, DC: Inter-American Development Bank, 1984), pp. 15–19, 24–25.

the 1970 level.[28] The 1969 Honduran–Salvadoran war calls attention to a recurrent Latin American outcome: simultaneous conflict and cooperation. Gains from CACM economic integration did not prevent war.

For most states, there is a gap between state interests and the rhetoric of its government leaders. The gap in the Americas is distinctive for three reasons. First, governments rarely acknowledge the existence of the gap. Officials continue to talk as if there were no gap. Second, states continue and, over time, heighten the rhetoric regarding the salience and utility of continental or subregional cooperation, regardless of lax enforcement. Third, states continue to sign treaties and other less formal agreements that sometimes reduce the gap between formal obligation and actual enforcement but just as likely widen the gap. Governments find it useful to sign agreements that they expect never to ratify because, on balance, these help them to manage relations with other states in the Americas, contributing to their reputation as inter-American or subregional team players. There is, therefore, an inter-American interstate "society" with a life of its own, with delayed impact on actual behavior, which engages time and attention from government officials. The US government, too, is as much a practitioner of the rule of laxity as are the Latin American governments, and the Latin Americans employ the rule of laxity at times as one tool to manage their relations with the United States.

Issue area subsystems: simultaneity of conflict and cooperation

Simultaneity of conflict and cooperation was also evident between states in southernmost South America during the last episode of widespread military government. In the mid and late 1970s, the same South American states that cooperated over counter-subversive operations came close to war with each other. In 1975, Chile's National Directorate of Intelligence (DINA) established Operation Condor, a means for military dictatorships to exchange intelligence about their opponents, coordinate trans-border counter-subversive operations and, in some instances, assist each other in murdering their opponents. Argentina, Bolivia, Brazil, Chile, Paraguay, and Uruguay participated in Operation Condor to varying degrees. The US government knew about Operation Condor and variously described it as counter-terrorist or counter-insurgency operations.

[28] Eduardo Lizano and José M. Salazar-Xirinachs, "The Central American Common Market and Hemispheric Free Trade," in Ana Julia Jatar and Sidney Weintraub (eds.), *Integrating the Hemisphere: Perspective From Latin America and the Caribbean* (Washington, DC: Inter-American Dialogue, 1997), pp. 111–12 and 117.

Operation Condor flourished because participating states were "modern" dictatorships, what Guillermo O'Donnell called "bureaucratic-authoritarian" regimes. They believed in technology, modern communications and transportation, psychological warfare, and similar means to counter the alleged threat of subversion. They thought that they had the right to kill the enemies of their regimes. In the name of national security, tens of thousands of civilians were murdered in the countries participating in Operation Condor. Intelligence services assisted each other in various ways, from issuing false passports to providing a safe haven to agents from a neighboring state tasked with assassinating a political exile. The extent of participation varied. Brazil was reluctant to extend their joint activities to Europe; Uruguay became inactive by 1978.[29]

The intelligence services operated with wide discretion. For example, on 24 August 1976, the US ambassador to Chile wrote to the US Secretary of State Henry Kissinger that "cooperation among southern cone national intelligence agencies is handled by the Directorate of National Intelligence (DINA), apparently without much reference to any one else. It is quite possible, even probable, that [President Augusto] Pinochet has no knowledge whatever of Operation Condor, particularly of its more questionable aspects."[30] If General Pinochet had the option of plausible denial of DINA-sponsored assassinations, surely the Argentine and Brazilian Congresses were kept in the dark when Operation Condor began in 1975. Operation Condor was a secret agreement.

These allies in the holy war against subversion had otherwise tense international relations, however, in those same years of intelligence cooperation. Argentina and Chile escalated their militarized conflicts throughout the 1970s. Argentina and Brazil differed seriously over a host of issues, especially those pertaining to the use of the Paraná river system's resources for hydroelectric power and navigation. Respective military missions envisaged combat against neighbors. The US government feared that Argentine–Brazilian rivalry would lead these governments to develop nuclear weapons.

In 1978, the military governments of Argentina and Chile mobilized for war against each other. Their armies went on alert; citizens prepared for the worst. Argentina's military government had refused to accept an international arbitration award concerning the lands and waters in the

[29] J. Patrice McSherry, "Operation Condor: Clandestine Inter-American System," *Social Justice*, 26 (Winter 1999), pp. 144–74; Esteban Cuya, "La 'Operación Cóndor:' El Terrorismo de Estado de Alcance Transnacional," www.derechos.org/koaga/vii/2/cuya.html; www.gwu.edu/~nsarchiv/news/20010306/condortel.pdf; www.gwu.edu/~nsarchiv/news/20010306/condor.pdf; www.gwu.edu/~nsarchiv/news/20001113/760901.pdf

[30] www.gwu.edu/~nsarchiv/news/20001113/760824.pdf

Beagle Channel, even though Argentina had been bound in advance to abide by the arbitral award.

In 1975, the military dictatorships in Bolivia and Chile re-established diplomatic relations severed in 1962 because of Bolivia's insistence hitherto that Chile award it a sovereign corridor to the Pacific Ocean. Perhaps in the context of increased collaboration between their intelligence services, Bolivia and Chile negotiated actively in 1975–1976 over such a corridor. The negotiations failed, however, and Bolivian–Chilean relations again became adversarial thereafter.[31]

These could be called "functional" or "issue area" specialized international subsystems. The same states, in the same subregion, cooperate over one issue and fight over another. Cooperation-inducing institutions and rules that govern in one issue area (trade, counter-subversion) have not always prevented war or threats of war, nor did cooperation in one issue area, with the partial and brief exception of Chilean–Bolivian relations, facilitate cooperation in another issue area.

The transformation of international and domestic politics in the 1980s

On the eve of Latin America's great economic depression of the 1980s, its international regional institutions had a mixed record. Its best accomplishments were long-term. The territorial integrity of states was accepted. External powers no longer deployed their navies to collect public debts. The institutions stopped relatively frequent militarized interstate disputes from escalating into war, or stopped war when it (rarely) broke out. The United States intervened recurrently in the domestic affairs of states but only to stamp out leftists.

The region's continental or subregional international institutions had not succeeded at economic integration or even accelerating trade, however. In the area of human rights and democracy, hypocrisy reigned: lofty pronouncements alongside systematic violations. The gap between formal assent and actual implementation was noteworthy in many issue areas. The same governments collaborated in some issue areas and risked conflict or even war in others. International subsystems in the Americas retained a certain insulation from the international system, enabling Argentina and Chile as well as Honduras and El Salvador, among others, to pursue possession goals relatively independent of wider trends or the

[31] Ronald Bruce St. John, "Chile, Peru, and the Treaty of 1929: The Final Settlement," *Boundary and Security Bulletin* 8:1 (Spring 2000), pp. 92 and 94–5.

distribution of power in the international system. There was, in short, remarkable path dependence in structures and rules over a long time.

Three fundamental changes swept through Latin America in the 1980s: economic liberalization, the end of the Cold War, and democratization. Each had a significant impact on each country's international relations and cumulatively affected international regional and subregional institutions in the Americas.

The economic depression that hit Latin America in the 1980s was the world's most severe outside of Sub-Saharan Africa. Its depth and duration forced most Latin American governments first to modify economic policies and in due course to adopt a new liberalizing macroeconomic framework. Between 1985 and 1991, unweighted average tariff rates dropped in Argentina from nearly 40% to about 14%; in Brazil, from above 55% to about 20%; in Mexico, from above 33% to less than 13%. The same happened in other countries.[32] In each case, these were unilateral decisions. Dormant regional institutions did not mandate them. Unilateral tariff reduction preceded and facilitated the creation of the North American Free Trade Agreement (NAFTA) and the Southern Common Market (MERCOSUR). The international financial institutions aided and abetted the process of economic restructuring and liberalization, especially the Inter-American Development Bank.

The end of the Cold War in Europe had a decisive impact in Central America, where since the late 1970s internal and international wars had been impregnated by US–Soviet–Cuban rivalries. The Cold War's end freed the US government from anti-communist demons so that it could foster, and participate in, negotiations to end wars in Nicaragua, El Salvador, and Guatemala – negotiations that the US government had opposed and undermined during most of the 1980s. Such bargaining brought peace to Nicaragua in 1990, El Salvador in 1992, and Guatemala in 1996.

The long night of military dictatorship ended gradually in Latin America. In 1979, Ecuador's military government was the first to transfer power to a freely elected civilian government. Most South American countries followed suit in the 1980s, with Chile the last to democratize in 1990. Democratization in South America occurred for the most part for autonomous reasons, with little impetus from outside (and no assistance from the United States during the first half of the 1980s).[33] In Central

[32] Robert Devlin, Antoni Estevadeordal, and Luis Jorge Garay, "Some Economic and Strategic Issues in the Face of the Emerging FTAA," in Jorge I. Domínguez (ed.), *The Future of Inter-American Relations* (New York: Routledge, 2000), p. 157.

[33] See general discussion in Laurence Whitehead, "International Aspects of Democratization," in Guillermo O'Donnell, Philippe Schmitter, and Laurence Whitehead (eds.),

America, in contrast, pacification and democratization proceeded hand in hand. Central American democratization would have been unthinkable without the end of the Cold War; this subregion's democratization is closer to Eastern European than South American patterns.

In sum, Latin America's economic liberalization and South American democratization began largely unaided by international regional institutions. Central America's pacification and democratization, in contrast, occurred simultaneously with changes in the international system and subsystem and, as we will see, with valuable roles for the OAS and especially the United Nations. The difference between these subsystems can be attributed to the deep US involvement in the domestic affairs of Central American countries and its greater aloofness from those in the South American cases. The United States found it expedient to empower international institutions to help it extricate itself from Central America and, as corollaries of that process, positive externalities resulted – peace and constitutional government.

The triumph of regionalist multilateralism in the 1990s

The three great transformations of the 1980s made room for innovations in the 1990s. First, the United Nations and the OAS became means to pacify Central America. Peace-making elsewhere in the Americas would also make effective use of international institutions. Second, the changed conditions of domestic political regimes changed the incentives regarding some international rules: democratic regimes welcomed international intervention to defend them.[34] Third, economic liberalization, notwithstanding its origin in domestic circumstances, engaged countries in the global economic system; in this issue area, too, domestic changes increased incentives for international cooperation.

International institutions facilitated the bargaining and implementation that brought peace and democratization in Nicaragua, El Salvador, and Guatemala.[35] In all three countries, negotiations went forward under

Transitions From Authoritarian Rule: Comparative Perspectives (Baltimore: Johns Hopkins University Press, 1986), pp. 3–47.

[34] For a persuasive articulation of this point, see Jon C. Pevehouse, *Democracy From Above: Regional Organizations and Democratization* (Cambridge: Cambridge University Press, 2005), especially chapters 6 and 7.

[35] For a partial assessment, see Teresa Whitfield, "The Role of the United Nations in El Salvador and Guatemala: A Preliminary Comparison," in Cynthia Aronson (ed.), *Comparative Peace Processes in Latin America* (Stanford: Stanford University Press, 1999), pp. 257–90. See also Mônica Herz, "Límites y Posibilidades de la OEA en la Esfera de la Seguridad," in Wolf Grabendorff (ed.), *La Seguridad Nacional en las Américas* (Bogotá: Fondo Editorial CEREC, 2003), pp. 133–54.

the auspices of the UN Secretary-General and the intrusive and effective involvement of his representatives. UN and OAS observers monitored the elections that were key to the transition. During the first half of the 1990s, the OAS International Commission for Support and Verification monitored and facilitated the demobilization and resettlement of the Nicaraguan insurgents. The United Nations played this implementation role in El Salvador.[36] Both the OAS and the United Nations worked effectively on Guatemala's pacification and democratization. In the early 1990s, the OAS also helped to end Suriname's internal war.

Most new democratic regimes in South and Central America and the long-standing democracies of the Anglophone Caribbean joined forces with the George H. W. Bush (Bush I) administration to breach one of the hemisphere's oldest rules: non-intervention in domestic affairs, weakening the protection for the rights of tyrants to abuse their people. In June 1991, the OAS General Assembly adopted the Santiago Commitment to Democracy (Resolution 1080), converting the OAS into a club of democracies. It was a simple rule. The interruption of constitutional government would henceforth automatically trigger an OAS meeting to discuss a response. The rule did not mandate any specific action other than convening a meeting, with the behavioral expectation that the risk of shameful failure would increase the likelihood that the member states would act indeed to defend democracy under threat.

The OAS defended constitutional government in the 1990s in Guatemala, Haiti, and Peru. Its effectiveness varied, but its engagement differed from its passive acquiescence to military coups in decades past. Success was greatest in defending constitutional government in Guatemala in 1993. Domestic circumstances in Haiti made success more difficult to achieve but the 1991 military coup would be reversed in 1994 in part thanks to the pressures and legitimation for such reversal that international institutions provided. Success in Peru was deferred because Alberto Fujimori's 1992 coup against the Congress and the courts stood, but the OAS facilitated the transition that terminated Fujimori's rule in 2000.[37]

A second old "founding rule," laxity, suffered a dozen-year setback as a result of the enforcement of the new defense-of-democracy rule. The rapid response of the OAS to interruptions of constitutional government

[36] Luis Guillermo Solís, "Collective Mediations in the Caribbean Basin," in Carl Kaysen, Robert Pastor, and Laura Reed (eds.), *Collective Responses to Regional Problems: The Case of Latin America and the Caribbean* (Cambridge, MA: American Academy of Arts and Sciences, 1994), pp. 95–125.

[37] Acevedo and Grossman, "The Organization of American States and the Protection of Democracy," pp. 132–49.

and the generally unhesitant response of member states to defend democratic institutions was a marked contrast to the past. The united democratic front cracked only in April 2002, when the George W. Bush (Bush II) administration behaved either ineptly or anti-democratically during the slow-moving attempt to overthrow Venezuela's President Hugo Chávez. In March 2004, the Bush II administration decisively induced Haiti's constitutional president, Jean-Bertrand Aristide, to resign in the face of a growing insurgency.

Regionalist multilateralism got a boost in December 1994 when the Miami Summit of Heads of State of the Americas launched the process to create a Free Trade Area of the Americas (FTAA). States would negotiate, as a single undertaking, a comprehensive hemispheric free-trade agreement by 2005. These negotiations had been made possible by the prior unilateral economic trade liberalization in Latin America, the increased political compatibility between democratic regimes, and the practical commitment (see below) to settle also territorial and other security-related issues between states.[38] The negotiations bogged down because the US Congress did not grant the President unfettered trade negotiating authority (at the time known as "fast track").

In late 2003, to rescue the negotiations, the United States and Brazil crafted an agreement that came to be known as "FTAA light." All eventual signatories would accept a "common and balanced set of rights and obligations applicable to all countries" but, beyond that, a cafeteria menu approach would prevail. Countries would be free to adopt, or opt out of, other provisions in the FTAA.[39] As originally conceived, the FTAA thus aborted, its real future more likely to depend on the Doha Round of negotiations of the World Trade Organisation. The practical consequences of signing and ratifying "FTAA light" remain unclear.

In April 2001, however, the FTAA negotiations adopted a democracy-promotion feature. The Quebec Summit of Heads of State of the Americas, at the initiative of the southern South American states and Mexico, inserted a "democracy clause" in the FTAA process. Only democratic regimes could sign or remain FTAA members. This broke with past US government preferences. The United States, Canada, and Mexico had signed the NAFTA with no democracy clause (NAFTA still lacks such a clause). The Quebec Summit agreement was the first-ever link between trade negotiations and the continental defense of democratic regimes.

[38] Devlin, Estevadeordal, and Garay, "Some Economic and Strategic Issues in the Face of the Emerging FTAA," p. 153.

[39] Free Trade Area of the Americas, 8th Ministerial Meeting, Miami, 20 November 2003: Ministerial Declaration, www.ftaa-alca.org/Ministerials/Miami/Miami_e.asp

In September 2001, the OAS adopted the Inter-American Democratic Charter, which authorizes the OAS Permanent Council to intervene in circumstances when constitutional democracy is threatened.[40]

The multilateralist revival in the 1990s had four key traits:

(1) For the first time ever, the American Republics welcomed the United Nations to play a leading role in conflict settlement. The United Nations performed ably in three Central American cases.

(2) The American Republics linked the democratic nature of the domestic political regime to the prospects for international trade negotiations. No economic integration agreement before 1990 had this feature.

(3) A democratic exception was carved out of the hard-shell rule of non-intervention. Democratic constitutionalism would henceforth be defended, even if direct intervention in domestic affairs were required. This new rule was enforced until 2002, although it lies in doubt since then.

(4) The United States, the Anglophone Caribbean, and the Latin American states agreed on these new systemic traits, until the United States broke the constitutionalist consensus in 2002.

Coalitions of the willing

The new multilateralism of the 1990s did not displace the coalitions of the willing that had been crucial in the region's past, that is, a subset of states that cooperate outside the framework of existing regional or subregional institutions. Examples in the political–military arenas include the collective interventions in Haiti in 1994 and 2004, the definitive settlement of the Ecuador–Peru boundary in 1998, and the repeated defense of constitutional government in Paraguay.

In 1994, in an historic first, in advance of deployment the United States asked the UN Security Council to authorize the use of force in Haiti. Illegal migration from Haiti to its neighbors was a legal consideration, but the intervention sought to evict the military junta that had overthrown the constitutionally elected president in 1991. The United States supplied most of the forces for the intervention. After the invasion, Canada provided the next largest contingent. Argentina contributed a warship to help enforce the naval quarantine of Haiti prior to the invasion. Argentina and several Anglophone Caribbean countries also supplied police forces afterwards. The event demonstrated the new US commitments to

[40] For discussion, see Francis Adams, "The Emerging Hemispheric Democracy Regime," *FOCAL Point*, 2:2 (February 2003), pp. 1–3.

multilateralism and the defense of democracy in the Americas but in actual implementation the intervention in Haiti was a coalition of the willing with UN and OAS blessings.

The March 2004 military intervention in Haiti was also a coalition of the willing, with security forces at first deployed mainly by the United States but also Canada, Chile, and France. This time, however, the UN Security Council authorized the deployment only after the US government had eased President Aristide out of office. The subsequent military occupation was the first-ever UN force anywhere most of whose troops were South Americans (Brazil with the largest force; Argentina, Chile, and Uruguay also important) operating under Brazil's military command.[41]

In April 1996, a military coup nearly overthrew Paraguay's constitutional president. Dramatic mobilization by Paraguayans thwarted the coup, but a key element in stopping it was international support for President Juan Carlos Wasmosy. The key members of this coalition of the willing were Argentina, Brazil, Uruguay (Paraguay's MERCOSUR partners), and the United States. All four governments reacted immediately through their ambassadors in Asunción. OAS Secretary-General César Gaviria was also quick (though acting on his own authority because the OAS could not meet in time). These actions were consistent with the new OAS rule of democratic defense adopted in Santiago, Chile, in 1991, but the most general characteristic of the response was an *ad hoc* coalition of the willing.[42] In 1997, MERCOSUR members amended the founding Treaty of Asunción (1991) to limit membership to constitutional democracies – the first example in the Americas of such a democratic clause in an economic integration treaty.[43]

In 1995, war broke out between Ecuador and Peru. Argentina, Brazil, Chile, and the United States stopped the war, acting under the authority of the Rio Protocol (1942) that terminated the Ecuador–Peru 1939–1941 war. The Rio Protocol called these four states the "Guarantors," obligated them to resolve disputes between Ecuador and Peru, and required them to play an ongoing role until the border was demarcated definitively.

[41] *The New York Times*, 1 August 2004, p. 4.

[42] See Arturo Valenzuela, "Paraguay: The Coup That Didn't Happen," *Journal of Democracy*, 8:1 (January 1997), pp. 43–55. See also Frank O. Mora, "Paraguay y el Sistema Interamericano: Del Autoritarismo y la Parálisis a la Democracia y la Aplicación de la Resolución 1080," in Arlene Tickner (ed.), *Sistema Interamericano y Democracia: Antecedentes Históricos y Tendencias Futuras* (Bogotá: Ediciones Uniandes, 2000), pp. 251–7.

[43] Rut Diamint, "Evolución del Sistema Interamericano: Entre el Temor y la Armonía," in Arlene Tickner (ed.), *Sistema Interamericano y Democracia: Antecedentes Históricos y Tendencias Futuras* (Bogotá: Ediciones Uniandes, 2000), pp. 12–13.

The Rio Protocol "institutionalized the role of outsiders in the Ecuador–Peru dispute" and represented "multilateral commitment to a bilateral settlement."[44] The Guarantors brokered the 1998 settlement of the Ecuador–Peru dispute. The parliaments of Ecuador and Peru supported the settlement, thereby employing the procedures of democracy to credibly commit the actions of their countries in the future.

Noteworthy in these three examples was the transformation of Argentina and Brazil into internationally active pro-democracy dispute-settling states. South America's giants demonstrated that they had been directly impacted by the triple transformation of the 1980s and were committed to sustaining it.

These coalitions of the willing in military and security arenas respected international institutions and treaties and acted within their parameters; acted principally at the initiative of a subset of states, not at the direction or even the urging of the international institutions; involved the United States along with other countries of the region; and went beyond merely supplying "good offices" to act decisively and often intrusively in particular cases.

Subregional trade agreement may also be considered coalitions of the willing. MERCOSUR, the CACM, and NAFTA are examples. In the mid-2000s, US negotiations with Central American countries and the Dominican Republic to create a Central American Free Trade Agreement (CAFTA) were new examples. We now examine MERCOSUR and the CACM as both political and economic agreements.

Southernmost South America and MERCOSUR

Until 1979, relations between Argentina and Brazil had been tense. Military missions envisaged combat against each other. The two countries seemed engaged in the early stages of a nuclear arms race.[45] In November 1979, however, the military dictatorships of Argentina, Brazil, and Paraguay signed the Itaipú-Corpus Treaty, governing the distribution of the Paraná river system waters to permit the construction of two hydroelectric projects, one by Brazil and the other by Argentina.[46]

[44] Ronald Bruce St. John, "Ecuador–Peru Endgame," *Boundary and Security Bulletin* 6:4 (Winter 1998–1999), p. 79.

[45] Subsequent research has shown that Argentina was not developing nuclear weapons, however. See Jacques Hymans, "Of Gauchos and Gringos: Why Argentina Never Wanted the Bomb, and Why the United States Thought it Did," *Security Studies*, 10:3 (Spring 2001), 153–85.

[46] This section draws from Jorge I. Domínguez (ed.), *International Security and Democracy: Latin America and the Caribbean in the Post-Cold War Era* (Pittsburgh: University of

This treaty engineered not just dams but also peace. Argentina and Brazil reached additional agreements to reduce the probability of military confrontation and a nuclear weapons race and, in 1986, signed economic integration accords. The 1991 Treaty of Asunción founded the Southern Common Market, MERCOSUR; its original members were Argentina, Brazil, Paraguay, and Uruguay. From the start, MERCOSUR was envisaged as a shared political project, not just a trade agreement.

The development of this integration process closely paralleled the chronology of broader trends in the world. The member states of the European Community signed the Single European Act in February 1986 to deepen the creation of a single European market. With the collapse of European communist regimes in Eastern Europe in 1989, Western European attention focused on the new European democratizing regimes and emerging markets. In mid-1990, Mexico, the United States, and Canada began negotiations to establish the North American Free Trade Agreement (NAFTA). In each case, South American governments reacted defensively to strengthen their ties to each other, fearing a loss of markets and influence in their relations with both Europe and North America.[47]

Intra-MERCOSUR trade did grow. Tariff barriers on goods fell, trade boomed. From 1990 to 1998 – the eve of Brazil's financial panic in 1999 and the start of Argentina's prolonged economic recession – intra-MERCOSUR exports grew by 23% per year from $4.1 billion in 1990 to $20.4 billion in 1998. The intra-MERCOSUR share of exports relative to the total exports of MERCOSUR countries grew from 9% in 1990 to 25% in 1998.[48]

MERCOSUR's trade integration narrowed the gap with other regional organizations. In 1989, before its founding, the MERCOSUR countries' intra-regional exports accounted for about 8% of their total trade in comparison to about 18% for the same statistic for countries within the Association of Southeast Asian Nations (ASEAN). MERCOSUR countries' intra-regional exports accounted for less than 0.5% of their

Pittsburgh Press, 1998), especially chapters by Jorge I. Domínguez, "Security, Peace, and Democracy in Latin America and the Caribbean: Challenges for the Post-Cold War Era;" Carlos Escudé and Andrés Fontana, "Argentina's Security Policies: Their Rationale and Regional Context;" Francisco Rojas Aravena, "Transition and Civil-Military Relations in Chile: Contributions in a New International Framework;" and Mônica Hirst, "Security Policies, Democratization, and Regional Integration in the Southern Cone."

[47] Walter Mattli makes these points especially. See his *The Logic of Regional Integration: Europe and Beyond* (Cambridge: Cambridge University Press, 1999), 139–63.

[48] Devlin, Estevadeordal, and Garay, "Some Economic and Strategic Issues in the Face of the Emerging FTAA," pp. 166–7; Inter-American Development Bank, *Integration and Trade in the Americas: A Preliminary Estimate of 2003 Trade* (Washington, DC: 2003), p. 5.

combined regional gross domestic product, whereas this same statistic was over 9% for ASEAN countries. In 2000, MERCOSUR intra-regional exports accounted for 21% of total exports, approximately the same as the intra-regional-to-total export proportion among ASEAN countries. Nonetheless, the ASEAN/MERCOSUR trade gap in 2000 was still substantial. MERCOSUR intra-regional exports accounted for a bit over 2% of regional gross domestic product, whereas that statistic was nearly 15% in the ASEAN region.[49] (With the Brazilian 1999 financial crisis followed by an even more severe economic depression in Argentina, intra-MERCOSUR exports fell sharply, recovering thereafter. In 2003, they were worth $12.7 billion and 12% of total exports.[50])

Simultaneous with MERCOSUR's development, Argentina and Brazil signed a nuclear safeguards agreement to provide for transparency and mutual guarantees in their respective nuclear power industries; they also installed an array of confidence-building and cooperative military measures.[51]

Chile did not join MERCOSUR but signed an agreement of association. It has behaved in many respects in accordance with the new pattern of interstate relations in the southern cone. In 1978, as noted, the military governments of Argentina and Chile mobilized for war. The Pope's mediation prevented war. In 1984, Argentina (then under a democratic government) and Chile (still under General Pinochet's rule) signed the Treaty of Peace and Friendship whereby Argentina accepted the award of the disputed Beagle Channel islands to Chile. Argentine–Chilean relations improved across the board. Trade and other economic relations intensified in the 1990s. At the start of the 1990s, the two democratic governments settled twenty-four unresolved boundary disputes, still extant 170 years after their independence. Chile and Argentina, too, created many confidence-building security measures and promoted substantial economic cooperation.[52]

The structure of the southern South American international subsystem changed after 1979, nurtured by the triple transformation of the

[49] Banco Interamericano de Desarrollo, *Más Allá de las Fronteras: El Nuevo Regionalismo en América Latina. Progreso Económico y Social en América Latina. Informe 2002* (Washington, DC: Banco Interamericano de Desarrollo, 1982), p. 163.

[50] Inter-American Development Bank, *Integration and Trade in the Americas: A Preliminary Estimate of 2004 Trade* (Washington, DC: 2004), Table 3.

[51] For a thoughtful analysis, see Arturo C. Sotomayor Velázquez, "Civil-Military Affairs and Security Institutions in the Southern Cone: The Sources of Argentine-Brazilian Nuclear Cooperation," *Latin American Politics and Society*, 46:4 (Winter 2004), pp. 29–60.

[52] For examples, see Francisco Rojas Aravena, "Building a Strategic Alliance: The Case of Chile and Argentina," *Pensamiento Propio*, 14 (July–December 2002), pp. 61–97.

1980s.[53] In the Argentina–Brazil and Argentina–Chile dyads, the initiative regarding both peace and trade began without reference to inter-American or subregional institutions. MERCOSUR is a product of prior democratization in southern South America; it was not a contributor to the transition to democracy.[54] MERCOSUR is a product of the prior bilateral improvement of political and security relations and the reactivation of trade between Argentina and Brazil, not the cause of such processes, although MERCOSUR did intensify the trends previously set in motion.[55] The Argentine–Chilean across-the-board improvement of political, security, boundary, and economic relations never developed under the aegis of inter-American or subregional institutions. Chile is associated with MERCOSUR but it eschewed formal membership in order not to subscribe to its common external tariff and to retain flexibility to sign free trade agreements with other countries, including the United States.[56] These southern cone processes resemble coalitions of the willing, albeit formalized through MERCOSUR.

MERCOSUR is "light" on institutionalization. Its key operative mechanism is presidential initiative. Parliaments ratified the Treaty of Asunción but have otherwise been passive and at times been bypassed, notwithstanding the existence of a Joint Parliamentary Commission constituted of sixteen parliamentarians per member country. Implementation depends on inter-executive relations, not supranational institutions. Presidents are both decision makers and dispute settlers. MERCOSUR's only permanent institutions are its Administrative Secretariat whose primary task is to supply documents and information regarding new protocols and agreements to member governments and its Permanent Commission whose main job is outreach to parliamentarians and civil society entities. There is no MERCOSUR parliament or commission similar to those of the European Union. The 2004 Olivos Protocol created a permanent MERCOSUR court, but it has yet to function properly. The

[53] See also David Pion-Berlin, "Will Soldiers Follow? Economic Integration and Regional Security in the Southern Cone," *Journal of Interamerican Studies and World Affairs*, 42:1 (Spring 2000), pp. 43–69.

[54] This differs, therefore, from other cases that Pevehouse discusses in *Democracy From Above*, chapters 4–5.

[55] Freund and McLaren have shown that trade accelerates in anticipation of the formal start of trade agreements based on prior credible negotiations (such as the European Union, NAFTA, and MERCOSUR). See C. Freund and J. McLaren, "On the Dynamics of Trade Diversion: Evidence From Four Trade Blocks" (Washington, DC: Federal Reserve Board, 1999, mimeo), cited in Robert Devlin and Antoni Estevadeordal, "¿Qué Hay de Nuevo en el Nuevo Regionalismo de las Américas?" *Documento de Trabajo*, 7 (Buenos Aires: INTAL-ITD-STA, 2001).

[56] David R. Mares and Francisco Rojas Aravena, *The United States and Chile: Coming in From the Cold* (New York: Routledge, 2001), pp. 40–1.

top-ranking representatives of each member government (Foreign and Finance Ministers) constitute the MERCOSUR Council. Its Common Market Group performs technical tasks of implementation; the foreign ministries of member governments staff it.

MERCOSUR suffers, too, from the lax applications of the decisions of its entities. Between 1991 and 2002, the MERCOSUR Council approved 149 decisions that require their incorporation to the domestic legal system of each member country, of which 70 percent remained unenforced in 2002. The Common Market Group approved 604 resolutions for those same years, of which 63 percent remained unenforced in 2002.[57] The 1991 Treaty of Asunción, short and vague, does not cover security issues; a 1997 amendment requires members to be constitutional democracies. Between 1991 and 1998, nearly all trade disputes between members were addressed through bilateral negotiation, and the most serious through direct presidential involvement.[58]

One consequence of this institutional design is that MERCOSUR has fallen short of many of its goals. The MERCOSUR project depends on ongoing political negotiations to achieve most goals. Little happens as a consequence. The liberalization of trade in services has lagged considerably. The common external tariff is in a shambles. There has been little effective harmonization of macroeconomic and microeconomic policies, including no competition policy. Coordination of policy toward foreign direct investment is poor, and little has been done to coordinate social policy.[59]

MERCOSUR's formal dispute settlement mechanism for trade disputes had been used only twice before the Brazilian financial panic of January 1999 that was followed by Argentina's steep 2001–2003 economic recession. Between 1999 and 2001, however, fifteen disputes came before its dispute settlement mechanism. MERCOSUR's institutions were thus moderately helpful as its states navigated through serious

[57] Félix Peña, *Concertación de Intereses. Efectividad de las Reglas del Juego y Calidad Institucional en el MERCOSUR*, www.fundacionbankboston.com.ar. I am grateful to Juan Cruz Díaz for bringing this work to my attention.

[58] More generally, see Luigi Manzetti, "The Political Economy of MERCOSUR," *Journal of Interamerican Studies and World Affairs*, 35:4 (Winter 1993–1994), pp. 105 and 116–20; Andrés Malamud, "Presidential Diplomacy and the Institutional Underpinnings of MERCOSUR: An Empirical Examination," *Latin American Research Review*, 40:1 (February 2005), pp. 138–64; Celina Pena and Ricardo Rozemberg, "MERCOSUR: A Different Approach to Institutional Development," FOCAL FPP-05-06 (Ottawa: 2006), pp. 1–14.

[59] Nicola Phillips, "Moulding Economic Governance in the Americas: US Power and the New Regional Political Economy," in Michèle Rioux (ed.), *Building the Americas* (Bruyland, 2005). More generally, see her *The Southern Cone Model: The Political Economy of Regional Capitalist Development in Latin America* (London: Routledge, 2004).

economic troubles. Yet, bilateral Argentine–Brazilian inter-executive negotiation remained the key means to manage the fallout on MERCOSUR from their intertwined economic crises (1999–2003). The presidents of Argentina and Brazil have come to see the MERCOSUR partnership as a strategic alliance.[60] In addition, the two governments and respective business groups negotiated individual deals over voluntary trade restraint, special tariffs, etc. MERCOSUR's thin institutionalization – its relatively few, limited-scope formal treaty-mandated organizations – accommodated these *ad hoc* responses reasonably well but the longer-term effects of this improvised adjustment may have adverse effects on trade growth and macroeconomic coordination.[61]

In contrast to that dismal record with regard to politicized negotiations, the two most effective institutional rules in MERCOSUR, as in NAFTA, have been automatic, unencumbered by political negotiations, and thus self-enforcing. One has been the automatic, pre-programmed, and systematic lowering or elimination of tariff barriers on goods, in marked contrast to cumbersome Latin American integration schemes from the 1960s to the 1990s. By 1995, each MERCOSUR country had liberalized at least eighty-six percent of rubrics for trade in goods.[62] This rule was battered during the 1999–2003 economic crises; there was some backtracking and new negotiations, yet continued commitment to joint problem-solving. The automatic rule worked effectively and better than alternatives. The second most effective rule has been the requirement that members be democracies, which helped to dissuade potential business elite supporters of a military coup in Paraguay, and that all members would act automatically to defend a member constitutional government under threat of coup. These two most effective rules do not depend on MERCOSUR's small staff or weak organization.

The southern South American balance of power system, founded in the 1860s, ended in the 1990s, replaced by a pluralistic security community. As originally explained by Karl Deutsch, this is a set of states in which "there is real assurance that the members of the community will not fight each other physically, but will settle their disputes in some other way."[63] Within such a community there are reliable expectations of

[60] Laura Gomez Mera makes this point forcefully in her "Explaining Mercosur's Survival: Strategic Sources of Argentine-Brazilian Convergence," *Journal of Latin American Studies*, 37 (2005), pp. 109–40.

[61] Banco Interamericano de Desarrollo, *Más Allá de las Fronteras*, pp. 105 and 192–93.

[62] Robert Devlin and Antoni Estevadeordal, "¿Qué Hay de Nuevo en el Nuevo Regionalismo de las Américas?"

[63] Karl W. Deutsch *et al.*, *Political Community in the North Atlantic Area* (Princeton: Princeton University Press, 1957), pp. 5–6.

peaceful change, with military force disappearing as a thinkable instrument of statecraft. War is not simply absent. The demon of conflictual possession goals has been exorcized. State elites constructed new interests and identities and internalized norms to ban the likelihood of war in a subregion where not so long ago it still seemed likely.[64]

Presidential decisions based on domestic political calculations, not "spillovers" from one issue area to another fostered by supranational technocrats, explain the change in the international subsystem.[65] ("Spillover" would imply perceived linkages between problems arising out of their inherent technical characteristics and linkages deliberately created or overstated by political actors.[66]) The international behavior that flows from the preferences of actors, not the rules of specific institutions, explains the outcomes.

MERCOSUR has no formal role with regard to security issues, though its promotion of trade and foreign economic policy coordination indirectly help peace maintenance. Thus MERCOSUR's direct contribution to the formation and sustenance of the southern South American security community is less important than ASEAN's, as other papers in this project indicate, even though a pluralistic security community is better consolidated in southern South America than in Southeast Asia.

The internalization of commitments to defend democracy mattered. Among the motivations to resolve all twenty-four boundary disputes between Argentina and Chile in the 1990s was the shared wish of their respective democratic governments to eliminate the likelihood of war. Success in boundary limitation would also reduce the significance of the armed forces in each country and consolidate civilian authority over the military. The agreements on nuclear cooperation between Brazil and Argentina were similarly motivated by the shared desire of their civilian governments to govern the military more effectively.[67] Argentine

[64] Andrew Hurrell, "An Emerging Security Community in South America?," in Emanuel Adler and Michael Barnett (eds.), *Security Communities* (Cambridge: Cambridge University Press, 1998), pp. 228–64. Southern South American changes occurred through processes unlike those that Paul Huth identified for the peaceful resolution of territorial disputes. See his *Standing Your Ground: Territorial Disputes and International Conflict* (Ann Arbor: University of Michigan Press, 1996), chapter 6.

[65] For a thoughtful explanation of changes in southern South America in terms of domestic coalitional change in the 1980s and 1990s, see Etel Solingen, *Regional Orders at Century's Dawn: Global and Domestic Influences on Grand Strategy* (Princeton: Princeton University Press, 1998), chapter 5.

[66] Nye, *Peace in Parts*, p. 65.

[67] Sotomayor Velázquez, "Civil Military Affairs and Security Institutions in the Southern Cone." More generally, this use of international agreements to lock in domestic democratic commitments is consistent with Pevehouse's general argument in *Democracy From Above*.

President Raúl Alfonsín's incentives to accept the Papal arbitral award regarding the Beagle Channel were also the same. Democratic governments in Argentina and Brazil in the 1990s shared similar dispositions. (These cases contradict the argument that new democracies are more likely to engage in war with each other.[68]) Domestic democratic concerns underpinned the shift toward international dispute settlement. In 1991, Chile and Argentina led the effort to adopt the new inter-American rule of defense of democracy for similar reasons.

In conclusion, in the 1990s trade grew, other economic cooperation developed, democracies became stronger, boundary disputes were settled, and security cooperation intensified in southern South America. MERCOSUR was organizationally thin but its automatic trade-in-goods liberalization and democracy requirement rules worked; its specific contribution to the construction of a security community was indirect, however. Inter-executive and specifically inter-presidential relations and a few institutionalized conflict-resolution rules handled disputes and crises. The result was a pluralistic security community – South America's interstate achievement of the 1990s.

MERCOSUR's troubles: expansion or deepening?

The failure of the negotiations regarding the Doha Round of the World Trade Organisation and the possible Free Trade Agreement of the Americas (FTAA) induced Brazil, in particular, but all the MERCOSUR partners to explore alternatives. The members faced a choice between deepening cooperation within MERCOSUR to achieve greater efficiencies, and expanding the partnership to include other countries that might bring fresh assets. In the distressed circumstances of the MERCOSUR economies in the early 2000s, expansion seemed less politically burdensome at home.

From the early 1990s, Brazil had considered fostering a South American Free Trade Area (SAFTA), built around MERCOSUR; this project re-emerged late in the presidency of Fernando Henrique Cardoso, and during the Lula presidency, as one way to advance Brazil's interests along with its partners.[69] The sustained increase of the world's price of energy in the early 2000s focused attention on Venezuela – South America's preeminent holder of petroleum and natural gas reserves. Venezuela's President Hugo Chávez was eager to expand his influence in South America.

[68] Edward D. Mansfield and Jack Snyder, 'Democratic Transitions, Institutional Strength, and War," *International Organization*, 56:2 (Spring 2002), pp. 297–337.

[69] See especially Gomez Mera, "Explaining Mercosur's Survival," p. 131.

Brazil was nearly energy sufficient but not quite, while Argentina had a complicated political situation with regard to its domestic energy policies.

In July 2004, MERCOSUR expanded in lieu of deepening. It granted associate member status to Ecuador, Colombia, and Venezuela to supplement the special MERCOSUR arrangements already in existence with Bolivia and Chile. In November 2005, MERCOSUR members and Venezuela stood apart from the rest of the governments at the Mar del Plata inter-American summit in voicing their reservations regarding the FTAA negotiations. In December 2005, MERCOSUR accepted Venezuela as a full member. In pursuit of such membership, in 2005 the Venezuelan government had already purchased $1.6 billion in Argentine debt to help Argentina become free of its obligations to the International Monetary Fund; in 2006, Venezuela purchased another $600 million of Argentine debt.[70] Soon President Chávez and his new MERCOSUR partners focused on a mega project, the "great pipeline of the south," through the Amazon rainforest to deliver Venezuelan natural gas to southernmost South America, even though liquefying natural gas would be a financially more viable project.

Natural gas had already become a source of southern cone international disputes, however. In 2002, Argentina lowered and froze the domestic price of natural gas; gas shortages appeared when demand recovered. Argentina then cut off natural gas exports to Chile, breaking an international agreement.

In 2005 President Chávez backed the election campaign of Evo Morales for the presidency of Bolivia; in December, Morales won the presidency. At the end of April 2006, Morales flew to Havana to secure political and material support from Venezuela and Cuba and, on 1 May 2006, he announced the nationalization of Bolivia's natural gas sector. One of the two most affected companies was Brazil's Petrobras; half of the natural gas consumed in Brazil comes from Bolivia. Bolivia also decided to double the price for its natural gas exports to Argentina. At a presidential summit on 4 May 2006, Argentina and Brazil accepted Bolivia's nationalization but their ardor for Chávez's involvement in the southern cone cooled.[71]

A parallel dispute had also broken out between Uruguay and Argentina. In early 2006, Argentina objected to the building of two large cellulose factories by Finnish and Spanish investors on the Uruguayan bank of the Uruguay River, which is also the binational border. Argentine protestors,

[70] Credit Suisse First Boston, *Emerging Markets Economics Daily*, 13 February 2006, p. 6.

[71] International Crisis Group, "Bolivia's Rocky Road to Reforms," *Latin America Report*, 18 (3 July 2006), pp. 5–10; *The Economist*, 11 February 2006, pp. 36–7; ibid., 13 May 2006, pp. 43–4; Credit Suisse First Boston, *Emerging Markets Economics Daily*, 27 June 2006, p. 2.

with the backing of Argentina's government, blocked a busy binational bridge to halt construction of the paper factories. After weeks of sustained protests and serious losses to tourism and trade, Argentina's Congress voted to sue Uruguay before the International Court of Justice while Uruguay took its case before the OAS. The OAS indicated its support for Uruguay, and a nearly unanimous international court ruled against Argentina. While this dispute was under way, Uruguay announced that it would negotiate a free trade agreement with the United States, breaking with MERCOSUR's posture hitherto of negotiating as a single bloc.[72]

These events have weakened MERCOSUR. The inclusion of Chávez's Venezuela as a full member dilutes MERCOSUR's commitment to liberal democratic institutions. Chile and Bolivia are not full MERCOSUR members, but their respective associations with MERCOSUR should have led Argentina to honor its natural gas agreement with Chile and it should have led Bolivia along a different path in making its natural gas decisions as they bear on Argentina and Brazil. Argentina and Uruguay, both MERCOSUR full members, were unable to resolve their serious differences within the MERCOSUR framework. Uruguay unilaterally broke ranks with MERCOSUR's common external trade policy.

Nevertheless, these serious disputes have been handled without resort to armed force or military coups. Uruguay and Argentina have made use of proper international means for dispute resolution. Evo Morales' democratic election as President of Bolivia was instantly accepted, as it should have been. Bolivia's decision to nationalize its natural gas sector has been accepted while negotiations on trade and financial issues continue. Venezuela's purchase of Argentina's international bonds was a valuable contribution to Argentina's economic recovery. Intra-MERCOSUR trade remains strong. MERCOSUR's core commitments to peace, security, inter-presidential negotiations, respect for democratic elections, and trade persist.

Central America and the Central American Common Market

The Central American Common Market (CACM) stagnated in the wake of the 1969 war between Honduras and El Salvador and weakened severely during the 1980s under the impact of region-wide economic depression and its internal and international wars. With the peace settlements reached in Nicaragua, El Salvador, and Guatemala in the

[72] *The Economist*, 18 March 2006, p. 40; Credit Suisse First Boston, *Emerging Markets Economics Daily*, 3 May 2006, p. 6; ibid., 16 May 2006, p. 7; ibid., 14 July 2006, p. 4.

1990s, the economies recovered. CACM reactivation began with the Puntarenas Declaration in December 1990, benefiting from the end of the Nicaraguan international and civil wars earlier in 1990, and mindful that NAFTA negotiations had begun also earlier that year without the Central Americans and that European assistance and attention had focused on former communist Eastern Europe.

The CACM has been rich in organizations, poorer in results. In the early 1990s, there was a fresh attempt to revitalize its institutions. The common external tariff, established at its founding, had lapsed; it was restored in 1993. The 1993 Tegucigalpa Protocol (ratified by all members) created the Central American Integration System, establishing regional executive, parliamentary, and judicial functions, Ministerial Commissions for regional cooperation, and technical secretariats.[73] The Central American Bank for Economic Integration finances joint development projects. The Central American Economic Integration Secretariat provides technical support. Both are long-standing CACM institutions, badly battered in the 1980s, but modernized in the early 1990s. A more recent creation, the Central American Parliament, is a forum to hold integration institutions accountable. In 2003, intra-CACM exports reached 27% of Central America's total exports, surpassing the 1960s level; at $3.1 billion, the value of intra-CACM exports was the highest ever. In 2000, CACM intra-regional exports accounted for about 7% of the CACM's gross domestic product, compared to not quite 5% in 1989.[74]

And yet, the rule of laxity in implementation still haunts Central America. Only three of the five CACM countries ratified the agreement to establish a Central American Court of Justice. Even those that ratified have made little use of its procedures to resolve commercial disputes. No fewer than sixteen trade disputes broke out between CACM members from 1993 to 2001 but in only one case did the parties resort to the Central American Court. Moreover, an important segment of regional production – agriculture and services – has never been part of free trade in Central America. The born-again common external tariff covered 95% of all tariffs in 1993, dropped to 50% in 2001, and rose to 80% in 2002.[75]

[73] Lizano and Salazar-Xirinachs, "The Central American Common Market and Hemispheric Free Trade," pp. 122 and 125.

[74] Devlin, Estevadeordal, and Garay, "Some Economic and Strategic Issues in the Face of an Emerging FTAA," pp. 166–7; Inter-American Development Bank, *Integration and Trade in the Americas: A Preliminary Estimate of 2004 Trade*, Table 3; Banco Interamericano de Desarrollo, *Más Allá de las Fronteras*, p. 163.

[75] Devlin and Estevadeordal, "¿Qué Hay de Nuevo en el Nuevo Regionalismo de las Américas?," p. 21; Banco Interamericano de Desarrollo, *Más Allá de las Fronteras*, pp. 32, 98–9, and 104–5.

Central America exhibits moderate levels of foreign policy coordination. Central American governments negotiated as a block with the European Union, the United States, Mexico, and Venezuela, respectively, regarding possible trade agreements. In the early 2000s, they negotiated as the CACM with the US government to sign the US–Central American Free Trade Agreement (CAFTA) in mid-2004. But Central American governments repeatedly broke ranks to make individual deals. Never during the 1990s did MERCOSUR countries, for example, sign bilateral framework agreements with the United States as part of negotiations for a free trade area of the Americas; the MERCOSUR bloc negotiated as a unit. Yet, within the first three years after the Bush I administration proposed inter-American free trade, each Central American government reached a separate trade deal with the United States.[76] Between 1994 and 2000, Mexico signed separate bilateral free trade agreements with Costa Rica and Nicaragua, and another jointly with El Salvador, Guatemala, and Honduras. In the 1990s, the CACM as a bloc signed a free trade agreement only with the Dominican Republic.[77] And in 2005 CAFTA went into effect without Costa Rican participation.

Central American governments also coordinated to some extent their foreign policy responses to the changes in US immigration law enacted in 1996. In 1997, the foreign ministers of Guatemala, El Salvador, Honduras, Nicaragua, and Costa Rica journeyed to Washington to make a joint case. The respective presidents also did so as a bloc during the summit meeting with President Bill Clinton in Costa Rica later that same year. However, each Central American government responded mainly on its own to the new US immigration law. The final outcome reflected the efficacy of such independent lobbying: Nicaragua succeeded the most thanks to its long-standing ties to the Republican Party, which then held a majority in the US Congress, Honduras the least, with El Salvador and Guatemala with intermediate results.[78]

Regarding international security, Central America's record in the 1990s and the first decade of the twenty-first century is poor, even though all states in the region are constitutional democracies. Militarized

[76] Ennio Rodríguez, "Central America: Common Market, Trade Liberalization, and Trade Agreements," in Roberto Bouzas and Jaime Ross (eds.), *Economic Integration in the Western Hemisphere* (Notre Dame: University of Notre Dame Press, 1994), pp. 152–65.

[77] Devlin and Estevadeordal, "¿Qué Hay de Nuevo en el Nuevo Regionalismo de las Américas?," p. 31.

[78] Christopher Mitchell, "The Future of Migration as an Issue in Inter-American Relations," in Jorge I. Domínguez (ed.), *The Future of Inter-American Relations* (New York: Routledge, 2000), pp. 221–2; Rafael Fernández de Castro and Carlos Rosales, "Migration Issues: Raising the Stakes in US–Latin American Relations," in Jorge I. Domínguez (ed.), *The Future of Inter-American Relations*, pp. 242–7 and 252–3.

interstate disputes increased in frequency since the Cold War ended in the region. Disputes involving some use of force broke out between Honduras and Nicaragua in 1991, 1995, 1996, 1997, 1998, and 2000; between Nicaragua and El Salvador in 1996 and 2000; between El Salvador and Honduras in 1996 and 2000; between Guatemala and Belize in 1997, 1999, and 2000.[79] Although larger-scale war did not break out, these cases support the key propositions advanced by Mansfield and Snyder to explain why early democratizers may be belligerent even toward other constitutional democracies.[80] Nicaraguan President Arnoldo Alemán, in particular, mobilized belligerent nationalism to bolster his flagging political support. The armed forces of Nicaragua, El Salvador, Guatemala, and Honduras also welcomed external defense missions to resist downsizing in the aftermath of civil-war pacification.

On the other hand, repeated OAS mediations helped to keep the peace. Since 1990, the Central American record is consistent with Huth and Allee's hypothesis, on the basis of large-N statistical research, that "democratic dyads are very unlikely to see their military confrontation escalate to high levels of force."[81] An optimistic view is that interstate militarized disputes in Central America might have been worse in the absence of the CACM. Perhaps so, but the CACM did not prevent the 1969 war between Honduras and El Salvador when the record of trade growth had been more impressive. The more likely causal path is that militarized interstate disputes prevent the intensification of cooperation within the region and impede greater advances in economic integration.

Regarding the defense of democracy, in 1993 the OAS intervened to stop a coup in Guatemala, staged by President Jorge Serrano with initial military support against Congress, the courts, and the political parties.[82] Other Central American democracies supported OAS action. Left to their own devices, however, Central American governments performed less well. In 1995, CACM members signed a treaty obligating each other to

[79] David R. Mares, "Boundary Disputes in the Western Hemisphere," *Pensamiento Propio*, 14 (July–December 2001), pp. 46–8. For a detailed study, see Manuel Orozco, "Boundary Disputes in Central America: Past Trends and Present Developments," *Pensamiento Propio*, 14 (July–December 2001), pp. 99–134.

[80] Mansfield and Snyder, "Democratic Transitions, Institutional Strength, and War."

[81] Paul Huth and Todd Allee, "Domestic Political Accountability and the Escalation and Settlement of International Disputes," *Journal of Conflict Resolution*, 46:6 (December 2002), p. 781.

[82] Jorge Luis Borrayo Reyes, "Aplicación de la Resolución 1080 del Compromiso de Santiago para la Democracia y la Renovación del Sistema Interamericano. El Caso de Guatemala," in Arlene Tickner (ed.), *Sistema Interamericano y Democracia: Antecedentes Históricos y Tendencias Futuras* (Bogotá: Ediciones Uniandes, 2000), pp. 227–33.

sustain democratic regimes, but not enough states ratified for it to go into effect – another example of the rule of laxity.[83]

In conclusion, since 1990 regional coordination in Central America has become more effective in trade liberalization and growth, foreign policy coordination, and, possibly, democratic accountability. Yet the extent of improvement was limited and inferior to that achieved in southern South America. Central America performed poorly in the international security issue area, saved from wider war by the OAS. Guatemala's claim to Belize's territory is a clear rejection of *uti possidetis juris*. Central America remains an example of lax implementation of agreements but it benefits from the inter-American vocation to address and contain militarized interstate disputes and, in the 1990s, from the new inter-American commitment to intervene in defense of constitutional government.

Assessing hypotheses

International regional and subregional institutions in the Americas have been constructed over a long time but they were revitalized and reinvented in the early 1990s.[84] The idea that regional institutions are good is a legacy of the aftermath of independence in the 1820s. The structure of the international system in the Americas, differentiated into subsystems, fostered subregional patterns. The rules of the continental system (respect for territorial integrity, activist commitment to interstate mediation, laxity in implementation) are also of long standing and changed very slowly. Indeed, only the "hard shell" view of sovereignty, averse to intervention in the domestic affairs of states, changed. In the 1990s, it was replaced by a rule permitting and obligating states to defend democracy everywhere in the Americas – a new rule that weakened in the early 2000s.

Between 1990 and 2002, the OAS and MERCOSUR performed well in collectively defending constitutional government. The OAS' effectiveness in democratic defense weakened thereafter, and Venezuelan membership in MERCOSUR may dilute the latter's commitment to democratic constitutionalism. Both the OAS and MERCOSUR improved the likelihood that interstate peace would be constructed and sustained (see summary in Table 3.2). They facilitated better foreign policy coordination and MERCOSUR had a significant role in the expansion of trade in goods. Their automatic rules helped to defend democracy and promote trade in goods.

83 Diamint, "Evolución del Sistema Interamericano: Entre el Temor y la Armonía," p. 14.

84 For a theory-based assessment of regionalism sensitive to the Latin American experience, see Andrew Hurrell, "Regionalism in Theoretical Perspective."

Table 3.2 *Latin American regional and subregional institutional outcomes, 1990–2006*

Organization	Organizational design	Laxity	Trade growth	Financial adjustment	Security	Foreign policy coordination	Democracy defense
OAS	Thick	Down	NR	NR	++	+	+
MERCOSUR	Thin	Down	+	–	++	+	++
CACM	Thick	Same	+	~	–	+/~	+/~

NOTE: Organization of American States (OAS); Southern Common Market (MERCOSUR); Central American Common Market (CACM). + implies good performance; – implies poor performance; ~ implies middling performance; NR means the category is not relevant. Ratings under "laxity" are comparisons to pre-1990 patterns. "Thick" and "thin" refer to the number and scope of treaty-mandated formal organizations.

MERCOSUR was unprepared for the financial crises of its members in the1999–2002 period, however.

The CACM is a more modest achiever with regard to the promotion of trade, and since 1990 it performed less well than the OAS and MERCOSUR in defending constitutional democracy. The rule of laxity continued to bedevil this subregion. Central American governments managed foreign policy coordination and financial adjustment marginally better than the MERCOSUR countries but the Central Americans did not handle well their shared international security problems. Finally, organizational design had little impact on the likelihood of achieving successful outcomes. Organization-poor MERCOSUR performed reasonably well. The organization-rich OAS and CACM had varying levels of performance but they were not better performers than MERCOSUR.

We now consider plausible hypotheses that bear on the explanation of the change in institutional performance before and after 1990.

Hypothesis rejection

(1) Domestic **political culture and identity** did not change and consequently they cannot explain the changes in the "thickness" (the number and scope of treaty-mandated organizations), formality, or effectiveness of institutional arrangements in the 1990s. The Latinobarómetro public opinion polls continue to show skepticism about democracy and free markets.[85] After 1990, new government policies in defense of constitutional government and freer trade did not respond to public opinion changes. Instead, the shocks of the 1980s (end of the Cold War in Europe, the decade-long economic depression, and the democratization wave), exogenous to the international regional institutions, broke moorings for states in the Americas.

(2) **Membership** in organizations and the **number of state actors** varied little over time. Membership has always been inclusive for all Latin American countries for each pertinent level, except for Cuba's suspension from OAS active membership in 1962. Since 1870 no state has disappeared. No secession past independence succeeded since 1903. Membership in the OAS increased in the 1960s and 1970s thanks to the addition of newly independent Anglophone Caribbean countries, but the change in OAS efficacy did not occur until much after that increase in membership. Canada joined the OAS in 1989 and contributed to the adoption of the 1991 Santiago Declaration on

[85] Marta Lagos, "Public Opinion," in Jorge I. Domínguez and Michael Shifter (eds.), *Constructing Democratic Governance in Latin America*, 2nd edn. (Baltimore: Johns Hopkins University Press, 2003), pp. 137–61.

democracy, but the key actors in adopting the rule change regarding the collective defense of democracy were the old members, namely, Latin American states and the United States. Cuba's suspension from active OAS membership in 1962 was unrelated to the OAS' disposition to defend democracy from the 1960s to 1990; instead, it was an episode in the Cold War. Membership in the CACM remained unchanged since its foundation. Venezuela joined MERCOSUR in December 2005, well after MERCOSUR's characteristics were set.

(3) Organizational **decision-making rules** remained the same in MERCOSUR and the CACM combining elements of formality and informality. MERCOSUR *de facto* operated under leadership from Argentina and Brazil, with Paraguay and Uruguay as bandwagoners. However, *de facto* rules changed over time in the OAS from a supermajority to "consensus." The OAS dispute-mediating effectiveness was about the same under both decision-making rules. The change from strict non-intervention to the collective defense of democracy occurred for reasons other than this shift in decision-making rules and well after the *de facto* rule had shifted to consensus.

(4) **Institutional scope** changed dramatically after 1990 at both the regional and subregional levels. The institutions undertook many more tasks and sought to affect domestic politics more intrusively. This was equally true regardless of the relative reliance on internal organizations, that is, it was comparably the case for the organizationally "thick" OAS as for the organizationally "thin" MERCOSUR. But the change was so uniform that it is difficult to make much of this variable either to explain effectiveness or variation between institutions.

(5) In a hemisphere marked since the birth of Latin American states by the rule of laxity, hypotheses about **centralization and flexibility** are difficult to specify.[86] In a pinch, each and every Latin American organization has been "flexible" to the point of ineffectiveness. Such flexibility and, for prolonged periods, irrelevance help to explain why the institutions (OAS and CACM in the 1970s and 1980s) did not just fade away. However, these variables do not explain the resurrection of the OAS and the CACM or the birth of MERCOSUR in the early 1990s. The single most effective design feature in these three institutions was automaticity, not flexibility.

(6) The OAS began to defend democracy only after its **mandate** changed in 1991. However, the change in the OAS is better explained as

[86] Koremenos, Lipson, and Snidal argue that centralization and flexibility are among the most important design features in institutions. See their "Rational design," p. 1054.

the result of changes exogenous to the organization. MERCOSUR acted to defend Paraguayan democracy in 1996 before its mandate changed, and a treaty to mandate the defense of democracy as part of the CACM went unratified. Mandate change thus fails as a systematic explanation of cross-institutional behavior. The fact that the OAS and MERCOSUR were more effective in defending democracy in the 1990s is unrelated to a change in their formal mandate.

(7) The Latin Americans sought economic integration under both state-led and open-market **economic models**. At first the CACM and LAFTA were attempts to lengthen the useful life of import-substituting industrialization – the same economic model but within a hoped-for larger integrated protected economy. Economic integration developed or re-shaped in the 1990s took place in market-friendlier contexts. Economic model is unrelated to the likelihood of undertaking an economic integration project because such projects were undertaken regardless of the prevailing economic model. In the 1990s, trade integration succeeded more in southern South America than in Central America but the prevalence of market-oriented policies varied a good deal by country within each subregion. Semi-protectionist LAIA went nowhere; the market-based FTAA project has also gone nowhere. The choice of economic development model thus explains little about the likelihood or effectiveness of international economic cooperation in the Americas.

(8) **Country size and power** does not explain success at integration efforts, which have been as likely when large or small countries lead them. The participation of large countries in an integration scheme does not ensure its success, or their absence doom such a scheme to failure. The sources of leadership have also varied in the political and security arenas. The key actor in Central America's pacification in the late 1980s was Costa Rica. The 1994 intervention in Haiti gained a modicum of legitimacy from the deployment to Haiti of Afro-Caribbean police officers from democratic Anglophone Caribbean countries. Yet the United States played a major role in the intervention in Haiti in 1994 and the larger countries were also essential in bringing about the Ecuador–Peru settlement in 1998 and in defending constitutional government in Paraguay in the late 1990s.

(9) **Enforcement and uncertainty problems** explain little about the results in the 1990s. The enforcement of a "relative absence-of-war" system predates the foundation of all the formal regional and subregional organizations. The OAS and the southern South Americans dealt capably with interstate security disputes in the 1990s but the Central American governments on their own did not. The OAS was more effective than the Central Americans acting on their own at

addressing Central American interstate security problems. The OAS and MERCOSUR ratified and acted on their respective democracy clauses; the CACM approved a democracy clause that went unratified. The CACM clearly had an enforcement problem but the nature of the problem was the same as for those other states and institutions that overcame the problem. Moreover, the level of uncertainty explains little about the changes in the 1990s or the variation across institutions.

Hypotheses with mixed results

(1) The democratic regimes of Central America performed poorly but those in South America performed well in responding to interstate disputes since the regime transitions of the 1990s. Central America's democratic regimes have been less effective at fostering intra-regional trade than have the democratic regimes in southern South America. Southern South American dictatorships cooperated in specific issue areas in the 1970s – as Central American dictatorships did at times – but they could not reach more comprehensive forms of security cooperation. The mixed membership of the OAS – with dictatorships and democracies for most of its history – did not impair the organization's capacity to mediate between states in security disputes but, of course, its capacity to defend democracy depended on the prior change in the domestic political regime of all member states by 1990. Thus **domestic political regime** seems unrelated to the likelihood or efficacy of trade promotion or specific dispute settlement, but democratic regimes are more likely to succeed at continental international security cooperation and in democratic regime defense.

(2) The **presence of interstate militarized conflict** greatly impairs international cooperation across the board, as evident in both Central and South America in the 1970s and in Central America since the end of the Cold War. The absence of militarized interstate conflict was a contributing but not the predominant factor in fostering such cooperation as in southern South America.

(3) In the 1980s, the **United States** played a salient role promoting free-market ideas but only a delayed and secondary role in promoting democratization. In the 1990s, the US played a key role in institutionalizing the OAS rule regarding the collective defense of democracy and fostering inter-American trade. After 2002, the United States weakened the defense of democracy rule. The US role in interstate boundary dispute settlement was embedded within the OAS or

coalitions of the willing; the US role in such disputes had little significance outside of collective efforts.

Hypothesis acceptance

(1) The likelihood of regional and subregional institutional effectiveness responds strongly to **prior and independent structural and normative changes in the international system**. The birth of the OAS after World War II and MERCOSUR in the 1990s, the revitalization of the OAS and the CACM in the 1990s, greater bilateral or *ad hoc* international problem-solving, are best explained with reference to prior normative and structural changes in the international system – the ends of World War II and the Cold War and, since the 1980s, the global spread of democratic and free-market norms. The critical juncture of the 1980s brought together an economic great depression that unleashed free-market alternatives, a continent-wide democratization, and the end of the Cold War (Cuba excepted). The interaction between these three variables – exogenous to the continental and subregional institutions – facilitated international regional and subregional institutional revitalization and effectiveness in the 1990s.

(2) **International non-governmental organizations**, especially those concerned with human rights, and **international political party federations**, especially the Socialist International and the World Federation of Christian Democrats, played significant roles in assisting Latin America's democratization in the 1980s. The **United Nations** played an indispensable role in Central American pacification in the 1990s.

(3) The commitment to the collective defense of democracy since 1990 and toward market-friendlier economic integration can only be explained with reference to the **changes within countries** during the 1980s. Changes in the preferences of actors affected how they used the institutions and how they complied with their decisions.

(4) **Automatic rules** have been most effective since 1990, when two new rules were adopted: the reduction of tariffs on goods and (for the OAS until 2002) the obligation to defend constitutional democracy under threat. These are self-implementing rules, independent of organizations or their staffs past the very moment of agreement. Liberalization of tariffs on goods succeeded the most (NAFTA and MERCOSUR) wherever the rule of automaticity applied.[87] Although the OAS must meet to act to defend democracy under threat,

[87] For a comparison between NAFTA and MERCOSUR, see Ivan Bernier and Martin Roy, "NAFTA and MERCOSUR: Two Competing Models?," in Gordon Mace and

member states and the OAS Secretary-General came to feel sufficiently authorized to act in many cases on their own.

Nearly as automatic is an older rule: by the 1920s the habit developed that coalitions of the willing act in instances of international security threat and seek to mediate between disputants. In the 1990s, the rule was extended to the defense of democracy, too. Thus Rio Protocol Guarantors fashioned the peace between Ecuador and Peru in 1998 and coalitions of the willing defended democracy in Paraguay and, in 1991–1994, Haiti. Between 1991 and 2002, once a dispute broke out or democracy was threatened, regional or subregional institutions or sets of states automatically offered their good offices to stop and settle conflicts and defend constitutional government.

(5) The presence of **distributional problems** affects the likelihood of success of international economic institutions. LAFTA and the early CACM privileged distributional issues in their agreements and, as a result, found it nearly impossible to liberalize trade effectively. At the end of the great depression of the 1980s, governments privileged growth over distribution, permitting the foundation of MERCOSUR and the refurbishing of the CACM. The weakening of both MERCOSUR and the CACM during the economic slowdown that began in the late 1990s can be traced to the reappearance of distributional concerns within both organizations.

(6) International cooperation in the Americas has been most successful when it is both **voluntary and comprehensive** in its origins and purposes. Southern cone cooperation in the 1970s was strictly utilitarian and limited to some issue areas. Southern cone cooperation since 1990 has been comprehensive, crossing many issue areas, seeking both material utility and peace and democracy. In the 1990s, less successful institutions such as the CACM did not address issues comprehensively; the CACM failed to settle interstate security disputes. The least successful interventions in the domestic affairs of states, even if the OAS authorized them, are those that felt coerced or "bought" – the US-led intervention in the Dominican Republic in 1965 is the most prominent example.

Two other hypotheses should also be accepted because they help to explain important continuities between the pre- and post-1990 periods.

(1) Latin Americans have been **international rule innovators**. They are not just "price takers." They developed the doctrine of *uti possidetis juris* a century before its spread throughout Africa, Asia, and

Louis Bélanger (eds.), *The Americas in Transition: The Contours of Regionalism* (Boulder, CO: Lynne Rienner, 1999).

the former Soviet Union. They pioneered the defense of "hard shell" notions of sovereignty and non-intervention. Their coalitions of the willing succeeded more often at interstate dispute resolution than did the League of Nations. The OAS has been more successful in such endeavors than other regional organizations. Latin Americans began serious economic integration efforts coincident with the efforts that led to Western Europe's Treaty of Rome. They lagged behind Western Europe in implementing a commitment to defend democratic institutions but they improved their own performance since 1990. There has been, therefore, significant ideational, normative political autonomy in the Americas. The Latin Americans have been innovation receivers in the design of economic development models at times in their histories, however.

(2) **Legacies** matter. The structure of international subsystems in the Americas, first developed in mid nineteenth century, persists into the twenty-first century. The subregional organizations created in the 1990s respond to international subsystemic structures that date from the nineteenth century. The rules of territorial integrity, activist mediation, and laxity in implementation are also of very long standing. Success in avoiding major interstate war is also an accomplishment of old. The only old rule reversed in the 1990s was the absolute prohibition to intervene in the domestic affairs of states; intervention to defend democracy became possible.

Conclusions

From the nineteenth to the twenty-first centuries, Latin American governments fashioned international rules to order their relations. In the second half of the twentieth century, they constructed international organizations to institutionalize those rules. The efficacy of these organizations rests on their intergovernmental character; they are not supranational. These organizations succeed or fail in response to the preferences of their member states. For the most part, institutional design features have explained little about the efficacy of organizations. The key exception has been automaticity. From *uti possidetis juris* or the propensity for instant international mediation in the face of the threat of war, to the defense of democracy in the 1990s, or NAFTA and MERCOSUR reduction of tariffs on goods, international rules work absent a role for any international organization, or minimalist organizations succeed when the founding actors bind themselves to act automatically and link the rule to their interest in complying with it.

Past 1990, there was success. Scores of boundary disputes were settled in South America. Trade in goods grew in MERCOSUR and the CACM. No constitutional democracy was dismantled in the Americas outside Haiti. Foreign policy coordination improved in southern South America and somewhat in Central America. The Isthmus of Panama had not yet become like the Isthmus of Corinth, as Bolívar in 1826 had hoped it would become, but the Americas became more prosperous, peaceful, and freer thanks to the greater effectiveness of international regional and subregional institutions.

4 Crafting regional cooperation in Africa

Jeffrey Herbst

Numerous attempts at creating formal regional organizations have failed in Africa, leaving a veritable organizational junkyard of unsuccessful attempts to reduce the continent's balkanization. The assumption has therefore been that regional cooperation has failed, and will continue to do so, in Africa because the domestic and regional environments are so different from Europe, which has the highest density of successful regional experiments. In fact, while the failures in crafting regional organizations have been numerous, there have also been occasional examples of dramatic success. In particular, the Organization of African Unity managed to establish an improbable continental norm that boundaries should not be altered and large parts of Africa had a common currency decades before the euro. More generally, African states continue to devote enormous amounts of time and energy to creating continental, regional, and bilateral treaties, organizations, and forums, suggesting by their revealed preferences that they do not believe that pursuing regional cooperation is fruitless.

In fact, regional cooperation is largely initiated and designed in Africa to promote the security and interests of rulers, rather than the more generally assumed goals of increasing the size of economic markets, ensuring the rights of citizens, or overcoming capricious national boundaries. The key to understanding the fate of regional cooperation in Africa is to discard the assumption that there is an inevitable conflict between sovereignty (or, more precisely, the prerogatives of individual leaders) and regional cooperation. African leaders usually seek to promote regional or continental agreements in order to enhance their own domestic standing and to cement their state's sovereignty. Regional institutions usually work in Africa when they help African leaders with their domestic problems. As a result, regional cooperation is not necessarily a good thing in Africa, or elsewhere, because leaders may be using regional or continental mechanisms to augment their own stature, rather than to promote regional and international peace and prosperity. Of course, regional cooperation in other regions of the world is also often designed to help the interests of leaders. However, African leaders are the weakest in the world and realistically have to be much more concerned about their immediate positions than other rulers. As African countries, on average, are as a group the farthest from having a monopoly on legitimate violence in their countries, the immediate need to constantly reiterate the sovereign nature of the state is more important in Africa than elsewhere.

This perspective is also radically different from the work done recently on the Rational Design of International Institutions project. This recent approach asks how states design international institutions to promote their *international* goals. For instance, Koremenos, Lipson, and Snidal argue that "institutions are considerably more than empty vessels. States spend significant amounts of time and effort constructing institutions precisely because they can advance or impede state goals in the international economy, the environment and national security."[1] Indeed, they explicitly focus much of their own analysis of how states respond to new international problems.[2] African leaders are, in fact, quite attentive to the rational design of institutions but their focus, more often than not, is to protect and extend their domestic standing rather than strengthen their states' standing on international issues. The reason, of course, is that domestic forces threaten African leaders much more palpably than international problems, especially given the context of extraordinary poverty and weak institutions. Indeed, the rational design literature takes, seemingly as a given, that states are well-ordered enough that worries about international problems can be separated from domestic politics. That assumption needs to be questioned in some parts of the world.

There is a clear style of African regional cooperation. Cooperation tends to be extremely inclusive (a large number of participants), formal (in the sense that organizations are well-defined and their rules elaborated at length), non-hierarchical (no country is privileged and secretariats are generally weak), and attentive to national sovereignty. It would be hard to argue that this style emerges from a particular African way of conducting business because cultural styles vary immensely across the continent and because there was no history of interaction between territorially-defined sovereign nation-states before the advent of independence in the early 1960s.[3] Rather, the African style of international coordination developed because African leaders face generally similar problems in securing their

[1] Barbara Koremenos, Charles Lipson, and Duncan Snidal, "The Rational Design of International Institutions," *International Organization*, 55:4 (Autumn 2001), p. 762.
[2] Ibid., p. 768.
[3] There was, of course, in Africa a history of international relations before colonialism but precolonial states were not territorially defined and the notion of sovereignty as currently understood was absent.

rule and have a common set of concerns about foreign interference in their domestic affairs.

A record of failed cooperation?

Regional cooperation is associated with failure in Africa in good part because the process of independence required, in many cases, the destruction of large territorial units. The two large French colonial federations (Afrique Occidental Français and Afrique Equatorial Français) devolved into more than a dozen countries; Kenya, Tanzania, and Uganda emerged out of the British East Africa Federation while Malawi, Zambia, and Zimbabwe eventually came to independence after the Federation of Rhodesia and Nyasaland collapsed. Dissolving these colonial groupings often involved the destruction of important common institutions. The East Africa Federation, for instance, had a common currency, university, and airline. Many other colonial arrangements that allowed for significant cross-border cooperation were also eliminated in the headlong march toward independence. For instance, the West Africa Currency Board that provided one currency linked to sterling for all of Great Britain's colonies in West Africa was wound down shortly after independence. The colonial period was clearly the high point of regional cooperation.

After independence, across Africa, there was a feeling of profound ambivalence about the attainment of sovereign power. On the one hand, leaders and citizens were committed to guaranteeing the viability of their own states, even if the independence of their states had not even been imaginable a few years before and irrespective of the profound problems that affected many countries, including their size and geographic location (especially the large number of land-locked states). On the other hand, it was understood that the balkanization of Africa into, eventually, four dozen countries was a betrayal of the pan-African ideal that had motivated many early proponents of independence and left the new countries exceptionally vulnerable to divide-and-rule tactics by the ex-colonial powers, the superpowers, and, through the 1980s, white-ruled regimes in Southern Africa.

African countries therefore embarked on a large number of projects to promote economic integration to ameliorate the effects of the balkanization produced by independence. The legacy of these attempts has been a large number of failures. As Christopher Clapham has argued:

> Classically, Africa regional integration schemes have been established in terms of a completely misperceived analogy with the Europe Union, in terms of which a process of progressively closer economic integration was (at least rhetorically)

expected to lead to a political union implicit in the Pan-African project. These schemes varied in the number of states involved, from a minimum of two (like the Senegambian Confederation or the Mano River Union) to 15 (the Economic Community of West African States) . . . They likewise differed in the complexity of their institutional arrangements, the level of common services that they already possessed, and the ambition of their goals. None of them achieved very much.[4]

Africa is indeed littered with the carcasses of failed economic unions (e.g. the Economic Community of West African States) and the volumes planning putative continental organizations that were never realized are legion. Thus, the 1980 *Lagos Plan of Action*, the apotheosis of the Organization of African Unity's desire to create pan-African institutions, asked for the creation of an African Economic Community, supported by an African Monetary Fund and an African Mutual Guarantee and Solidarity Fund.[5] Of course, none was even attempted because the hopeful architects of these new creations, like the planners of many aborted groupings, could not offer leaders significant enough incentives to abdicate even small bits of power. The regional organizations failed despite the fact that many donors were sympathetic to them because Africa's political fragmentation made aid to individual countries problematic.[6] It is therefore easy to conclude that regional integration has failed because international cooperation has been too difficult in Africa.

International cooperation as a source of domestic power

African leaders, as a group, are profoundly insecure. Many leaders have been forcibly deposed; indeed, coup d'états are the single greatest cause of regime change in Africa. While there has been a significant number of African leaders who have been elected recently, very few of the new democracies in Africa can be considered institutionalized. For instance, Madagascar, which was one of the leaders in democratization in the early 1990s with two regime changes after free and fair elections, descended into a devastating civil war after a contested election in 2002. Further, African leaders must continually confront the problems of extraordinarily

[4] Christopher Clapham, "The Changing World of Regional Integration in Africa," in Christopher Clapham *et al.* (eds.), *Regional Integration in Southern Africa: Comparative International Perspectives* (Johannesburg: South African Institute of International Affairs, 2001), pp. 59–60.

[5] Organization of African Unity, *Lagos Plan of Action for the Economic Development of Africa, 1980–2000* (Geneva: International Institute for Labour Studies, 1982), pp. 87 and 126.

[6] See, for instance, a paper prepared by the US State Department's Policy Planning Council, "Selected Aspects of US Economic Aid Policy for Africa," PPC 61–7, 1961, reprinted in Nina Davis Howland (ed.), *Foreign Relations of the United States: Africa, 1961–1963* (Washington, DC: Government Printing Office, 1995), p. 296.

low per capita incomes, poorly functioning administrative systems, immature market mechanisms, and a large peasant population that is sometimes only peripherally ruled by the state. Fluctuations in the prices of commodities, the vagaries of international aid donors who supply much of government revenue, and instability in neighboring countries further threaten many rulers.

African leaders have therefore always looked to the international system as a source of domestic power. As Robert Jackson has effectively argued, the granting of sovereignty to African nations in the early 1960s was a fundamental change in international relations. He noted that starting with the famous Harold Macmillian "wind of change speech" in 1960, "empirical statehood went rapidly into eclipse" and a new form of juridical statehood based on a "rights-model of international relations" became dominant. In the new model of international relations, epitomized by United Nations' General Assembly Resolution 2621, states no longer had to earn sovereignty (through the establishment of a national government that could enforce its authority) but deserved it simply on the basis of being decolonized and then becoming members of the United Nations.[7] As a result, from the birth of their countries, African leaders have seen membership and participation in international organizations and agreements as critical to alleviating their own insecurities rather than being a threat to their prerogatives.

The OAU

Thus, the first regional organization that Africans created – the Organization of African Unity – was, despite its name, devoted to ensuring the division of Africa was viable by strengthening individual states. In particular, the OAU's 1964 resolution on border problems pledged member states "to respect the frontiers existing on their achievement of national independence."[8] There was an almost immediate determination that the OAU Charter, written in 1963 and demanding (Article III, paragraph 3) "Respect for the sovereignty and territorial integrity of each State and for its inalienable right to independent existence,"[9] meant the states as mapped by the Europeans.

[7] Robert H. Jackson, "The Weight of Ideas in Decolonization: Normative Change in International Relations," in Judith Goldstein and Robert Keohane (eds.), *Ideas and Foreign Policy* (Ithaca, NY: Cornell University Press, 1993), pp. 117 and 125.

[8] Organization of African Unity, "OAU Resolution on Border Disputes, 1964," reprinted in Ian Brownlie (ed.), *Basic Documents on African Affairs* (Oxford: Clarendon Press, 1971), p. 361.

[9] Organization of African Unity, "Charter of the OAU," reprinted in Ian Brownlie (ed.), *Basic Documents on African Affairs*, p. 3.

One implication of the OAU's solution to the boundary problems faced by the African countries was to effectively quash the right of self-determination. This right, which all African nationalists had relied upon during the fight to gain independence, posed an extraordinary threat to the leaders of the newly independent countries because it implied that the many disgruntled minorities in these countries had a legal right to destroy the territorial integrity of their states through secession. While the OAU Charter recognized "the inalienable right to all people to control their own destiny," the OAU Principles were designed to promote the rights of states rather than individuals. The first three items of the Principles (in Article III of the Charter) affirm sovereign equality of all member states, non-interference in the internal affairs of member states, and respect for their sovereignty and territorial integrity.[10] Self-determination was deemed only to apply to those countries which were still colonies or which were still under white minority control. The African decisions on boundaries both reinforced the United Nations' decision to recognize the sovereignty of each former colony and further emphasized the legitimacy of giving sovereignty a clear priority over self-determination. To some extent, the OAU decisions helped explain "what came next" after the UN decision that all former colonies would become sovereign states.

The OAU boundary regime was strongly supported by African leaders who did not know how their state would fare if boundaries were changed and therefore were happy to embrace the state design of their colonial predecessors. Indeed, despite the fact that most African countries cannot physically defend their boundaries, the only example of forced boundary change in Africa's history has been the independence of Eritrea from Ethiopia. While many countries have violated the boundaries of their neighbors (especially in the continental war that raged in Democratic Republic of the Congo in the late 1990s), the norm of boundary stability has been successfully institutionalized. This has been a tremendous boon to the numerous leaders across the continent: they do not have to worry, by and large, about the external threats that have obsessed most weak rulers throughout history, instead the regional system they created calls for respect for the states they lead and non-interference in their internal affairs.

Given how improbable the map of Africa seemed in the early 1960s, the preservation of the boundaries over two generations has to be one of the more extraordinary successes in regional cooperation. The boundary maintenance regime has successful secured the sovereignty of countries

[10] Ibid., pp. 2–3.

that often could not defend themselves if attacked and helped leaders who often do not have a monopoly on legitimate violence across their territories. Indeed, a reasonable argument could be made that the African boundary maintenance regime was one of the most successful instances of regional cooperation in the last third of the twentieth century.

The boundary maintenance regime has all of the characteristics of African style cooperation. It is extremely inclusive, as all of the countries except Somalia (which had irredentist goals in the 1960s) agreed to retain the boundaries. It is formal as the OAU declared its intentions immediately and did not hide the fact that self-determination was to be declared non-legitimate. It is non-hierarchical in that all countries are treated the same way. Africa's large, powerful countries, in particular, agreed to the boundary maintenance regime. This was done not out of charity but because Nigeria, Ethiopia, and Zaire (three of the largest African countries and ones that traditional international relations theory might predict to have their own territorial ambitions) were threatened by secessionist movements themselves and therefore were especially committed to the boundary maintenance regime. While the OAU had a very weak secretariat, these boundary rules were enforced more by consensus and by mediation by *ad hoc* committees of heads of state rather than an intrusive secretariat. Finally, the boundary regime is exceptionally attentive to national sovereignty.

Whether this success is a good thing generally is a separate issue. The boundary regime did not prevent African states from failing. African states fail at an unsurprising rate because it is difficult to establish national authority. After all, Tilly estimates that the "enormous majority" of states in Europe after 1500 failed,[11] and conditions in Africa are no more conducive to state formation than in other areas of the world. What is different in Africa is that states fail within their boundaries. The response to state failure elsewhere in the world has been for non-viable units to break up, to be taken over by neighbors, or to otherwise be reconstituted. In Europe, stronger units eventually emerged as a result of these processes. However, in Africa, a similar sequence of state reconstitution cannot get started because it has proven to be impossible to detach sovereignty from even collapsed states. Thus, the international community continues to try to make Somalia function although that state has never worked and shows no sign of being viable in the future. At the same time, Somaliland – the break-away part of Somalia that has made some progress – has largely

[11] Charles Tilly, "Reflections on the History of European State-Making," in Charles Tilly (ed.), *The Formation of National States in Western Europe* (Princeton: Princeton University Press, 1975), p. 38.

been ignored by the international community because many aid agencies, in particular, do not know how to relate to subnational units that have declared independence. Similarly, African communities and the international community continue to pledge fealty to the territorial integrity of the Democratic Republic of the Congo (the former Zaire), despite the lack of evidence that the country can ever be ruled successfully.

In 2002, African countries created the African Union (AU) to succeed the OAU. The new organization has, not unexpectedly, continued to guarantee most of the perquisites that were institutionalized within the OAU. The founding act of the African Union repeats the old OAU's determination to preserve the boundaries inherited from the colonialists and pledges the AU to "Defend the sovereignty, territorial integrity and independence of its Member States."[12] Of course, it would hardly be surprising if a group of leaders whose common characteristic is their internal weakness created anything other than an organization that could be used as a resource while confronting their endless domestic problems. However, the AU is notable for the Africans' ability to replicate their previous success in the area of boundary maintenance.

General enthusiasm for international agreements

Not surprisingly, African countries have always been among the most enthusiastic signers of international and regional agreements, ranging from the Convention on the Rights of the Child to the International Criminal Court, to the many UN and OAU documents on human rights. African countries have also been enthusiastic participants in the large international conferences that have, in the last decade, focused on such issues as the environment, women, and human rights. Finally, African countries have continued to design regional political (the AU) and economic agreements. Thus, the recently promulgated New Partnership for Africa's Development (NEPAD) is based on the idea that African countries should conduct peer review of each other's policies in order to reduce the role of the World Bank and the International Monetary Fund (IMF). African countries continue to try to cooperate despite the fact that few have either the intention or the capability to meet their obligations under the international human rights agreements, or the final proclamations of the meetings that they were attending, or the new strictures of NEPAD. For instance, the 1990s were notable for the number of international

[12] African Union, "Constitutive Act of the African Union," Article 3, July 2000. Available online: www.au2002.gov.za/docs/key_oau/au_act.htm, date accessed, July 29, 2002.

agreements that African countries signed to try to regulate the laws of war even while civil wars were killing an unprecedented number of civilians across the continent.

However, signing international human rights accords, designing new regional and continent agreements, and participating in the vast United Nations conferences are reaffirmations of African countries' sovereignty and thus helpful in augmenting the domestic power bases of leaders. The United States has traditionally been reluctant to join in all kinds of international agreements because, by acceding to them, Washington will feel compelled to enforce them. The United States, and many other countries, also worry that such international agreements are an infringement on their sovereignty. African countries have no such concerns; indeed, they view their very participation as a solidification of their sovereignty. Thus, African leaders enthusiastically applauded Zimbabwe President Robert Mugabe's speech at the 2002 World Summit on Sustainable Development in Johannesburg. Mugabe, whose land seizure policies have caused millions to suffer from malnutrition, is hardly an exemplar of sustainable development. Rather, Mugabe was applauded while demanding that Prime Minister Tony Blair stop criticizing his regime because the UK was interfering with Zimbabwe's sovereignty. Similarly, few believe that African leaders would actually police each other's policies under NEPAD. Rather, the new economic gambit is seen as a way of reducing IMF and World Bank oversight, a particularly grievous violation of sovereignty for African leaders. Again, regional cooperation is not always an obvious "good," motivations must always be considered.

It is therefore hardly surprising that African cooperation has a bias toward including a relatively large number of countries. The larger the number of countries that have agreed to an accord, the more likely it is to be seen as a marker for sovereignty. The coordination problems posed by large memberships are not that significant an issue because these cooperative arrangements are not designed to actually do something. The last thing that African leaders want is a democratic deficit in their international institutions. Ostentatious procedures promote the ideal of each country being equal, and therefore having equivalent claims to sovereignty. Of course, highly democratic international institutions are also unlikely to take action against any particular country.

Cooperation that fails

Not surprisingly, the type of cooperation that is most likely to fail in Africa actually does challenge the sovereignty of countries. That is why the early attempts to ameliorate Africa's balkanization – including the Mali Federation, the East African Federation, the aborted Ghana–Guinea–Mali Union, and "Senegambia" – all either did not get off the ground or rather quickly crashed.[13] These attempts, like the many regional attempts at economic organization, failed because they could not offer leaders significant enough incentives to abdicate even small bits of power. However, membership in these organizations continually amplified the notion that African countries are sovereign; therefore, they served a purpose, even if not the one commonly thought. Thus, African leaders continue to participate in organizations that have long records of failure, a puzzling trait for those who believe that regional institutions exist to solve regional problems but one that is understandable from a domestic perspective.

Formal efforts at promoting cooperation in security have also failed in Africa. Perhaps in no area of the world was the need to create an international force greater than in Africa. Despite the achievement of independence by most African countries in the early 1960s, foreign military intervention by the ex-colonial powers and others highlighted the fragility of the newly won political power and served to strengthen the historic memory of colonial domination. Thus, *West Africa*, the major news weekly on the continent, called in 1964 for an "African Fire Brigade" that could serve as an interpositional force in international conflicts (e.g. between Ethiopia and Somalia, Rwanda and Burundi, and Morocco and Algeria) and that would also address domestic upheavals in individual countries. *West Africa*'s motivation was the debacle in Tanganyika where British troops had to intervene to quell a revolt by the East African country's restive army, a profound embarrassment given then President Julius Nyerere's clarion calls for an end to all foreign influence and his criticism of Western powers during the Cold War.[14] However, it was the catastrophe in the Congo, where outside intervention by the United Nations, Belgium (the former colonizer), and other powers, apparently motivated by Cold War concerns, ended in the death of Congolese President Patrice Lumumba, that solidified the African view that foreign intervention, even under humanitarian guise, would always be problematic. Yet, no all-African force was created. Such a force, by definition, would have the potential to threaten African leaders and would have had a call on the most precious resource that African leaders have: loyal soldiers.

[13] Claude E. Welch Jr., *Dream of Unity: Pan-Africanism and Political Unification in West Africa* (Ithaca, NY: Cornell University Press, 1966), p. 356.

[14] "African Fire Brigade," *West Africa*, 15 February 1964, p. 169.

The SADC

The Southern African Development Community (SADC) is a particularly vivid example of the dynamics of regional cooperation in Africa. The SADC was originally the Southern African Development Coordination Conference (SADCC) when it was founded by nine Southern African countries in 1980 (after the independence of Zimbabwe). The goals of SADCC were to lessen the region's dependence on white-ruled South Africa and to promote economic development in the region. The SADCC became the SADC in 1992 when the independence of Namibia and the imminent transition in South Africa caused the organization to move away from its goal of economic autarky toward the more traditional goal of regional integration, especially economic development. In 1996, the then Zaire (now the Democratic Republic of the Congo (DRC)), the Seychelles, and Mauritius joined the organization. The cost of adding the giant Congo was to completely confuse the organization's agenda because the DRC is actually not in Southern Africa. In addition, the Congo would soon become a battleground that would drag in some of the SADC countries while effectively splitting the organization over the war.

The SADCC and then the SADC has always had a privileged place in Africa. During the difficult 1980s, when much of the world's attention was focused on apartheid South Africa and especially Pretoria's campaign of destabilization against its neighbors, the SADCC was very much in the frontline of global opposition to minority rule. Giving money to SADCC was seen explicitly as a way of signaling opposition to apartheid, a position especially convenient to the Reagan and Thatcher governments in light of severe criticism in the United Kingdom and the United States that these administrations were soft on apartheid. Indeed, the World Bank estimated that per capita aid to the Southern Africa region, much of it either going to SADCC projects or attracted by the SADCC, was three times the average for Third World countries. Praise from the international community was plentiful. For instance, Edward Jaycox, former World Bank Vice-President for Africa, said in 1988 that the SADCC was "a functional example of how regional cooperation in Africa might work."[15]

More importantly for African countries, SADCC was enormously successful in serving as an aid platform for African countries that enabled leaders to garner more resources from the international community than they would have as individual supplicants. Indeed, the reality of the

[15] Statistic and quote from Nana Poku, *Regionalization and Security in Southern Africa* (Basingstoke: Palgrave, 2001), pp. 103–4.

SADCC and the SADC has been quite different from regional integration as it is understood in Europe. They have been careful to guard the sovereign prerogatives of the member states. As Peter Takirambudde has noted:

With respect to the perennial problem of implementation of SADCC and PTA [Preferential Trade Agreement of Eastern and Southern Africa] decisions, the Achilles heel of the founding text is the unanimity rule and the requirement for domestic ratification and incorporation of regional instruments into the domestic laws of member states. The implication is that each member state reserves the right to pursue an independent line of action if it does not agree with a particular measure . . . Both Secretariats remain hampered by the leeway enjoyed by member states in terms of honoring regional commitments, despite the trappings of supranationality which the founding treaties have conferred upon them. The legal structure of the PTA and SADC therefore contrasts sharply with the EU Treaty. In the EU model, the Treaty takes precedence over domestic law and national governments cannot take measures which are liable to impair the effect of the Treaty. Moreover, unlike the unanimity rule under the SADC/PTA Treaties, the EU Treaty has been characterized by an increase in majority voting.[16]

Reflecting the leaders' domestic imperatives, the organization's record over twenty-four years, and after consuming billions of dollars in aid, is limited. Cleary calls the SADC a "hollow shell" because of its inability to develop a consensus about trade liberalization, failure to implement many accords, and especially, disagreements about the use of certain regional structures, especially after Angola, Namibia, and Zimbabwe claimed in 1997 the SADC mantle to intervene in the Congo.[17] Williams argues that, after the Congo intervention, "SADC became, from early 1997 onwards, essentially a bipolar subregional entity with its two subregional powers and their respective allies adopting strategies toward the resolution of the conflict within the DRC that were qualitatively and quantitatively dissimilar."[18] Indeed, despite the amount of time and attention that has been lavished on the southern African region by the international community, "Aggregate indicators of their economic performance do not suggest that, for the period of its existence, SADC had any significant impact on improving the economic circumstances of its member states."[19]

[16] Peter Takirambudde, "The Rival Strategies of SADC and PTA/COMESA in Southern Africa," in Daniel C. Bach (ed.), *Regionalisation in Africa: Integration and Disintegration* (Oxford: James Currey, 1999), p. 157.

[17] Séan Cleary, "Variable Geometry and Varying Speed: An Operational Paradigm for SADC," in Christopher Clapham *et al.* (eds.), *Regional Integration in Southern Africa: Comparative International Perspectives*, p. 87.

[18] Rocky Williams, "From Collective Security to Peace-building? The Challenges of Managing Regional Security in Southern Africa," in Christopher Clapham *et al.* (eds.), *Regional Integration in Southern Africa: Comparative International Perspectives*, p. 106.

[19] Poku, *Regionalization and Security*, p. 104.

It might be perplexing, if the usual logic of international relations was applied, why the SADCC/SADC had been so unsuccessful given the amount of attention it has received. However, the point of regional integration in Africa has never been to unite to create a supranational identity that might supplant the state, and thus the prerogatives of the ruler. It is true that during the apartheid era, "the SADC united against a massive and singular threat in the form of South Africa" and that "this rendered the formulation of policies, strategies and plans within and between SADC states a relatively easy exercise."[20] However, apartheid South Africa was a unique threat to southern African states and to their leaders. Once the threat of white South Africa disappeared in 1994, it was utterly predictable that African leaders would go back to their regular practice of embracing regional organizations only so far as they would enhance their domestic standing and that they would not hesitate to weaken regional organizations to satisfy their other imperatives. Indeed, it is one of the SADC's great ironies that hope was continually expressed during the days of apartheid that the admission of a non-racial South Africa would be the final step in building a profound regional organization that would finally overcome the balkanization induced by colonialism. Instead, since the South African non-racial elections of 1994, the organization has become less and less of a regional force as differing national agendas roar, unbridled by the nominal regional apparatus.

Cooperation with external pressure

While most attempts at economic cooperation in Africa have failed, a notable exception was the so-called franc zone. Indeed, this highly successful monetary cooperation surpassed what Europe has been able to do until recently. Why the franc zone has been successful says much about the dynamics of regional cooperation in Africa and highlights the role that an external power can play.

After independence in the 1960s, fourteen African countries retained their link to the French currency via the Communauté Financière Africaine (CFA) franc, originally established in 1946. The French Treasury guaranteed that the CFA franc was directly convertible into the French franc at a fifty to one gearing ratio. Two regional banks, the Banque des Etats de l'Afrique Centrale (BEAC) and the Banque Centrale des Etats de l'Afrique de l'Ouest (BCEAO), were established as the instruments of monetary policy. They were originally headquartered in Paris but have been based since the early 1970s in Yaoundé and Dakar

[20] Williams, "From Collective Security," p. 108.

respectively. The political price of the CFA currency was to shift much of the decision-making power to the metropole. France exercised a veto over policies related to the CFA and the rules, enforced by France, demand extremely conservative policies, including an emphasis on positive balance of payments and tight control over credit.

The franc tie was retained by the francophone countries, in part, because French colonies in West Africa were much poorer and more dependent on aid than their anglophone neighbors.[21] Also, the French, because West Africa was much more important to them, were more willing to provide inducements to their former colonies to retain the link to the franc. The French, for instance, made it very clear to Mali that its future aid levels were dependent on it returning to the franc zone,[22] a demand that apparently never even occurred to the British as the West African Currency Board dissolved. Thus, a critical aspect of this successful cooperation was the provision of assistance by France since independence.[23] Francophone countries, unlike their anglophone neighbors, therefore had profound incentives to retain a common currency that was not congruent with their distinctive national boundaries. However, this incentive came, ironically, not from a desire to maintain pan-African institutions that might ameliorate the damage of territorial balkanization but from a need for the elites, in particular, to stay close to France.

The CFA arrangement was especially successful in controlling monetary policy. Francophone countries essentially did not have their own currencies as their monetary supply was determined by the French Treasury. They could not print money and were therefore exceptionally successful at controlling consumer price inflation.[24] The restraint provided by the CFA franc was particularly important because the propensity in the francophone countries was to replicate the same destructive economic policies that occurred in West Africa. For instance, fiscal policy was not nearly as conservative as monetary policy. Control over fiscal policy was noticeably lax in some francophone countries and governments in the region consistently failed to coordinate their fiscal policies.[25] Guinea, the

[21] Anthony G. Hopkins, *An Economic History of West Africa* (London: Pearson Professional Education, 1973), p. 289.

[22] David Leith Crum, "Mali and the UMOA: A Case-Study of Economic Integration," *The Journal of Modern African Studies*, ii (September 1984), p. 469.

[23] See Sir H. Poynton, "The Currency System in West Africa: Memorandum," reprinted in Richard Rathbone (ed.), *British Documents on the End of Empire: Ghana*, series B, vol. 1 (London: Her Majesty's Stationary Office, 1992), p. 56.

[24] Ibrahim Elbadawi and Nader Majd, "Adjustment and Economic Performance under a Fixed Exchange Rate: A Comparative Analysis of the CFA Zone," *World Development*, 24 (May 1996), p. 942.

[25] David Stasvage, "The CFA Franc Zone and Fiscal Discipline," *Journal of African Economies*, 6 (1996), p. 134; and Christoph Rosenberg, "Fiscal Policy Coordination

one country to go off the French franc for a significant period of time, did experience a quick overvaluation of its currency which made it "effectively worth nothing outside Guinea and very little inside Guinea."[26] It is therefore not unreasonable to claim that the institutional arrangements governing the CFA were the primary determinant of the relative soundness of francophone West African monetary policy until the late 1980s.

While the credibility provided by the CFA was a benefit for roughly the first twenty-five years of independence, a determination to keep the currency linked to the franc played havoc with francophone economies in the late 1980s and early 1990s. The CFA became overvalued when the (traditionally weak) French currency appreciated after the Plaza Accords in 1985 while the prices for the African commodities declined. As a result, in the late 1980s and early 1990s, the francophone economies suffered tremendously due to the progressive overvaluation of the currency. Output stagnated in the CFA countries between 1986 and 1994 even while expanding by 2.8 percent in other countries.[27] While the price stability of the CFA zone was still impressive, it seemed that the cost in forgone growth had become too great.[28]

However, despite the economic disaster, the Africans and France seemed committed to the old rate for fear that the CFA would lose the credibility that it had built up over the years if there was a devaluation. Of course, elites in the francophone countries also had their own interests in keeping the exchange rate stable even if their countries were in an economic tailspin. A devaluation would have made affluent Africans far less rich in French franc terms, an important consideration for elites that often considered Paris home and that had found it convenient over the years to export money to France. The CFA value of government debt owed abroad would also have been greatly increased by a devaluation. Indeed, then French President François Mitterand was supposed to have promised his good friend President Houphouet-Boigny of Côte d'Ivoire that the CFA would not be devalued as long as the Ivorian was alive. Bowing to the economic crisis and strong pressure from the international

in the WAEMU After the Devaluation," *International Monetary Fund Working Paper*, WP/95/25 (February 1995), pp. 12–14.

[26] Douglas Rimmer, *The Economies of West Africa* (New York: St. Martin's Press, 1984), pp. 136–8. He is quoting R. W. Johnson, "Guinea," in John Dunn (ed.), *West African States: Failure and Promise* (Cambridge: Cambridge University Press, 1978), p. 48.

[27] Jean A. P. Clément *et al.*, *Aftermath of the CFA Franc Devaluation* (Washington, DC: International Monetary Fund, 1996), p. 1.

[28] See, for instance, Shantayanan Devarajan and Dani Rodrik, "Do the Benefits of Fixed Exchange Rates Outweigh the Costs? The CFA Zone in Africa," in Ian Goldin and L. Alan Winters (eds.), *Open Economies: Structural Adjustment and Agriculture* (Cambridge: Cambridge University Press, 1992), p. 83.

financial institutions and non-French donors, the CFA franc was eventually devalued to a gearing ratio of one hundred to one in January 1994, after Houphouet died but before he was buried. Elite politics, rather than national interest, has driven much of the politics behind the CFA. With the abolition of the French franc, the CFA is now linked to the euro.

Conclusion

African leaders cooperate when it is in their interest. However, "interest" must be carefully defined. African leaders cannot divorce the pressures they feel from their domestic constituencies when making calculations about diplomatic efforts. Indeed, the international realm has often been far more comforting for African leaders than domestic politics. Thus, African leaders are extremely enthusiastic about particular types of regional cooperation, especially those that highlight sovereignty, help secure national leaders, and ask little in return. These desires lead to a particular style of regional cooperation that is effective in promoting domestic interests but not necessarily a normative improvement over other paths. As demonstrated by the case of the CFA franc, if an outside power is willing to provide inducements and a certain amount of coercion, more traditional types of regional cooperation are certainly possible in Africa. However, there have been very few outside powers, and almost no African states, which have been willing to provide such inducements.

5 Functional form, identity-driven cooperation: institutional designs and effects in post-Cold War NATO

Frank Schimmelfennig

Introduction: new partners, new tasks

According to an oft-quoted aphorism of Lord Ismay, NATO's first Secretary-General, the purpose of the North Atlantic Alliance during the Cold War was "to keep the Americans in, the Russians out, and the Germans down." In functional-institutionalist parlance, NATO as an international institution served to provide a high level of US and European military resources for the collective deterrence and defense of Western Europe against the Warsaw Pact, while making it hard for the US to defect in case of a Soviet attack and avoiding rivalries among the alliance members from resurfacing and escalating.

With the collapse of communism, the Soviet Union, and the Warsaw Pact, on the one hand, and the progress of European integration, on the other, the original purposes of NATO receded into the background. Instead, in a declaration agreed at NATO's London summit in July 1990, the alliance offered the Central and Eastern European transition countries to formally put an end to confrontation, establish permanent diplomatic relations with NATO, and base the future relationship on the principle of common security. In its Strategic Concept adopted in Rome in November 1991, NATO established a new, cooperative relationship with the countries of Central and Eastern Europe as an integral part of the Alliance strategy.

At the same time, NATO began to develop a set of new forums and frameworks to institutionalize this new relationship: *NATO partnership*. Over time, partnership led to both a deepening of cooperation between NATO and the Central and Eastern European countries (CEECs) and an increasing differentiation among them. The Liaison Concept of June 1991 was followed by the establishment of the North Atlantic Cooperation Council (NACC) in December of the same year as an inclusive forum for consultation and exchange. In January 1994, NATO agreed on the Partnership for Peace (PfP) program, which deepened security cooperation and consultation between NATO and the CEECs, differentiated among the CEECs through Individual Partnership Programs, but was still open to all Organization for Security and Cooperation in Europe (OSCE) countries. In 1997, the Euro-Atlantic Partnership Council (EAPC) was established, which serves as an umbrella organization for both former NACC and PfP activities. Also in 1997, NATO invited the first CEECs (the Czech Republic, Hungary, and Poland) to join the alliance and, in 1999, established the Membership Action Plan (MAP) for the remaining CEECs interested in becoming full members. Seven of them joined NATO in March 2004. In lockstep with the enlargement decisions, NATO upgraded its institutionalized relationship with Russia and Ukraine in 1997 (NATO–Russia Founding Act; Charter on a Distinctive Partnership between Ukraine and NATO) and 2002 (NATO–Russia Council, NATO–Ukraine Action Plan).[1]

During the same period, NATO has begun to transform its organizational and force structure and security strategies and policies to respond to the disappearance of the common Soviet threat and the rise of new, more diverse and unpredictable risks and challenges to the security of its members. At its 1994 Brussels summit, NATO endorsed the Combined Joint Task Force (CJTF) concept calling for "easily deployable, multinational, multi-service military formations tailored to specific kinds of military tasks."[2] In 1996, NATO agreed to build a European Security and Defense Identity (ESDI) within NATO, which would permit and support autonomous military operations led by the European Union (EU). At the Washington summit of 1999, NATO launched the Defense Capabilities Initiative to equip its forces for new tasks of crisis management and intervention. The Prague summit in October 2002 gave new impetus to the transformation of NATO. In June 2003, NATO defense ministers agreed on a new and streamlined command structure with a single command (Allied Command Operations) with operational responsibility and another command (Allied Command Transformation) responsible for overseeing the transformation of NATO forces and capabilities. In October 2003, NATO inaugurated a highly flexible, globally deployable, and interoperable NATO Response Force based on a pool of troops and military equipment. In sum, the main thrust of transformation to the *new NATO* has been flexibilization and diversification.

Finally, and paradoxically at first sight, it was *after* the end of the Soviet threat, for which it was established, that NATO has been involved in

[1] The Mediterranean Dialogue follows a similar approach in relations with Mediterranean non-member countries but is less institutionalized and will not be further discussed here.

[2] NATO Handbook at www.nato.int/docu/handbook/2001/hb1204.htm [last accessed 2 August 2006].

actual warfare, invoked the mutual assistance and consultation articles of the North Atlantic Treaty (NAT), and sent member state troops outside the North Atlantic region – each for the first time in its history. In 1995 and 1999 NATO used its airpower to intervene in Bosnia-Herzegovina and Kosovo and put an end to ethnic violence in these parts of former Yugoslavia. On 12 September, 2001, the North Atlantic Council agreed to regard the terrorist attacks on New York and Washington as an attack on all alliance members according to Article 5 NAT, and in October 2003, NATO assumed the command and coordination of the International Security Assistance Force (ISAF) in Afghanistan. At the same time, however, NATO member states were deeply split over the war on and occupation of Iraq in 2003 and any NATO involvement in it. The strongest opponents of the Iraq war (Belgium, France, and Germany) for some time failed to agree to NATO preparations to protect their ally Turkey against a possible Iraqi counter-attack and have rejected any substantial NATO role in Iraq to this day.

It is the aim of this chapter to explain the variation in institutional design and cooperation in post-Cold War NATO. In the first part, I describe and categorize the elements of institutional design in NATO partnership and the new NATO in comparison to the old, Cold War NATO. Second, I explain these elements and their variation on the basis of the main explanatory variables presented in the introductory chapter. The third part deals with the quality of NATO post-Cold War cooperation. Above all, I seek to account for the variation in member state cooperation on the core policies and decisions of the past decade: enlargement and the decisions to intervene in Yugoslavia and the Middle East.

In terms of research design, the chapter tries to capitalize on the insights of "within-case variation" and comparison. The fact that post-Cold War NATO has changed and differentiated its institutional design and has exhibited highly different degrees of member state cooperation allows me to probe systematically into alternative explanations of institutional design and cooperation while holding constant the region (Europe), the organization (NATO), the issue-area (security), and other systemic parameters typical of the post-Cold War era (such as "unipolarity"). The explanations I offer on the basis of these comparisons do not consist of absolute or "point explanations" of a specific institutional design or quality of cooperation but take on the less demanding form of relative statements. For instance, rather than trying to explain why the quality of NATO cooperation was high on enlargement, I ask why it was *higher* than on Afghanistan or Iraq.

The main argument of the chapter draws on different theoretical approaches. First, I argue that the constant features of NATO's institutional design (liberal ideology, high member state control, and low agent autonomy) can be attributed to the liberal identity of the transatlantic community and the hegemonic structure of its membership. These are the enduring structural (intersubjective and material) features of NATO. The variation in institutional design between the old NATO, the new NATO, and NATO partnership, however, is best explained in functional terms by the nature of the core cooperation problem that these security arrangements were made to address. The old NATO faced a common and certain threat and the enforcement problems of extended deterrence: to "keep the Americans in" and to prevent the allies from free-riding under the US nuclear umbrella. The functional response to this situation was a restriction of membership and flexibility.

In contrast, post-Cold War NATO has not been confronted with common or clearly identifiable threats. Within NATO, the core cooperation problem was potential deadlock caused by divergent strategic views, threat perceptions, and security interests. The functional response to this problem was institutional flexibility. With regard to the former Warsaw Pact countries, the main problem was uncertainty resulting from a lack of information on security problems and preferences in this region and a lack of trust. Under these conditions, the inclusive membership, broad issue scope, high flexibility, and process-oriented mandate made sense in a functional perspective, as instruments to gain knowledge and create trust.

In contrast, I find that the presence or strength of actual international cooperation is underdetermined by institutional design and unrelated to the level of the threat to the member states' security. On the one hand, given the high flexibility of post-Cold War NATO security arrangements, institutional design cannot predict or explain when members will actually cooperate. On the other hand, the quality of cooperation – high in the cases of enlargement and the Balkan interventions and low with regard to Afghanistan, Iraq, and Sudan – has not been systematically related to the intensity of the material security threat to NATO members. Rather, it varies with threats or challenges to the identity of NATO as a transatlantic community of liberal states. The quality of cooperation has been highest when liberal community values and norms are at stake in the transatlantic home region of the community – either as a result of their massive violation (as in the "ethnic cleansing" in the Balkans) or their strong reaffirmation (as in the candidates for NATO membership).

The findings thus seem to suggest that while the change and variation in institutional design follow functional requirements, actual cooperation in the absence of a common and clearly identifiable security threat is determined by the identity and ideology of the Euro-Atlantic community. Hence the title of the chapter: functional form, identity-driven

Table 5.1 *Elements of institutional design in NATO*

	Old NATO	New NATO	NATO partnership
Membership	Restrictive		Inclusive
Scope	Narrow (military security)		Broad (comprehensive security)
Formal rules: control	High (consensus)		
Formal rules: flexibility	Low (military integration)	High (task-specific coalitions of the willing)	
Norms	Liberal ideology		
Mandate	Product-oriented, distributive		Process-oriented, deliberative
Agent autonomy	Low		

cooperation. In other words, whereas institutional design appears to follow considerations of utility, actual cooperation varies with legitimacy. At least for post-Cold War NATO, the chapter puts into question the assumed causal relationship between institutional design and quality of cooperation.

The institutional design of NATO

Table 5.1 gives an overview of common and varying design elements in the old NATO, the new NATO, and NATO partnership.

Membership

NATO applies different criteria for partnership and full membership. Both are in principle open to all European countries (in addition to the US and Canada). But whereas geography (being part of Europe broadly defined) is the main criterion for partnership, full membership requires a common identity based on liberal norms in addition. I therefore categorize NATO partnership as "inclusive" and both old and new NATO as "restrictive" in comparison.[3]

Since its beginnings with the NACC, partnership has been based on the objective of including all countries of the former Soviet sphere, that is, both the Warsaw Pact member states and the successor states of the

[3] Barbara Koremenos, Charles Lipson, and Duncan Snidal, "The Rational Design of International Institutions," *International Organization* 55:4 (2001), 783–85.

Soviet Union. Later, partnership was extended to the non-aligned countries of Europe. According to the Basic Document of EAPC, adopted in May 1997, the EAPC "is open to the accession of . . . OSCE participating states."[4] Currently, there are 49 EAPC members: 26 NATO member states and 23 partner countries. Only Cyprus and the European micro-states are missing.

Full NATO membership is, in principle, open to all European countries, too. Although NATO has only admitted ten new members in the post-Cold War era, it has consistently declared and pursued an "open door" policy for all partner countries that meet the prerequisites. In addition to being part of Europe geographically, outside countries must primarily fulfill political conditions to qualify for full membership. They must share and adhere to fundamental liberal-democratic norms: democracy and human rights, multilateralism, and peaceful conflict management.[5] Put negatively, "Countries with repressive political systems, countries with designs on their neighbors, countries with militaries unchecked by civilian control, or with closed economic systems need not apply."[6]

Scope

All NATO-based arrangements remain within the issue area of security but NATO partnership follows a much broader definition of security than both old and new NATO. As even a brief glance at NACC or EAPC Work Plans or PfP Working Programmes will reveal, NATO partnership covers an extremely broad scope of activities, some of which are only weakly related to military security. They range from narrow security issues such as defense planning, arms control, peacekeeping and, more recently, the fight against terrorism to issues such as defense economics and conversion, environmental problems emanating from defense-related installations, the military protection of cultural monuments, civil emergency planning, responses to natural and technological disasters, international humanitarian law, and scientific cooperation.

In contrast, the Membership Action Plan for NATO aspirants already focuses more narrowly on the political, military, financial, security, and

[4] NATO Basic Document of the Euro-Atlantic Partnership Council, available at www.nato.int/docu/basictxt/b970530a.htm [last accessed 2 August 2006].

[5] Frank Schimmelfennig, "NATO Enlargement: A Constructivist Explanation," *Security Studies*, 8:2 (1999), pp. 198–234; Frank Schimmelfennig, *The EU, NATO and the Integration of Europe. Rules and Rhetoric* (Cambridge: Cambridge University Press, 2003), pp. 92–9.

[6] "The US and Central and Eastern Europe: Forging New Partnerships – President Bill Clinton," US Department of State Dispatch, 16 January 1995.

legal prerequisites of and preparations for alliance membership. Correspondingly, the work of NATO, even though it comprises a broad range of security-related activities for member states, too, is focused on the core activities of collective defense and military exercises and operations.

In the course of the transformation from the old to the new NATO, however, the focus among the core military security activities has shifted significantly. In the Cold War era, it was (nuclear) deterrence supplemented by the conventional defense of NATO territory should deterrence fail. These issues have not been discontinued but strongly deemphasized. NATO activities have shifted toward "out-of-area operations" (as military activities outside the transatlantic region used to be called in the "old NATO days") and military intervention.

Formal rules: control and flexibility

Generally, NATO has few formal rules. The North Atlantic Treaty is short – fourteen single-paragraph articles – and has remained unchanged in the post-Cold War period. Here I understand "control" as the control that the organization's decision-making and voting arrangements accord to individual member states and "flexibility" as the degree to which NATO's rules and arrangements allow member states to choose their level of participation and commitment. Whereas inflexible rules and arrangements bind all member states all of the time, highly flexible or fragmented ones permit varying participation across member states and time.

The North Atlantic Treaty does not include precise rules for decision-making. Article 9 simply states: "The Parties hereby establish a Council, on which each of them shall be represented, to consider matters concerning the implementation of this Treaty." In practice and self-understanding, however, the Alliance is an intergovernmental organization with consensus-based decision rules.[7] The most important decision-making body is the North Atlantic Council (NAC), which meets at different levels from ambassadors to heads of government and state. Decisions are reached in a process of consultation, exchange of member-state points of view, and via consensus or common consent. There are no formal voting procedures either for or against decision proposals. To facilitate decision-making in situations of conflict, NATO uses the "silence procedure." A decision is laid on the table and regarded as adopted if no member government openly objects. If, however, a single member

[7] A good source for this official self-image is "Extending Security in the Euro-Atlantic Area. The Role of NATO and its Partner Countries," available at www.nato.int/docu/ext-sec/a-cover.htm [last accessed 2 August 2006]. See also Sean Kay, *NATO and the Future of European Security* (Oxford: Rowman and Littlefield, 1998), pp. 36–8.

"breaks silence," NATO decision-making and operations are blocked. Thus, member states have a *de facto* right of veto, although it is not explicitly mentioned in the Treaty. In addition, according to NATO, "the same process of building consensus between countries applies to decisions taken with Partner countries on cooperation with the Alliance."[8]

There is a growing difference, however, in the flexibility of NATO's old and new security arrangements. Although the NAT is again not very specific, it is clear that collective deterrence and defense was designed to include all member states. Article 5, the core of the treaty, reads: "The Parties agree that an armed attack against one or more of them . . . shall be considered an attack *against them all* and consequently they agree that . . . *each of them* . . . will assist the Party or Parties so attacked . . ." (my omissions and italics). Moreover, the integrated military command structure and the forward stationing of allied forces (mainly in Germany) in the 1950s were designed to reduce the member states' flexibility in responding to military attacks. As a consequence, member states would have been involved immediately in combat as well as in executing defense plans; their room for political decision-making and maneuvers would have been severely curtailed. To be sure, even during the Cold War, France was able to formally withdraw from military integration (in 1966) while remaining a NATO member and cooperating *à la carte* with its Supreme Command. Many other member states have traditionally had specific arrangements with NATO, for instance, with regard to the stationing of nuclear weapons on their territory. But the general thrust of institutional design was to include all member states in the deterrence of the Soviet threat and in the collective defense of NATO territory and to restrict the flexibility of their participation.

In contrast, in the post-Cold War period, the general thrust of institutional design has been reversed. Partnership follows the principle of differentiation. The Individual Partnership Programs negotiated between NATO and the partner countries allow for varying degrees of cooperation. Partnership thus varies from virtually suspended activities (such as in the case of Belarus) to intensive cooperation with the participants of the Membership Action Plan. The main transformation decisions of the new NATO have also been decisions in favor of flexibility. According to the CJTF concept, forces would "vary according to the circumstances"; headquarters would be formed *ad hoc*; members and partners would contribute "as necessary, using a modular approach, in order to meet the

[8] "The principles of consensus and common consent," available at www.nato.int/docu/ext-sec/m-consen.htm [last accessed 2 August 2006].

requirements of the specific mission."[9] The ESDI permits the use of NATO capacities for operations led by the EU, that is, without US participation. Both follow the principle of "separable but not separate" forces allowing "coalitions of the willing" to take advantage of NATO's organizational assets. In addition, while NATO operations do not require actual participation of all NATO members any more, they are open to participation by non-members, partners, or non-partners. For instance, twenty-two non-NATO countries participated in the Stabilization Force (SFOR) in Bosnia and nineteen non-NATO countries did so in the Kosovo Force (KFOR) under NATO command – including, for instance, Argentina and Morocco in both cases.

Norms

The formal ideology of NATO consists in a *liberal theory* of peace and security. This liberal theory postulates liberal-democratic statehood plus multilateral and peaceful conflict management.[10] In the preamble to the North Atlantic Treaty of 1949, the signatory states declare the protection of their liberal values as the basic purpose of NATO: "They are determined to safeguard the freedom, common heritage and civilization of their peoples, founded on the principles of democracy, individual liberty, and the rule of law." Article 1 underlines their commitment to "settle any international dispute in which they may be involved by peaceful means . . . and to refrain from the threat or use of force." Article 2 refers to the "democratic peace" and adds another important strand of the liberal theory of peace – "commercial liberalism" or "peace through trade" (and the intensification of other transnational transactions):

> The Parties will contribute toward the further development of peaceful and friendly international relations by strengthening their free institutions, by bringing about a better understanding of the principles upon which these institutions are founded, and by promoting conditions of stability and well-being. They will seek to eliminate conflict in their international economic policies and will encourage economic collaboration between any or all of them.

Furthermore, NATO practices are governed by multilateralist alliance norms. As Article 4 of the North Atlantic Treaty prescribes, "The Parties

[9] NATO Handbook at www.nato.int/docu/handbook/2001/hb1204.htm [last accessed 2 August 2006].

[10] Thomas Risse-Kappen, *Cooperation Among Democracies. The European Influence on US Foreign Policy* (Princeton: Princeton University Press, 1995); Schimmelfennig, *Integration of Europe*, pp. 81–3; Steve Weber, "Shaping the Postwar Balance of Power: Multilateralism in NATO," in John Gerard Ruggie (ed.), *Multilateralism Matters. The Theory and Praxis of an Institutional Form* (New York: Columbia University Press, 1993), pp. 233–92.

will consult together whenever, in the opinion of any of them, the territorial integrity, political independence or security of any of the Parties is threatened" and, in Article 5, they agreed that "an armed attack against one or more of them . . . shall be considered an attack against them all."

The same liberal principles underlie NATO partnership. According to the final communiqué of the North Atlantic Council preceding the establishment of the NACC, the new institution was designed not only "to aid in fostering a sense of security and confidence among" the CEECs but also "to help them transform their societies and economies, making democratic change irreversible."[11] The 1994 PfP Framework Document also emphasized the liberal foundations of partnership:

> Protection and promotion of fundamental freedoms and human rights, and safeguarding of freedom, justice, and peace through democracy are shared values fundamental to the Partnership. In joining the Partnership, the member States of the North Atlantic Alliance and the other States subscribing to this Document recall that they are committed to the preservation of democratic societies, their freedom from coercion and intimidation, and the maintenance of the principles of international law.[12]

Mandate

The mandate of NATO security arrangements varies between a predominant process orientation in partnership and a predominant product orientation in the old as well as the new NATO. In other words, the mandate of NATO partnership is primarily deliberative, whereas NATO proper distributes the burdens and benefits of collective security. Moreover, as partners intensify their partnership and move toward membership, product orientation increases.

Except under special circumstances, the NACC was originally planned to meet once a year for plenary sessions of state representatives to discuss pan-European security issues. Meanwhile, the EAPC meets more frequently and at different levels. In addition, the NACC – and later the EAPC – set up annual work plans which focus on programs of contact, consultations, and information dissemination and exchange, and include activities such as meetings between officers and staff of the former adversary alliances including "familiarization courses," fellowships for the

[11] Press Communiqué M-NAC-2(91)110, available at www.nato.int/docu/comm/49-95/c911219a.htm [last accessed 2 August 2006].

[12] NATO Partnership for Peace Framework Document, available at www.nato.int/docu/basictxt/b940110b.htm [last accessed 2 August 2006], §2.

study of democratic institutions, and seminars, workshops, and "open-ended Ad Hoc Working groups" on a great variety of topics. Jonathan Eyal characterized the NACC as "no different from the OSCE: a gigantic talking shop."[13] However, just as the OSCE, NACC/EAPC activities have included product-oriented activities, too. For instance, since their beginnings in 1991, they were intended to support the implementation of the CFE Treaty on conventional arms control in Europe. The PfP added more product-oriented elements. For the first time, it envisaged direct military cooperation such as the training of partner forces and the enhancement of interoperability for joint military (mainly peacekeeping) operations.

In contrast, NATO proper goes beyond deliberative and process-oriented activities and focuses on producing and sharing collective security gains. The traditional products of the old NATO were collective deterrence and defense. Assuming common security interests, its mandate has been to develop effective and efficient capabilities and procedures of collective defense including standardization and interoperability of military equipment and common infrastructure projects, to increase the member states' investment in military manpower and technology, and to arrive at an acceptable sharing of defense burdens among the allies. Likewise, the new NATO strives to "produce" command structures and military capabilities that are adapted to the change in its security environment and to new tasks such as peacekeeping and military intervention out of area.

Agent autonomy

Formal agent autonomy in NATO is generally low. In this respect, NATO is much closer to a traditional international organization than its Brussels neighbor, the EU. This design feature corresponds closely with the high degree of member state control in decision-making. NATO's international staff consists in a civilian and a military "branch."

Created in 1951 and mainly based at NATO's Headquarters in Brussels, NATO's (civilian) International Staff does not have any treaty-based formal competencies. Officially, its role is summarized as "an advisory and administrative body that supports the work of the national delegations at different committee levels and assists in implementing their decisions."[14] According to the NATO Handbook, it "supports the process of consensus-building and decision-making between member and

[13] Jonathan Eyal, "NATO's Enlargement: Anatomy of a Decision," *International Affairs*, 73:4 (1997), p. 701.

[14] See "NATO's International Staff," available at www.nato.int/issues/international_staff [last accessed 2 August 2006].

Partner countries and is responsible for the preparation and follow-up of the meetings and decisions of NATO committees, as well as those of the institutions created to manage the different forms of bilateral and multilateral partnership with non-member countries established since the end of the Cold War."[15] Correspondingly, in interviews, members of International Staff illustrated their role as one of a "pen" or "facilitator" for member state governments: "Substance is not our role." Rather, staff members see their role in facilitating consensus-building by targeting the lowest common denominator and finding compromise formulas, either in written reports or through chairmanship in discussions among member states.[16] Traditionally, NATO staff were recruited directly by NATO or seconded by member governments for a limited time period (renewable contracts for usually no longer than ten years). Under a reform started in 2003, contracts may be renewed indefinitely after three years. It remains to be seen whether this reform enhances the autonomy of NATO's staff.[17]

NATO's International Military Staff consists of military personnel sent by the member states and is "responsible for planning, assessing and recommending policy on military matters for consideration by the Military Committee, as well as ensuring that the policies and decisions of the Committee are implemented as directed."[18] Both International Staff and International Military Staff are expected to work in an international capacity for the Alliance rather than taking orders from their home countries. They are responsible to the Secretary-General and the Director of the International Military Staff, respectively, rather than to the National Delegations of the member states. However, the Iraq crisis showed the limits of staff autonomy clearly when, to the public dismay of US Secretary of State Colin Powell, those governments that opposed the Iraq war and a NATO role in it refused to allow international military staff from their countries to be sent to Iraq to participate in a NATO-led training mission.[19]

In sum, the design of the three NATO institutional designs is characterized by both constant and varying features. Consensus-based decision-making, a liberal theory of peace and security, and a low degree of agent autonomy are common to NATO old and new as well as to NATO

[15] NATO Handbook at www.nato.int/docu/handbook/2001/hb1004.htm [last accessed 2 August 2006].

[16] Interviews by the author with members of NATO International Staff, Brussels, May 1999.

[17] Annalisa Monaco, "Reshuffle of NATO International Staff: A Change for the Better?," *NATO Notes*, 28 May 2003.

[18] NATO Handbook at www.nato.int/docu/handbook/2001/hb1103.htm [last accessed 2 August 2006].

[19] *The Washington Post*, 10 December 2004, p. A25.

partnership. Based on these common features, NATO can be classified as a *liberal* and *intergovernmental* regional security organization. The variation between the old NATO and the new NATO mainly consists in a move toward *flexibility*; that between the old NATO and NATO partnership in the latter's more *open and diffuse* design. In partnership, membership is inclusive, scope is broad, flexibility is high, and the mandate is deliberative and process-oriented. This descriptive analysis is the starting point for the remaining two parts of the chapter. First, how can we explain both the constant design features of NATO and the variation and change between the three institutional arrangements? Second, how and to what extent does the variation in design produce a variation in the quality of cooperation?

Sources of institutional design

The functional explanation: threats, cooperation problems, and institutional design

According to the functional theory of international institutions, institutional design will vary with the type and seriousness of international cooperation problems.[20] In the case of security institutions, this general condition can be specified further: design varies with the nature of the threat and the problems of security cooperation that arise from countering it.

In the old NATO, the *core threat* was *clearly identifiable* and *common* to all member states: the Soviet Union. However, while all member states had a common interest in "keeping the Soviets out," their capabilities and vulnerabilities differed. On the one hand, the West European countries were immediately threatened by the massive conventional forces of the Warsaw Pact on their borders, against which they were not capable of defending themselves alone. In addition, most West European countries did not possess nuclear weapons and those that possessed nuclear weapons (Britain and France) had only limited capabilities that might not have been sufficient to deter a conventional or nuclear Soviet attack. For this reason, the West European countries had an interest in a security guarantee by the United States, above all in a place under its nuclear umbrella.

[20] See for example George W. Downs, David M. Rocke, and Peter N. Barsoom, "Managing the Evolution of Multilateralism," *International Organization*, 52:2 (1998), pp. 397–419; Koremenos *et al.*, "Rational Design."

Because of its geographic position, the United States, on the other hand, was not directly threatened by the conventional forces of the Soviet Union and the Warsaw Pact. It has usually had a technological edge over the Soviet Union and a superior capability of projecting military power globally. In the early days of NATO, its nuclear capabilities trumped those of the Soviet Union. Later, it has always preserved a credible second-strike capability. Whereas its homeland has generally been safe (with the exception of the Cuban missile crisis), the US was in a disadvantaged geographic position with regard to the control of the Eurasian landmass. Above all, it sought to deny the Soviet Union access to and control of the highly industrialized and wealthy Western Europe. For this reason, the US was interested in a military presence on Western European territory and in finding allies for the defense of the region.

The common interests *cum* different capabilities and vulnerabilities created sufficient interdependence between the US and Western Europe to promote the building of a transatlantic alliance, but, as the functional theory of institutions leads us to expect, they also created cooperation problems. The *enforcement problems of extended deterrence* were at the core of the transatlantic alliance. On the one hand, under the US nuclear umbrella, the Western European countries had a rational incentive to minimize their military contributions to the alliance. If, as they assumed, US nuclear capabilities were sufficiently strong to deter the Warsaw Pact from attacking Western Europe, why should they invest heavily in expensive conventional military forces (except to pursue their own specific strategic interests)? In a system of mutual nuclear deterrence, investments in conventional defense are militarily irrelevant but rather signal mistrust in the credibility of deterrence. In short, Western Europe had the incentive of *free-riding under the US nuclear umbrella.*

On the other hand, the credibility of extended deterrence in a system of mutual nuclear deterrence is always questionable. Whereas the US had a credible incentive in using nuclear weapons to retaliate against an attack against its own territory, it was doubtful whether it would really use nuclear weapons in the case of a conventional attack on Western Europe and thereby invite a Soviet nuclear attack on US territory in retaliation. In short, the US had the incentive to *defect from the nuclear defense of Western Europe.*[21]

[21] On alliance dilemmas in general, see Glenn H. Snyder, "The Security Dilemma in Alliance Politics," *World Politics*, 36 (1984), pp. 461–95. For conflicting views on the effectiveness of extended deterrence, see Paul Huth, *Extended Deterrence and the Prevention of War* (New Haven: Yale University Press, 1988), and Richard Lebow and Janice Gross Stein, "Deterrence: The Elusive Dependent Variable," *World Politics*, 42:3 (1990), pp. 336–69.

Given these two enforcement problems of extended deterrence, the alliance partners had an interest in making each other's commitments as credible as possible. The US was keen on committing the Europeans to do as much as possible for their own defense. This would not only reduce the costs of US military engagement in Western Europe but, above all, reduce and protract the need to revert to the use of nuclear weapons and thus to test the credibility of US extended deterrence. In contrast, Western Europe was interested in limiting the US room for discretion and increasing the pressure on the US administration to use nuclear weapons early in the case of attack and thereby increasing the credibility of extended deterrence.

The nature of the threat and the cooperation problems changed fundamentally with the demise of the Soviet Union and the Warsaw Pact. As the main successor state to the Soviet Union, Russia inherited its nuclear forces but suffered a loss in territory, population, and allies. Above all, however, it was not so much the balance of power but the balance of threats that changed to the advantage of NATO.[22] Under the Yeltsin presidency of the 1990s, Russia was generally perceived as a country that had terminated the Soviet legacy of enmity to the West and sought a cooperative relationship with Western organizations. Already in its 1991 "Strategic Concept," NATO stated that "the threat of a simultaneous, full-scale attack on all of NATO's European fronts has effectively been removed."[23] Four years later, in its "Study on NATO Enlargement," the organization added, "Since then, the risk of a re-emergent large-scale military threat has further declined."[24]

The *disappearance of the Soviet threat* strongly reduced the alliance dilemmas of extended deterrence. The nuclear umbrella became less important in guaranteeing the security of Western Europe. The US administration had less reasons to fear that it might be drawn into a nuclear exchange because of the weak conventional forces of its alliance partners, and European governments needed to be less concerned about the credibility of the US nuclear security guarantee.

At the same time, however, the clearly identifiable and common threat that had generated the common interest of the alliance members ceased to exist. The military interdependence of the United States and Western Europe diminished and so did the need for NATO as an organization

[22] Stephen M. Walt, *The Origins of Alliances* (Ithaca, NY: Cornell University Press, 1987).
[23] "The Alliances' Strategic Concept agreed by the Heads of State and Government participating in the meeting of the North Atlantic Council," Rome, 8 November 1991, available at www.nato.int/docu/basictxt/b911108a.htm [last accessed 2 August 2006].
[24] "Study on NATO Enlargement," available at www.nato.int/docu/basictxt/enl-9501.htm [last accessed 2 August 2006], §10.

of collective defense and deterrence. Realist theory expected the end of NATO to follow the end of the Soviet Union and the Warsaw Pact as a result of the allies' primary interest in autonomy and the Western Europeans' need to balance the emerging US hegemony.[25] In contrast, the functional theory of international institutions explains the persistence of NATO as a result of high sunk costs stemming from prior investments in the institutionalization of the alliance and of general and specific institutional assets that were seen to be "cost effective in the new security environment."[26] In addition, however, we should observe change in and adaptation of the institutional design reflecting this new security environment and the new cooperation problems it created.

What were these new cooperation problems? Among NATO members, *the absence of a common and clearly identifiable external threat* brought the *heterogeneity of strategic views and security interests* among the allies to the fore. Prominent descriptions of the divergences (between the US, on the one hand, and many European countries, on the other) include global versus regional security interests and strategies and a militarized foreign policy (attributed to the United States) versus the emphasis on diplomatic, legal, and economic tools of foreign policy (attributed to Europe). To be sure, these differences did exist during the Cold War as well and led to debates and conflicts among the allies. Yet the Soviet threat provided a strong focus, which urged the allies to cooperate despite their divergences. The divergence was put into stark contrast again after the 9/11 terrorist attacks on the United States. In the United States, they created an unprecedented sense of insecurity and a strong preference to combat them by the global projection of military force. Both were much weaker in Europe. For NATO as an organization operating on the principle of consensus, the absence of a clear and common threat and the prominence of diverging strategic views and security interests decreased the likelihood of reaching agreement and created the cooperation problem of *deadlock* or decision-making blockades. Generally speaking, if an individual member state or a group of member states wants to act on a security issue that it considers relevant according to its strategic views and security interests and wants to use NATO resources for that purpose, it is likely faced with other member states that do not share its concerns and reject collective action.[27]

[25] See for example Kenneth N. Waltz, "The Emerging Structure of International Politics," *International Security*, 18:2 (1993), pp. 44–79.

[26] Celeste A. Wallander, "Institutional Assets and Adaptability: NATO After the Cold War," *International Organization*, 54:4 (2000), p. 711.

[27] This is different from free-riding insofar as collective action is *not* in the common interest.

In NATO's relations with its former enemies, the Central and Eastern European countries and the successor countries of the Soviet Union, the core problem was *uncertainty* – about the security preferences of the new and transformed states and about the emergence of new security threats in this region. Would the post-communist regimes consolidate democracy or develop into authoritarian states? Would these states seek friendly relations with the West or follow new anti-Western ideologies rooted in nationalism or traditionalism? What would happen to the enormous armaments of the Soviet Union including its nuclear weapons now located in several independent states? Where would its military technology and knowledge spread? And finally, would the new states develop peaceful relations among each other or would they become mired in new hegemonic struggles and ethnic strife? In other words, the cooperation problems for NATO in this region resulted from both a *lack of reliable information* about the new security environment and a *lack of trust* in the newly emerging state actors of the region.[28]

Can we attribute the variation in institutional design between the old NATO, the new NATO, and NATO partnership to variation in threats and cooperation problems as the functional theory of institutional design would suggest? More specifically, does the disappearance of a common and clearly identifiable threat – and the concomitant shift from enforcement to deadlock as the core cooperation problem – explain the flexibilization of NATO? And does the emergence of uncertainty in the East account for the rather open and diffuse design of NATO partnership?

I argue that the functional account is largely plausible. First, international institutions designed to solve an enforcement problem require low flexibility because flexible rules allow countries to decide their level of commitment autonomously and thus further defection and free-riding. Thus, it made sense for old NATO to constrain institutionally the rather flexible treaty commitments to mutual assistance and defense, e.g. through an integrated command and the forward stationing of allied troops. Conversely, the higher flexibility of post-Cold War NATO is a functional response to the deadlock problem it faces. It allows the task-specific creation of "coalitions of the willing," that is, of those member states that share security concerns on specific issues. These coalitions need the basic consent of the Allies to use NATO assets but do not require the participation of those member states with other threat perceptions and security interests. In addition, flexibility allows member states to participate to different degrees reflecting their capabilities and their

[28] See for example Andrew Kydd, "Trust Building, Trust Breaking: The dilemma of NATO enlargement," *International Organization*, 55:4 (2001), 801–28.

interests in a security issue. An agreement to make an organization more flexible is likely if all member states expect to need alliance resources and the cooperation of other member states at some point for their specific security concerns but do not expect to generate general consensus and participation.

Second, the reduction of uncertainty with regard to the security environment requires different institutional features than the creation of binding commitments to counter a highly certain security threat. The more *open and diffuse character of NATO partnership* compared to NATO membership reflects this. The inclusiveness of NATO partnership helps the member states to learn about the specific knowledge, the preferences, the problems, and the trustworthiness of as many as possible potential partners (or rivals and enemies) in the new security environment – without incurring the potential costs of defending them against an attack or giving them a say in NATO decisions.[29] The broad issue scope again maximizes knowledge about the security issues in the new environment and the preferences of the neighboring states. It also helps to explore the potential need and efficiency of international cooperation.[30] The same is true of the process-oriented and deliberative mandate of NATO partnership. It is useful to learn as much as possible about the concerns and preferences of other actors, helps to build trust and a common definition of the situation, and to explore possibilities for more product-oriented cooperation. Finally, the high flexibility of partnership allows NATO to differentiate between partners and vary the intensity of cooperation with them on the basis of the acquired knowledge and according to their relevance to NATO security concerns, their trustworthiness, and the scope of common interests.[31]

Although the functional account is plausible overall, it has its limits and shortcomings. First, it is entirely based on relative statements explaining more or less issue scope, flexibility, etc. It does not claim to account for absolute levels of the individual elements of institutional design. For instance, given the enforcement problems of the old NATO, one might have expected even less flexibility. Second, not all of the conjectures of the Rational Design of International Institutions project are corroborated by the evidence on NATO. For instance, according to Koremenos, Lipson, and Snidal, restrictive membership, issue scope, and centralization should

[29] This statement does not necessarily contradict the hypothesis by Koremenos *et al.*, "Rational Design," p. 784, namely that "restrictive membership increases with uncertainty about preferences," if "membership" refers only to full membership in the organization, not to participation in the looser partnership arrangements.

[30] Ibid., pp. 785–86. [31] Ibid., p. 793.

decrease with the easing of the enforcement problem.[32] Yet, there has not been any significant change in these design features after the end of the Cold War. What is more, the higher uncertainty about the post-Cold War security environment should have generated higher centralization and higher member state control. Again, this has not been the case. Thus, these design features seem to be constants unexplained by the changing nature of the threat and the dominant cooperation problem. Finally, the norms of the organization (the liberal ideology of NATO) are exogenous to the functional approach.

The constructivist explanation: identity and community

While the functional theory of rationalist institutionalism offers a plausible, albeit not fully determinate, account of institutional change in NATO, it may not be the only plausible account. For this reason, I now turn to a constructivist or sociological-institutionalist alternative explanation. The basic proposition here is that the design of international institutions will vary with the collective identities and norms of the international community that establishes them[33] and with the requirements of community-building and community representation.[34] Can this perspective shed light on the variation of institutional designs in NATO security arrangements?

First of all, the *liberal ideology* and the *multilateralist alliance norms* of NATO reflect the *liberal democratic identity* of the transatlantic or Western international community which established NATO.[35] The preamble to the NAT, for instance, speaks of a "common heritage and civilisation of their peoples." Second, the partnership and membership arrangements of NATO reflect a variation in identity. Whereas full members are assumed to share the common liberal identity, values, and norms of the transatlantic community, partners still need to learn them. The *open and diffuse NATO partnership*, then, is designed to promote the *international socialization* of the partners to NATO values and norms. The process-oriented,

[32] Ibid., pp. 783–94.

[33] Michael N. Barnett and Martha Finnemore, "The Politics, Power, and Pathologies of International Organizations," *International Organization*, 53:4 (1999), p. 703; Christian Reus-Smit, "The Constitutional Structure of International Society and the Nature of Fundamental Institutions," *International Organization*, 51:4 (1997), p. 569; Steven Weber, "Origins of the European Bank for Reconstruction and Development," *International Organization*, 48:1 (1994), pp. 4–5 and 32.

[34] Kenneth W. Abbott and Duncan Snidal, "Why States Act Through Formal International Organizations," *Journal of Conflict Resolution*, 42:1 (1998), p. 24.

[35] Christopher Hemmer and Peter J. Katzenstein, "Why is There no NATO in Asia? Collective Identity, Regionalism, and the Origins of Multilateralism," *International Organization*, 56:3 (2002), pp. 575–607.

deliberative mandate facilitates persuasion and learning processes. Seminars, workshops, and open-ended discussion groups behind closed doors or without much public attention are the most suitable forums. The broad range of security and security-related issues multiply the opportunities for interaction, exchange, and familiarization and amplify the messages of the NATO community.[36] If the socialization of NATO partners is successful and partners conform reliably to the liberal alliance norms, they qualify for membership.[37] Membership (both in its old and new NATO versions) can then focus more narrowly on the production of military security for the existing community.[38]

In contrast, a constructivist explanation based on community identity and norms has problems to account for the flexibility that is the hallmark of the new NATO. A constructivist account would need to explain flexibilization as a result of identity change resulting in different identities in the transatlantic community or varying strengths of liberal transatlantic identity.[39] There is little evidence for this. First, the identity of the transatlantic Western community has been reaffirmed rather than changed by the end of the Cold War. The opposite is true for the nature of the threat and the cooperation problems. Second, different identities or degrees of transatlantic identity have existed in the old NATO as well (think of Turkey or France). Rather than being a new feature of the post-Cold War era, they had been deemphasized by the common Soviet threat and reemphasized by the disappearance of this threat. In sum, the flexibilization of NATO reflects a change in the nature of the threat and cooperation problems rather than a change in the nature of identities in the transatlantic community.[40]

The realist explanation: US hegemony

Neither the functional theory of rationalist institutionalism nor the identity-based theory of constructivist institutionalism gives a plausible

[36] Jeffrey T. Checkel, "Why Comply? Social Learning and European Identity Change,' *International Organization*, 55:3 (2001), pp. 553–88; Alexandra Gheciu, "Security Institutions as Agents of Socialization? NATO and the 'New Europe'," *International Organization*, 59 (2005), pp. 973–1012.

[37] Schimmelfennig, *Integration of Europe*.

[38] Note that the constructivist account in no way contradicts the functional account. Uncertainty and the lack of trust are the common starting point in both accounts for the explanation of NATO partnership.

[39] To give an example from another European organization: The opt-out of Britain, Denmark, and Sweden from participating in the Euro cannot be explained by economic variables but reflects a less "Europeanized" identity of these countries including a longstanding skepticism toward supranational political integration.

[40] Note also that flexibilization predates 9/11/2001.

explanation for two of the constant features of NATO's institutional design: high member state control and low agent autonomy. As pointed out above, the changes in the nature of the threat or the core cooperation problems of NATO did not produce change in these two elements of institutional design. Nor are they characteristic for a liberal international community. A quick comparison with the EU, the other major organization of the liberal international community in Europe, shows this. Not only do the formal rules of the EU allow for (qualitative) majority voting on a great number of issues but member states have also delegated major competences to supranational organizations: the European Commission, the European Court of Justice, and the European Parliament. On the other hand, a major characteristic of NATO is absent in the EU: hegemonic power.

The preponderance of the military power of the United States in NATO is such that the label "hegemonic" is justified. The hegemonic structure of NATO provides a plausible explanation for the low agent autonomy and high member state control. On the one hand, one may argue that there was no functional need for the pooling and delegation of sovereignty in NATO insofar as the hegemon was able to enforce cooperation and compliance in dilemma situations.[41] On the other hand, realism would argue that hegemons generally seek to avoid being bound by decisions of other governments or supranational organizations.

By contrast, hegemony cannot account for the variation in NATO's institutional designs. US military hegemony has not diminished in relation to Western Europe after the Cold War and has replaced Soviet hegemony in large parts of Central and Eastern Europe. What has changed, though, is the relevance of hegemony. Whereas Western Europe was strongly dependent on US military power during the Cold War, the disappearance of the Soviet threat has strongly reduced this dependence.

Conclusion

There is not a single comprehensively or exclusively valid explanation of the institutional design of NATO and its variation across different security arrangements. The functional theory of institutions explains the post-Cold War changes in NATO's institutional design plausibly by changes in the nature of the threat and the core problems of security cooperation. However, it does not account for the constants in formal institutional

[41] This is the core proposition of hegemonic stability theory; see Charles P. Kindleberger, "Dominance and Leadership in the International Economy. Exploitation, Public Goods, and Free Rides," *International Studies Quarterly*, 25:2 (1981), pp. 242–54.

design: liberal ideology, low agent autonomy, and high member state control. These constants are better explained by other theoretical approaches, social constructivism in the case of liberal alliance norms and realist hegemonic theory in the case of autonomy and control. In turn, these two approaches have difficulties in explaining change and variation. Constructivism aptly conceptualizes NATO partnership as an institutional design conducive to international socialization and community-building but is less convincing on the flexibilization of NATO. Hegemonic theory fails to account for variation and change precisely because hegemony has remained unchanged. In sum, the change in the nature of the threat and the cooperation problems explain institutional change and variation within a liberal and hegemonic organization.

Institutional design and international cooperation

The final part of the analysis asks whether and how institutional design shapes the quality of cooperation in post-Cold War NATO. Since rationalist institutional theory provided the best account of institutional variation and change for this time period, I will primarily focus on the definition of cooperation that is closest to this theory: *degree of policy convergence across actors*.[42] To assess the degree of policy convergence, I analyze the *major post-Cold War decisions of NATO*: NATO enlargement and the military interventions and operations in Bosnia-Herzegovina, Kosovo, Afghanistan, Iraq, and Sudan. On the basis of two main indicators – *participation and resourcing* – I roughly distinguish between areas of low and high cooperation or policy convergence. First, if only a part of NATO members agreed to a NATO decision or participated in a NATO action, cooperation qualifies as low. Conversely, an area of high cooperation involves the consent and participation of the large majority or all NATO member states. Moreover, high cooperation is indicated by a high level of financial and military commitment to a NATO policy. After describing the variation among NATO policies with regard to policy convergence, I will try to explain it. In order to do so, I analyze the *routes to policy convergence*.[43]

Policy convergence in post-Cold War NATO decisions

Table 5.2 gives an overview of policy convergence in the major post-Cold War NATO policies. Whereas policy convergence has been high overall in NATO Eastern enlargement and NATO interventions in

[42] Acharya and Johnston, ch. 1, this volume. [43] Ibid.

Table 5.2 *Policy convergence in post-Cold War NATO*

Policy	Participation	Resourcing	Policy convergence
Eastern enlargement	Consensual decision	Treaty commitment	High
Bosnia-Herzegovina	Consensual decision, NATO operation	Joint military combat and peacekeeping operation	High
Kosovo	Consensual decision, NATO operation	Joint military combat and peacekeeping operation	High
Afghanistan	NATO sidelined by US-led coalition of the willing, broad participation in war and ISAF	Joint peacekeeping operation with comparatively weak resources	Medium high
Iraq	Decision blockade, partial participation in war	Training of police forces	Low
Sudan	Consensual decision	Logistic support to African Union	Medium low

Bosnia-Herzegovina and Kosovo, it has been comparatively low with regard to military operations in Afghanistan, Iraq, and Sudan.

When the Central European governments first expressed their interest in joining NATO in the course of 1991, they were confronted with a general reticence among the member states. Although NATO was prepared to establish and expand institutionalized cooperation with the former members of the Warsaw Pact, the expansion of NATO *membership* was initially rejected. In 1993, a few policy entrepreneurs within alliance governments – most notably US National Security Adviser Anthony Lake and German Defense Minister Volker Rühe – began to advocate the expansion of NATO against an overwhelming majority of member governments and even strong opposition within their own governments. It took until the end of 1994 to make enlargement official NATO policy. Enlargement requires the consensus of all member states, and this consensus was reached in 1997 on the first round of enlargement and in 2002 on the second round.[44] Although Eastern enlargement entailed a rather low risk of actual military involvement to defend the new members, the treaty-based commitment to mutual assistance is the strongest

[44] Schimmelfennig, *Integration of Europe*, pp. 182–6.

commitment that NATO can make. In addition, NATO enlargement caused immediate costs to the member states: the adaptation of NATO's headquarters and staff as well as of the common infrastructure as well as support for the upgrading and "interoperability" of military forces in the new member states.[45] In sum, the consensual decision to expand treaty-based alliance commitments to ten Central and Eastern European countries after initial reluctance and member state divergence qualifies *NATO enlargement* as a significant *policy of high convergence.*

The war in *Bosnia-Herzegovina* broke out in March 1992. Initially, neither individual member states nor NATO as an organization were prepared and willing to deny Serbia control of the new state and to protect civilians and refugees by military force. NATO repeatedly threatened the Serb forces with air strikes in case they attacked UN protected areas and peacekeeping forces but it was not before 1994 that the NATO threats became more frequent and credible. Yet they could not prevent repeated Serb attacks on the civilian population, kidnappings, and killings. In the summer of 1995, however, after Serb forces overran the protected areas of Srebrenica and Zepa and killed thirty-seven people in a shelling of the Sarajevo marketplace, the major NATO powers (the US, Britain, and France) overcame their initial policy differences. As a result, NATO decided to exclude the United Nations from participating in NATO military decisions on Bosnia-Herzegovina and initiated its Operation Deliberate Force. This operation consisted in massive air strikes on Serb forces on the entire territory of Bosnia-Herzegovina, which continued until Serbian commander Ratko Mladic gave in to the NATO ultimatum and agreed to a ceasefire. In December 1995, the Dayton Peace Accord was signed and NATO deployed the 60,000-strong Implementation Force (IFOR) to guarantee the peace and oversee the implementation of the Dayton Accord. In 1996, and until the end of 2004, IFOR was replaced by SFOR (Stabilization Force). NATO's intervention in Bosnia-Herzegovina constituted the first active combat mission of NATO since its establishment and its first large-scale operational peacekeeping mission. This indicates a high level of resourcing. In addition, the level of participation was high. Not only did the US, Britain, and France agree on a joint military strategy but IFOR and SFOR involved almost all member states and up to 22 partner countries. In sum, *policy convergence* was *high* on both accounts.

The analysis of NATO's involvement in the war in *Kosovo* comes to a similar conclusion. In 1989, under the leadership of Slobodan

[45] Gary L. Geipel, "The cost of enlarging NATO," in James Sperling (ed.), *Two Tiers or two Speeds? The European Security Order and the Enlargement of the European Union and NATO* (Manchester: Manchester University Press, 1999), pp. 160–78.

Milosevic, Serbia abolished the autonomous status of Kosovo that the province with its predominantly ethnic Albanian population had enjoyed since World War II. After almost ten years of peaceful but unsuccessful resistance against the Serbian oppression, a Kosovo Liberation Army (UCK) emerged and initiated an armed struggle for the independence of Kosovo in 1998. The Serbian Police and the Yugoslav Army responded with the pillaging of Kosovo villages in the summer of 1998; almost 500,000 ethnic Albanians were expelled from their homes. Given the policy convergence already achieved on the similar case of Bosnia-Herzegovina, NATO reacted quickly to the outbreak of violence. Already in June 1998, the alliance began to study possible military options; in October, the NAC authorized activation orders for air strikes. Faced with the threat of NATO bombings, the Serbian leadership accepted a ceasefire and the deployment of an OSCE peacekeeping mission in Kosovo. In March 1999, however, after Serbia started a new offensive in Kosovo and rejected a peace agreement, NATO initiated air strikes against Yugoslavia (Operation Allied Force) that lasted for seventy-two days before the Serbian leadership began to withdraw from Kosovo. Operation Allied Force was the result of a consensual decision of the NATO allies, run by the Supreme Allied Command, and politically directed by the NAC. General Wesley Clark, the Supreme Allied Commander Europe at the time, called it "the first Alliance-wide air operation of its type."[46] Although the US provided most of the military equipment and conducted most of the military operations by far, other allies contributed according to their capabilities. Despite persistent political disagreement on the conduct of the air campaign – and heavy complaints by US officials and militaries on the constraints and inefficiency of "war-by-committee" – alliance cohesion and the intergovernmental steering of the military operation in NATO were preserved until the end.[47] In addition, NATO provided humanitarian assistance to the ethnic Albania refugees in Kosovo and the neighboring countries and led the Kosovo Force (KFOR) established in June 1999 to monitor and enforce the peace. In KFOR, just as in IFOR and SFOR, almost all member states and many partner countries participated. At its full strength, KFOR consisted of approximately 50,000 troops.

In other cases, policy convergence has been weaker. Compare the interventions in Afghanistan, Iraq, and Sudan with those in Bosnia-Herzegovina and Kosovo. The terrorist attacks on New York and Washington on 11 September 2001 were followed by a strong wave of solidarity and sympathy for the US in the transatlantic community. For the

[46] See www.nato.int/kosovo/press/p990325a.htm [last accessed 2 August 2006].
[47] See Wesley K. Clark, *Waging Modern War* (New York: Public Affairs, 2001).

first time in its history, NATO invoked Article 5 of the Treaty, in effect declaring the attack on the US to be an attack on the entire Western alliance. In terms of practical policy convergence, however, the effects have been much weaker. The war in *Afghanistan* has not been a NATO-led but a US-led military operation – in cooperation with a coalition of willing NATO member countries. Initially, the International Security Assistance Force (ISAF) – established to keep the peace in the country after the defeat of the Taliban regime – was not led by NATO but by individual nations (UK, Turkey). It was not before August 2003 that NATO took command of ISAF, and October 2006 that it included the US-led coalition forces in eastern Afghanistan. Meanwhile, all NATO member states and partner countries (totalling thirty-seven) participate in one way or another in ISAF. Force levels have gradually increased with the expansion of ISAF to all parts of Afghanistan. Yet compared with the Balkan missions of NATO, the level of resourcing and commitment has remained lower. As of may 2007, ISAF numbered some 30,000 troops – that is around 60 percent of the size of KFOR in a country about sixty times the size of Kosovo. In addition, participating countries have been reluctant to commit additional troops to Afghanistan and to move ISAF from an exclusively peacekeeping to more of a combat mission.[48] In sum, I rate policy convergence in the Afghanistan case as *medium high*.

In the *Iraq* case, policy convergence has even been *extremely low*. From the beginning, the Bush administration's case and plans for war with Iraq divided the NATO allies. In February 2003, the conflict culminated in probably the most severe crisis in the history of the transatlantic alliance. First, NATO failed to agree to a formal request by the US administration for limited support of NATO. Then, Belgium, France, and Germany blocked advance planning for NATO support of Turkey in the event of a war with Iraq. In response, Turkey called for consultations according to Article 4 of the Treaty. This was the first time in the history of the alliance that Article 4 was invoked. After a week-long standoff, the crisis could only be formally solved by passing the issue from the North Atlantic Council to the Defense Planning Committee, on which France does not sit, thereby excluding France from the decision. In the end, whereas NATO would have been ready to support Turkey against a possible Iraqi counter-attack (which did not occur), it did not lend support to the "coalition of the willing" that fought the war side by side with the

[48] See "NATO in Afghanistan," available at www.nato.int/issues/afghanistan/index.html [last accessed 2 August 2006]. After the expansion of ISAF to Southern Afghanistan, the number of troops is planned to rise to 18,500.

US. Moreover, the coalition was much smaller than in the Afghanistan case. Also in contrast with the Afghanistan case, NATO has not taken over peacekeeping tasks to assist or replace the coalition combat troops after the regime of Saddam Hussein had been defeated. To this day, the opponents of the war reject any official NATO presence in Iraq. The only minor commitment that NATO was able to make consensually was the training and equipment of Iraqi security forces.

In the Darfur region of *Sudan*, a rebellion broke out in 2003, which was brutally suppressed by the government with the help of the *janjaweed*, a mounted Arab militia. The *janjaweed* burnt villages, uprooted crops, raped women, and is estimated to have killed almost 200,000 people. Two million have been displaced. The NATO allies have been united in condemning the acts of the Sudanese government, imposing trade sanctions, giving aid to the displaced people, and putting pressure on the Sudanese government to enter into negotiations with the rebels and to declare a ceasefire in 2004. On request from the African Union (AU) in April 2005, NATO quickly agreed on a package of support measures, most importantly the provision of airlift facilities for AU peacekeepers. In a humanitarian crisis similar to Kosovo in 1998 and 1999, NATO members have thus consensually agreed in the NAC on providing military support. The level of support, however, has remained restricted to small-scale logistical support despite the fact that AU peacekeeping has failed, the ceasefire has broken down, and the killings have resumed at the end of 2005. The deployment of NATO troops to Darfur is still ruled out. The combination of high participation and inadequate resourcing makes Sudan a case of *medium low policy convergence*.

Routes to policy convergence (and divergence)

Most of the major post-Cold War NATO decisions were not harmonious. Enlargement met with the overwhelming resistance of the member governments initially. It took NATO three years to agree on a full-scale air campaign in Bosnia-Herzegovina. NATO was initially sidelined in the case of Afghanistan and could not agree in the case of Iraq. Even in the Kosovo case, in which the general decision to act militarily was quick and rather consensual, the actual conduct of war caused strains among the allies. After the disappearance of the clear and common Soviet threat, against which NATO had originally been established, the allies had to negotiate in each case whether it required a NATO response and was able to generate consensual commitments. The question then is how policy convergence was produced and why it succeeded in some cases but failed in others. I begin with rational institutionalism, because it explained the change and variation in the institutional design of post-Cold War NATO best.

There are two theoretical problems with the *rational* or *functional* explanation of international cooperation by institutional designs – one general, the other one particular to post-Cold War NATO. First, functional theory assumes that states choose and design international institutions to produce and stabilize international cooperation in order to achieve gains that they could not achieve otherwise. In this view, it is the rational anticipation of gains from cooperation that drives the establishment and design of international institutions in the first place. Thus, the finding that effective cooperation resulted from a specific institutional design would be trivial. On the other hand, any observation of non-cooperation or weak policy divergence would put in question the assumption of rational actors, because this would mean that the actors were not able to anticipate the consequences of their design choices correctly.

Second, and more importantly in the context of this volume, if the rational choice of institutional design is high flexibility because the need for cooperation and the partners in cooperation are not obvious, the explanation of international cooperation is institutionally underdetermined. This is the case in the new NATO. In the face of uncertainty and member state divergences concerning the potential threats in a new security environment, the member states opted for a more flexible institutional design of the alliance. Consequently, whether or not policy divergence actually occurs cannot be inferred from institutional design.

Rather, international security cooperation in a flexible institutional context must be explained, first, by the need to cooperate to counter a common threat effectively and, second, by the higher efficiency of international cooperation as compared to autonomous action. I argue, however, that policy convergence (and its variation) in post-Cold War NATO still cannot be explained on the basis of threats and security interests. In the case of enlargement, the member states did not face a military threat or the growing power of an adversary in Europe that they would need to have balanced by adding new members. Rather, NATO enjoyed a higher degree of security and relative power than at any time before. What is more, given their military and economic weakness, the new Central and Eastern European members rather diluted than strengthened the military power and effectiveness of NATO.[49] Similarly, neither Bosnia-Herzegovina nor Kosovo were of any major strategic, let alone vital interest to NATO and its member states. After the end of the Cold War, Yugoslavia had lost

[49] Schimmelfennig, *Integration of Europe*, pp. 40–50.

its geopolitical relevance. Moreover, there was no need to intervene in order to prevent or stop negative security externalities of the civil wars for the NATO members. By sealing off their borders, NATO countries were able to protect themselves effectively from the consequences: they were able to keep the refugee problem in manageable proportions and were neither threatened nor drawn into the wars by any of the participants.[50] Thus, in the absence of a relevant threat, security interdependencies, or strategic gains, why should the NATO members have cooperated particularly strongly with regard to enlargement and intervention in the Balkans? At any rate, in the rationalist perspective, the initial divergence of preferences and absence of cooperation is much easier to explain than the eventual policy convergence. Moreover, it is not clear in this perspective why policy convergence should have been lower in the Afghanistan and Iraq cases. At least, Islamist terrorism presented a real and proven security threat to the member states of NATO. Even if one argues that this threat was perceived differently in the US and Europe and that the connection between Islamist terrorism and the regime of Saddam Hussein in Iraq was highly doubtful, this might explain the weak cooperation in these cases – but not why cooperation was stronger in the Balkan cases and enlargement.

As an alternative to functional reasoning, *sociological or constructivist institutionalism* proposes two main links between institutional design and international cooperation. First, institutional designs may be more or less conducive to processes of institutional learning and socialization.[51] This line of explanation, however, is not helpful in accounting for the variation in post-Cold War NATO cooperation. All decisions analyzed here were made in the same institutional context (the NAC). In addition, the time dependency of learning and socialization can be dismissed, too, because instances of high and low policy divergence occurred almost simultaneously – such as the second round of Eastern enlargement in late 2002 and the Iraq crisis in early 2003.

Second, international organizations institutionalize the fundamental values and norms that constitute the identity of an international community. They are established in the treaties and other basic documents of the organization and regularly invoked in its official discourse. In this view, the more these fundamental community values and norms are at stake in a given situation or issue, and the more a proposed collective

[50] Andreas Hasenclever, *Die Macht der Moral in der internationalen Politik. Militärische Interventionen westlicher Staaten in Somalia, Ruanda und Bosnien-Herzegowina* (Frankfurt: Campus, 2001), pp. 362–80.

[51] Acharya and Johnston, ch. 1, this volume; Checkel, "Why Comply?".

decision is in line with them and serves to uphold and defend them, the more member state policies will converge. In line with this theoretical argument, cooperation in the alliance will be high if *fundamental human rights and liberal-democratic norms are at stake in the transatlantic community*. This will either be the case, negatively, when they are challenged by grave and systematic human rights violations in the Euro-Atlantic region (such as in Bosnia-Herzegovina and Kosovo) or, positively, when they are reaffirmed, strengthened, and expanded (such as in the democratic consolidation of Central and Eastern Europe that preceded the enlargement of NATO). Either way, the consensual decisions and cooperative actions were not driven by security threats and interests but by the liberal democratic and Euro-Atlantic identity of NATO. NATO members felt compelled to intervene in the civil wars in Yugoslavia insofar as "ethnic cleansing" on the European continent violated the most basic norms of the community and to admit new members from Central and Eastern Europe insofar as they had embraced liberal democracy and a Western identity.

As the brief case studies have shown, consensus and cooperative action were not the immediate responses of the NATO member states to either the CEECs' bid for membership or the human rights violations on the Balkans. Initially, the member states have been reluctant to offer membership to the CEECs or to intervene decisively in Bosnia-Herzegovina precisely because strategic relevance was low and expected costs were high. In both cases, processes of rhetorical action and shaming produced cooperation in the absence of egoistic material and political incentives.

In the enlargement case, the Central and Eastern European governments and the advocates of enlargement within NATO successfully portrayed the CEECs as traditional members of the Euro-Atlantic community now "returning to Europe" and to liberal democracy. At the same time, they stressed the instability of democratic achievements in their region. In addition, they framed NATO as a democratic community rather than a military alliance, and enlargement as an issue of democracy promotion and protection rather than an issue of military necessity or efficiency. On this basis, they argued the case that NATO's liberal values and norms obliged the member states to stabilize democracy in the CEECs and, for that purpose, to grant them membership in NATO.[52] Based on the fundamental identity of the transatlantic community, this framing and justification made it difficult for the opponents to openly oppose enlargement without putting into question their commitment to the community values and norms. It also gave the proponents of

[52] Schimmelfennig, *Integration of Europe*, pp. 230–5.

enlargement considerable normative leverage in putting this policy on the agenda and working toward its implementation. Thus rhetorically entrapped, the skeptical majority of member states acquiesced to the increasingly concrete planning for NATO enlargement and did not block the enlargement decisions – even though they remained unconvinced of their utility.[53]

In the case of Bosnia-Herzegovina, for a long time, the allies shied away from the risks and costs of an intervention and could not agree on a common strategy to help. In the summer of 1995, however, it had become clear that low-risk and low-commitment strategies such as humanitarian assistance, peacekeeping, diplomatic mediation efforts, and momentary threats or uses of force were not sufficient to stop the human rights violations in Bosnia-Herzegovina and end the plight of the population. In particular, when Serbian forces overran the UN-protected areas of Srebrenica and Zepa and killed some 7,000 people that had trusted the UN's and NATO's safety guarantee – while Dutch peacekeeping forces stood by helplessly – Western governments came under strong public criticism and moral pressure to act.[54]

In contrast, the Middle East cases were not only "out of area" but also outside the Euro-Atlantic region to which the identity of NATO applied. Yet the intervention in Afghanistan could be justified as a legitimate act of self-defense against a terrorist organization that not only rejected the fundamental values and norms of the West but also was determined to use violence against NATO member states. This explains the strong show of alliance solidarity after 9/11 and the general readiness of NATO members to join the US in fighting al-Qaida and stabilizing Afghanistan. That the war in Afghanistan was not fought under NATO command did not result from a lack of consensus in NATO but from a deliberate choice of the Bush administration to prevent intergovernmental political constraints in the conduct of war. In contrast, the Iraq war failed to generate consensus and policy convergence in NATO because it lacked legitimacy. It was outside the community region, not an act of self-defense, and initially not primarily motivated by the defense of community values (although it was later increasingly justified as a war to end tyranny and establish democracy in the Middle East). Finally, the fact that the Darfur case

[53] Ibid., pp. 242–50. On the mechanism of social influence that is central here, see Alastair Iain Johnston, "Treating International Institutions as Social Environments," *International Studies Quarterly*, 45:4 (2001), pp. 487–515.

[54] Hasenclever, *Macht der Moral*, pp. 407–19. In addition, it must be said that the military situation on the ground had improved due to the Croatian offensive in the west of Bosnia and the pullout of peacekeeping forces. As a result, the risks had decreased with the increase of moral pressure.

also qualifies as a case of "ethnic cleansing" explains the high level of consensus among NATO countries; however, because this genocide takes place outside the Euro-Atlantic community region, the commitment of resources has remained low. In sum, alliance cooperation has varied with the degree to which a security issue was relevant to the identity of the Euro-Atlantic liberal community.

Which alternative explanations could be brought up to challenge the identity-based explanation of cooperation in NATO? I distinguish between capabilities, hegemony, and partisan alternative explanations and argue that none of them accounts plausibly for the variation in cooperation.

According to the first alternative explanation, the *divergence in capabilities* is at the core of the cooperation problem in NATO.[55] In this view, most European allies lack airlift capacities and globally deployable and useable military forces. Therefore, NATO cooperation becomes increasingly inefficient and useless as the most important security problems move away from the European region. Thus, NATO cooperation was strong in the European conflicts where the allies' military capabilities were marginally useful in supporting the US armed forces and, above all, in providing peacekeeping forces. By contrast, in the Middle Eastern wars, the capabilities of the allies were too limited for NATO involvement to be useful (with the exception of some allied forces like the British or post-war peacekeeping in Afghanistan). Whereas the description of the gap in capabilities is correct, it does not convincingly account for the variation in cooperation. Most importantly, the decisions for or against NATO involvement and individual participation were political not military decisions. Whereas the decision for NATO-led air strikes in Bosnia-Herzegovina was made consensually, the actual combat only involved a few NATO member states. In the Iraq crisis, it was the US administration that asked for NATO support of the war and preparations for a possible defense of Turkey. These requests were not rejected because they would have been beyond NATO's capabilities but because they were contested. Moreover, the Bush administration was highly interested, for reasons of legitimacy, in enlisting as many countries as possible in the coalition, including many that made no or only minor contributions to the actual warfare. In other words, cooperation in NATO is about coalitions of the *willing*, not coalitions of the *capable*.

According to the second alternative explanation, it was *American hegemony and leadership* in NATO rather than value commitments that led to policy convergence and cooperation. Indeed, all cases of high policy

[55] See most prominently Robert Kagan, *Of Paradise and Power: America and Europe in the New World Order* (New York: Knopf, 2003).

convergence are cases of strong and essential US leadership. The US administration was the main driving force behind the air campaigns in Bosnia-Herzegovina and Kosovo, and without the US military, the interventions would just not have been possible militarily. The US administration was also the main driving force of NATO enlargement. NATO's main decisions on the PfP, the Study on Enlargement, the setting of a date for enlargement, and the selection of new members mirrored US preferences and were predetermined by US domestic decisions.[56] Nevertheless I argue that it was not the bargaining power of US hegemony but the normative power of US moral entrepreneurship that produced cooperation. First, whereas there is abundant evidence of US use of arguments based on the identity, values, and norms of the Euro-Atlantic community, explicit bargaining was conspicuously absent from the process. There is no evidence – either in newspaper reports or in interviews – of US material threats to the reluctant European allies in case they vetoed enlargement. Moreover, US leadership has only been successful when it was in line with and legitimated by the fundamental community values. Conversely, US leadership was not sufficient to produce policy convergence when this legitimacy was absent or weak – as in the Iraq crisis. Thus, whereas US leadership may well have been a necessary condition of policy convergence in the cases analyzed here, it was sufficient only in conjunction with value and norm conformance. What is more, when it was successful, US leadership did not need to use bargaining and coercion but consisted mainly in moral entrepreneurship.

Third, it seems at first glance that whereas the cases of high policy convergence occurred during the Clinton administration, those of low policy convergence fall into the "unilateralist" *Bush administration*. Yet the second round of NATO enlargement was launched mainly by the Bush administration and consensually approved at the end of 2002 when the Iraq crisis was looming already. In the constructivist perspective, it was approved precisely because the Bush administration argued the case for enlargement on very much the same identity-based grounds as the Clinton administration.[57]

Conclusions

In the post-Cold War era, NATO has become more flexible and developed an open-ended and process-oriented partnership with the countries of Central and Eastern Europe. The change and variation in institutional

[56] James M. Goldgeier, *Not Whether but When: The US Decision to Enlarge NATO* (Washington, DC: The Brookings Institution, 1999).

[57] Schimmelfennig, *Integration of Europe*, pp. 255–60.

design can be explained plausibly as a functional response to the disappearance of the common and certain Soviet threat and its replacement with a diversity of less common and clear security issues and with uncertainty about the new security environment in the East. At the same time, however, the more flexible institutional design of post-Cold War NATO, which allows for varying degrees of cooperation among NATO members and partners, is indeterminate with regard to the actual degree of cooperation. It does not tell us why and how member state policies sometimes converge and sometimes don't. I have argued in this chapter that, in the absence of a common and clearly identifiable threat to their security, the member states of NATO are mainly held together – and bound to act together – by their common liberal democratic identity and the shared liberal values and norms of the transatlantic community of all member states. Whenever this identity was at stake, member states eventually felt compelled to cooperate even in the absence of a threat to their own security.

What does the analysis of post-Cold War NATO tell us about the sources and effects of institutional design? First, the study suggests that institutional design cannot be fully explained by the functional theory of rational institutionalism. On the one hand, the findings of this chapter corroborate the long-standing liberal or constructivist criticism that rational institutionalism does not account for the principles of institutional forms and the varying social purposes of international organizations.[58] In the NATO case, the liberal ideology and norms of the organization are exogenous to the functional explanation, and control and centralization remained constant despite a change in functional exigencies. This being said, however, the variation and change in the institutional design of post-Cold War NATO, the more open, diffuse, and process-oriented partnership and the more flexible new NATO, can be plausibly understood as functional responses to the challenges of the post-Cold War era: uncertainty about the new security environment and diversity of security issues and preferences. Thus, there seems to be a distinction between "first-order" institutional design features that are determined by relatively durable (intersubjective and material) structural features of the international system and will not be affected by changes in the specific cooperation problems, and "second-order" features that will vary with the functional exigencies of changing cooperation problems.

Second, the NATO case casts serious doubts on the causal link between institutional design and international cooperation. First, in a functional

[58] See e.g. John G. Ruggie, "Multilateralism: The Anatomy of an Institution," in John G. Ruggie (ed.), *Multilateralism Matters*, p. 31; Reus-Smit, "Constitutional Structure."

perspective, this link is rather trivial – and underdetermined if institutions are purposively designed to allow for high flexibility in cooperation. Second, the identity-based explanation for varying degrees of cooperation advanced here relegates institutional design to a merely intervening variable and the relationship between design and cooperation to a spurious relationship. In other words, it is the identity of the Euro-Atlantic community that shapes both the norms of NATO (institutional design) and the extent of policy convergence (cooperation).

6 Designed to fail or failure of design? The origins and legacy of the Arab League

Michael Barnett and Etel Solingen

In its nearly sixty years of existence the Arab League has achieved a relatively low level of cooperation. Although the League has had a measure of influence in socializing some Arab elites, it has fallen short in changing state preferences, in forcing significant adjustment of prior policies, or in achieving a pan-Arab blueprint to guide their collective behavior. At the same time, to the extent the League was *designed* to enhance state sovereignty, it has certainly succeeded in doing so. *Prima facie*, this relatively limited cooperation is something of a surprise for several reasons. First, the League of Arab States was the first regional organization established after 1945. Second, its members share a common language, identity, and culture. Third, there is an arguable shared threat in Israel and continuing suspicions of the West. Fourth, there have been expectations of joint gains from trade and commerce, although similar production patterns detracted from benefits achievable through complementarity.[1] Such shared identities and interests would surely place the Arab states system high on most predictors of regional institutionalization. Yet, the most that can be said is that a shared Arab identity keeps Arab states oriented toward one another, but obstacles toward meaningful institutionalization and cooperation of any depth have never been surmounted.

Why such disappointing results? We reject several conventional explanations for sub-Pareto outcomes and failure to cooperate. First, we find very limited evidence that extra-regional actors or Cold War politics played much if any role in the original design or ongoing failures of the League. British Prime Minister Eden supported a framework to enhance

[1] Stanley Fischer, "Prospects for Regional Integration in the Middle East," in Jaime de Melo and Arvind Pangariya (eds.), *New Dimensions in Regional Integration* (New York: Cambridge University Press, 1995), p. 440. Note: The authors would like to acknowledge the helpful comments of two anonymous reviewers, the editors, and other participants at workshops held at Harvard University and Singapore IDSS. Etel Solingen also thanks the United States Institute of Peace and the University of California's Institute on Global Conflict and Cooperation for research support. The opinions, findings, and conclusions expressed in this publication do not necessarily reflect the views of the USIP.

Arab ties in 1943 but it was regional leaders who spearheaded the process that led to the League's creation. The Cold War may have certainly accentuated internal divisions in the Arab world – but it did not determine them. Nor were external actors the source of disappointing results in the multilateral peace process of the 1990s. Indeed extra-regional actors – from the US to the EU, Russia, and Japan – provided extensive support for these alternative institutional efforts. Second, there is little evidence that the number of actors hindered cooperation. The original League had only seven members, hardly daunting. Third, the regional distribution of power, at least as conventionally understood, also played a limited role. In fact, some analyses suggest that a hegemon willing to play a leadership role is necessary in order to subsidize the costs of cooperation, while other analyses offer that it might be an obstacle to cooperation because of the fear hegemony engenders in other states. In the Arab world, Egypt might have played a hegemonic role, but Egypt appeared to define cooperation in ways that reflected its own interests. Hence, other states feared Egypt, though not because of the threat of a conventional military attack of the sort associated with most balance of power arguments but rather because of the *competitive politics of regime survival* across the Arab world. Lastly, while some scholars believe that a shared identity necessarily helps to overcome collective action problems, in fact, as we will argue here, *a shared identity represented an obstacle.*

Our argument focuses on two main – mutually reinforcing – explanatory variables: identity and domestic politics. Together they account, in our view, for weak cooperation among Arab states and an institutional design for the Arab League that reflected leaders' primary concerns with domestic regime survival. Specifically, the politics of Arab nationalism and a shared identity led Arab states to embrace the rhetoric of Arab unity in order to legitimize their regimes, and to fear Arab unity in practice because it would impose greater restrictions on their sovereignty. The Arab League was a reflection of these interests and fears. Consequently, the League's design should not be seen as an unintended outcome but instead as the result of the clear imperative of regime survival that led Arab leaders to prefer weak regional institutions. Such institutions were specifically designed to fail at producing the kind of greater collaboration and integration that might have weakened political leaders at home. In that sense, our case provides some support for the general hypothesis that regimes enjoying weak legitimacy fear compromising sovereignty and their own survival through the establishment of strongly binding regional institutions.

Yet exactly how the logic of regime survival led to the desire for weak regional institutions has differed substantially over the sixty years of regional independence. To explore these issues, we compare two time periods, one from the 1940s through the late 1960s, and the other from the late 1970s to the present. Although these two periods are similar because the logic of regime survival led to the creation and design of weak regional institutions, they differ on the sources of institutional design, and the low level of cooperation.

We follow the evolution of the normative variable throughout the first period, at which time Arab leaders could not live with pan-Arab nationalism but also could not live without it, since it legitimated their activities. Arab leaders feared that, left unchecked, pan-Arab nationalism would undermine their own state sovereignty: unity and cooperation in this context implied surrendering political authority to a pan-Arab state. Consequently, leaders labored to create the myth and ceremony of Arab nationalism while limiting the possibility that it would impose any unwanted demands. These imperatives led to and shaped the design of the Arab League, which we examine in section I. *The Arab League was designed to fail as supranational entity, and in that sense it reflects the triumph of domestic regimes with little interest in developing robust regional institutions.*

Yet the creation of the League had unintended effects. Although Arab leaders wanted to ensure that the League would not restrict their movements or leave them beholden to the norms of Arabism (i.e. a stronger union), over time their interactions created what they had hoped to preclude, a dynamic we explore in section II. As the Arab identity and the broad goal of Arab unity lingered, Arab leaders still wanted to be associated with these aspirations even as they worked to frustrate them, and the Arab League became the institutional forum where they worked out these tensions. The result was that cooperation could mean policy coordination of one of two kinds: a shift of their foreign policies so that they were consistent with some of the more ambitious demands of Arab nationalism, including a common security and foreign policy, economic integration, and political unification; or a convergence of policies around a more modest Arab nationalism that prohibited them from undertaking policies that could be perceived as threatening the security of the Arab nation. Conversely, defection from the status quo could mean either: an Arab leader attempted to push others to coordinate their policies in ways that would demand greater integration and thus subordinate their sovereignty to the Arab nation; or an Arab leader violated existing norms of Arabism. There were different incentives for defection. A leader could gain tremendous status by being perceived as ready to demand regional integration. But if all Arab leaders acted accordingly, attempting to outbid each other on who was the most committed Arab nationalist, it might have led to a suboptimal outcome (from their perspective) because it would have reduced their individual autonomy and sovereignty. However, they had little incentive to violate the existing norms of Arabism because doing so could challenge a regime's very legitimacy and stability.

These different "games" were associated with different enforcement mechanisms and penalties for those who violated existing norms. Although Arab states worried about any dynamic that might lead to integration, they could hardly invest the League with sanctions against such a possibility because it would only reveal how little they wanted to integrate. Consequently, they had to utilize extra-institutional means, such as creating symbolic institutions and using shaming techniques. For these social mechanisms (sanctioning others to adhere to the norms of Arabism) to have their intended effects, there had to exist regional attachments and a collective identity. We explore these dynamics and enforcement mechanisms in several instances: the attempt by King Abdullah to violate an existing norm when he threatened to establish a separate peace with Israel and annex the West Bank in 1949; the creation of the Arab Collective Security Pact of 1950 as a way of halting a drive for unification between Syria and Iraq; and the successful attempt by Nasser to develop a norm against alliances with the West in response to the Baghdad Pact of 1955.

The effects of Arabism on the regional order were reinforced by the nature of domestic regimes in the Arab world from the 1950s onwards, our second explanatory variable. Most Arab states were ruled by different variants of inward-looking domestic coalitions emphasizing import-substitution, state entrepreneurship, and civic (*wataniya*) – as well as Arab (*qawmiya*) – nationalism and populism.[2] The armed forces played a central role in imposing this grand strategy, usually through centralizing leaders that maintained the coalition, nearly invariably through authoritarian institutions.[3] Massive nationalizations of oil (Algeria, Libya, Iraq), of the Suez canal (Egypt), and of other industrial and physical capital, allowed these ruling coalitions to appropriate monopoly rents and to convert them into sources of political support.[4] The military appropriated gargantuan proportions of that rent, transforming the Middle East into

[2] On *wataniya* and *qawmiya*, see Adeed Dawisha, *Arab Nationalism in the Twentieth Century: From Triumph to Despair* (Princeton: Princeton University Press, 2003). In our subsequent discussion the term "statism" is used interchangeably with *wataniya* (local nationalism) whereas the term *qawmiya* relates to pan-Arabism.

[3] Grand strategies help identify potential threats to a coalition's survival at home, in the region, throughout the world, and to devise political, economic, and military means to counter such threats. Etel Solingen, *Regional Orders at Century's Dawn: Global and Domestic Influences on Grand Strategy* (Princeton: Princeton University Press, 1998).

[4] A. Richards and J. Waterbury, *A Political Economy of the Middle East – State, Class, and Economic Development* (Boulder: Westview 1990), p. 362; Michael Barnett, *Confronting the Costs of War: Military Power, State, and Society in Egypt and Israel* (Princeton: Princeton University Press, 1992); Ellis Goldberg, "Why Isn't There More Democracy in the Middle East?" *Contention*, 5:2 (Winter 1996), pp. 141–50; Lisa Anderson, "The State in the Middle East and North Africa," *Comparative Politics*, 20:1 (October 1987), pp. 1–18.

one of the most heavily militarized regions in the world, with the highest levels of military expenditures relative to both GDP and government expenditures, and the largest-sized military establishments relative to the general population.[5]

State entrepreneurship and low integration with the global economy (except of the kind fostered by some rentier states in the Gulf) suppressed the emergence of a strong and independent private entrepreneurial class throughout much of the Arab world.[6] Under this model, the typical Middle East state employed over 50 percent of the workforce and accounted for three-quarters of industrial production. Despite intermittent efforts in Lebanon, Jordan, Tunisia, and Morocco to develop more market-friendly political economies, the region's political center of gravity for many decades remained with inward-looking regimes, particularly following the inauguration of Nasserism in the early 1950s. Vastly protectionist political economies, pivoting on state entrepreneurship, came to characterize mostly the radical-praetorian, but also monarchic versions of ruling coalitions. Competition along coalitional lines and efforts to impose their respective models over neighboring states foiled cooperative efforts. The very logic of these import-substituting models precluded effective economic integration, despite a rhetoric that paralleled the normative calls for Arabism.

In sum, the pull toward both cooperation and conflict stemming from Arabism and the imperatives of regime survival help explain the nature of institutional design, the low level of institutionalization, and why the Arab League and other all-Arab institutions (including the summit system) produced very little policy convergence. Arabism oriented Arab states toward each other (and therefore created a demand for normative integration) and pulled them apart (and therefore created a dynamic of fragmentation). The political logic of inward-looking strategies reinforced those barriers to regional cooperation and integration. Leaders committed to their own domestic political requirements got the weak

[5] On military expenditures throughout the Arab world, see *The Military Balance*, 1992–1993; James A. Bill and Robert Springborg, *Politics in the Middle East*, 3rd edn. (Glenview, IL: Scott, Foresman/Little, Brown Higher Education, 1990), p. 247; Richards and Waterbury, *A Political Economy*, p. 362; Baghat Korany and Ali Hillal Dessouki, "The Global System and Arab Foreign Policies," in B. Korany and A. Dessouki (eds.), *The Foreign Policies of Arab States: The Challenge of Change* (Boulder: Westview, 1991), p. 38; and Yahya M. Sadowski, *Scuds or Butter? The Political Economy of Arms Control in the Middle East* (Washington, DC: Brookings Institution, 1993). On Middle East militarization relative to other regions, see Etel Solingen, "Mapping Internationalization: Domestic and Regional Impacts," *International Studies Quarterly* 45:4 (2001), pp. 517–56; and Etel Solingen, "Pax Asiatica versus Belli Levantini: The Foundations of War and Peace in East Asia and the Middle East," *American Political Science Review*, 10:4 (November 2007).

[6] Anderson, "The State in the Middle East and North Africa."

institutions they wanted: just enough to demonstrate their commitment to Arabism but not so much as to allow Arabism to threaten their individual sovereignties, domestic political alliances, and power base. The two key variables – Arabism and statist interests – were interactive, conjunctural, and mutually reinforcing at this point. Both dimensions are critical to explain the design of the Arab League and its low levels of cooperation.

The norms of Arabism weakened after the 1970s, when collective aspirations had less salience and new state-building projects and evolving domestic arrangements enabled Arab leaders to emphasize their respective interests over common identity. The role of Arabism under the new circumstances declines significantly whereas statism assumes greater centrality. The domestic logic of regime survival shifted in some cases and, with it, new regional institutional possibilities came to the fore. Section III examines this shift and its effects on institutional design and the nature of regional cooperation. In particular, a new domestic coalitional dynamic enabled the emergence of a Multilateral Middle East Peace Process, with the participation of several Arab states (but not others) as well as Israel, Turkey, and extra-regional supporting actors, including the US, the EU, Japan, and Russia. Section IV provides a snapshot of the evolving dynamic between regime survival and institutional challenges to the Arab League in the aftermath of 9/11 and the 2003 Gulf War.

I: A league of their own

To understand the origins and design of the Arab League requires recognition of its historical context. The issue of Arab unity lay dormant for the first three decades of the twentieth century as Arab lands struggled for independence against colonialism. By the late 1930s, however, as an independent Arab world emerged on the horizon, the race for statehood among Arab states was "taken over by the struggle for unity."[7] Newspapers, popular magazines, and political commentaries increasingly featured the topic of Arab unity and the practical steps that might foster this outcome. Arab leaders were beginning to speak of life after colonialism and the political opposition in many Arab countries began using the theme of Arab unity to embarrass the government and to score easy political points.[8] Although there were strong divisions among Arab

[7] Patrick Seale, *The Struggle for Syria: A Study of Post-War Arab Politics, 1945–1958*, new edition with a foreword by Albert Hourani (London: I.B. Tauris, 1986), p. 1; also see Mary C. Wilson, *King Abdullah, Britain, and the Making of Jordan* (New York: Cambridge University Press, 1987), pp. 129 and 140.

[8] Yehoshua Porath, *In Search of Arab Unity, 1930–1945* (London: Cass, 1986), p. 189.

leaders, social movements, and intellectuals concerning what unity meant and what practical form it should take, there was an emerging consensus that an Arab association of some sort was necessary for an Arab revival and commendable on strategic, political, cultural, and economic grounds.[9]

Two distinct camps viewed Arab unity differently. The maximalist camp defined unity as entailing unification or federation among the Arab states in order to bring into correspondence "state" and "nation," to erase the residues of colonialism, and to fulfill Arab nationalism's ultimate aspirations. Even where unification was most favored – largely in Transjordan, Syria, and Iraq, and among the lower and middle classes – support was hardly overwhelming. Yet Iraqi, Syrian, and Transjordanian political elites kept unification alive, matching and sometimes outpacing their societies to advance personal, political, and strategic calculations. King Abdullah of Transjordan aired various Greater Syria plans primarily to achieve his long-standing personal ambition to be crowned King of Damascus and to lay claim to part of Palestine as well as to encourage Britain to expedite the timetable for Transjordan's independence.[10] Beginning with King Faysal and continuing over the years, the Iraqi Palace saw Syria as having been promised and then denied to the Hashemites, and held that a reclaimed Syria also would advance Iraq's economic interests and leave it more secure from Turkey and Iran.[11] Iraq's interest in some sort of federation increased: with formal independence in 1930; when the rather ambitious Nuri al-Said was Prime Minister; when such proposals might increase Iraq's other foreign policy objectives vis-a-vis Britain or the other Arab states; and on occasion for domestic political purposes. Numerous Syrian nationalists desired a "Greater Syria" that included parts of Transjordan and Lebanon, territories that they viewed as ancestral parts of Syria, severed by colonial whims.[12] In general, these and other Arab officials might have been sincere champions of unification, but it just so happened that the discourse of unification served to legitimate their rule. And in the highly unlikely event that their proposals became reality, the result would

[9] Ahmed Gomaa, *The Foundation of the League of Arab States* (London: Longman, 1977), p. 114.

[10] Porath, *In Search of Arab Unity*, p. 36; Wilson, *King Abdullah, Britain, and the Making of Jordan*, pp. 135–40; Ron Pundik, *The Struggle For Sovereignty: Relations Between Great Britain and Jordan, 1946–1951* (Oxford: Basil Blackwell, 1994), pp. 37–9.

[11] Porath, *In Search of Arab Unity*, chap. 1. For a detailed overview of shifting trans-regional coalitions or groupings in the Arab world, see Mark Zacher, *International Conflicts and Collective Security, 1946–77: The United Nations, Organization of American States, Organization of African Unity, and Arab League* (New York: Praeger, 1979).

[12] Daniel Pipes, *Greater Syria: History of an Ambition* (New York: Oxford University Press, 1990).

be an increase in their own political power because each had a favored proposal that always led to their self-aggrandizement.[13]

The minimalist camp included Saudi Arabia, Yemen, Lebanon, and Egypt, who opposed unification and pressed for a regional association that exhibited some modest moves toward cultural, economic, and political cooperation within the very constraining parameters of state sovereignty. Saudi Arabia was suspicious of Arab nationalism or any related scheme that increased the political power of the Hashemite states in Transjordan and Iraq. Yemen was equally distant from the flag of Arab unification. Lebanese officials could not help but translate Greater Syria into Lesser Lebanon. Since Lebanon had been administratively created from part of historical Syria, many Lebanese, and especially the Maronite population, feared that Syria would use the facade of Arabism to make a territorial claim.

Egypt's initial attitude toward unification was not merely dismissive but derisive. Its pre-1930 position was famously captured by Sa'ad Zaglul, the great Egyptian nationalist: "If you add one zero to one zero, then add another zero, what will be the sum?"[14] The Arab countries, in his view, were zeros. Most Egyptian officials and intellectuals feared becoming entangled in Arab politics.[15] As Egyptians became more attached to Arab nationalism and concerned with Palestine, however, the government began to take a greater interest in regional politics on account of two calculations. First, they believed that it was in their own, and Egypt's, strategic and political interests to become more involved in Arab affairs. Becoming identified as a leader of Arab politics could elevate Egypt's political importance in global affairs, increase its commercial relations with the Arab east, and perhaps even further its ultimate goal of independence. Second, if Arab nationalism's growing appeal at home would render Egypt vulnerable to pan-Arab issues then Egypt might as well control the Arab agenda rather than be controlled by it.[16]

[13] The idea of unification also gained some support in response to the ongoing crisis in Palestine. See Porath, *In Search of Arab Unity*, chap. 2; Gomaa, *Foundation of the League of Arab States*, chap. 2. Various Arab leaders and British officials toyed with the notion of halting the crisis by absorbing Palestine into a unified Arab state, and various Fertile Crescent leaders encouraged such thoughts as a way to increase their own domestic fortunes and symbolic capital.

[14] Quoted from Anwar G. Chejne, "Egyptian Attitudes on Pan-Arabism," *Middle East Journal*, 11:3 (Summer, 1957), p. 253.

[15] Gomaa, *Foundation of the League of Arab States*, pp. 49 and 50–1.

[16] Eran Lerman, "A Revolution Prefigured: Foreign Policy Orientation in the Postwar Years," in Shimon Shamir (ed.), *Egypt: From Monarchy to Republic* (Boulder, CO: Westview Press, 1995), pp. 291–2. Economic elites, particularly those part of the Bank Misr group, also calculated that they might profit from greater exchange with the Mashreq. Porath, *In Search of Arab Unity*, pp. 155 and 188. Egypt's centrality in Arab circles

Discussions surrounding Arab unity lay dormant until World War II, when the possibility of independence appeared on the horizon. One of the defining characteristics of these discussions was the pull and push of Arab identity and regime survival, with Arab states declaring the desirability of some sort of unity but fearing that such a unity might undermine their political authority and regime survival. The first set of discussions on unity were triggered by British Foreign Secretary Anthony Eden's Mansion House speech of 29 May 1941, when he declared Britain's support for any proposal that strengthened ties among Arab states. Although these discussions did not lead to any concrete proposals, they did lead Iraqi Prime Minister Nuri al-Said to forward a Fertile Crescent plan defined by a Greater Syria and a union between Arab states that most resembled each other in their general political and social conditions, that is, those of the Fertile Crescent but not Egypt and Saudi Arabia.[17] Negotiations turned serious in 1943, a development, once again, triggered by a speech by Anthony Eden.[18] At the suggestion of Nuri al-Said, on 30 March Egyptian Prime Minister Nahhas proposed that Cairo host a preparatory conference on the subject of Arab unity.[19] Although Nahhas had never been a champion of Arab nationalism, he believed that by hosting such a conference he could associate himself with an emerging sentiment and extend Egypt's power and influence.[20]

Over the next several months Arab officials conducted a series of negotiations over who were the Arabs and what should be the regional architecture and its organizing principles.[21] Nahhas of Egypt and Nuri of Iraq opened informal discussions regarding who were the Arabs and whether to include Egypt and the Sudan; the form and system of governance of any future federation; Greater Syrian schemes and the future status of Christian and Jewish minorities; the willingness of states to renounce their sovereignty; and the potential danger of Jewish expansion within a

increased during World War II because of its role in the Middle Eastern Supply Center and corresponding political and economic linkages to other parts of the Arab world. Cecil Hourani, "The Arab League in Perspective," *Middle East Journal*, 1:2 (April, 1947), p. 129.

[17] Cited from Hourani, "The Arab League in Perspective," p. 128. Also see Seale, *The Struggle for Syria*, pp. 11–12; Porath, *In Search of Arab Unity*, pp. 51–3; Bruce Maddy-Weitzman, *The Crystallization of the Arab State System* (Syracuse: Syracuse University Press, 1993), p. 12; Gomaa, *Foundation of the League of Arab States*, pp. 69–71.

[18] Porath, *In Search of Arab Unity*, pp. 248–50.

[19] Ibid., pp. 54 and 258; Wilson, *King Abdullah, Britain, and the Making of Jordan*, pp. 142–3; Tawfig Y. Hasou, *The Struggle for the Arab World: Egypt's Nasser and the Arab League* (Boston: Routledge and Keegan Paul, 1985), pp. 6–10.

[20] Maddy-Weitzman, *The Crystallization of the Arab State System*, p. 14.

[21] Mohammad Iqbal Ansari, *The Arab League, 1945–1955* (Aligarh, India: Institute of Islamic Studies, Aligar Muslim University, 1968), pp. 15–20 and 25.

federation that included Palestine.[22] The most important results of this discussion were the conclusion that Egypt had to be included in any future regional association, that unification was inconceivable and federation was politically unlikely, and that future discussions should concentrate on more practical possibilities.

Further negotiations produced three related patterns that would shape future discussions. The first was the contradictory logics of *wataniya* (state interests) and *qawmiya* (pan-Arab interests). While Arab leaders had become quite comfortable with the territorial entities created by the West, the transnational dimension of Arab nationalism led to the expectation that Arab states would pool their separate sovereignties. Arab leaders routinely handled this tension by proclaiming their devotion to Arab unity while opposing most proposals intended to bring about unification on the grounds that they were impractical for the moment, not easily salable at home, and would possibly leave them vulnerable to unwanted outside interference. Second, Arab leaders looked upon each other as a potential threat to their own sovereignty, autonomy, and survival. While they could hardly resist the opportunity to score some easy political points by calling for unification or federation, almost all proposals were viewed as a Trojan Horse and their proponents as a potential threat.[23] After all, no Arab leader would advance or associate himself with a proposal that did not leave him better off and with more power. Consequently, while Arab leaders needed to create some regional association in order to satisfy the aspirations of some domestic constituencies, they also feared that such an association would leave them vulnerable to other Arab leaders and compromise their own political survival. Third, Arab leaders were converging on a practical meaning of "Arab unity" that dismissed unification (at least in the near term) but allowed for a formal association that did not threaten their sovereignty and autonomy.

Following months of informal negotiations and a convergence on a "practical" meaning of Arab unity, the Arab states gathered in Alexandria from 25 September through 6 October 1944 for the first formal round of negotiations. The early part of the conference revolved around unification and various Fertile Crescent schemes, the need for a formal organization, and its possible architecture and machinery.[24] Consistent with prior consultations, Arab delegations quickly discarded unification or federation in favor of a less ambitious design.[25] After two weeks of

[22] Gomaa, *Foundation of the League of Arab States*, p. 165.
[23] Wilson, *King Abdullah, Britain, and the Making of Jordan*, pp. 143–4.
[24] Ansari, *Arab League*, p. 25.
[25] Gomaa, *Foundation of the League of Arab States*, p. 219.

preparatory discussions, the conference created a series of resolutions that became known as the Alexandria Protocols, which attended to five principal issues surrounding the future regional order: (1) creation of the League of Arab States, which included in its constitution pacific dispute settlement, binding decisions, and inter-Arab cooperation; (2) cooperation in social, economic, cultural, and other matters; (3) consolidation of these ties in the future; (4) a special resolution allowing Lebanon to retain its independence and sovereignty; and (5) a special resolution on Palestine and the need to defend Palestinian Arabs.[26] The Protocols were signed on 7 October by all representatives except for Saudi Arabia and Yemen, whose signatures were delayed because they did not have prior authorization,[27] a sure sign of their governments' deeply-held suspicions.

The Protocols had something for everyone. Egyptian Prime Minister Nahhas could feel satisfied that he had controlled the Arab agenda, and, more importantly, scored some political points with domestic opponents of unification. The Lebanese government was pleased to express its Arab orientation without sacrificing its sovereignty or threatening its important Maronite constituency. The Syrian government was able to assert its independence vis-a-vis the French and to move toward a greater alliance with their Arab brethren, a priority of its strong pan-Arab constituencies. Abdullah of Transjordan, though still waiting for Syria, emerged as one of the elder statesmen of the conference. Iraq's Nuri al-Said, though still hoping for something resembling a Fertile Crescent orientation, believed that the conference had taken an important step toward inter-Arab cooperation. Saudi Arabia and Yemen, while concerned with various features of the Protocols, were gratified to realize that there probably would not be either a Fertile Crescent scheme or federation.[28] And the general Arab public greeted the Protocols with accolades and as a symbol of a more independent and grander Arab future.[29]

After six months of negotiations Arab representatives met in Cairo on 22 March and signed the Charter of the League of Arab States (which came into effect on 10 May 1945). Although celebratory toasts boasted of how they had fulfilled Arab nationalism's vision, the Charter in fact represented a victory for sovereignty. Led by Egypt, Saudi Arabia, and Lebanon, the post-Alexandria negotiations had transformed an organization whose ties were supposed to bind into one that clung to sovereignty as an organizing principle and as a defense against both each other's possi-

[26] Ansari, *Arab League*, pp. 28–30; Porath, *In Search of Arab Unity*, pp. 278–83.
[27] Ansari, *Arab League*, pp. 23–5.
[28] Gomaa, *Foundation of the League of Arab States*, pp. 226–35. [29] Ibid., p. 232.

ble intrusions and Arab nationalism's transnational traits.[30] Whereas the Protocols did not prescribe any basis of inter-Arab cooperation except with the goal of unity, the Charter insisted on the "respect for the independence and sovereignty of these states." Whereas the Protocols insisted on periodic meetings, the Charter did no such thing. Whereas the Protocols discussed the importance of binding decisions, the Charter reserved veto power for states. Whereas the Protocols demanded that Arab states adopt a common foreign policy, the Charter insisted that each state be free to pursue its own foreign policy. Whereas the Protocols made no mention of domestic forms of government, the Charter insisted that states respect each other's choice of a system of government. Whereas the Protocols hinted of Arab states yielding their sovereignty to unification, the Charter insisted on the retention of sovereignty (although Article Nine paid homage to the possibility of unification). And, finally, the Arab states debated and eventually discarded any mention of a collective security system or institutionalized military cooperation.[31] Although the Protocols had not demanded much, even that seemed more than Arab states were willing to bear as they watered it down to the point that it demanded very little. This development led Abdullah of Transjordan to characterize the League of Arab States as "a sack in which seven heads have been thrust."[32]

The actual design and scope of the institution reflected the sense that the very Arab identity that brought them together also was viewed by the regimes as a potential threat. *Membership* was limited to independent Arab states, excluding states under colonial arrangements that did not enjoy sovereignty.[33] This was not a "regional" organization to the extent that geography itself determined eligibility for membership. Turkey or Iran were never considered as possible members. Israel, sitting in the middle of the Arab world, would never be invited to the table. To be a member of the *Arab* League meant, quite obviously, that the state be *Arab*.

The general purpose and mandate of the organization was threefold: to strengthen relations between member states; to coordinate their policies to further cooperation and maintain their independence and sovereignty; and to promote the general welfare and interests of the Arab states.

30 Ansari, *Arab League*; Cecil Hourani, "The Arab League in Perspective," pp. 131–2; T. R. Little, "The Arab League: A Reassessment," *Middle East Journal*, 10 (Spring, 1957), pp. 140–1; Baghat Korany, "The Dialectics of Inter-Arab Relations, 1967–87," in Yehuda Lukacs and Abdalla Battah (eds.), *The Arab-Israeli Conflict: Two Decades of Change* (Boulder, CO: Westview Press, 1988), p. 165.

31 Gomaa, *Foundation of the League of Arab States*, p. 240.

32 Ibid., p. 265.

33 According to Article 4 of the Charter, non-members could participate in discussions in technical committees. But, we do not know of a single instance in which that occurred.

Although this might suggest that Arab states were planting the seeds of Arab unity and a federated state, the issues included and excluded suggest otherwise. Areas of close cooperation were limited to technical and non-political issues such as health, economic and financial concerns, communication, and social and cultural affairs. Although Article 9 did mention the desire to strengthen relations between states, the language was watered down and did not explicitly advocate the goal of a unified Arab state. More strikingly, unlike the Alexandria Protocols which explicitly advocated the coordination of foreign policy, the League Charter did not consider the idea of collective defense or a common foreign policy. As Macdonald concludes, "In the vocabulary of functionalism, the primary purpose of the League is to foster non-political activities and only incidentally to enter the political arena."[34] By and large the organization was not intended to promote anything more than functional cooperation and, significantly, was prohibited from engaging in any action that even hinted of circumscribing state sovereignty.

The *formal institutional structure and rules* also reflected the desire to produce a status quo organization with little autonomy to challenge it. The chief organs of the League were the Arab League Council and the Secretariat. The Council's principal duties were to moderate disputes among members and between members and non-members, to deal with relations with the United Nations, and to help coordinate their foreign and defense policies. All members of the Arab League became members of the Council, and each member had a vote. The *formal voting rules* tilt toward consensus on substantive matters. Article 7 stipulates that all substantive matters related to political or security issues, to become binding, require unanimity; majority decisions are binding only on those members that vote for them. The effect of this voting rule was to give each Arab state virtual veto power over any proposed policy and to drive the Arab League to the lowest common denominator on matters of Arab unity. None of this was unintended; they knew that a unanimity principle would make the organization highly inflexible and earth-bound.

There were several reasons for this rule and the drive for a status quo organization.[35] It was in keeping with the times, especially given that the role model was the Council of the League of Nations and the UN Security Council. It reduced the probability that a single power or power bloc might dominate the organization. It also was intended to protect their sovereignty and independence. Macdonald concludes "that the

[34] Robert Macdonald, *The League of Arab States: A Study in the Dynamics of Regional Organization* (Princeton: Princeton University Press, 1965), p. 43.

[35] Ibid., pp. 58–9.

unanimity rule of the League Council serves as a brake on the inherent tendency of the organization either to evolve into a unitary state or to collapse completely."[36] A consequence of this orientation and these various control mechanisms was an Arab League Secretariat that had little autonomy or discretion. Its principal responsibilities were to carry out the instructions of the Council, but the creators showed little interest in investing it with any independent initiative. In sum, Arab leaders designed the Arab League to be an expressive institution emphasizing rhetoric over action, one with little autonomy that would not challenge the status quo or initiate changes that might undermine regime survival.

II: Life after creation

The creation of the Arab League represented a victory for statism. Yet its very creation also gave fundamental and symbolic expression to a shared Arab identity which, leaders proclaimed, was connected to Arab national interests to reduce foreign control, to confront Zionism, and to search for Arab unity.[37] Because these were presumably shared Arab interests, leaders were obligated to proceed multilaterally. By publicly acknowledging a class of issues that properly belonged to the Arab nation they conceded that unilateralism violated norms of Arabism and that Arab states would be mutually accountable and thus mutually constrained in these critical areas. If the Arab League was not exactly empowering the unification movement, at least its hallways created a place for Arab states to congregate, express their preferences, channel their grievances, and, most important, symbolize their commitment to Arab nationalism. This process nearly guaranteed that Arab nationalism would become expressive of their national identity and compelled "every Arab state to become 'unity-minded'."[38]

The Arab League thus became a forum of collective legitimation.[39] Several aspects of this legitimation process shaped the potential opportunities and constraints on the foreign policies of Arab states. To begin, Arab states began to look to the League to establish their Arab

36 Ibid., p. 58.

37 According to a commentator from *The Jerusalem Post*, Arab states had three principal concerns: "Palestine: unity and defiance; the outside world: unity and hope; home politics of the Arab countries where dynastic and economic rivalries are still unsolved: circumspection." 25 March 1945; cited in Gomaa, *Foundation of the League of Arab States*, p. 264.

38 Ansari, *Arab League*, p. 123.

39 Inis L. Claude, Jr., "Collective Legitimization as a Political Function of the United Nations," *International Organization*, 20 (Summer 1966), pp. 368–74.

credentials. An Arab leader seeking to demonstrate that he was a member in good standing would use the League toward this end by participating in its proceedings and by honoring its resolutions. This opportunity also represented a constraint on their foreign policy activities. In order to be counted as a member in good standing, leaders had to abide by the norms of Arabism. Having conceded in practice that on certain issues they must proceed multilaterally, the construction of the League formalized this process. Whatever formal or informal decisions would emerge from their discussions would now act as a normative constraint lest they be accused of violating the norms of Arabism. However much they emphasized sovereignty, they were bound by identity.

These symbolic effects of the League begin to explain two striking features of inter-Arab cooperation between 1945 and 1970. The first was the creation of more restrictive norms that increased constraints on their respective foreign policies. The norms of Arabism created and enshrined in the 1945 Charter of the Arab League imposed very few specific demands on Arab states and were nearly identical to the norms of international society, most importantly, the recognition of state sovereignty. Yet over the next several decades Arab leaders began using norms of Arabism to further their individual interests, thus imposing greater constraints on their own foreign policy.[40] An Arab leader could gain tremendous status if he was viewed at home and abroad as a stalwart champion of Arab nationalism. Each leader had an incentive to demonstrate leadership, and upon taking this stand, it was difficult for other Arab leaders to remain behind for fear of being portrayed as outside the Arab consensus.

The second feature was the enforcement mechanisms that were used to ensure that leaders did not defect from the previously established regional norm. Arab leaders had little incentive to defect from an existing norm when defection was perceived as violating a basic tenet of Arab nationalism; various institutional and extra-institutional mechanisms could punish defection and enforce compliance. However, they did have an incentive to defect from an existing norm if doing so was perceived as a contribution to the goals of Arab nationalism; such defections had immediate payoffs for the leader's regional and domestic standing. Yet because most Arab leaders viewed the norms of Arabism as a potential threat that could reduce their autonomy, they generally preferred

[40] Michael Barnett, *Dialogues in Arab Politics: Negotiations in Regional Order* (New York: Columbia University Press, 1998) calls this symbolic entrapment; and Jack Snyder, *Myths of Empire: Domestic Politics and International Ambition* (Ithaca, NY: Cornell University Press, 1991) calls it blowback.

to avoid a collective defection (a suboptimal outcome) that increased political, economic, and security integration. Leaders could not publicly oppose these attempts to strengthen the Arab nation because doing so would enable others to challenge their credentials. Hence, they had to develop extra-institutional mechanisms to enforce compliance with the *status quo ante*. We explore how the politics of Arab identity and regime survival, alongside the existence of institutional and extra-institutional enforcement mechanisms, led to symbolic cooperation in the cases of King Abdullah's aborted peace treaty with Israel in 1949, the Arab Collective Security Pact of 1950, and the Baghdad Pact of 1955.

A separate peace?

Following the UN partition of Palestine in 1947, the Arab League declared that it would not recognize a state for the Jews in Palestine and encouraged members to act militarily.[41] Egypt, Syria, Lebanon, Transjordan, and Iraq attacked the newly created state of Israel in 1948. The 1948–1949 war represented a defeat not only for Palestinians but also for all Arab leaders associated with the war, who mistrusted each other's personal ambitions vis-a-vis Palestine. Many had committed troops to the cause of Palestine because they wanted to appear to be contributing to the Arab cause, but their half-hearted efforts did little for either the Palestinians or their own goal of self-aggrandizement. The loss of Palestine suggested that the immediate causes of Arab weakness were irresoluteness, incompetence, corruption, rivalries, and disunity, and "served to confirm pre-existing beliefs about the perennial backwardness of Arab society."[42] Consequently, not only did the war deposit greater animosity toward the new Jewish state, but the masses, the military, and the intelligentsia were now more than ever opposed to the regimes in power and more emboldened in indicting their leadership and legitimacy. Military officials returning from Palestine, intellectuals, and the masses arrived at the conclusion that "the enemy is us."[43]

While various Arab states dealt with the practical need of establishing armistice agreements with Israel, Jordan used the armistice discussions to continue pre-war negotiations with the Israelis regarding the possibility of commercial dealings, a non-aggression pact, and a peace treaty. Although Abdullah hoped that a peace treaty might accomplish a variety of goals, his

[41] Dawisha, *Arab Nationalism*, pp. 128–9.
[42] Leila S. Kadi, *Arab Summit Conferences and the Palestine Problem* (Beirut: Research Centre, Palestine Liberation Organization, 1966), p. 85.
[43] Itamar Rabinovich, *The Road Not Taken: Early Arab-Israeli Negotiations* (New York: Oxford University Press, 1991), p. 19.

primary desire was to complete his annexation of the West Bank.[44] Israel and Jordan neared a non-aggression pact in the early months of 1950, and to prepare the groundwork Abdullah attempted to force his Council of Ministers to accept the principle of commercial relations with Israel. This ultimatum produced a governmental crisis that eventually led to the collapse of the cabinet and publicized Abdullah's plans for a separate peace with Israel and annexation of the West Bank. Arab governments responded swiftly and severely. Egypt portrayed Jordan as an enemy of Arabism and Israel's co-conspirator, Abdullah was vilified throughout the region, many recommended Jordan's expulsion from the League if Abdullah concluded a separate peace treaty or annexed the West Bank, and the Syrian prime minister threatened to close the Syrian border if Abdullah proceeded as planned. While Abdullah attempted to deflect the criticism by claiming that his approach alone would solve the refugee crisis and produce a just peace,[45] he was increasingly isolated.

Arab leaders gathered in Cairo for the twelfth Arab League session from 25 March through 13 April 1950, focusing on how to stop Abdullah and, if that failed, how to punish him. At stake, however, was not only Abdullah's plan but perhaps the very future of the Arab League. Much commentary at the time revolved around the fact that the League had been ineffectual in confronting the Zionist challenge and that Arab states had negotiated separately rather than collectively after the war. Now it appeared that Abdullah, and perhaps others, were about to conclude a separate peace treaty with Israel leading some to wonder: what was the point of the League?[46] Arab leaders rejected Egypt's proposal that they expel Jordan from the Arab League in favor of a strongly worded resolution, adopted unanimously on 1 April, that prohibited any Arab state from negotiating or concluding "a separate peace or any political, military or economic agreement with Israel."[47] A few days later the League determined that a possible violation would be referred to the Political

[44] Avi Shlaim, *Collusion Across the Jordan: King Abdullah, the Zionist Movement, and the Partition of Palestine* (New York: Columbia University Press, 1988), pp. 359–60; Rabinovich, *The Road Not Taken*, pp. 118–19.

[45] Rabinovich, *The Road Not Taken*, pp. 139–41.

[46] "League's Future Hangs on Cairo Session," Tunis, in Arabic, 26 March 1950; cited in *Foreign Broadcast Information Service (FBIS)*, 28 March 1950, no. 60, p. 3. Although Jordan initially refused to attend the meetings, citing a hostile Egyptian press and Egypt's failure to carry out their previous agreement that Egypt was to oversee Gaza and Jordan the West Bank, it quickly determined that it had more to lose by staying away than by facing a hostile crowd. "Amman States Position on Arab League," Jerusalem (Jordan), March 28, 1950; cited in *FBIS*, 29 March 1950, no. 63, p. 1.

[47] "Arab League's Resolution," Beirut, 30 March 1950; cited in *FBIS*, 31 March 1950, no. 63, p.14. "League Approves Defense, Economic Pact," Cairo, Egyptian Home Service, 14 April 1950; cited in *FBIS*, 17 April 1950, no. 74, p.1.

Committee to consider whether such a violation had occurred; that such a decision would be binding if four states agreed to it; and that possible penalties included severing political and diplomatic relations, closing common borders, and prohibiting all financial or commercial transactions with the violator. Relations of any kind with Israel were now taboo.

Although Abdullah bristled at this intrusion on his foreign policy, he eventually listened to his advisers, who warned him that flaunting the League's decisions would invite further domestic and regional condemnation, and jeopardize his ultimate goal of smooth elections on the West and East Banks – if not also his crown.[48] After holding a quick-and-dirty local election, on 24 April Abdullah announced the unity of the two banks under the Hashemite crown, citing the legality of his actions from past Arab League resolutions and from a plebiscite on the West Bank, portraying his decision as a step toward "real union."[49] His announcement led to widespread disapproval, charges of betrayal, and calls for his expulsion from the League, and an unconciliatory Abdullah dared other Arab leaders to punish him.[50]

Seeing a good opportunity to solidify its Arab credentials, Egypt called Abdullah's bluff and pushed for expulsion, all the while assuming that other Arab states would oppose such a severe sentence. Eventually the Arab League struck upon a compromise charging that Jordan's decision was a product of expediency dictated by the facts on the ground, and that the territories should be held in trust until the liberation of all the pre-1948 territories (i.e. until Israel itself was undone). In the end, Arab leaders resigned themselves to Jordan's annexation of the West Bank, though none ever formally acknowledged the move.[51] Although the Arab League never did punish him, he met a harsher fate and the most violent

[48] Shlaim, *Collusion Across the Jordan*, pp. 554–5; Maddy-Weitzman, *The Crystallization of the Arab State System*, pp. 130–5; Rabinovich, *The Road Not Taken*, pp. 148–9; Aqil Hyder Hasan Abidi, *Jordan: A Political Study* (New York: Asia Publishing House, 1965), pp. 77–8.

[49] "Jordan Announces Official Annexation," Jerusalem (Jordan), 24 April 1950; cited in *FBIS*, 25 April 1950, no. 80, pp. 7–10. Also see Abidi, *Jordan: A Political Study*, pp. 75–6; Shlaim, *Collusion Across the Jordan*, p. 558.

[50] "Abdullah's Real Motive Held Expansion," Cairo, Egyptian Home Service, 24 April 1950; cited in *FBIS*, 26 April 1950, no. 81, p. 10. "Syria States Case Against Annexation," Damascus, 22 April 1950; cited in *FBIS*, 24 April 1950, no. 79, pp. 1–4. "Abdullah Scorns League," 22 April 1950; cited in *FBIS*, 24 April 1950, no. 79, p. 5. Also see Martin Sicker, *Between Hashemites and Zionists: The Struggle for Palestine, 1908–1988* (New York: Holmes and Meier, 1989), p. 108.

[51] There is evidence, however, that King Faruq and King Abdullah made a backroom deal – that Abdullah would abandon his search for a separate peace with Israel in exchange for being allowed to annex the West Bank. Rabinovich, *The Road Not Taken*, p. 184.

of sanctions on 20 July 1951 when he was assassinated at the al-Aqsa mosque in Jerusalem.

Arab Collective Security Pact

During preparatory discussions Arab leaders had largely rejected a formal military alliance of any kind and closed the door to political integration, symptomatic of their general distaste for entangling alliances. Yet the discourse of Arabism, as embodied in the Arab League, held out the promise for just these sorts of collective projects. The challenge for Arab states such as Egypt and Saudi Arabia, who favored the status quo and were adamantly opposed to such possibilities, was to find various institutional and extra-institutional mechanisms to enforce this "cooperative" outcome and ensure that there were no defections. The trick, though, was to make it appear as if they were attempting to strengthen Arabism when they were doing nothing of the sort. These mixed motives help explain how and why Arab leaders decided to invest the League with the very security profile that they had previously rejected.

Although the Arab states had rejected unification during negotiations over the Arab League, a body of public opinion, particularly in the Fertile Crescent, continued to champion it, to view individual states as artificial entities, and to consider the idea of unification as a way to respond to their weakness, made apparent with the defeat in the Palestine war. There were various unification proposals between 1945 and 1955 but none more credible than a proposed Syrian–Iraqi unification in fall 1949.[52] This chapter opened on 30 March 1949, when Syrian Army Chief of Staff Husni Za'im overthrew President Qwattli, the first coup in the Arab world. Motivated largely by his desire to strengthen his hand vis-a-vis Israel at the Rhodes armistice talks and establish his Arab

[52] For instance, in March 1946 on the occasion of the first Parliament, and again in fall 1946 and early 1947 King Abdullah raised the idea of a "Greater Syria" to include Lebanon, Syria, and Transjordan. Seale, *The Struggle for Syria*, p. 13; Shlaim, *Collusion Across the Jordan*, pp. 85–6; Wilson, *King Abdullah, Britain, and the Making of Jordan*, pp. 157–60. This debate, like others that would transpire for the next decade, ended at the Arab League. Meeting in late November 1946, the Arab states agreed to honor each other's sovereignty and to cease all discussion of the Greater Syria proposal. Maddy-Weitzman, *The Crystallization of the Arab State System*, p. 39. In April 1947, Jordan and Iraq were rumored to be preparing a draft unification agreement, but ultimately signed only an alliance. Seale, *The Struggle for Syria*, p. 14; and "Iraq and Transjordan Sign Alliance," Sharq al-Adna, 14 April 1947; cited in *FBIS*, April 15 1947, no. 37. In fall 1947, Abdullah once again raised the idea of Greater Syria, though his timing, when the UN was debating Palestine, caused many Arab states to publicly ponder whether there was not a link between Abdullah's proposals and British and Zionist interests in the region. Maddy-Weitzman, *The Crystallization of the Arab State System*, p. 42.

credentials, Za'im immediately proposed that Iraq and Syria conclude a defense treaty.[53] Although a defense treay proved elusive, its very prospect stimulated discussions about future regional arrangements and competition among Arab states for Syria's favor.[54] Unification talk re-emerged after the overthrow of Za'im by Sami al-Hinnawi on 14 August 1949,[55] and soon thereafter Hinnawi recommended that Syria and Iraq unify, a proposal born from Arabist sentiments and fear of Israel.[56] Negotiations proceeded cautiously through the fall and then ultimately failed; a republican and independence-minded Syria was suspicious of a monarchical Iraq that had a defense treaty with Britain.[57]

Still, unification talk filled the airwaves. The debate shifted from the newspapers and the Syrian–Iraqi negotiating table to Cairo for the Arab League meeting in October, 1949 where Iraq presented the proposed union to the Council, emphasizing its consistency with Article 9 of the League Charter.[58] Jordan favored unification. However, Egyptian, Saudi, and Lebanese leaders had strong reservations although they could not publicly oppose unification.[59] As the Iraqi newspaper *al-Nida* wondered: how could Egypt oppose a plan that was designed to confront Israel and realize the aspirations of the Arabs?[60] The anti-union forces would have to devise another device to stop the drive for unification.

[53] Maddy-Weitzman, *The Crystallization of the Arab State System*, p. 107; Gordon H. Torrey, *Syrian Politics and the Military, 1945–1958* (Columbus: Ohio State University Press, 1964), pp. 134–5; Seale, *The Struggle for Syria*, p. 48.

[54] Malik Mufti, *Sovereign Creations: Pan-Arabism and Political Order in Syria and Iraq* (Ithaca, NY: Cornell University Press, 1996), pp. 51–2. Egypt and Iraq had a tendency to play out their own rivalries on Syrian soil, each buying Syrian politicians and competing for advantage in Syrian politics. Cairo and Baghdad tried to break this dynamic by drafting an agreement in December 1949 that pledged them to respect Syria's political integrity. The Iraqi architects of the agreement, who also pledged to help Syria forge a proper constitution that would facilitate stability, were accused of being weak on Egypt, and had to resign as a consequence. Elie Podeh, *The Quest for Hegemony in the Arab World: The Struggle over the Baghdad Pact* (New York: E. J. Brill, 1995), p. 82.

[55] See Seale, *The Struggle for Syria*, pp. 47–56, for a discussion of these talks.

[56] Torrey, *Syrian Politics and the Military*, pp. 153–4; Seale, *The Struggle for Syria*, pp. 77–83.

[57] Malcom H. Kerr, *The Arab Cold War, 1958–1964: A Study of Ideology in Politics* (New York: Oxford University Press, 1965), p. 3; Seale, *The Struggle for Syria*, pp. 15 and 79–81.

[58] "Iraq Press Comments on Council Union," Baghdad, 19 October 1949; cited in *FBIS*, 20 October 1949, no. 203, p. 2.

[59] "Shamoun States Arab Unity Conditions," Damascus, cited in *FBIS*, 8 September 1949, no. 173. Lebanon expressed its reservations toward the plan, including that it not intrude on Lebanon's sovereignty, not impose any military or financial obligations, and that it facilitate economic relations. "Lebanese Reservations," Jerusalem, Jordan-controlled, 6 November 1949; cited in *FBIS*, 7 November 1949, no. 212, pp. 4–5.

[60] "Egypt Blamed for Anti-Union Campaign," Baghdad, 20 October 1949; cited in *FBIS*, 21 October 1949, no. 204, p. 4.

Building on nationalism, the desire for unity, the reluctance to rely on Britain for defense assistance, and the fear of Israel, Egypt ingeniously proposed a collective security pact.[61] By injecting this motion, the meeting became a contest between Iraq's unification plan – an Iraq that was closely tied to Britain and a plan that was restricted to Syria – and Egypt's defense plan – which would be inclusive and perhaps a better solution to Syria's defense concerns because it included Egypt, the Arab world's largest state and one that also bordered Israel.

Egypt's strategy worked. The all-Arab military agreement became the focal point of the meetings, the Arab League adopted the military plan proposed by Egypt, and the League decided not to "touch the question of Iraqi–Syrian rapprochement since it is an internal affair which should not be interfered with."[62] Egypt used collective security to defeat a unification plan and to institutionalize sovereignty, and the League's decision not to formally consider the unification proposal under the guise of the principle of non-interference worked to the same end. Not unlike the talks that led to the creation of the Arab League, Egypt used a multilateral forum to, first, frustrate Iraq and its goal of unification, and, second, re-enforce the principle of state sovereignty and territoriality. Most importantly, Syrians who either opposed unification and/or saw the Iraqi proposal as a mechanism to increase Syria's security against Israel now embraced collective security as a viable alternative to unity with Iraq.[63] Iraq's pitch for unification had been thwarted. Visibly bitter about the League's deliberations and conclusions, Nuri al-Said characterized the military pact as a substitute for action and an attempt to block the proposed Iraqi–Syrian unification, and lamented the fact that "nations with no ties of language or religion or history [are] joining together through pacts and treaties [that are] stronger than those between the Arab League states." He also

[61] Egypt also submitted a memorandum requesting the Syrian government to reject the proposed agreement because it did not represent its people until after the elections. "Arab Political Discussions Cancelled," Tel-Aviv, 19 September 1949; cited in *FBIS*, 20 September 1949, no. 181.

[62] "Committee Adopts Military Plan," Sharq al-Adna, 23 October 1949; cited in *FBIS*, October 24 1949, no. 205, pp. 1–2. For the text, see "Clauses of the Arab Security Pact Revealed," Sharq al-Adna, 29 October 1949; cited in *FBIS*, 31 October 1949, no. 209, PP1–2. Also see Seale, *The Struggle for Syria*, pp. 90–1; Podeh, *The Quest for Hegemony in the Arab World*, p. 46.

[63] "Syria Tells Iraq Union Impossible Now," Beirut, in Arabic, 8 December 1949; cited in *FBIS*, 9 December 1949, no. 237, p. 4. "Hannawi Thinks Security Plan Essential," Beirut, in Arabic, 28 October 1949; cited in *FBIS*, 31 October 1949, no. 209, p. 4. Other reports, however, stated that the army was divided. See "Syrian Army Divided on Iraqi Union," Cairo, Egyptian Home Service, 7 November 1949; cited in *FBIS*, 8 November 1949, no. 215, p. 7. "Faris al-Khuri Speaks on Arab Unity," 21 September 1949; cited in *FBIS*, 23 September 1949, no. 184; 27 October 1949, no. 208, p. 3.

observed that the Arab League was founded on and continued to permeate "chaos," as evident from the Palestine war defeat. Not only did Arab states lack a union but they even lacked any "operative military alliance." He then issued a challenge. Either:

> we cooperate in a manner compatible with our Governments' responsibilities . . . , or we lay down another charter for our League under which every Arab government will openly give up some of its rights and authority as an independent sovereign state. A combination of these two alternatives is nothing but a kind of chaos which will lead us into stumbling upon one failure after another and going from bad to worse.[64]

Nuri dared Egyptian and other Arab leaders to stop using institutional devices and the cloak of collectivism to preserve their own independence and frustrate inter-Arab cooperation.

The Egyptian proposal provided the foundation for the Treaty of Joint Defense and Economic Cooperation Among the States of the Arab League, better known as the Arab Collective Security Pact (ACSP). Signed 13 April 1950, the Arab states pledged to settle their conflicts through non-violent means (Article 1), to engage in collective defense (Article 2), and to integrate their military and foreign policies (Article 5).[65] The Arab states never implemented the conditions of the treaty, which was hardly surprising since Egypt had proposed the treaty to block unification and not to further it.

Baghdad Pact

During conversations preceding the establishment of the League, Arab leaders had rejected restrictions on the sorts of alliances that they might entertain. At that moment many were receiving considerable economic and military assistance from Western powers and, while Arabism had an important element of anti-colonialism, it could include alliances if they did not appear to compromise Arab state sovereignty. However, the regional climate changed in the late 1940s. The Cold War descended on the Middle East and Western governments expected Arab leaders to fall into place in the emerging containment system. The West was making these demands at the very moment that a new generation of Arab leaders, many avowedly nationalist and highly sensitive to any hint of

[64] "Nuri: League Chaos Causes Problems," Beirut, 24 October 1949; cited in *FBIS*, 25 October 1949, no. 206, pp. 1–3.

[65] See Seale, *The Struggle for Syria*, pp. 90–1, for a discussion of the events leading to the Treaty. See Alan B. Taylor, *The Arab Balance of Power* (Syracuse: Syracuse University Press, 1982), pp. 125–7, for the text.

colonial privileges, began to push for full independence and to remove the stain of colonialism. The most famous was Nasser of Egypt. At first he was more an Egyptian than an Arab nationalist, but quickly discovered that Arab nationalism could be wielded to increase his own power and Egypt's role in regional and world politics. Importantly, he was not adamantly opposed to Arab alliances with the West, though he did expect that any such alliance must receive his personal blessing and improve Egypt's position. If not, he would find whatever means, institutional or extra-institutional, to stop it.

The prelude to the Baghdad Pact was the declaration of the Turko–Pakistani agreement of April 1954 that, although not including an Arab state, involved two Muslim states and was widely seen by Arab leaders as the West's "calling card" to the region. Egypt and Iraq took the lead in the region-wide debate over the Arab position on strategic relations with the West. Egypt's initial position was that any discussion was premature until the Suez Canal dispute was settled; this obstacle was overcome with the initialing of an agreement on 27 July 1954 (formally signed on 19 October). Still, Nasser and Egyptian public opinion remained cool to a Western-led defense arrangement. Indeed, Nasser and British Minister of State Nutting held talks on the subject after signing the Suez Canal Treaty.[66] Not so Iraqi Prime Minister Nuri al-Said, who welcomed the idea of an alliance and began seeking Arab allies to join him, or at least not block his path. Realizing that he needed Egypt's blessing, Baghdad and Cairo undertook a series of meetings, which resulted in either a green or red light, depending on whether one believes the Iraqi or the Egyptian version of events.[67]

The Arab foreign ministers met in Cairo in December, 1954, with the goal of creating some guidelines concerning their future relationship to the West and the conditions under which an Arab state might join a Western-led alliance.[68] Nasser took a rejectionist stance and urged those in attendance to follow Egypt's example by: constructing resolutions that reflected the needs of the Arab nation; pledging against joining any outside alliance; and emphasizing their reliance on the Collective Security Pact.[69] This they did. The foreign ministers crafted two

[66] Seale, *The Struggle for Syria*, p. 96.

[67] Podeh, *The Quest for Hegemony in the Arab World*, pp. 83–8; Seale, *The Struggle for Syria*, pp. 204–8; Mohamed H. Heikal, *Cutting the Lion's Tail: Suez Through Egyptian Eyes* (New York: Arbor House, 1987), pp. 53 and 57.

[68] These regional discussions over the West's overtures had domestic implications; for instance, they were a major topic of the Syrian elections in September, 1954. Seale, *The Struggle for Syria*, p. 164.

[69] "Egypt to Depend on Arab Defense Pact," Cairo, Egyptian Home Service, 10 December 1954; cited in *FBIS*, 10 December 1954, no. 239, A1.

resolutions: (1) "that no alliance should be concluded outside the fold of the Collective Arab Security Pact"; and (2) "that cooperation with the West was possible, provided that a just solution was found for Arab problems and provided the Arabs were allowed to build up their strength with gifts of arms."[70] Egypt, which had overseen the writing of the Arab League Charter with an eye toward stopping unification and preserving sovereignty and had then designed the ACSP as a method to halt the possible Syrian–Iraqi unification in 1949, now used the ACSP to slow down Iraq's planned alliance with the West. Echoing the neutrality that became a hallmark of Nasser's foreign policy, the foreign ministers proclaimed that the "burden of the defense of the Arab East should fall on the states of the area alone, and that the question of putting the Collective Security Pact into effect has become timely and inevitable if the Arab States are to form a united front in political affairs and defense against any foreign danger that may threaten any or all of them."[71] The foreign ministers publicly proclaimed that they must coordinate policies as Arab states.

No sooner had the meeting adjourned than rumors swirled concerning Iraq's possible alliance with the West. Nasser responded by unleashing a media tirade against Iraq, with his stated objections centering on the claim that any alliance would only safeguard the interests of the West and harm those of the Arab nation, and that Arab states should seek neutrality and security in their unity.[72] More importantly, such an alliance would also harm Egypt's standing, leaving it isolated and possibly facing the threat of Israel on its own.[73] Effectively, Nasser's own prestige was on the line, as King Hussein observed.[74] Nasser's efforts had little apparent effect for on 13 January 1955 Iraq and Turkey announced that they would sign a defense agreement in the near future. In presenting his case to the Iraqi people and the Arab world, Nuri claimed that the Pact was consistent with the Charter of the League of Arab States and Article 51 of the UN, and that it furthered the goals of the Arab world.[75]

[70] Seale, *The Struggle for Syria*, p. 211. Also see Podeh, *The Quest for Hegemony in the Arab World*, pp. 98–9.

[71] "Middle East Defense Talks Discussed," Cairo, Egyptian Home Service, 7 December 1954; cited in *FBIS*, 8 December 1954, no. 237, A2.

[72] Podeh, *The Quest for Hegemony in the Arab World*, p. 66.

[73] Podeh, *The Quest for Hegemony in the Arab World*; Fawaz A. Gerges, *The Superpowers and the Middle East: Regional and International Politics* (Boulder, CO: Westview Press, 1994), p. 25; Ali E. Hillal Dessouki, "Nasser and the Struggle for Independence," in Roger Owen and William Roger Louis (eds.), *Suez 1956: The Crisis and Its Consequences* (New York: Oxford University Press, 1989), p. 36.

[74] Hussein, King of Jordan, *Uneasy Lies the Head* (London: Heineman, 1962), p. 84.

[75] "Iraq Reaffirms Adherence to Arab League," Baghdad, Iraqi Home Service, 18 January 1955; cited in *FBIS*, 19 January 1955, no. 13, A5. "Iraq to Sign Defense Pact with

Iraq's announcement triggered outrage across the Arab world. Nasser framed the Baghdad Pact as a grave challenge to Arab nationalism and Arab security. Responding to whether Iraq, as a sovereign state, had the right to enter into any treaty it saw fit, Egyptian Interior Minister Salim Salim retorted: "Although Iraq is an independent sovereign state, she nevertheless has obligations and responsibilities toward the League of Arab States and the Arab Collective Security Pact. Is there any state, in the Atlantic Pact, for example, free to make any decisions it chooses even if it be contrary to that pact?"[76] If Arab states could not honor the decisions of the most recent conference and coordinate their foreign policies prior to any formal agreement with the West, then Arab nationalism and the Arab League were finished.[77]

To forge a common front against Iraq, Nasser hosted other Arab leaders from 22 January through 6 February. Although Arab representatives publicly proclaimed their outrage at Iraq's actions, privately they were less exercised and some even contemplated following Baghdad rather than Cairo. Saudi Arabia's position was closest to Egypt's for it feared that its traditional Hashemite rivals in Jordan and Iraq would use its new-found resources and prestige to launch another bid for Fertile Crescent unification, a threat to the Saudi regime's external and internal stability.[78] Yemen, too, came out against the Pact. Syria, Lebanon, and Jordan were less appalled and somewhat approving, in part because they saw little controversy in such an alliance and were actively contemplating offers from the West at that very moment.

Turkey," Baghdad, Iraqi Home Service, 13 January 1955; cited in *FBIS*, 13 January 1955, no. 9, A2. "Iraq Denies Disagreement on Pact," Baghdad, Iraqi Home Service, 21 January 1955; cited in *FBIS*, 24 January 1955, no. 16, A10. In a later attempt to defend himself against criticism and of having violated the norms of Arabism, Nuri al-Said claimed that Egypt had prior knowledge of and consented to Iraq's alliance with Turkey. "Premier Reviews Defense Talks with Egypt," Baghdad, Iraqi Home Service, 6 February 1955; cited in *FBIS*, 7 February 1955, no. 26, A6–10.

[76] "Salim Answers Questions," 16 January 1955; cited in *FBIS-MES*, 17 January 1955, no. 11, A7.

[77] Muhammad Khalil, *The Arab States and the Arab League: A Documentary Record*, vols. 1 and 2 (Beirut: Khayat's, 1962), pp. 229–30. "Arab Premiers Called to Discuss Iraqi Action," Cairo, Egyptian Home Service, 16 January 1955; cited in *FBIS*, 17 January 1955, no. 11, A1–2. "Iraq Action Endangers Arab Nationalism," Cairo, Egyptian Home Service, 17 January 1955; cited in *FBIS*, 18 January 1955, no. 12, A1. "Iraqi Moves Seen as a Plot Against Arab Unity," Cairo, Egyptian Home Service, 18 January 1955; cited in *FBIS*, 19 January 1955, no. 13, A2.

[78] "Amir Faysal's Statement," Cairo, Egyptian Home Service, 22 January 1955; cited in *FBIS*, 24 January 1955, no. 16, A5; Nadav Safran, *Saudi Arabia: The Ceaseless Quest for Security* (Ithaca, NY: Cornell University Press, 1988), pp. 78–9; Gerges, *The Superpowers and the Middle East*, p. 25; Podeh, *The Quest for Hegemony in the Arab World*, pp. 193 and 206.

Nasser attempted to convince Syria, Jordan, and Lebanon to condemn and censure Baghdad and challenged his fellow Arab leaders to answer Baghdad with strong action, including the "establishment of a unified Arab army under one command along the same lines as the proposed European army."[79] At first the other Arab leaders could not be moved, but Nasser's threat to go to the press and suspend Egypt's relations with them convinced them to fall into line.[80]

Iraq and Turkey formally signed the Pact on 24 February, which inaugurated a new round of competition between Nasser and Nuri for the hearts and minds in the Arab world. Initially many Syrian nationalists had welcomed the Pact because it might generate aid, increase security against Israel, and perhaps even professionalize the military and keep it in the barracks and out of politics.[81] To reinforce anti-Pact forces Egypt proposed a "federal union" with a joint military command and unified foreign policies in lieu of the now defunct collective security pact. Syrian leaders viewed this proposal with suspicion.[82] In his lobbying efforts, Nasser got some timely and unintended help from Israel. On 28 February, just four days after the Treaty's signing, Israel attacked a military installation in Gaza. Nasser quickly capitalized on the assault by claiming that it was coordinated with, and enabled by, the Baghdad Pact,[83] and found himself riding a tide of popular support as protests erupted against the Pact throughout the Arab world.[84] In Syria, Israel's attack increased domestic pressures against the Pact and in favor of an alliance with Egypt as a deterrent to Israel.[85] The army was now so determined to create a defensive alliance against Israel that several Syrian military officers threatened a coup d'état unless Syria joined an alliance with Egypt.[86]

[79] "Nasser Presents Joint Defense Plan," Limassol, Sharq al-Adna, 26 January 1955; cited in *FBIS-MES*, 26 January 1955, no. 18, A1.
[80] Heikal, *Cutting the Lion's Tail*, pp. 56–8.
[81] Torrey, *Syrian Politics and the Military*, p. 270.
[82] Seale, *The Struggle for Syria*, p. 223.
[83] "Israeli Attack the Result of Turko-Iraqi Pact," Cairo, Voice of Arabs, 1 March 1955; cited in *FBIS*, 2 March 1955, no. 41, A3–4.
[84] The Bandung conference took place during the debate over the Pact in mid-April. Its spirited rhetoric of anti-colonialism, independence, and rejection of alliances with the West had a major impact on Nasser as he became more insistent on the importance of "neutrality." Podeh, *The Quest for Hegemony in the Arab World*, p. 149, convincingly argues that the conference reinforced Nasser's understanding of the logical connection between neutrality and Arab nationalism, that nationalism could be best served through a policy of neutrality. Also see Georgiana Stevens, "Arab Neutralism and Bandung," *Middle East Journal*, 11:2, 1957, pp. 139–52.
[85] "Syria Supports United Army Plan," Cairo, Egyptian Home Service, 28 February 1955; cited in *FBIS*, 1 March 1955, no. 40, A1–2; Podeh, *The Quest for Hegemony in the Arab World*, p. 129; Seale, *The Struggle for Syria*, pp. 130–1.
[86] Podeh, *The Quest for Hegemony in the Arab World*, p. 144.

On 6 March Egypt, Syria, and Saudi Arabia pledged to create their own alliance, which they called the "Tripartite Alliance," and included among its provisions a rejection of the Baghdad Pact and the strengthening of collective Arab defense.[87] Syrian Foreign Minister Khalid al-Azm noted that Jordan could not join the alliance because its army was controlled by Britain and therefore ineligible to serve in the United Arab Command,[88] but nevertheless insisted that the pact not "exclude Iraq or preclude the possibility of member states joining the Iraq–Turkey Pact."[89] The value of the Egyptian–Syrian–Saudi alliance from the Egyptian and Saudi perspective was not its deterrent effect but rather its ability to halt Syria's leadership from following Iraq's footsteps.[90] Yet Syria's future relationship to the Baghdad Pact remained a matter of debate until Nasser signed the Czech arms deal, which suggested new possibilities for demonstrating autonomy and defiance of the West.

Jordan was the final battleground. Here Nasser demonstrated his ability to mobilize the streets in Amman in his favor and to essentially imprison the young King Hussein. Riots swept through Jordan, forcing one government after another to fall. After losing two prime ministers, experiencing a near civil war, and imposing a state of emergency, Hussein consented to allow the new Jordanian government to proclaim a "no new pacts" pledge. Hussein, reeling from the challenges to his rule, began an effort to repair his stained image by emphasizing his Arab credentials and espousing "anti-Western" leanings.

Summing up, these three snapshots – in 1949, 1950, and 1955 – reveal the centrality of regime survival to Arab leaders in the early decades of post-colonial state-building. Notwithstanding initial commitments to an institution asserting individual sovereignty, momentous domestic and trans-regional pressures to deliver on issues of Arab nationalism led to progressively more constraining norms and tougher penalties for defiance. Transformations in the domestic political economies, beginning with Egypt's 1952 revolution, solidified these tendencies to resort to Arabism as a powerful instrument of domestic mobilization. Leaders and

[87] Torrey, *Syrian Politics and the Military*, pp. 279–80; Podeh, *The Quest for Hegemony in the Arab World*, p. 129; "Communiqué on Talks Between Egypt, Syria, and Saudi Arabia," in Muhammad Khalil, *The Arab States and the Arab League: A Documentary Record*, vols. 1 and 2, p. 240; "Arab States Sign New Alliance," Damascus, 6 March 1955; cited in *FBIS*, 7 March 1955, no. 45, A1–3. Soon thereafter Yemen announced its support for the alliance. "Yemen Announces Support of New Arab Pact," Damascus, 10 March 1955; cited in *FBIS*, 10 March 1955, no. 48, A7.

[88] "Azm Comments on New Arab Alliance," Damascus, 10 March 1955; cited in *FBIS*, 11 March 1955, no. 49, A7.

[89] Quoted from Podeh, *The Quest for Hegemony in the Arab World*, p. 144.

[90] Seale, *The Struggle for Syria*, pp. 224–25.

their supportive coalitions emphasized economic self-reliance and state dominance of the economy while warning against Western colonialism. The concept (albeit not the reality) of Arab unity provided an invaluable tool to mask what was at heart an inward-looking, state-building political strategy of regime survival. Arabism became a powerful tool of domination in the hands of regimes that relied on the military as an instrument of control by ethnic minorities or tribes, as with Syria's Alawi, Jordan's Hashemite officer corps, and Iraq's predominantly Takriti Sunni military command.[91]

Our account highlights how Arab leaders competed for the status of standard-bearer of Arab ideals and interests, a competition that worked to undermine regional institutional cooperation. This competitive outbidding extended to a contest over who would provide the best exemplar of a self-reliant, military-endowed, import-substituting, state entrepreneurial model capable of guiding the rest of the Arab world into a more powerful future. While proposing a union with Syria in 1958 (and Iraq later), Nasser attempted to impose Egypt's own version of political and economic institutions, triggering anti-union opposition among adversely affected Syrian factions, from agriculture and commerce to the military itself. The very nature and logic of these regimes – protectionist, inward-looking, and pivoted on the military – created strong incentives against more binding regional institutional forms that might put coalitional allies (state and military enterprises, for instance) literally out of business.[92]

As a result of these competitive dynamics, economic barriers never receded, inter-Arab trade remained between seven and ten percent of their total trade since the 1950s, and intra-regional capital movements within the Arab world stayed insignificant. The Arab Common Market (1965, Egypt, Iraq, Jordan, and Syria) and many other similar efforts and agencies under the Arab League existed largely on paper, without much effective impact. Integrative political schemes among Egypt, Syria, Iraq, Libya, Algeria, Sudan, and Tunisia never lasted far beyond the declaratory stage. This historical account confirms Noble's depiction of interactions among Arab regimes during this period, where persuasion, diplomacy, or economic inducements were not a favored strategy. Instead, he argues, "Arab governments relied primarily on unconventional coercive techniques," including "strong attacks on the leadership of other states, propaganda campaigns to mobilize opposition, and intense subversive

[91] Saudi Arabia's Sudairi clan was more oriented to an Islamist collective referent, rather than a pan-Arab one, Solingen, *Regional Orders*. See also Solingen, "Pax Asiatica versus Belli Levantini."

[92] On Syria's Ba'ath military's lack of enthusiasm for "unions," see Stephen M. Walt, *The Origins of Alliances* (Ithaca, NY: Cornell University Press, 1987), p. 209.

pressures, including cross-frontier alliances with dissatisfied individuals and groups. The aim was to destabilize and ultimately overthrow opposing governments."[93] The Arab League not only failed to tame competitive outbidding along political, economic, and normative lines but indeed provided a stage for that competition.

III: The Arab League and its alternatives after the 1970s

The 1970s unleashed changes in both the domestic coalitional landscape and the content of Arabism that had repercussions for regional institutional cooperation. First, severe strains in the inward-looking strategy forced incipient policies of economic liberalization (*infitah*), exports, and growth, particularly in Egypt, Tunisia, and Morocco. The policy required fostering new political sources of support, at home and abroad (i.e. in the West), even as it triggered significant opposition from domestic beneficiaries of the old strategy. Second, these trends reinforced a weakening of Arabism and its perceived legacy of failed unity, truncated progress, and futile promises of collective empowerment through the Arab League. An implicit belief began taking hold among some Arab leaders and government officials that the rise of territorial nationalism (*wataniya*), that is, the acceptance of each other's separate sovereignties, might actually make cooperation less threatening and more efficacious.

Although *infitah* progressed excruciatingly slowly, it did provide modest new incentives to transform domestic political arrangements, relations with the West, and, in time, some regional interactions. To a significant extent, Sadat's initiatives must be seen in that light. Specifically, facing a country bankrupted by war and by Nasser's policies, Sadat calculated that the only way to attract scarce investment capital was to tap into Saudi Arabia's amazing oil wealth and to orient Egypt away from the Soviet Union and to the West. Coming to terms with Israel and convincing the US that he was ready to switch sides was all part of Sadat's grand strategy to restructure Egypt's foreign policy alignments and domestic political economy. The Camp David peace accords (1979) were a natural corollary of this shift and its repercussions for the viability of the Arab League were shattering. Egypt was expelled from the League, which moved its headquarters out of Cairo.

By the 1980s, some Arab leaders attempting to refashion domestic arrangements throughout the region came to the realization that sclerotic states could hardly compete with other regions for foreign investment,

[93] Paul C. Noble, "The Arab System: Pressures, Constraints and Opportunities," In Bahgat Korany and Ali E. Hillal Dessouki (eds.), *The Foreign Policies of Arab States*, p. 75.

financial assistance, and Western technology. Furthermore, the absence of regional stability and cooperation were a main barrier to pursuing these objectives, as were outmoded domestic political economies with vast military-industrial complexes (Solingen 2006). At this time a pattern of "subregionalism" began to emerge. Beginning with the Gulf Cooperation Council (GCC, 1981), it was later followed by the Arab Maghrebi Union (1989, Algeria, Libya, Mauritania, Morocco, and Tunisia) and then the Arab Cooperation Council (1989, Egypt, Jordan, North Yemen, and Iraq).[94] For the most part these subregional organizations were not much more successful than the Arab League, although the GCC registered successes that surprised even its members, particularly on common internal security issues.[95]

By the late 1980s, the winding down of the Cold War, expanding globalization, and a developing thaw in the Arab–Israeli conflict provided even stronger incentives and political covers for alternative regional institutional settings. Specifically, the "decline of identity," the rise of international market and institutional pressures, and the emergence of new particularistic interests and new domestic coalitions led to growing interest in new forms of interstate cooperation outside the umbrella framework of the Arab League. In the early 1990s, a stale Arab League had become even more discredited as an institutional option for a new era. The 1991 Gulf War had shattered what little remained of Arabism, pitting Arab regimes along competing sides of the war. The League was the chief institutional casualty and Arab leaders now began to think of new regional arrangements that might accommodate changing domestic dynamics. New and evolving requirements for political survival (particularly pressures to address mounting economic crises and slow growth) widened the regional institutional repertoire to include innovative approaches to regional cooperation that might encourage regional stability, foreign investment, and economic recovery.

In the early 1990s, the interrelated dynamics of a changing domestic political landscape, an enveloping *zeitgeist* of globalization, and the 1993 Oslo process, made the emergence of a Multilateral Middle East Peace Process (MMEPP) possible. This was an unprecedented effort to

[94] Michael N. Barnett, *Dialogues in Arab Politics: Negotiations in Regional Order*; Ghassan Salamé, "Integration in the Arab World: The Institutional Framework," in G. Luciani and G. Salamé (eds.), *The Politics of Arab Integration* (New York: Croom Helm, 1988).

[95] Charles Tripp, "Regional Organizations in the Arab Middle East," in Louise Fawcett and Andrew Hurrell (eds.), *Regionalism in World Politics: Regional Organization and International Order* (New York: Oxford University Press, 1995), pp. 283–308; Fred H. Lawson, "Theories of Integration in a New Context: The Gulf Cooperation Council," in Kenneth P. Thomas and Mary Ann Tefreault (eds.), *Racing to Regionalize: Democracy, Capitalism, and Regional Political Economy* (Boulder, CO: Lynne Rienner, 1999).

tackle core sources of conflict in the arms control, economic, refugee, water, and environmental arenas, bringing together Israel and its Arab neighbors for the first time ever under a common, if fledgling, regional institutional framework. It is undeniable that the US played a key role in launching and steering this process but it would be a mistake to ignore the domestic and regional forces that made some actors in the region more receptive to this development in the mid-1990s than ever before.[96] There were expectations (moderate in most cases) that the MMEPP, or at least its externalities (Middle East and North Africa [MENA] economic summits, a regional bank), would enable ruling coalitions to revert the socio-economic devastation left by declining oil prices, bloated bureaucracies, economic mismanagement, overpopulation, militarization, and foreign-policy adventurism on all sides. A complementary multilateral framework came into being in the context of the Euro-Med process (Barcelona Declaration) gathering the European Union and the Eastern and Southern Mediterranean states, including the Palestinian Authority.[97]

To be sure, the MMEPP cannot be divorced from the domestic interests of the ruling coalitions that underpinned its brief existence. Each delegation approached the process with separate agendas but also converging objectives. The newly-minted Palestinian Authority saw the MMEPP as an opportunity to bridge between Israel as a perceived "newcomer" into the region and the rest of the Arab world. It thus insisted on hosting a number of emerging institutions that would indirectly buttress Palestinian claims for statehood. The Jordanian leadership, under perennial threats to its political survival, approached the MMEPP as a means to increase predictability and stability for the small kingdom. Jordanian participants thus spearheaded significant achievements in the multilateral context and became pivotal brokers. Egyptian leaders hoped that the

[96] This section builds heavily on Etel Solingen, "The Multilateral Arab–Israeli Negotiations: Genesis, Institutionalization, Pause, Future," *Journal of Peace Research*, 37:2 (March 2000), pp. 167–87 including personal interviews in Amman (August 1997), Cairo (March 1998), and Jerusalem (August 1997 and March 1998). See also Joel Peters, *Building Bridges: The Arab–Israeli Multilateral Talks* (London: Royal Institute of International Affairs, 1994); Joel Peters, *Pathways to Peace: The Multilateral Arab–Israeli Peace Talks* (London: Royal Institute of International Affairs, 1996); Bruce Jentleson and Dalia Kaye, "Explaining the Limits of Regional Security Cooperation: The Middle East ACRS Case," paper presented at the Annual Conference of the American Political Science Association, Washington, DC, 28–31 August 1997; and Dalia Kaye, *Beyond the Handshake* (New York: Columbia University Press, 2001). Technically, the multilaterals were first conceived at the Madrid Conference (1991) but only the Oslo processes provided them with momentum.

[97] On the institutional design of the Barcelona process see Etel Solingen, "The Triple Logic of the European-Mediterranean Partnership: Hindsight and Foresight," *International Politics*, 40:2 (June 2003), pp. 179–94.

MMEPP would cement Egypt's leadership of the Arab world as the first Arab state to sign a peace treaty with Israel. Israel's Likud-led coalition under Yitzhak Shamir approached the MMEPP as a diversionary instrument to avoid concrete concessions in the Palestinian–Israeli arena. However, with Labor's return to power in 1992 and the unprecedented breakthrough in Oslo, Israeli leaders interested in internationalizing Israel's economy and normalizing relations with the region and the rest of the world embraced the MMEPP in earnest.

For all participants, the MMEPP was a regional institutional arena with some potential for collectively strengthening each other's domestic position while weakening that of their rivals, by tying the hands of current competitors and successive leaders and making reversals harder to implement. Residual supporters of pan-Arabism and newly reinvigorated proponents of Islamist and pan-Islamist movements were staunch opponents of this process. Jordan's Foreign Minister Dr. Kamel Abu Jaber sought to counter the Islamist opposition by citing a Koranic verse at the MMEPP inaugural meeting in Madrid: "Let not a people's enmity toward you incite you to act contrary to justice; be always just, that is closest to righteousness" (*Koran*, Sura 5:8).[98] The MMEPP also provided inducements (the promise of investments, aid, and other support) and signaled opportunity costs to "outsiders" who stayed away, including Iran and Iraq. At the same time, participants stressed an "open door" policy to broaden the circle of support and strengthen regional stability, foreign investment, and economic reforms. On the one hand, the MMEPP provided a respectable international cover for reformers who favored those policies for their own domestic reasons (lowering military expenditures, liberalizing the economy, and the like). On the other hand, the MMEPP became a direct threat to the continuity of competing political-economic models in Syria which, with occupied Lebanon, became reluctant partners of the MMEPP, frequently boycotting its activities.

Given the shadow of the past in both inter-Arab and Arab–Israeli relations, as described in earlier sections, the multilaterals could be no more than a fledgling institutional form with little formal structure. On the one hand, Arab parties insisted on linking effective progress in the MMEPP with progress in bilateral Palestinian–Israeli relations. On the other hand, Israel was concerned with any rigid rule-making procedure that could automatically overwhelm it by an Arab majority. Yet the MMEPP brought about significant breakthroughs, particularly considering the legacy of conflict but also considering its brief duration. Its achievements were more symbolic than effectively constraining on its members. They were

[98] 31 October 1991. www.mfa.gov.il/mfa

often a "consummation" of progress achieved elsewhere (primarily the bilateral track between Israelis and Palestinians) but nonetheless transformed what had been an inert process before 1992 into a vibrant undertaking that included a "vision paper," a draft "Declaration of Principles" on regional peace and security, an environmental code of conduct, a monitoring committee and permanent Secretariat for the Regional Economic Development Working Group (REDWG), a proposed "vision chapter" on refugee issues, a regional desalination center, and other substantive and procedural focal points. This record makes the MMEPP a near revolutionary institution in the region, even with its informal and tentative structure. It superseded what had been the organizing (Arab) identity basis for membership in regional institutions, allowing not only other Muslim states (such as Turkey) but also Israel in its midst. Notably, no Arab head of state (except the host, President Mubarak) participated in the celebrations of the Arab League's fiftieth anniversary in 1995.[99]

Alas, the promise and expectations from the MMEPP were truncated by the resilience of decades-old path-dependent processes throughout the region that resisted the domestic and regional changes of the 1990s and were reinforced by a newer and more explosive component: Islamist radicalism. Not only had internationalizing coalitions in the Arab world remained quite fragile in key states (such as Egypt and Jordan) but their competitors (in Syria, Libya, and Iraq) gained ground and actively bolstered the domestic opposition to Oslo and the MMEPP in neighboring states. In doing so, they relied on many of the same tactics of shaming and providing material support to their rivals' opposition that had characterized earlier periods in inter-Arab relations. Islamist terror against Israeli civilians helped elect Likud's Benjamin Netanyahu, thus ending the MMEPP cooperative episode and providing new life to institutional alternatives pivoted, once again, on Arab identity and interests.[100]

IV: Not quite an epilogue

Our overview suggests that the sources of institutional design, as defined in Acharya and Johnston's introductory chapter, were primarily in the

[99] Clovis Maksoud, "Diminished Sovereignty, Enhanced Sovereignty: United Nations-Arab League Relations at 50," *The Middle East Journal*, 49:4 (Autumn 1995), pp. 582–94.

[100] Netanyahu's coalition included hypernationalists (including settler constituencies), populists, developing-towns, and protected business and labor, which were all dependent on state subsidies and housing. Neither this agenda nor that of imperial infrastructural projects in the West Bank and Gaza were particularly sensitive to the synergies required by internationalizing strategies (macroeconomic as well as regional stability, *inter alia*).

symbolic-instrumental and domestic politics-centered dynamics that led to the demand for the League in 1945. Institutional design was characterized by an (Arab) identity-based membership, an exclusive pan-Arab ideology or normative framework, a desire to preserve state sovereignty, and a related commitment to consensus rules. The domestic survival of ruling coalitions was always a pivotal consideration in the design of the Arab League, trumping an effective norm of unification.[101] In the 1950s and 1960s symbols associated with Arabism (*qawmiya*) were deftly deployed by Arab rulers in managing inter-Arab conflict and cooperation.[102] At the same time, the interests of rulers in individual states (*wataniya*) were rarely sacrificed in that process, only strengthened. Political survival at home was at least partly a function of how rulers defined their place within Arabism. What was good for swaying the neighbors' publics was also good for maintaining influence within one's own. Throughout this period Arab governments embarked on state-building projects and inward-looking survival strategies that had little economic and political affinity with cooperative, let alone integrative, regional efforts.

The League's low institutionalization was thus over-determined by both shared culture and contested norms (i.e. efforts *not* to institutionalize shared norms) and by rulers' efforts to maximize individual utilities (i.e. their own domestic survival and that of their political allies). One indication of the endeavor to make the Arab League "be seen but not heard" was that – even as it was specifically deprived of any monitoring or formal sanctioning mechanisms – the League had passed over 4,000 resolutions by the 1980s, of which 80 percent were never implemented. As Salamé argued, "there is no need to establish majority rules, since even when unanimity is possible it remains ineffective."[103] Furthermore, the "need to be seen" is reflected in the League's baroque bureaucratization, encompassing internal and affiliated agencies such as an Economic and Social Council, a permanent military command, an Arab Development Bank, an Arab union for communications, an Arab Postal Union, a union of Arab radio stations, ALECSO (akin to UNESCO), an Arab Labor Organization and Arab Labor Bureau, Arab Fund for Economic and Social Development, and Arab Monetary Fund, among others. Not

[101] Charles Tripp, "Regional Organizations in the Arab Middle East," pp. 283–308. In their study of Arab foreign policies, Korany and Dessouki (*The Foreign Policies of Arab States*, p. 3) notice "a difference between the sources of a particular policy, which are in many cases specific state interests, and the justification of that policy – usually articulated in pan-Arab rhetoric."

[102] Michael Barnett, *Dialogues in Arab Politics: Negotiations in Regional Order.*

[103] Ghassan Salamé, "Inter-Arab Politics: The Return to Geography," in W. Quandt (ed.), *The Middle East: Ten Years After Camp David* (Washington, DC: Brookings Institution, 1988), p. 276.

unsurprisingly for an institution relegated to manufacturing appearance more than substance, between 25 and 30 percent of the Arab League's budget was historically devoted to "information."[104]

The League's design could not help it fulfill the mission – even if not formally enshrined – of resolving conflict among its members. Indeed, it should come as no surprise that the League succeeded in only six of the seventy-seven inter-Arab conflict situations it dealt with between 1945 and 1981.[105] As Zacher reports, the League abstained from intervening at all in many conflicts involving competing blocs of transnational coalitions (quite often "rejectionists" versus "pro-Western" blocs) between 1946 and 1977. For example, both Lebanon's plight against subversion by the United Arab Republic in 1958 and Jordan's call for Arab League action following Syria's military intervention against Jordan in 1970 fell on deaf ears. Nor did the League intervene during Iraq's 1973 attack on Kuwait, the 1976–77 conflict between Algeria, Morocco, and Mauritania, or the brief war between Egypt and Libya in 1977. Oftentimes aggrieved parties did not even appeal to the League, knowing that the balance of forces in the region would not allow the League to redress grievances. Two important exceptions were the League's effective intervention during Iraq's threat to Kuwait in 1961 and Algeria's invasion of Morocco in 1963.[106] A subsequent "success," following a devastating civil war in Lebanon, was the League's sponsorship of the Taif accord which helped chart a less violent path in war-torn Lebanon even as it legitimized Syria's extended control of Lebanon.

The dynamics that had led to this state of affairs did not disappear but was progressively overlaid with changes in the 1960s and 1970s, hastened in the 1980s and particularly the 1990s by global "world time" effects and their reverberations in the domestic politics of Arab states. Rising pressures to reform (from both markets and global institutions) and the decline of Arabism deepened the cleavages between regimes more oriented to global economic exchange and those striving to preserve relative economic closure and the political economy of military and *mukhabarat* states. This cleavage ruled out a common regional strategy but also widened the repertoire for individual survival strategies. Some (prominently Jordan) began unilateral efforts to improve their own position

[104] Macdonald, *The League of Arab States*, p. 144.

[105] Ibrahim Awad, "The Future of Regional and Subregional Organization in the Arab World," in Dan Tschirgi (ed.), *The Arab World Today* (Boulder, CO: Lynne Rienner, 1994), p. 153; Hussein A. Hassouna, *The League of Arab States and Regional Disputes: A Study of Middle East Conflicts* (Dobbs Ferry, NY: Oceana Publications, Inc, 1975).

[106] Mark W. Zacher, *International Conflicts and Collective Security, 1946–77: The United Nations, Organization of American States, Organization of African Unity, and Arab League.*

vis-a-vis global markets, institutions, and powerful states. A multilateral alternative to the Arab League that would strengthen regional stability and domestic reform became more attuned to such objectives. The Arab League's rigid, identity-based criteria for institutional membership were thus superseded by a new framework that now included Turkey, Israel, and a range of extra-regional supporting actors.

Because the logic of regime survival prevailed in both periods, our sense is that the prisoner's dilemma is the game that most closely approximates the nature of strategic interaction among Arab states, although the substance of this "cooperation" changed over the two periods. There was a progressive erosion of the norms of Arabism after 1967 even if their effect never disappeared, as evident in Egypt's expulsion from the League after Camp David, from 1979 to 1989. The region's diversity of domestic regimes had always imposed important barriers to collaboration but evolving ruling coalitions since the 1980s reinforced the prisoner's dilemma, making cooperation through the Arab League even more difficult to attain. The collapse of the Soviet Union as protector of some regimes, globalization pressures in the 1990s, the Oslo process, and the prospects of political and economic links with the West, combined to heighten incentives to defect from Arabist norms. Competition between *ancien regime* coalitions, such as Syria, and proto-reformers, such as Jordan, became more pronounced. The latter's incentives to defect into alternative institutional forms such as the MMEPP became stronger, and the costs of doing so in the mid-1990s were more bearable than at any time before.

At the same time, the strains accompanying incipient reform and regional initiatives in the 1990s, and the failure of Oslo, doomed this institutional episode by the latter half of the decade. Subsequently, both harsh Israeli responses to the second intifada (2000 onwards) and international pressures stemming from 9/11 brought the Arab League back from obscurity but only to face ever more difficult challenges. Among them was the Saudi February 2002 initiative pushing for a joint declaration to "normalize" relations with Israel in exchange for full Israeli withdrawal. The initiative was later watered down at the 2002 Summit meeting in Beirut, and its impact was truncated by Palestinian suicide attacks on civilians and Israeli reprisals.

Even more ominous for the League's continued existence was the Second Gulf War, which led Arab League Secretary-General Amr Moussa to declare that weakness and disunity had precluded the League from playing a meaningful role in preventing the war. The League, he argued, could be replaced by a new system, just as the UN had replaced the League of Nations. In Moussa's own words: "Arab states wanted the war and I do not care if the Arab League remains or goes. I excuse the strong bitterness in Kuwait, but I believe they should not help invade Iraq."[107] Moussa had reportedly ignored an initiative by Shaykh Zayid Bin-Sultan al-Nuhayyan, Crown Prince of Abu Dhabi, calling on Saddam Hussein to resign in order to prevent the war.[108] Saddam had apparently responded favorably to the proposal but demanded that the Arab League back the offer. The initiative was circulated but never debated by the League.[109] Instead, Moussa indicted Arab leaders, declaring that: "The Arabs are not united; the people are. All Arab people reject the war." When asked whether the Arab League was "dead," Moussa replied that the League could not work as long as the Arab body remained weak, that the entire Arab order had to be reconsidered, and that some "Arab forces" were interested in activating the League only slightly but never as a major voice in the Arab world.

What is remarkable about Moussa's analysis is how closely it resembles vestigial tensions from earlier decades about the League's role. While several Gulf states provided facilities for the coalition forces (Kuwait, the UAE, Qatar, Bahrain, and Oman) and others extended more indirect assistance (Egypt, Jordan, and Saudi Arabia), the Sharm al-Shaykh meeting called for a common Arab position rejecting war and the League's foreign ministers' council labeled the war an aggression against an Arab state. The pressure to publicly conform to a common stand while retaining divergent private preferences (i.e. the gap between rhetoric and practice) was not much different from that characterizing the Baghdad Pact events. Moussa even proclaimed his own understanding of why "brother Taha Yasin Ramadan" (Saddam's Vice-President) would not be satisfied with mere "words" of support from Arab League members.

This last statement raises one important issue regarding the League's *modus operandi*. Its refusal to condemn genocidal human rights abuses by the Iraqi regime – including the use of chemical weapons in Halabjah, the extermination of 400,000 Shia in March 1991, and the torture and killing of many others – was in line with its stated principles of "sovereignty"

[107] Al-Sharq al-Awsat, London, in Arabic, 1 April 2003; cited in Global News Wire – Asia Africa Intelligence Wire, p. 6. Copyright 2003 BBC Monitoring/BBC, BBC Monitoring International Reports. Iraqi leader Izzat Ibrahim al-Douri was more direct, interrupting Kuwait's foreign minister at a meeting while urging him "to shut up you little man, you stooge, you monkey! . . .You are facing Iraq, may God curse you," John F. Burns and Edward Wong, "Death of Hussein Aide is Confirmed," *The New York Times*, 13 November 2005, p. A8.

[108] Al-Sharq al-Awsat, London, in Arabic, 3 May 2003; cited in Global News Wire – Asia Africa Intelligence Wire, p. 6. Copyright 2003 BBC Monitoring/BBC. BBC Monitoring International Reports.

[109] Hassan M. Fattah, "Arab League Plan for Hussein Exile Went Sour, Arab Leader Says," *The New York Times*, 2 November 2005, p. A12.

and non-intrusion in domestic affairs. After all, massive killings within Syria (al-Hama), Sudan, and elsewhere had received the same treatment. However, as earlier sections recount, intrusions into others' domestic affairs were legendary if and when the theme could be coined in pan-Arab terms. This should come as no surprise since Arab nationalism could be more easily manipulated as a tool of regime survival than could demands for democratization. Abstaining from intervention on account of human rights violations was among the few truly consensual principles guiding Arab League members, reflecting the common rejection of democratic institutions by most of its leaders.[110] The Arab Charter for Human Rights issued by the Arab League in 1994 has not been endorsed by a single Arab country.

Soon after the March 2003 war Moussa retracted his earlier statements, now arguing that "the Arab League must remain intact because it is the only organization assembling the Arabs."[111] Another particularly difficult and momentous test for the League arose when the new Iraqi Governing Council (IGC) claimed its right to represent Iraq at the League's meetings in September 2003. Denying the IGC's claim on the basis of its presumed lack of sovereign legitimacy was particularly poignant for an institution that lacked a single democratically elected member. The League had no choice but to accept Iraq's Foreign Minister Hoshyar Zebari (the first ever Kurdish foreign minister of Iraq) who laid out a challenging blueprint for the League: "The new Iraq will stand against the culture of rejection and isolation of others and would be established on bases of multiplicity as well as democratic and constitutional rules."[112] The League refrained from establishing a collective framework for aiding in Iraq's post-war reconstruction. Furthermore, much in the tradition of earlier periods, Arab leaders used their own state-controlled media to inflame pan-Arab sentiment against the US and Iraq's leadership. This time, however, they did so from within Iraq itself, the Arab state with the region's freest media.[113]

Various other crises in the region reaffirmed the League's inability to resolve matters afflicting Arab states in recent years. First and foremost was the continued debacle in Iraq and growing influence of Iran, leading to widespread Sunni concerns throughout the region. Potential talks

[110] On how the absence of democratic institutions dooms effective regional cooperation in the Middle East, see Tripp, "Regional Organizations in the Arab Middle East."

[111] Text of recorded telephone interview with Amr Moussa, in Tunis by Nabawi al-Mallah in Cairo, broadcast by Egyptian radio on 9 May 2003. Copyright 2003 BBC Monitoring Middle East – Political. Supplied by BBC Worldwide Monitoring.

[112] Cairo MENA government news agency, Financial Times Information, Global News Wire, NTIS, US Department of Commerce, World News Connection, 9 September 2003.

[113] Al-Bayan, Baghdad, 2 January 2004, *FBIS-NES*-2004-0102.

between the US and Iran led Moussa to declare that "any solution for the Iraqi problem cannot be reached without Arabs."[114] The fear of "losing" Iraq led to pledges to reopen diplomatic missions in Baghdad and the threat of a nuclear Iran triggered expressions of concern from predominantly Sunni League members. Moussa also denounced Iraq's new constitution – particularly provisions for regional autonomy and describing Iraq as a Muslim but not an Arab state – although the absence of a Constitution under Saddam never triggered such criticism.[115] The League never endorsed a common statement clearly condemning massacres of Shiites by Sunni terrorists in Iraq, although it invited contending Iraqi factions to a meeting in Cairo. Ultimately the League has remained marginal to developments in Iraq and, two years after the war, it had yet to cancel Iraq's debts and contribute to building Iraqi security forces.[116]

A second recent challenge to the League related to international pressure on Syria's control of Lebanon in the aftermath of the alleged assassination of Prime Minister Rafiq Hariri by Syrian agents. On the one hand the League proclaimed its "solidarity" with Syria and rejected "foreign intervention," including UN Security Council Resolution 1559 calling on Syria to pull out of Lebanon. On the other hand it gently encouraged Bashar al-Assad to continue with Syria's own plan for withdrawal. Syria's eventual withdrawal had far more to do with pressure from beyond the region than with any Arab League decisions. In the words of Lebanon's *Daily Star* editor Rami Khouri, "as the gravity of the crises continues to rise, so does the irrelevance of the Arab League response – or the lack of it . . . It's an institution of the 1960s and hasn't changed, even though the world and the region has."[117] Meanwhile, Assad transformed Syria's Ba'ath party, which for decades advanced a pan-Arab vision, into one focused only on Syrian needs. A third conundrum for the League was posed by the genocidal massacre by Sudanese-supported Arab militias (*janjaweed*) in Darfur of at least 400,000 innocent civilians, and the displacement of at least one million people in what the UN called "the world's worst humanitarian crisis." Moussa insisted that Arab countries help Sudan end the violence in Darfur but the League opposed both UN sanctions and disarming the *janjaweed*. However, Arab states continued their support for the Sudanese leadership and, according to a Japanese

[114] Abeer Allam, "Influence in Iraq Emerges as Key Issue as Arab Conference Opens," *The New York Times*, 29 March 2006, p. A8.

[115] Robert F. Worth, "Leader Says Other Arabs Are Insensitive to Iraq's Plight," *The New York Times*, 6 September 2005, p. A9.

[116] Hassan M. Fattah, "Iraqi Factions Seek Timetable for US Pullout," *The New York Times*, 22 November 2005, p. A1.

[117] Hassan M. Fattah, "Conference of Arab Leaders Yields Little of Significance," *The New York Times*, 24 March 2005, p. A3.

source, "Canada, by itself, [had] pledged more aid [to Darfur] than all the Arab countries combined."[118] Nor did the League contribute relief workers.[119] Indeed, Arab leaders scheduled their 2006 Summit in Khartoum, legitimizing Sudan's leadership and opposing UN troops.

Finally, the issue of democratization has posed yet another test to the League, in the form of the Bush administration's proposed Greater Middle East Initiative announced in early 2004. Preparatory negotiations for the Tunis Summit scheduled for 29–30 March failed to reach an agreement on an Arab homegrown counter-proposal on political reform. Egypt, Saudi Arabia, and Syria opposed the US initiative most forcefully, while liberalizing regimes in some Gulf states, Tunisia, and Morocco were more favorable to reform. The first group refused to include words like "democracy," "parliament," and "civil society" in any declaration, or to support the idea of NGOs as building blocks of civil society.[120] Continued divisions over political reform and a perceived boycott of the Summit by leaders from the Gulf and Egypt moved Tunisia to postpone the Summit. When the meeting was finally held two months later, only two-thirds of the leaders attended, dwindling to four before it ended. Beyond cleavages on political reform (including human rights, women's rights, political participation, and judicial reforms) there was also disagreement over reform of the Arab League (including the possible creation of an Arab parliament, an Arab security council, and an Arab court), whether to reinvigorate the 2002 Beirut summit declaration on the Palestinian–Israeli conflict (with Jordanians and Palestinians favoring it, Syria and Lebanon opposing it), and rifts between "major" and "minor" states as well as between *Mashriq* and *Maghrib* states.[121] Muammar Qaddafi repeatedly called for dismantling the League, calling the entire agenda flawed.

An editorial in a London-based daily with some sympathy for Bin Laden summed up one response to these events: ". . . the official Arab

[118] Joseph Britt, "Deafening Arab Silence on Arab Genocide," *The Japan Times*, 16 July 2005, p. 16.

[119] Lebanon's *Daily Star* discussed the silence of the Arab world on Darfur, in "Symptomatic Arab Silence on Darfur," reproduced in the *International Herald Tribune*, 13 August 2004, p. 6.

[120] Neil MacFarquhar, "Arab Summit Meeting Collapses Over Reforms," *The New York Times*, 28 March 2004, p. 10.

[121] Al-Quds al-Arabi, London, 7 April 2004; cited in *FBIS-NES*-2004-0407, p. 19. The heightened violence in Israel/Palestine remained a core challenge. After all, as Awad ("The Future of Regional and Subregional Organization," p. 150) suggested, the Arab League has "lived by and for the Arab-Israeli conflict." Yet, a consultative meeting in Cairo called by Palestine's permanent representative on 12 December 2003 was boycotted by most Arab ambassadors and permanent representatives, with only Syria, Algeria, and Tunisia attending. "Unprecedented Boycott of Arab League Consultative Meeting." Al-Sharq al-Awsat, London, 1 January 2004, cited in *FBIS-NES*-2004-0102, p. 1.

order does not want reforms and democracy but wants the present stagnant situation to continue. Therefore any new summit will be just an act and an attempt to save face, the face of the regimes of course, and will therefore be useless."[122] A more optimistic perspective advanced that "the Tunis summit has succeeded without the need to hold it. It is the first time that we have seen such projects, ideas, and various political debates that talk about political reform of the Arab order and correction of the operating procedures within the Arab League itself. Raising these two issues is more important than discussing the Palestinian and Iraqi issues, which are both the subject of agreement and about which nobody can do anything other than issue a statement of support and expressing solidarity."[123] These competing interpretations suggest that the Arab League will continue to provide an arena on which to imprint contending views on the relationship between domestic politics and regional order in this part of the world. As Shafeeq Ghabra suggests, political survival remains "the core of the weakness of the Arab League."[124]

[122] Editorial: "Reasons for Arab Summit's Failure," Al-Quds al-Arabi, 30 March 2004, NTIS: World News Connection.

[123] Abd-al-Rahman al-Rashid, "The Tunis Summit was the Most Successful," Al-Sharq Al-Awsat, London, 29 March 2004, NTIS: World News Connection.

[124] Quoted in Susan Sachs, "Internal Rift Dooms Arab League Plan to Help Avert a War by Pressing Iraq," *The New York Times*, 14 March 2003, p. A11.

7 Social mechanisms and regional cooperation: are Europe and the EU really all that different?

Jeffrey T. Checkel

Introduction

Many analysts would characterize the European Union (EU) as a unique case among the panoply of regional organizations, with a level of cooperation that is wider and deeper than elsewhere. Moreover, recent years have witnessed a seeming acceleration of the Union's uniqueness. A common currency has been successfully introduced, a constitutional convention held, and a (supranational) constitution is now up for adoption. In social science terms, it would seem that actors have undertaken major adjustments in favor of group norms through the internalization of shared preferences and normative understandings.

The key word in that last sentence is "seem," for there is broad disagreement across the EU literature on this basic issue. In part, this is simply a function of analysts employing different social-theoretic toolkits (contractionalist-rationalist versus sociological) to structure their studies. However, equally important is a state of affairs where normative claim-making and abstract theorizing have outrun carefully designed and methodologically sound empirical studies.[1]

To be fair to EU scholars, their object of study is extraordinarily complex and is a moving target. The degree of cooperation varies tremendously depending upon the institution (the supranational Commission versus the intergovernmental Council, say) or policy area studied. Moreover, EU institutions have evolved significantly over the past half century, in directions often at variance with the original desires of the member states.[2] For example, the European Court of Justice has crafted for itself an extraordinarily important role as a supranational legal organ and quasi-supreme court – functions foreseen by virtually no one fifty years ago.

[1] Jeffrey T. Checkel and Andrew Moravcsik, "A Constructivist Research Program in EU Studies? (Forum Debate)," *European Union Politics*, 2 (June 2001), pp. 219–49.

[2] Paul Pierson, "The Path to European Integration – A Historical Institutionalist Analysis," *Comparative Political Studies*, 29 (April 1996), pp. 123–63.

Analysts thus face a daunting task when seeking to establish clear causal connections between the design and effect of EU institutions. In this essay, I employ the language of social mechanisms to advance some conceptual nuts and bolts for thinking more systematically about such connections. These theoretical propositions are illustrated with materials drawn from two projects, which focus on the EU as well as other European institutions. A first examines regional cooperation over questions of citizenship and membership in post-Cold War Europe. Its main focus is the Council of Europe, a pan-European human rights organization based in Strasbourg. A second project explores the relation between international institutions and socialization. While its central focus is socialization, several contributions examine how institutional design affects the degree of cooperation in European regional organizations.

The analysis proceeds in three steps. First, I discuss three generic mechanisms – strategic calculation, role playing, and normative suasion – that can provide causal micro-foundations to arguments connecting regional institutions and cooperation. For each mechanism, particular conditions (so-called scope conditions) for its operation are highlighted.[3] In doing this, I focus on the last two stages – design elements and outcomes – in Acharya and Johnston's three-stage framework.[4] In part, this is simply a matter of space constraints. However, a good bit of excellent work has already been done on the sources of European regional institutions, both from rationalist and ideational perspectives.[5] I thus thought it wise to focus on those elements of the puzzle where the greatest value added was likely.

Second, I provide examples of these mechanisms at work. The illustrations highlight two important findings: (1) the difficulties of achieving agent preference change even in a thickly institutionalized setting such as Europe; and (2) the key role of national institutions and traditions in affecting the degree of regional institutional cooperation. I thus agree with other contributors to this volume on the need to bring domestic politics back to the study of regional institutions. Third, I explore the *sui generis* question. What is it, if anything, about European institutional

[3] These scope conditions are inferred from a number of different empirical studies and, thus, need to be treated as preliminary subject to their extension and testing on new cases.

[4] Acharya and Johnston, Chapter 1 this volume.

[5] Andrew Moravcsik, *The Choice for Europe: Social Purpose and State Power from Messina to Maastricht* (Ithaca, NY: Cornell University Press, 1998); Andrew Moravcsik, "The Origins of Human Rights Regimes: Democratic Delegation in Postwar Europe," *International Organization*, 54 (Spring 2000), pp. 217–52; Kathleen McNamara, *The Currency of Ideas: Monetary Politics in the European Union* (Ithaca, NY: Cornell University Press, 1998).

dynamics that makes them unique when seen in a broader, cross-regional perspective?

Before proceeding, I should be clear about my intent here. The chapter's purpose is not so much to tell us about this or that European institution – how it works or how it may differ from those found in other regions. Such analysis is provided in many existing – and excellent – studies.[6] Rather, I seek to use findings from Europe to make the case for a focus on causal mechanisms in the study of international institutions – and why this is important for researchers interested in questions of institutional design.

Social mechanisms and regional institutions

Both empirical observation and social theoretic common sense suggest three forms of rationality – instrumental, bounded, and communicative – shaping human behavior or, in our specific case, cooperation in regional institutions.[7] From each of these, one can deduce a generic social mechanism under girding cooperation: strategic calculation, role playing, and normative suasion.

For my purposes, a mechanism is "a set of hypotheses that could be the explanation for some social phenomenon, the explanation being in terms of interactions between individuals and other individuals, or between individuals and some social aggregate." This language of mechanisms is particularly helpful in reducing the lag between input and output, between cause and effect.[8]

In operational terms, I seek to minimize the lag between international institutions and their design (the input or cause), and the nature of cooperation (strategic adaptation, role adoption, preference change), and do so by theorizing three mechanisms connecting the former to the latter.

[6] For a state-of-the-art analysis of the EU along such lines, see Knud Erik Joergensen, Mark Pollack, and Ben Rosamond (eds.), *Handbook of European Union Politics* (London: Sage Publications, 2006).

[7] Of course, the instrumental version is well known to US students of international institutions, while bounded or communicative understandings of rationality have received much greater attention elsewhere – in organizational/institutional work and continental social theory, respectively. See also Alexander Wendt, *Social Theory of International Politics* (Cambridge: Cambridge University Press, 1999), pp. 120–2.

[8] Peter Hedstroem and Richard Swedberg (eds.), *Social Mechanisms: An Analytical Approach to Social Theory* (Cambridge: Cambridge University Press, 1998), pp. 25 and 32–3. This definition of mechanisms is one that is common in both the philosophy of science and international relations theory literatures. See Jon Hovi, "Causal Mechanisms and the Study of International Environmental Regimes," in Arild Underdal and Oran Young (eds.), *Regime Consequences: Methodological Challenges and Research Strategies* (Boston: Kluwer Academic Publishers, 2004), for an excellent discussion.

These are incentives and cost/benefit calculations, role playing, and normative suasion.

Incentives and cost/benefit calculations[9]

This particular mechanism has deep roots in rationalist social theory. While incentives and rewards can be social (status, shaming) as well as material (financial assistance, trade opportunities), one would expect both to play some role in determining the nature of cooperation.[10]

With this mechanism, the pathway to cooperation is first and foremost via instrumentally rational agents who carefully calculate and seek to maximize given interests; behaviorally, they adapt strategically. Of course, the key question is one of scope and domain, that is, under what conditions will incentives and rewards promote cooperation of this sort? Work on European institutions suggests several possibilities, all of which emphasize the importance of domestic politics and of conditionality.

Conditionality – the use of material incentives to bring about a desired change in the behavior of states – is the quintessential incentives-based policy. It has also long been a favored instrument of international financial institutions like the World Bank and the International Monetary Fund (IMF).[11] More important for my purposes, conditionality has been utilized extensively by European regional institutions in recent years.

Its role can be explored more specifically by considering what Schimmelfennig calls intergovernmental reinforcement. Intergovernmental reinforcement by reward refers to a situation where an international institution offers the government of a target state positive incentives – rewards like aid or membership – on the condition that it adopts and complies with the institution's norms. This is a classic use of political conditionality. Transnational reinforcement by reward refers to the same process, but now directed at non-governmental actors in target states. Given these definitions, cooperation based on behavioral adaptation is more likely under the following conditions.

[9] The following draws extensively on Jeffrey T. Checkel, "International Institutions and Socialization in Europe: Introduction and Framework," *International Organization*, 59 (Fall 2005), pp. 801–26, where more detailed discussions, as well as full citations to the relevant theoretical literatures can be found.

[10] On social incentives/rewards and the more general class of social-influence processes to which they belong, see Alastair Iain Johnston, "Treating International Institutions as Social Environments," *International Studies Quarterly* 45:4 (December 2001), pp. 499–506.

[11] Jeffrey T. Checkel, "Compliance and Conditionality," *ARENA Working Paper*, 00/18 (Oslo: ARENA Centre for European Studies, University of Oslo, September 2000), pp. 2–9.

- *Targeted governments expect the promised rewards to be greater than the costs of compliance (Intergovernmental Reinforcement).*
- *Targeted societal actors expect the costs of putting pressure on the government to be lower than the benefits of conditional external rewards, and they are strong enough to force the government to comply with the international norms (Transnational Reinforcement).*[12]

Like much research in the rational-choice tradition, these propositions are clear, more or less easy to operationalize and, for sure, capture an important part of the cooperation dynamics spurred by regional institutions. At the same time, their social-theoretic foundations limit the analysis. Most important, like all rational-choice scholarship, the ontology is individualist, where core properties of actors are taken as givens. While agreeing with others that the ontological differences separating rationalism and constructivism are often overstated,[13] the former is nonetheless ill equipped to theorize those instances of cooperation where basic properties of agents are changing.

Role playing

This mechanism of cooperation has roots in organization theory and cognitive/social psychology. Agents are viewed as boundedly rational, where it is not possible for them to attend to everything simultaneously or to calculate carefully the costs/benefits of alternative courses of action; attention is a scarce resource. Organizational or group environments provide simplifying shortcuts, cues, and buffers that can lead to the enactment of particular role conceptions among individuals.[14] The pathway to cooperation in regional institutions is now non-calculative behavioral adaptation – role enactment – without reflective internalization. In contrast to the previous mechanism, where patterns of cooperation can change quickly as agents recalculate, it now becomes more stable, with behavior and roles persisting absent any change in organizational or group setting.

[12] Frank Schimmelfennig, "Strategic Calculation and International Socialization: Membership Incentives, Party Constellations, and Sustained Compliance in Central and Eastern Europe," *International Organization*, 59 (Fall 2005), pp. 827–60. See also Judith Kelley, *Ethnic Politics in Europe: The Power of Norms and Incentives* (Princeton: Princeton University Press, 2004), chap. 2.

[13] James Fearon and Alexander Wendt, "Rationalism v Constructivism: A Skeptical View," in Walter Carlsnaes, Thomas Risse-Kappen, and Beth Simmons (eds.), *Handbook of International Relations* (London: Sage Publications, 2002), pp. 53–8.

[14] James March and Herbert Simon, "Decision-Making Theory," in O. Grusky and G. A. Miller (eds.), *The Sociology of Organizations. Basic Studies*, 2nd edn. (New York: The Free Press, 1981).

Proponents of this cognitive mechanism stress the key role of time/contact in small groups and organizational environments for inducing new roles. In doing so, they draw upon a rich laboratory-experimental research program in social psychology.[15] This allows them to provide carefully argued support for the old neo-functionalist claim that prolonged exposure and communication can promote a greater sense of we-ness.

Disaggregating contact, these researchers have developed more specific claims on how its duration and intensity, and the multiple-embeddedness of the agents involved, can lead to the development of new role conceptions in regional institutions. In particular, cooperation based on the adoption of new roles at the regional level is more likely under the following conditions.

- *The duration of the contact within regional institutions is long and sustained.*
- *The intensity of the interactions within regional institutions is high.*[16]

However, these arguments must control for the fact that individuals entering a new institutional arena are in no sense free agents; they are embedded in multiple domestic and international contexts. *Ceteris paribus*, when the latter dominates the former, role modification at the regional level should be facilitated. Thus, in addition to duration and intensity, cooperation based on the adoption of new roles is more likely when:

- *Agents have extensive previous professional experiences with regional or international policymaking settings.*[17]

These propositions and their careful testing begin to control for the elements of self-selection and pre-socialization that bedeviled earlier work in this tradition.[18]

This work on role playing captures an important, if understudied, dynamic in regional cooperation – one different from the instrumental or

[15] John M. Orbell, Robyn M. Dawes, and Alphons van de Kragt, "Explaining Discussion-Induced Cooperation," *Journal of Personality and Social Psychology*, 54:5 (1988), pp. 811–19, for example.

[16] These scholars operationalize intensity with some care – defining it as the number of committee meetings attended plus the number of informal contacts outside these formal sessions, for example. They also design their research to distinguish the independent causal effects of duration and intensity. Jan Beyers, "Multiple Embeddedness and Socialization in Europe: The Case of Council Officials," *International Organization*, 59 (Fall 2005), pp. 899–936.

[17] In contrast, agents with extensive domestic policy networks who are briefly "parachuted" into regional settings, will be less likely to adopt new role conceptions.

[18] Beyers, "Multiple Embeddedness and Socialization in Europe"; Liesbet Hooghe, "Several Roads Lead To International Norms, But Few Via International Socialization: A Case Study of the European Commission," *International Organization*, 59 (Fall 2005), pp. 861–98. See also Lisa Martin and Beth Simmons, "Theories and Empirical Studies of International Institutions," *International Organization*, 52 (Autumn 1998), pp. 735–6.

normative ones. We as individuals and states play roles because it is easier socially, as opposed to only and always acting strategically and instrumentally. Yet, these roles may later become taken for granted habits, without any conscious act of persuasion (see below).

This suggests a subtle, but important difference with the normative suasion mechanism. If role playing is at work, an agent will cooperate and comply with group/community norms, but in a non-reflective manner. That is, if asked about the source of compliance and cooperation, he/she – after conscious thought – might answer "well, I don't know whether it's right or wrong, it's simply what is done and, I guess, it's a habit of mine by now."[19]

Normative suasion

Recent work by international relations (IR) constructivists adds a communicative understanding of rationality to the instrumental and bounded versions seen above. Drawing upon Habermasian social theory as well as insights from social psychology, these researchers argue that communicatively rational social agents do not so much calculate costs and benefits, or seek cues from their environment when acting in regional institutions. Rather, they present arguments and try to persuade and convince each other; their interests and preferences are open for possible redefinition.[20]

Recall that role playing presupposes an agent's passive, non-calculative acceptance of new roles evoked by certain institutional-environmental triggers. When normative suasion takes place, agents actively and reflectively internalize new understandings of appropriateness. If asked about the source of cooperation, an agent – after conscious thought – might answer "well, this is the right thing to do even though I didn't used to think so." The switch from a logic of consequences to one of appropriateness is complete.

These insights give new meaning to the idea of regional institutions and organizations as talk-shops. Arguments and attempts at persuasion – talking in popular parlance – may change the most basic properties of agents. If the strategic calculation mechanism views language as a tool for self-interested actors to exchange information or engage in signaling games

[19] Methodologically, this difference has implications for the types of process-oriented questions we should be asking in studies of international institutions. Michael Zürn and Jeffrey T. Checkel, "Getting Socialized to Build Bridges: Constructivism and Rationalism, Europe and the Nation State," *International Organization*, 59 (Fall 2005), pp. 1045–79.

[20] Marc Lynch, *State Interests and Public Spheres: The International Politics of Jordan's Identity* (New York: Columbia University Press, 1999), Chap. 1; Thomas Risse-Kappen, "Let's Argue! Communicative Action in World Politics," *International Organization*, 54 (Winter 2000), pp. 6–11.

within institutions, then normative suasion embodies a much thicker role for it, as constitutive of agents and their interests.[21] The nature of cooperation now becomes more stable as agents learn new interests.

Most would agree that persuasion operates in international institutions. Indeed, two practitioner-scholars with considerable experience in the world of diplomacy describe it as a "fundamental instrument" and "principal engine" of the interaction within institutions.[22] While perhaps overstated, the real challenge has been to operationalize this commonsense insight in ways that allow for systematic empirical testing.[23]

Recent work on European institutions makes precisely this move, advancing specific propositions on the relation between social communication and preference change. In particular, it suggests that arguing and persuasion are more likely to change the interests of social agents and thus facilitate regional cooperation when the following conditions hold.[24]

- *The target of persuasion is in a novel and uncertain environment and thus cognitively motivated to analyze new information.*[25]
- *The target has few prior, ingrained beliefs that are inconsistent with the persuader's message.*
- *The persuader is an authoritative member of the ingroup to which the target belongs or wants to belong.*
- *The persuading individual does not lecture or demand, but, instead, acts out principles of serious deliberative argument.*
- *The persuader/persuadee interaction occurs in less politicized and more insulated, in-camera settings.*

[21] See Emanuel Adler, "Constructivism and International Relations," in Walter Carlsnaes, Thomas Risse-Kappen, and Beth Simmons (eds.), *Handbook of International Relations*, pp. 96–8.

[22] Abram Chayes and Antonia Handler Chayes, *The New Sovereignty: Compliance with International Regulatory Agreements* (Cambridge, MA: Harvard University Press, 1995), pp. 25–6. See also Harold Hongju Koh, "Review Essay: Why Do Nations Obey International Law?" *The Yale Law Journal*, 106 (June 1997), pp. 2599–659.

[23] See Checkel and Moravcsik, "A Constructivist Research Program in EU Studies?"; Andrew Moravcsik, 'Constructivism and European Integration: A Critique," in Thomas Christiansen, Knud Erik Joergensen, and Antje Wiener (eds.), *The Social Construction of Europe* (London: Sage Publications, 2001), pp. 176–88.

[24] Jeff Lewis, "The Janus Face of Brussels: Socialization and Everyday Decision-Making in the European Union," *International Organization*, 59 (Fall 2005), pp. 937–71; Alexandra Gheciu, "Security Institutions as Agents of Socialization? NATO and the 'New Europe'," *International Organization*, 59 (Fall 2005), pp. 973–1012. See also Johnston, "Treating International Institutions as Social Environments." More generally, see Philip Zimbardo and Michael Leippe, *The Psychology of Attitude Change and Social Influence* (New York: McGraw Hill, 1991); and Richard Brody, Diana Mutz, and Paul Sniderman (eds.), *Political Persuasion and Attitude Change* (Ann Arbor: University of Michigan Press, 1996).

[25] Put differently, agents are viewed as communicatively and not boundedly rational. With the latter, they would be much more likely to filter or ignore new information.

Cautions and caveats

There are two. First, when highlighting the effects of these differing mechanisms, I have followed common practice, arguing that patterns of cooperation become more stable as we move from incentive-based to normative ones. Indeed, social theorists have typically argued that change promoted by suasion and preference shifts should be more enduring than that promoted by incentives and strategic calculation. With the latter, newly adopted behaviors can be discarded once incentive structures change; with the former, they will show greater stickiness as actors have begun to internalize new values.[26]

Yet, this hierarchy of effectiveness can be questioned. Research on self persuasion and cognitive dissonance suggests that preference change and internalization can occur even in the absence of any attempts at persuasion. Consider an individual who, for purely strategic, incentive-based reasons, begins to act in a certain manner; at some point, she will likely need to justify these acts to herself and others. As a result, a cognitive dissonance may arise between what is justified and argued for, and what is (secretly, privately) believed. Laboratory and experimental work suggests that human beings have a tendency to resolve such dissonance by adapting their preferences to the behavior; that is, they internalize the justification.[27]

There is also growing empirical evidence that what starts as strategic, incentive-based cooperation within regional institutions often leads at later points to preference shifts and, thus, to more enduring change. For example, Kelley finds precisely this pattern at work in her research on the Baltic States, European institutions, and minority rights.[28] In several instances, she uncovers evidence of an initially highly strategic and instrumental process at work, as state elites carefully calculate how to change laws to ward off pressure from the EU, the Council of Europe, and the Organization for Security and Cooperation in Europe (OSCE). Yet, beyond the formal changing of laws, Kelley also finds evidence of changing practice and sustained compliance, patterns indicative of deeper socialization effects. Thus, on both theoretical and empirical grounds

[26] See Ian Hurd, "Legitimacy and Authority in International Politics," *International Organization*, 53 (Spring 1999), pp. 379–408, for an excellent discussion.

[27] Zürn and Checkel, "Getting Socialized to Build Bridges." This appears to be the implicit psychological dynamic behind Elster's argument regarding the "civilizing force of hypocrisy." Jon Elster (ed.), *Deliberative Democracy* (New York: Cambridge University Press, 1998). See also James Fearon, "Deliberation as Discussion," in Elster (ed.), *Deliberative Democracy*, p. 54.

[28] Kelley, *Ethnic Politics in Europe*.

and pending further research, it is perhaps more useful to view the three mechanisms as nominal rather than ordinal categories.[29]

Second, a focus on social mechanisms inevitably poses a micro/macro problem. Simply put, my analytic categories, research methods, and empirical illustrations are geared very much to the micro-level of specific agents operating in institutionalized environments in Europe. As a result, my stories largely end when agents leave a particular international institution. Yet, the efficacy of regional cooperation will be judged not only by interactions in Brussels or Strasbourg (or wherever). Rather, equally important will be what happens when these individuals return home. Do state policies and practices at the macro-level change as well and in ways consistent with newly learned behaviors, roles, or preferences?[30]

Regional institutions and cooperation in contemporary Europe

The following analysis is divided into four parts, all of which focus on the ability of European institutions to promote cooperation based on (possible) preference shifts. Obviously, this tells an incomplete story, in particular, slighting the strategic, incentives-based mechanism. However, much good work has already been done on the role of the latter in promoting European regional cooperation.[31] More important, there are ongoing, contentious, and unresolved policy and academic debates over the extent to which European integration promotes preference and identity shifts.[32] Indeed, with its thickly institutionalized regional environment

[29] That is, there is no assumption they are in any particular order. Robert Keohane, Gary King, and Sidney Verba, *Designing Social Inquiry: Scientific Inference in Qualitative Research* (Princeton: Princeton University Press, 1994), pp. 151–5.

[30] Methodologically, such concerns can be addressed in two ways – by establishing positive correlations between the effects of mechanisms at the individual level and later changes in state policy, or – better yet – by advancing a causal, process tracing argument that connects specific mechanisms to changes in policy. Checkel, "International Institutions and Socialization in Europe."

[31] Andrew Moravcsik, "Explaining International Human Rights Regimes: Liberal Theory and Western Europe," *European Journal of International Relations*, 1:2 (June 1995), pp. 157–89; Moravcsik, *The Choice for Europe*; Moravcsik, "The Origins of Human Rights Regimes"; Frank Schimmelfennig, "International Socialization in the New Europe: Rational Action in an Institutional Environment," *European Journal of International Relations*, 6:1 (March 2000), pp.109–39; Schimmelfennig, "The Community Trap: Liberal Norms, Rhetorical Action, and the Eastern Enlargement of the European Union," *International Organization*, 55 (Winter 2001), pp. 47–80; Schimmelfennig, *The EU, NATO, and the Integration of Europe: Rules and Rhetoric* (Cambridge: Cambridge University Press, 2003); Schimmelfennig, "Strategic Calculation and International Socialization"; Kelley, *Ethnic Politics in Europe*.

[32] On the former, see "The Brussels Consensus," *The Economist*, 7 December 2002; and "Cracks in the College," *The Economist*, 13 September 2003. On the latter, compare Brigid Laffan, "The European Union: A Distinctive Model of Internationalization,"

and a supranational, polity-in-the-making like the EU, Europe seems a most likely case for such dynamics to occur.[33]

Persuasion as a mechanism of European regional cooperation

There are two solid scholarly rationales for a focus on persuasion. Empirically, there are numerous tantalizing hints in the memoir literature and in journalistic accounts that it plays an important role – most recently, for example, in the EU's Convention on the Future of Europe.[34] Theoretically, sociological studies of cooperation and international institutions often hint at a key role for persuasion – for example, when they talk of institutions fixing meanings or diffusing norms. Yet, for the most part, these scholars have left the concept underspecified.[35]

The stage thus set, I define persuasion as a social process of interaction that involves changing attitudes about cause and effect in the absence of overt coercion. More formally, it is "an activity or process in which a communicator attempts to induce a change in the belief, attitude or behavior of another person . . . through the transmission of a message in a context in which the persuadee has some degree of free choice." Here, persuasion is a process of convincing someone through argument and principled debate.[36] To employ my earlier language, it is a social mechanism where the interactions between individuals may (potentially) lead to changes in the core properties – preferences or interests – of agents.

So defined, this is thick persuasion. For sure, there are different levels at which persuasion can occur.[37] Indeed, there is a long tradition in

Journal of European Public Policy, 5:2 (1998), pp. 235–53; and Wolfgang Wessels, "Comitology: Fusion in Action – Politico-Administrative Trends in the EU System," *Journal of European Public Policy*, 5:2 (1998), pp. 209–34.

[33] Steven Weber, "Origins of the European Bank for Reconstruction and Development," *International Organization*, 48:1 (Winter 1994), pp. 1–38.

[34] Paul Magnette, "Coping with Constitutional Incompatibilities: Bargains and Rhetoric in the Convention on the Future of Europe," paper presented at the ARENA Research Seminar, 2 March 2004 (Oslo: ARENA Centre for European Studies, University of Oslo).

[35] Michael Barnett and Martha Finnemore, "The Politics, Power, and Pathologies of International Organizations," *International Organization*, 53 (Autumn 1999), pp. 699–732; Michael N. Barnett and Martha Finnemore, *Rules for the World: International Organizations in Global Politics* (Ithaca, NY: Cornell University Press, 2004), chap. 2. See, however, Johnston, "Treating International Institutions as Social Environments."

[36] Richard Perloff, *The Dynamics of Persuasion* (Hillsdale, NJ: Erlbaum Associates, 1993), p. 14. See also Zimbardo and Leippe, *The Psychology of Attitude Change and Social Influence*; Brody, Mutz, and Sniderman, *Political Persuasion and Attitude Change*; and Robert Keohane, "Governance in a Partially Globalized World," *American Political Science Review*, 95 (March 2001), pp. 2 and 10.

[37] Peter A. Gourevitch, Peter J. Katzenstein, and Robert Keohane, "Memo on Persuasion." Presented at a workshop on "Arguing and Bargaining in European and International Affairs," April 2002 (Florence: European University Institute).

rational-choice scholarship emphasizing a thin, strategic, and manipulative understanding of persuasion – for example, Riker's work on heresthetics.[38] Common to these thin definitions is that persuasion does not bring about preference or attitude change. Given that manipulative understandings have received a good bit of attention in recent work on European institutions,[39] I focus on the thicker variant here.

Mandates and actor independence

As the earlier discussion of scope conditions suggests, persuasion as a mechanism of regional cooperation is crucially hindered or facilitated by certain factors. Here, I develop these in more detail and provide empirical illustrations. Regarding design features of institutions, mandates and actor independence play a key role, with persuasion more likely in brainstorming and depoliticized settings.[40]

Let me give an example from my work on European cooperation over questions of citizenship and membership. Here, one concern has been to document how European institutions – and, specifically, the Council of Europe – came to new, shared understandings on such issues over the past decade. When the Council seeks to develop new policy and norms in a given area, it sets up committees of experts, which are composed of representatives from Council member states as well as academic and policy specialists. Their mandate is to think big and puzzle through issues in an open way. In the early 1990s, two such committees were established: a Committee of Experts on National Minorities and a Committee of Experts on Nationality. If new norms were these committees' outputs, then the issue for me was the process leading to such outcomes. In particular, what role was played by persuasion?

[38] William Riker, *The Art of Political Manipulation* (New Haven: Yale University Press, 1986); and Riker, *The Strategy of Rhetoric* (New Haven: Yale University Press, 1996).

[39] This is especially the case with Schimmelfennig's notion of "rhetorical action," or the strategic use of norms and arguments. Schimmelfennig, "International Socialization in the New Europe"; Schimmelfennig, "The Community Trap"; Schimmelfennig, *The EU, NATO, and the Integration of Europe*. See also Rodger Payne, "Persuasion, Frames, and Norm Construction," *European Journal of International Relations*, 7:1 (March 2001), pp. 37–61; Matthew Evangelista, "Norms, Heresthetics, and the End of the Cold War," *Journal of Cold War Studies*, 3:1 (Winter 2001), pp. 5–35; and Kelley, *Ethnic Politics in Europe*.

[40] The comments here and below build upon other recent discussions that link institutional design to the nature and degree of international cooperation. See Acharya and Johnston, Chapter 1 this volume; Johnston, "Treating International Institutions as Social Environments," pp. 509–10; and Keohane, "Governance in a Partially Globalized World," pp. 8–9.

For the committee on national minorities, there were few attempts at persuasion – of any type – throughout its five-year life. Rather, committee members were content to horse-trade on the basis of fixed positions and preferences. Key in explaining this outcome was the politicization of its work at a very early stage. Events in the broader public arena (the Bosnian tragedy) and within the committee led to a quick hardening of positions.[41] Put differently, these (political) facts greatly diminished the likelihood that the committee's formal brainstorming mandate might lead Council member states to rethink basic preferences on minority policies.

The story was quite different in the committee on nationality. Through the mid-1990s, nationality was a rather humdrum issue – especially compared with the highly emotive one of minorities. Initially, much of the committee's proceedings were taken up with mundane discussions of how and whether to streamline immigration procedures and regulations. In this technical and largely depoliticized atmosphere, brainstorming and attempts at persuasion were evident, especially in a working group of the committee. In this smaller setting, individuals freely exchanged views on the meaning of nationality in a post-national Europe. They sought to persuade and change attitudes, using the force of example, logical argumentation, and the personal esteem in which one persuader was held. In at least two cases, individuals clearly did rethink their views on nationality in a fundamental way, that is, they were convinced to view the issue in a new light.[42]

That last sentence, however, raises an important methodological issue. How would I recognize persuasion if it were to walk through the door? In brief, the following can be said. I employed multiple data streams, consisting of interviews with committee members (five rounds spread over five years), confidential meeting summaries of nearly all the committee's meetings and various secondary sources – and triangulated across them. In the interviews, I asked two types of questions. A first touched upon an individual's own thought processes and (possibly) changing preferences. A second was more intersubjective, asking the interviewee to classify his/her interaction context. I gave them four possibilities – coercion, bargaining, persuasion/arguing, imitation – and asked for a rank ordering. Interviewees were also asked if their ranking changed over time and, if so, why.[43]

[41] At one of its first sessions, both France and Turkey declared that they had no national minorities and would countenance no change in this view.

[42] Jeffrey T. Checkel, "Going Native in Europe? Theorizing Social Interaction in European Institutions," *Comparative Political Studies*, 36:1/2 (February/March 2003), pp. 209–31.

[43] Ibid. On the use of triangulation to assess persuasion's causal role, see also the excellent application in Gheciu, "Security Institutions as Agents of Socialization?"

In sum, non-distributive mandates and actor independence promoted a form of cooperation where persuasion was able to play a role influencing preferences on nationality. Indeed, the regional norms to emerge from the committee's deliberations were different from what otherwise would have been the case. For example, on the question of dual nationality, a long-standing prohibitionary norm on it was relaxed, thus making European policies more open to the possibility of individuals holding two citizenships.[44]

Put differently, persuasion's causal role was facilitated as one moved from institutions as bargaining arenas to institutions as (possible) transformative settings marked by a thicker institutional context.[45] These findings are consistent with insights drawn from laboratory-experimental work in social psychology on the so-called contact hypothesis. They are also corroborated by results from two qualitative, case-study empirical research programs that emphasize non-bargaining dynamics in apolitical, technical settings – work on epistemic communities in IR theory and on comitology in EU studies.[46]

Membership and agency

Beyond the above, there is evidence that persuasive appeals are also promoted by institutional membership rules stressing exclusivity and by agency-level variables. Regarding the former, persuasion aimed at convincing an individual to change his or her basic attitudes appears to work best in front of groups with exclusive membership, where the emphasis is on small, knowledgeable, and private audiences.[47] This was the case in the small working group of the committee of experts on nationality discussed above. There is also evidence of such dynamics at work in small-group

[44] Council of Europe, European Convention on Nationality and Explanatory Report, Document DIR/JUR (97) 6 (Strasbourg: Council of Europe, 14 May 1997); Council of Europe, 1st European Conference on Nationality: Trends and Developments in National and International Law on Nationality, 18–19 October 1999, Document CONF/NAT (99) PRO 1 (Strasbourg: Council of Europe, 3 February 2000).

[45] Gourevitch, Katzenstein, and Keohane, "Memo on Persuasion."

[46] Respectively, Beyers, "Multiple Embeddedness and Socialization in Europe"; Peter Haas (ed.), "Knowledge, Power and International Policy Coordination." A special issue of *International Organization*, 46 (Winter 1992); Christian Joerges and Juergen Neyer, "From Intergovernmental Bargaining to Deliberative Political Processes: The Constitutionalisation of Comitology," *European Law Journal*, 3:3 (September 1997), pp. 273–99; and Joerges and Neyer, "Transforming Strategic Interaction into Deliberative Problem-Solving: European Comitology in the Foodstuffs Sector," *Journal of European Public Policy*, 4:4 (December 1997), pp. 609–25.

[47] Hooghe, "Several Roads Lead To International Norms, But Few Via International Socialization," however, it presents suggestive evidence that even in such exclusive, private settings, persuasion often fails. See below.

settings in post-Soviet Ukraine[48] and post-communist Eastern Europe,[49] as well as in a private monitoring procedure established by the Council of Europe to promote better compliance with human rights in its member states.[50]

A final factor linking persuasion to regional cooperation has nothing to do with institutions or their design. Instead, one needs to consider properties of the agents who may be at work within institutions. In particular, an individual's cognitive priors – that is, his/her background and previous thinking on the subject at hand – strongly affect the persuasion/cooperation linkage. A robust finding from several different research projects is that novices are much more likely to be open to persuasion.[51]

For example, in Ukraine, one reason the West was able to persuade and change minds on questions of citizenship and nationality in the first part of the 1990s was the newness of the Ukrainian participants in such exchanges. Many of these individuals were truly novices, with few ingrained cognitive priors on matters of nationality and citizenship. The recruitment of these novice outsiders was a direct consequence of Soviet policies, which saw major policy decisions taken in Moscow. The USSR thus bequeathed Ukraine few qualified home-grown personnel.

Consider the role played by Dr. Petro Chaliy, head of the Citizenship Department in the Presidential Administration through the mid-1990s. Before assuming this position, he was a researcher at the Institute of State and Law of the Ukrainian Academy of Sciences; his scholarly work examined constitutional law and local self-governance. Within the government, Chaliy therefore found himself in an unfamiliar position and uncertain environment, dealing with issues of first principle: the fundamental normative guidelines for Ukraine's conception of membership. He was a likely candidate for persuasion.

The evidence and research methodology behind such a claim are as follows. I interviewed Chaliy, his close collaborators and his Western interlocutors. I carried out a before and after comparison of Chaliy's writings on the subject (citizenship/nationality). I asked the counterfactual: absent intervention and attempts at normative suasion by regional institutions, would Ukrainian policy have been any different? Finally, I

[48] Jeffrey T. Checkel, "Why Comply? Social Learning and European Identity Change," *International Organization*, 55:3 (Summer 2001), pp. 553–88.

[49] Gheciu, "Security Institutions as Agents of Socialization?".

[50] Checkel, "Compliance and Conditionality."

[51] Johnston, "Treating International Institutions as Social Environments"; Gheciu, "Security Institutions as Agents of Socialization?" Material power asymmetries do not seem to be a relevant explanatory factor here as the finding holds for representatives from weaker states in Eastern Europe, as well as from strong ones in Asia (China).

compared word with deed, examining how and to what degree new beliefs translated into new policy.[52]

This claim about noviceness, which comes largely from work in social psychology, can be generalized. The issue is really one of embeddedness. Simply put, social actors, when entering a possible persuasive setting at the European regional level, are in no sense free agents; they arrive embedded in multiple contexts.

Consider the work of my EU collaborators in the project on international institutions and socialization in post-Cold War Europe. Their starting point is that individuals are embedded in multiple international and domestic institutions. However, these analysts go an important step further, theorizing and documenting how particular features of domestic and European organizations can hinder/promote persuasion or role enactment within a variety of EU institutions – including the Commission, Council working groups, or the Committee of Permanent Representatives (COREPER).[53] The clear conclusion is that efforts to explain the roles of these mechanisms and their link to regional cooperation will fail unless one systematically controls for prior national embeddedness.

The validity of the latter insight is further bolstered by the degree to which it overlaps with those drawn from other research traditions. This is particularly true of symbolic interactionism, where scholars have theorized multiple embeddedness in terms of role conflict.[54] Olsen makes a similar point in regards to the Europeanization literature, which explores the impact of the EU on nation states.[55]

The foregoing examples prompt two observations. First, while the results are intriguing from a broader disciplinary perspective (given how little attention the cooperation literature has paid to mechanisms like persuasion), in another, more important sense, they are surprising. This is,

[52] Checkel, "Why Comply?"

[53] See Morten Egeberg, "Transcending Intergovernmentalism? Identity and Role Perceptions of National Officials in EU Decision-Making," *Journal of European Public Policy*, 6 (September 1999), pp. 456–74; Egeberg, "An Organizational Approach to European Integration: Outline of a Complementary Perspective," *European Journal of Political Research*, 43 (March 2004), pp. 199–219; Beyers, "Multiple Embeddedness and Socialization in Europe"; Jeff Lewis, "Institutional Environments and Everyday Decision Making: Rationalist or Constructivist?" *Comparative Political Studies*, 36 (February/March 2003); Lewis, "The Janus Face of Brussels."

[54] Sheldon Stryker, *Symbolic Interactionism: A Social Structural Perspective* (Reading, MA: Benjamin-Cummings, 1980); John Meyer and David Strang, "Institutional Conditions for Diffusion," *Theory and Society*, 22 (August 1993); and, for an important application to international institutions, Michael N. Barnett, "Institutions, Roles, and Disorder: The Case of the Arab States System," *International Studies Quarterly*, 37 (September 1993), pp. 271–96.

[55] Johan P. Olsen, "The Many Faces of Europeanization," *Journal of Common Market Studies*, 40 (December 2002).

after all, Europe, where preference shifts are thought to be likely.[56] Yet, my collaborators and I found relatively few instances where persuasion played a role in changing basic attitudes.

Second, it is clear that domestic variables – the match between the structure of domestic and regional institutions, the embeddedness of agents in pre-existing national norms and values – play a central role in determining the degree of cooperation in European institutions. In one sense, this is not news. After all, in Moravcsik's liberal intergovernmentalist account, domestic interests are a driving force shaping the pattern of cooperation at the European level.[57] Moreover, several contributions to this volume emphasize domestic calculations of political survival as a key factor affecting the design and efficacy of institutions in other world regions.[58] However, the findings reported here reconceptualize and enrich our understanding of the domestic-regional nexus by moving beyond this narrow (instrumental) understanding of rationality.

One response to such cautions and caveats might be: "Good lord, you are looking in the wrong place!" Indeed, many of my examples come from the Council of Europe, which is a highly intergovernmental institution by purposeful design, or from EU units – COREPER and the European Council – where intergovernmental dynamics are thought to dominate. For evidence of preference shifts, I should have instead looked elsewhere – to that engine of Europe, the European Commision.

The European Commission

There have been many descriptive and policy studies of the Commission, and even more numerous claims about its power to alter the preferences of social actors ("going native," in Brussels-speak). However, only recently have such questions been subjected to sustained and rigorous social scientific analysis.[59]

[56] This is thought to be so for two reasons. Historically and compared to Asia, a distinct, more intense form of regionalism has developed in post-war Europe. This has facilitated the creation of a community, with common norms and rules. Theoretically, the IR literature on transnationalism and the sociological literature on organizations both suggest that value and preference change are more likely in institutionally thick environments. With its dense network of regional organizations, Europe easily qualifies as the thickest institutional environment beyond the nation-state anywhere on the globe. Zürn and Checkel, "Getting Socialized to Build Bridges."

[57] Moravcsik, *The Choice for Europe*.

[58] Barnett and Solingen; Herbst, both this volume.

[59] Liesbet Hooghe, "Top Commission Officials on Capitalism: An Institutionalist Understanding of Preferences," in Mark Aspinwall and Gerald Schneider (eds.), *The Rules of Integration: Institutionalist Approaches to the Study of Europe* (Manchester: Manchester University Press, 2001), pp. 152–73; Hooghe, *The European Commission and the*

From either a cross-regional or intra-regional (compared to other European institutions) perspective, the Commission of the European Union is unique. As Hooghe notes, the Commission:

is extraordinarily autonomous and powerful, and this, socialization theory predicts, should make it the most likely site for socialization. The European Commission is the steering body of the world's most encompassing supranational regime. It has a vocation to identify and defend the European interest over and above, and if need be, against, particular national interests. It is the agenda-setter in the European Union. It also has the authority to select and groom its employees with minimal national interference. So there are strong reasons to expect international socialization to be effective in the European Commission. If this powerful body cannot shape its employees' preferences, which international organization can?[60]

These features of the Commission are not simply a reflection of informal organizational norms, but, instead are anchored in EU treaties. For example, the Treaty on European Union instructs the Commission to serve the European interest and it requires Commissioners, who are appointed for five years by member states and the European Parliament, to be completely independent from any national government.

In addition to being bound by the Treaty, [Commissioners] are expected to adhere to the European Commission's internal staff regulations, which instruct that "an official shall carry out his duties and conduct himself solely with the interests of the Communities in mind; he shall neither seek nor take instructions from any government, authority, organisation or person outside his institution. . . . He shall carry out the duties assigned to him objectively, impartially and in keeping with his duty of loyalty to the Communities." Constitutional rules and house rules create clear expectations – norms – that are expressly designed to guide Commission officials, whether as political appointees or as permanent career officials. They prescribe the Commission and its employees to (1) put the Union interest first (supranationalism), (2) construe what this means pro-actively (agenda setting), and (3) promote the Union interest independently from national pressures (impartiality and autonomy).[61]

As this description makes clear, if there were ever a most likely case for cooperation in international institutions to be defined by the adoption of new roles or preference shifts, the Commission is it. Yet, in a striking finding, Hooghe finds little evidence of such dynamics at work.

Integration of Europe: Images of Governance (Cambridge: Cambridge University Press, 2002); Hooghe, "Several Roads Lead To International Norms, But Few Via International Socialization," pp. 861–98.

[60] Hooghe, "Several Roads Lead To International Norms, But Few Via International Socialization," p. 862.

[61] Ibid., pp. 863–4.

Based on two surveys of senior Commission officials conducted in 1996 and 2002, and controlling for a host of possible confounding factors,[62] her central conclusion is unambiguous. While support for the European project is extraordinarily high in the Commission, this has little, if anything, to do with preference shifts or the internalization of new values in it. Instead, top officials sustain Commission norms because national experiences motivate them to do so.[63] In her words, "these quintessentially European bureaucrats take their cues primarily from their national environment."[64]

For sure, Hooghe's survey/statistical techniques need to be supplemented with qualitative, process-tracing case studies that can better document causality and explore the role of specific mechanisms. Still, her preliminary results are a sobering reminder that even in the thickly and deeply institutionalized setting of Europe and, specifically, of the EU Commission, our arguments on regional dynamics will go astray if we fail to control for national variables.

Summary

It is domestic politics – broadly understood – that best explains the somewhat unexpected findings sketched above, where we see relatively few shifts – given Europe's most-likely-case status – in core properties of actors. Indeed, while Europe, when compared to other regions, may be head of class in designing robust and intrusive regional bodies, it also leads the others in having extraordinarily strong and historically rooted national traditions and institutions, which, in turn, decisively affect the degree of regional cooperation.

What makes Europe different – or is it different?

In many ways, European institutions – their design, effectiveness, domestic impact – are different from their counterparts in other world regions. Consider, for example, the fate of security institutions in Europe and

[62] Hooghe conducted in-depth interviews with all respondents in 1996, and shorter interviews with a subset in 2002. Of a total population of 210 or 230 officials at the respective time points, 105 responded in 1996 and 93 in 2002. For details on the data and methods, see www.unc.edu/%7Ehooghe/commission.htm.

[63] See also Beyers, "Multiple Embeddedness and Socialization in Europe"; Egeberg, "An Organizational Approach to European Integration."

[64] Hooghe, "Several Roads Lead To International Norms, But Few Via International Socialization," p. 862. See also Acharya and Johnston, Chapter 1 this volume, on "indigenous modes" of socialization.

Asia.[65] While NATO has become both a military alliance and a community of values,[66] the South East Asia Treaty Organization (SEATO) could not even make it as a weak security organization.

Beyond security, Europe is different in additional, important ways. Compared to other regions, it has a literal alphabet soup of institutions.[67] Moreover, in no other world region have the main regional institutions grown so rapidly over the past decade and a half – with the EU, OSCE, and Council of Europe alone nearly doubling their memberships. This rapid expansion has also made conditionality and its accompanying incentives-based approach to cooperation more evident in Europe than in other areas.[68] So, when viewed cross-regionally, there is little doubt that Europe is different.

Yet, for four reasons, we should be wary of claims that Europe and its post-World War II experience with crafting regional institutions represent a fundamental break with the past. First, if we shift the baseline and view Europe *intra-regionally over time* and not across separate world regions, a more sobering picture emerges. For example, claims are often made that European institutions – and especially the EU – have wrought dramatic changes in the core properties of European states over the past fifty years. If we define a change in core properties as shifts in preferences, then the empirical work reviewed above indicates such changes are less dramatic than first assumed.

If, instead, we define changes in core properties as shifts in national identities and cultures, then, here, too, a growing body of empirical research shows that the identities, discourses, and public spheres fostered by European institutions are still dominated by their national counterparts.[69] Even in cases such as Germany, where there is strong evidence

[65] Christopher Hemmer and Peter J. Katzenstein, "Why is There No NATO in Asia? Collective Identity, Regionalism, and the Origins of Multilateralism," *International Organization*, 56:3 (Summer 2002), pp. 575–607.

[66] Thomas Risse-Kappen, *Cooperation Among Democracies: The European Influence on US Foreign Policy* (Princeton: Princeton University Press, 1995); Alexandra Gheciu, *NATO in the "New Europe": The Politics of International Socialization after the Cold War* (Stanford: Stanford University Press, 2005). See also Henry Farrell and Gregory Flynn, "Piecing Together the Democratic Peace: The CSCE and the 'Construction' of Security in Post-Cold War Europe," *International Organization*, 53 (Summer 1999), pp. 505–36.

[67] Weber, "Origins of the European Bank for Reconstruction and Development."

[68] John Van Oudenaren, "The Limits of Conditionality: Nuclear Reactor Safety in Central and Eastern Europe, 1991–2001," *International Politics*, 38 (December 2001). I exclude here the global reach of the conditionality practiced by institutions such as the IMF or World Bank.

[69] Thomas Risse-Kappen and Matthias Maier (eds.), *Europeanization, Collective Identities, and Public Discourses*. Draft Final Report submitted to the European Commission (Florence: European University Institute and Robert Schuman Centre for Advanced Studies, 2003), and the research summarized therein.

of a Europeanized national identity,[70] there is a difficult methodological problem of multiple causality to sort out (impact of Allied occupation and denazification versus that of EU).

Second, even if we accept that European institutions have brought about dramatic domestic changes, a central argument of this essay – the importance of national contexts – needs to be kept in mind. As seen, national institutions and traditions have had a major influence in shaping the degree of cooperation at the European level. As European institutions and especially the EU begin to address policy areas (citizenship, immigration policy, fundamental rights) that are fundamentally and deeply constitutive of contemporary nation states, one might expect the importance of national contexts to increase – and to do so in a direction that likely weakens the degree of cooperation.

Indeed, a mini-test of this claim has already occurred. Over the course of 2003–2004, EU member states completed negotiations on a constitutional treaty for the Union. While a disappointment to the most ardent Euro-federalists, this treaty moved the EU further in a federal direction, with new competencies in such areas as citizenship and fundamental rights.[71] Yet, on the latter – to cite just one example – Eurobarometer polls consistently find concern for basic rights well down on the list of priorities of ordinary Europeans.[72] In retrospect, it is perhaps then not that surprising that two founding members of the Union – France and the Netherlands – rejected the treaty in referendums held in the early summer of 2005.

Third, the enhanced degree of cooperation scholars see in Europe may also be an artifact of theoretical underspecification, with research on European integration and cooperation consistently ignoring or bracketing off the domestic political.[73] In part, this choice was unintentional and simply influenced by broader trends in international relations theory,

[70] Peter J. Katzenstein (ed.), *Tamed Power: Germany in Europe* (Ithaca, NY: Cornell University Press, 1997).

[71] "Treaty Establishing a Constitution for Europe," *Official Journal of the European Union*, 47 (16 December 2004). For a concise summary of the constitution, see http://europa.eu.int/scadplus/constitution/index_en.htm [last accessed 25 September 2006].

[72] In July 1999, Europeans ranked "guaranteeing the rights of the individual and respect for the principles of democracy in Europe" sixth in a list of twelve priority EU actions. Eurobarometer, "Public Opinion in the European Union, Report Number 51" (Brussels: European Commission, July 1999), p. 56. Little had changed by late 2003, when they ranked the same question ninth in a list of fifteen priority actions. Eurobarometer, "Public Opinion in the European Union: Autumn 2003, Report Number 60" (Brussels: European Commission, February 2004), p. 20.

[73] Europeanists are certainly not alone in this regard. Similar critiques can be made of much of the new regionalism literature. Acharya and Johnston, Chapter 1 this volume.

where neglect of domestic politics is long-standing.[74] However, it was also intentional and driven by what scholars saw to be the main force behind European integration: elites. If integration was (mainly) about elites, why bother with more systematically integrating domestic politics into one's account?[75]

More recently, scholars are coming to recognize that the EU – and theory about it – is to some extent becoming a victim of its own success. The deepening of integration over the past decade and the current process of constitutionalization have spawned increasing domestic political resistance to and mobilization against the European project. In turn, this has led prominent theorists of integration to add a strong domestic politics-politicization element to their arguments.[76] In addition, new work on Europeanization emphasizes domestic cultural context, theorizing and documenting how religious communities that are at once both deeply national and transnational are likely to affect the degree of cooperation in an enlarged European Union.[77]

In both cases, the addition of an explicit domestic element leads analysts to evince more pessimism about the future of regional cooperation in Europe. For example, we now hear that "domestic support for European supranationalism is as weak as it has ever been," while "religion, as a political force, will be more likely to hinder the further integration of the European continent than to advance it."[78]

For sure, compared to other regions, Europe and its institutions are and will remain different. Yet, as the foregoing suggests, both developments on the continent and the bringing of domestic politics back to integration theory point to a narrowing of such differences – a lessening of Europe's uniqueness – as time passes.

Fourth, there is a data issue that complicates the drawing of comparisons between European institutions and those found elsewhere. Compared to virtually every other world region, there is lots of high-quality documentary, survey, and interview data available on the EU and other European organizations. In many other settings, where democracy

[74] Peter A. Gourevitch, "Domestic Politics and International Relations," in Walter Carlsnaes, Thomas Risse-Kappen, and Beth Simmons (eds.), *Handbook of International Relations*, pp. 309–25, for an excellent discussion.

[75] Zürn and Checkel, "Getting Socialized to Build Bridges," for details.

[76] Liesbet Hooghe and Gary Marks, "The Neo-functionalists Were (Almost) Right: Politicization and European Integration," Paper presented at the ARENA Research Seminar (Oslo: ARENA Centre for European Studies, University of Oslo, 5 October 2004).

[77] Timothy Byrnes and Peter J. Katzenstein (eds.), *Religion in an Expanding Europe* (Cambridge: Cambridge University Press, 2006).

[78] Hooghe and Marks, "The Neo-functionalists Were (Almost) Right," p. 15; Byrnes and Katzenstein, *Religion in an Expanding Europe*, p. 304, respectively.

and norms of transparency are not as advanced, it is hard to imagine researchers having access to such data. If they did, perhaps Europe would look a bit less different.[79]

Conclusions

The study of European regional institutions is in flux. Institutions like NATO and the Council of Europe have literally reinvented themselves to accommodate the realities of a post-Cold War setting where former dividing lines had vanished and earlier policies/strategies made no sense. For the European Union, its current process of constitutionalization suggests an institution poised on a precipice. To one side lie deeper integration, a constitutionalized future, and the emergence of a quasi-federal polity. To the other lies a return to a more intergovernmental way of operating. This change and flux make Europe and its institutions fun to study, but hard to compare to other regions. That's the bad news.

The good news is how scholars are studying this institutional dynamism. (Mostly) gone are the days when they drew upon EU-specific research traditions (neo-functionalism, intergovernmentalism, and their successors) to examine European institutions. Instead and as suggested throughout this essay, researchers are now more prone to embed their studies in broader social scientific debates and concepts. As the latter in principle travel easily across regions, the project of comparison is facilitated. If not yet completely gone, then the days of *sui generis* arguments about Europe are numbered, which is very good news indeed.

[79] Johnston's study of China and international institutions will be an important test of this argument. Alastair Iain Johnston, *Social States: China in International Institutions* (Princeton: Princeton University Press, forthcoming). See also Johnston, "Conclusions and Extensions – Toward Mid-Range Theorizing and Beyond Europe," *International Organization*, 59 (Fall 2005), pp. 1013–44.

8 Conclusion: institutional features, cooperation effects, and the agenda for further research on comparative regionalism

Amitav Acharya and Alastair Iain Johnston

By way of conclusion, we want to try to summarize a very rich set of studies. To this end we focus on four issues. First, we look at the variations in institutional design (our first dependent variable) among the regional institutions as a function of variation in the matrix of independent variables identified in the introduction. Second, we look at the variation in the nature of cooperation across regional institutions (our second dependent variable), as a function of institutional design (our first dependent variable now performing as an independent variable). Here we also highlight similarities and differences in the efficacy across regional institutions. Third, we highlight some tentative findings about the relationship between institutional design and the nature of cooperation. And finally, we set out some arguments and suggestions about extending the research agenda on comparative regional institutional design.

Although we presented the contributors with a list of variables on institutional design and indicators of the nature of cooperation, we did not insist that each chapter writer must address each of these variables and indicators. We allowed them the freedom to decide which of these were most relevant to their case study. In short, we recommended, but did not impose, a matrix of variables and indicators. The result, greater autonomy for the contributors, also created the condition for a rich set of empirical studies. But we are able to find important common ground and make generalizations about similarities and differences in meaningful ways.

Variations in institutional design, and their sources

At the outset, it may be useful to remind ourselves of a debate in the literature on regionalism, which formed the original rationale for this project. How unique are regional institutions in different parts of the world? Since the publication of Haas' influential article "International Integration: The

European and the Universal Process," much of the comparative literature on regional institution-building seems to be preoccupied with identifying and analyzing regional uniqueness and exceptionalism.[1] This tendency has been most notably replicated in the recent literature on European and Asian regional institutions. The EU is widely regarded as the most successful experiment in regional institution-building. For some it is seen as a model for the rest of the world to follow and a yardstick against which all other regional institutions are compared and their success measured. The fact that scholars and policymakers in Asia believe that the EU cannot be emulated underscores their concurrence that the EU model is descriptively very distinctive (though inappropriate for judging institutional effectiveness or the nature and quality of cooperation). They also add a normative argument, namely that the EU's sovereignty-challenging approach should not be emulated in an area where sovereignty is a hard-earned and, to this day, novel idea. Instead, regional institutions in the developing world should develop their own distinctive approach, perhaps emulating ASEAN, one of the most successful experiments in regional cooperation outside the West. Moreover, many claim, the ASEAN model has elements of uniqueness which ought to be highlighted and analyzed in the theoretical literature on regionalism.

One of the most important contributions of this volume is to consider this debate about regional exceptionalism by comparing the findings of the chapters on the design and effectiveness of various regional institutions. In their own ways, the four non-European chapters speak to such patterns.

In the case of Asian institutions, Khong and Nesadurai note a distinctive "ASEAN way" which emphasizes informality, flexibility, non-confrontation, and consensus. These features derive from Southeast Asian cultural practices and sustain the domestic autonomy of ruling regimes. In other words, the "ASEAN Way" is also a relatively efficient way of protecting fragile domestic political arrangements.[2] Africa too has a style of regional cooperation which has been identified by Herbst. African regional cooperation "tends to be extremely inclusive (a large number of participants), formal (in the sense that organizations are well-defined and their rules elaborated at length), non-hierarchical (no country is privileged and secretariats are generally weak), and attentive to national sovereignty."[3] Unlike Khong and Nesadurai, he does not, however, see these traits as being rooted in African cultural styles. Instead, he attributes

[1] Ernst B. Haas, "International Integration: The European and the Universal Process," *International Organization*, 15:3 (Summer 1961), pp. 366–92.
[2] Khong and Nesadurai, this volume. [3] Herbst, this volume, p. 130.

the African style of socialization and regional institution-building to a shared predicament of the rulers in securing regime legitimacy and a common aversion to external interference in their domestic affairs. One might note here that regime legitimation and non-interference also drives Asian regional cooperation, reinforced, at least in the case of ASEAN, by cultural affinities.

The institutional design of the Arab League also shows distinctive features including, as Barnett and Solingen note, a pan-Arab ideology, an identity-based membership, the protection of state sovereignty, and a commitment to consensus rules. Moreover, domestic survival of regimes was a crucial factor in the design of the Arab League, "trumping an effective norm of unification."[4]

Finally, in his chapter on Latin American regionalism, Domínguez also generalizes about "style." Latin American institutions have been innovative and their development autonomous of much of the institutional development in the rest of the world. Domínguez labels Latin Americans as "international rule innovators," rather than "price takers."[5] Among these rule innovations was the doctrine of *uti possidetis juris* (inviolability of colonial boundaries), a century before its spread throughout Africa, Asia, and the former Soviet Union. Other innovations concern rules supporting the defense of "hard shell" notions of sovereignty and non-intervention and interstate dispute resolution.

One of the main lines of difference is between the "formal" informality of Asian institutions and the "formal" formality of those in other regions. That is, ASEAN states, for instance, have deliberately and carefully designed their institutions to be informal. And in other regions the formality of the institutions has been a cover for the informality or the weakly legalized way in which they have functioned.

One common feature of these regional "ways" is that notwithstanding geographic, cultural, and political differences and the time lag in their evolution, the emphasis on sovereignty and non-interference has remained a powerful constant. This is the case even in Latin America, where a distinct shift in recent decades from sovereignty and non-intervention toward a more intrusive form of regionalism does not undermine its original credentials as an innovator of this norm. It also extends to Europe, where, as Checkel argues, the differences between Europe and the rest of the world remain, but are often overstated. He questions some of the more exceptionalist claims about the EU which contrasts the supranational, legalistic, and highly formal or institutionalized nature of European regionalism against Asia's "soft institutionalism." While European institutions "are

[4] Barnett and Solingen, this volume, p. 213. [5] Domínguez, this volume, p. 126.

and will remain different," he notes, "developments on the continent and the bringing of domestic politics back to integration theory point to a narrowing of such differences – a lessening of Europe's uniqueness – as time passes."[6]

These similarities help to keep in perspective the variations that do exist. As these chapters suggest, the differences cannot easily be attributed to big "capital C" culture – the broader social mores, norms, and habits that characterize daily social interaction. For example, when Herbst speaks of a "clear style of African regional cooperation," he is not referring to a big "capital C" culturally generated style. If anything, he dismisses the broader society's cultural variables as a general explanation, pointing to the sheer diversity of cultures across the continent. Instead, he focuses on a common predicament: "similar problems in securing their rule and a common set of concerns about foreign interference in their domestic affairs." Hence, regional norms and institutional styles reflect regime security and domestic politics, rather than cultural styles per se.

Following from the above, one can look at generalizations from the case studies in terms of the key elements of institutional design outlined in the introduction (see Tables 8.1 and 8.2).

Elements of institutional design

Recall that the project disaggregated institutional design into six elements or features. We summarize below the main variations in these elements uncovered by the empirical chapters.

Membership The most important variation here is between Asia, the EU, and NATO on the one hand, and the OAS, the OAU/AU, and the Arab League on the other. ASEAN, the EU, and NATO all started stressing exclusivity on the basis of political, ideological, and security considerations and criteria. This in turn was partly a reflection of Cold War geopolitics. On the other hand, the OAS, the OAU, and the Arab League remained open to all regional states with the exception of Cuba (suspended), South Africa, and Israel. South Africa has now joined the OAU/AU, and Cuba is likely to join the OAS after the end of the Castro regime, although Israel is unlikely to be invited to the Arab League (or an Arab-dominated Middle East Organization) even after the resolution of the Palestinian issue with the creation of a Palestinian state.

With the end of the Cold War, almost all exclusionary regional groups have undertaken significant initiatives toward expanding their

[6] Checkel, this volume.

Table 8.1 *Explanations for institutional design*

	Type of cooperation problem	Number of actors	Ideology and identity (liberalism; post-colonialism)	Systemic and subsystemic power distribution	Domestic politics (regime type; salience of ethnic conflict; state authority)	Extra-regional institution OR non-state actors as agents of change (e.g. do templates for institutions come from outside the region?)	Geography
Africa (**OAU**, **AU**)	• functional problem type relatively unimportant	• large numbers, accentuates joining as a marker of independence • regional pariah (South Africa) key for development	• weak regional identity • initially strong identity as victim of colonialism	• French power important for creation of CFA	• regime legitimacy and survival critical • regime types varied	• NGOs play limited role • attempt to emulate EU	• helps determine boundaries of membership
Asia (**ASEAN**, **ARF**)	• functional problem type relatively unimportant	• small numbers (ASEAN) • the ARF larger	• moderately strong sub-regional identity (ASEAN) • weak regional identity (ARF)	• Indonesian power important for ASEAN's creation • uncertainty about shifts in regional power distribution critical (for ASEAN and the ARF)	• regime legitimacy and survival critical • regime types varied	• NGOs (Track II) play some role • other regional models explicitly rejected	• important for ASEAN in determining boundaries of membership, not important for the ARF

				• uncertainty about future economic growth due to economic rise of China a key factor in economic cooperation (AFTA)			
Europe (NATO, EU)	• functional problems important for multiple designs of NATO's security arrangements	• small numbers, conditioned expansion	• strong political/regional identity as democracies	• bipolarity critical to development of NATO • US hegemony critical for high level of control and low level of state autonomy in NATO	• regime type (shared democracy) critical • regime types similar	• NGOs play limited role	• helps define boundaries of membership. Some territorial link to Europe a condition for NATO
Latin America (OAS)	• functional problem type relatively unimportant	• regional pariah (Cuba) key for development in 1960–1980 period	• weak regional identity, divided mainly into Latin American and Anglo-Caribbean	• systemic power distribution not very important for creation • collapse of bipolarity encouraged spread of economic liberalism	• regime type varied	• NGOs important for democratization processes	• helps determine boundaries of membership
Middle East (Arab League)	• functional problem type relatively unimportant	• regional pariah (Israel) key for Arab solidarity	• strong shared identity	• systemic power distribution not very important	• regime types varied • regime legitimacy and survival critical	• NGOs play limited role	• not so important in determining boundaries of membership. Language and identity more important.

Table 8.2 *Features of institutional design*

	Membership	Scope (e.g. intrusiveness in domestic politics)	Rules	Norms (e.g. ideology of institution)	Mandate (e.g. process vs. outcome; deliberative vs. distributive
Africa (**OAU**, **AU**)	inclusive	• unintrusive, no emphasis on democracy expansion or defense	• consensus • fairly elaborate and detailed • respect for sovereignty and independence	• tension between formal pan-continentalism and defense of sovereignty • more embrace of economic liberalism over time • minor weakening of non-intervention norms	• process-oriented
Asia (**ASEAN**, **ARF**)	• exclusive (ASEAN) • inclusive (ARF)	• AFTA mechanisms intrusive • new security roles with the development of the ARF • unintrusive, some gradual and limited movement toward concern about domestic governance (ASEAN), or more proactive preventive diplomacy activities (ARF)	• flexible consensus (chair has some leeway to declare consensus) • legalistic rules for AFTA • relatively non-legalistic rules for the ARF • respect for sovereignty and independence	• pan-continentalism weak, defense of sovereignty primary • convergence around market-oriented economic regionalism	• deliberative, process-oriented

Europe (**EU, NATO**)	• exclusive	• highly intrusive in domestic politics; strict domestic governance requirements for membership • NATO expanding missions from collective defense to peace-making and peace-keeping	• consensus, *de facto* veto (NATO) • flexible procedures, not especially elaborate or detailed (NATO) • EU moving toward majority voting on non-sensitive issues	• strong influence of liberal theories of security and development	• distributive (access to economic and political benefits are conditional)
Latin America (**OAS**)	• inclusive	• increasingly intrusive over time, with more emphasis on defense of democracy	• *de facto* shift from super-majority to consensus (?) • elaborate and detailed • respect for sovereignty and independence	• tension between formal pan-continentalism and defense of sovereignty • some redefinition of pan-continentalism to include promotion of democratic values	• minor distributive (controls access to limited economic benefits) • outcome-oriented (defense of democracy)
Middle East **(Arab League)**	• inclusive, based on shared Arab identity	• very unintrusive – no effort to deal with domestic governance issues	• consensus • fairly elaborate and detailed • respect for sovereignty and independence	• tension between formal pan-continentalism and defense of sovereignty, latter clearly dominant • little or no consensus behind promotion of liberal political and economic values	• deliberative?

membership. Maximum inclusiveness is now a common feature of all the regional organizations under investigation here. The partial exception is NATO. While it is expanding to include Eastern European states, its membership is still ideologically exclusive. NATO restricts full membership to an exclusive and trustworthy group of consolidated liberal democracies and uses partnership as a process to reduce uncertainty and socialize its partners with regard to a broad range of security-related issues.

Scope As the chapters demonstrate, there is considerable variation across regions in the scope of institutions. At one end of the spectrum is the Middle East. The Arab League, ironically for an organization which under the Arabism framework disdained national sovereignty, is least involved in domestic affairs.

At the other end is the European Union and NATO. The EU has seen an expanded mandate toward citizenship and fundamental rights, even without the constitution whose future now appears to be in some doubt. As for NATO, while it remains focused on traditional collective security activities, it has expanded its activities to include, essentially, socialization and security management functions, including counter-terrorism, defense economics, environmental protection, disaster relief, and humanitarian intervention. Moreover, many of these functions are now "out of area."

In Asia, there was no macro-regional political organization during the Cold War. ASEAN did combine political and economic functions, but had no direct security role. In the post-Cold War era, the institutional scope of ASEAN has expanded to include economic integration, financial cooperation, trans-boundary environmental problems, and non-traditional security issues such as environment, transnational crime, terrorism, and infectious diseases. ASEAN has also created new ASEAN-plus institutions to deal with new transnational issue areas that involve states outside Southeast Asia and which could not be addressed exclusively on a subregional (Southeast Asian) basis. But while Asian institutions have expanded dramatically in embracing transnational issues, they have shied away from expanding into domestic matters. Asian institutions are least prone to domestic intrusion and constitute one end of the spectrum.

The scope of regional institutions in Latin America has expanded both at regional and subregional levels, increasingly covering domestic political issues especially related to democratization. In Asia, security has been brought onto ASEAN's regional agenda, and it has also appeared in the form of an entirely new institution, the ARF. Regional institutions in Africa remain somewhere in between Asia and Latin America.

As a multipurpose organization, the OAU/AU always had a theoretically broad agenda. While the AU has accepted the need for regional action in humanitarian disasters, unlike the OAS, Africa has seen no comparable extension of its agenda to domestic issues, such as the promotion of democracy, although it has moved to some extent in that direction.

Formal rules Here, the major variations are really between European and non-European organizations. Most of the latter operate on the consensus principle, and there is really little variation among them. Moreover, their formal or constitutional norms read alike, including respect for sovereignty and territorial integrity, non-interference in the internal affairs of states, the pacific settlement of disputes, and renunciation of the threat or use of force. But despite the declaratory commitment to all these rules, the relative salience of these rules does vary across regional institutions. In this regard, Asia and the Middle East have moved the least; Africa has shifted somewhat, with Latin America changing the most.

Apart from these behavioral norms, regional institutions also have procedural norms. In ASEAN, these norms are collectively known as the "ASEAN Way." Once again, the consensus principle is pretty much the same in other regional organizations outside Europe. But one may note an important variation between Asia and Africa. Asia's general avoidance of formal legalistic rules differs markedly from Africa, where cooperation is very "formal (in the sense that organizations are well-defined and their rules elaborated at length)."[7] But this does not necessarily mean African nations are more likely to comply with these rules. Rather, these rules serve mainly a symbolic function as indicators of sovereignty. Asia may be moving in a more formal, legalized direction, as Khong and Nesadurai point out in the discussion of economic cooperation in ASEAN. But it is still, and will remain, a far cry from European institutions.

Why the commitment to consensus? While in Southeast Asia, consensus has been linked to local "cultural practices," in reality the preference for consensus reflects, as Barnett and Solingen point out in relation to the Arab League, the salience of state sovereignty rather than traditional culture ("a desire to preserve state sovereignty, and a related commitment to consensus rules").[8] Consensus rules prevent any radical change in the limits on institutions to develop more intrusive principles and roles. The reasons for the preference for consensus found in the case of the Arab League can easily apply to other Third World regional groups. The consensus/unanimity rule of the League is meant to check any tendency toward a unitary state or supranationalism. Among the implications for

[7] Herbst, this volume, p. 130. [8] Barnett and Solingen, this volume, p. 213.

consensus in the case of the League are control mechanisms that limit the autonomy of the secretariat: "Arab leaders designed the Arab League to be an expressive institution emphasizing rhetoric over action, one with little autonomy that would not challenge the status quo or initiate changes that might undermine regime survival."[9] Once again, this is similar in the case of Africa and Asia, and to some extent the OAS.

But the OAS is distinctive in one respect: the most formal rules of cooperation outside Europe can be found here. The formality of these rules does not mean they are watertight and not subject to flexible interpretation. Hence, Domínguez notes that while the Spanish American Republics and Brazil developed four "international rules" to govern their intra-mural relations, such as honoring the boundaries inherited from empires, upholding sovereignty and non-intervention, and active resort to mediation of disputes, the fourth of these rules (practices) was laxity in the implementation of agreements. This laxity dilutes the overall effect of legalism and makes it more comparable to Asia and Africa than would be expected. This is reinforced by the fact that the OAS' *de facto* rules have "changed over time . . . from a super-majority to 'consensus'."[10]

NATO has few formal rules, and these show a clear preference for consensus-based decision procedures which are typically found in an intergovernmental organization. Indeed, decision-making in the North Atlantic Council (NAC) is marked by processes of consultation, and attempts to reach consensus, without formal voting procedures either for or against decision proposals. The same consensus principle also applies to decisions taken with NATO's Partner countries. With the expansion of the alliance in the post-Cold War era, there has been a trend toward even greater flexibility in decision-making. Overall then, there is less variation over time in rules across regional institutions than meets the eye.

The European Union is making significant moves toward majority voting. Changes to decision-making procedures adopted by the Constitutional Treaty adopted by the European Council in Brussels in June 2004 ensure that more decisions are reached through majority decision-making, rather than unanimity. The procedures of consensus and veto mechanisms, however, will continue to apply to the politically sensitive issues of foreign policy, security, and defense.[11] And the EU's march to constitutionalism is subject to limits, as Checkel noted, even before the French and Dutch opposition to the constitution effectively killed it. Checkel foresees continued tensions between a constitutionalized future

[9] Ibid., p. 193. [10] Domínguez, this volume, p. 122.
[11] "Toward a European Constitution," http://europa.eu.int/constitution

and intergovernmentalism. If the latter trend is to find stronger expression, then it would make the EU less distinctive than it was thought to be at one point.

Norms and ideology The most specific and striking statement about the ideology of a regional institution has been made by Schimmelfennig, who, drawing on Risse-Kappen, identifies the formal ideology of NATO to consist of a *liberal theory* based on liberal-democratic governance plus multilateral and peaceful conflict management. The same liberal principles underlie NATO's partnerships. This is not surprising, as NATO was an ideological Cold War alliance. The EU is also strongly wedded to a liberal ideology, which encompasses democracy, but also extends specifically to liberal economies, the EU's original focus.

Outside of the Euro-Atlantic area, the chief ideology of regional institutions, especially in their formative years, was different forms of pan-continentalism: pan-Americanism in the case of the OAS, pan-Arabism for the Arab League, and pan-Africanism for the OAU/AU. In Asia, a limited degree of pan-Asianism was evident in early post-war efforts to build regional institutions, but failed to gain ground. In Africa and the Middle East, regional institutions emerged from a contestation between pan-ideologies and the secular claim of state sovereignty. While this contestation seemed initially to favor the former, it was not long before the latter prevailed. These tensions between continental solidarity and state sovereignty have been brought out most clearly in the Barnett and Solingen chapter. The architects of the Arab League "designed it to fail," in the sense that they placed a premium on maintaining statist notions, and had no intention of political integration. It is important to note that while ideology was crucial to the formation of the Arab League and the OAU, this did not ensure their effectiveness. By contrast, Asia, which did not develop a regional organization based on pan-Asianism, despite some efforts in this regard by leaders like India's Jawaharlal Nehru, saw the emergence of a form of regionalism underpinned by sovereignty norms that was arguably more effective in ensuring regional order.

Another ideological factor that has shaped regional institutional design in the developing world is variation in the impact of political and economic liberalism. Initially, regional organizations in the Third World shunned both liberal politics and economics. Non-intervention assumed priority over democracy promotion, and having a democratic political system was not a criterion for membership, and their economic approaches were geared toward collective self-reliance, rather than participation in the globalization process. But this has changed significantly, with regional institutions across the Third World embracing market economies.

The same is not true of ideological variations in the political sphere. Unlike the EU and NATO, in recent years Asian institutions have not made any specific political ideology their criterion for membership. Hence communist Vietnam (and Laos) have been co-opted into ASEAN, whose members continue to be ruled by political regimes of all hues: military dictatorship, communist government, presidential and parliamentary democracies (with varying degrees of civil liberties), and an absolute monarchy. This ideological diversity is replicated at the wider Asian level, where communist China has become the lynchpin of regional institution-building activities in the post-Cold War era.

Unlike Asian regional institutions, the OAS has openly embraced liberal democracy, with a marked shift from non-intervention to democracy promotion, although this is subject to limits. Other non-Western regional institutions continue to embrace ideological diversity. Africa is increasingly receptive to liberal economics, and is more willing to move away from non-intervention to allow for a limited embrace of the democracy promotion objective. The situation in the Middle East is similar to that in Asia in the political respect, with regional institutions especially reluctant to embrace political liberalism, and they lag significantly behind Asia in promoting liberal economics.

Mandate The mandates of Asian, African, and Middle Eastern regional groupings share common features and may be contrasted with that of the EU, with the OAS closer to the former than the latter. Initially, most adopted a mandate which Khong and Nesadurai describe in the ASEAN context as "decidedly deliberative, stressing regular consultations and dialogue among its members on a host of shared intra-regional problems and wider concerns."[12] The ARF has thus far stressed "brainstorming, developing habits of dialogue and consensus on threat sources, and has, in the main, avoided more intrusive mechanisms" such as preventive diplomacy measures.[13] But some shift in this mandate has occurred, although none have come close to the EU style mandate, which covers distributive issues (e.g. access to economic and political benefits). The ARF has discussed sensitive regional issues, and set up institutions such as the inter-sessional support group meetings. But it is important to bear in mind that regional organizations can undertake new roles without a formal change of mandate; the OAS' mission of defense of democracy did not require a formal change of mandate.[14]

[12] Khong and Nesadurai, this volume, p. 40. [13] Ibid., p. 62.
[14] Domínguez, this volume, pp. 122–23.

Sources of continuity and change in institutional design

What explains the variations in institutional design outlined above? The chapter writers explored a variety of plausible independent variables from a wide range of theoretical perspectives.

Type of cooperation problem Most chapters dealing with non-Western regional institutions provide little evidence of the salience of functional considerations. In the case of the ARF "the functional variable is of least help in understanding . . . institutional design," because its founders "were uncertain about the kind of strategic interaction or game that was being played; one of the main purposes of the ARF was to clarify the nature of the game."[15] In Latin America, despite having a number of "functional" or "issue area" "specialized international subsystems," there is not much functionality in institutional design overall. Moreover, "The same states, in the same subregion, cooperate over one issue and fight over another. Cooperation-inducing institutions and rules that govern in one issue area (trade, counter-subversion) have not always prevented war or threats of war."[16] Functional considerations may be more important than cultural forces as in Africa, as Herbst points out ("the African style of international coordination developed because African leaders face generally similar problems in securing their rule and have a common set of concerns about foreign interference in their domestic affairs"),[17] and also in Asia, but that does not make them the dominant factor shaping institutional design.

Number of actors Among other determinants of institutional design, the number of actors has been especially important in the case of Africa where large membership is seen as a "marker for sovereignty."[18] But as noted in the earlier section dealing with membership, this has not been important for Asian organizations before the end of the Cold War. ASEAN was not especially inclusive, but post-Cold War ASEAN and the new ARF have been very inclusive-minded. The Arab League, the OAU/AU, and the OAS have not seen much expansion because they were already fairly inclusive, their membership has always been open on the basis of the geographic principle. During the Cold War, a common feature of three major macro-regional institutions was the existence of a regional pariah: South Africa in the case of the OAU, Israel in the case of the Arab League, and Cuba in the case of the OAS. This might have an important effect in shaping their economic and security agenda, but this

[15] Khong and Nesadurai, this volume, p. 70. [16] Domínguez, this volume, p. 99.
[17] Herbst, this volume, pp. 130–31. [18] Ibid., p. 137.

has already ended in the case of the OAU/AU, and will most certainly end with the demise of the Castro regime in Cuba, but will remain in the case of Israel. The most significant expansion of the OAS has been in the earlier period, from Spanish America to all of America, but there has been little change since then. In principle, membership of the OAS is open to all Latin American countries, except for Cuba's suspension from OAS active membership in 1962. The increase in the membership in the OAS in the 1960s and 1970s was due to the addition of newly independent Anglophone Caribbean countries.

The most dramatic changes in membership have taken place in Europe, with the EU, the OSCE, and the Council of Europe nearly doubling their memberships. In the case of NATO, exclusivity was important from the outset, due to the nature of the institution, collective defense, rather than collective security or cooperative security. But NATO too has expanded as part of its post-Cold War restructuring.

The trend toward greater inclusiveness is likely to affect the principle of consensus decision-making. In the case of ASEAN, it is already making consensus-building difficult and contributed to growing recognition for further institutionalization of its hitherto informal decision-making procedures. In the EU, it's likely that the membership expansion would reinforce the perceived need for majority voting.

Identity In the Middle East, the Arab League's identity-based membership and exclusive pan-Arab ideology imposed very few specific demands on Arab states and were nearly identical to the norms of international society in terms of the recognition of state sovereignty. In Asia, regional identity mattered even less, given a very weak notion of pan-Asianism after World War II. More important in Asia have been subregional identities, especially that of ASEAN.[19] In Africa, regional cooperation and integration was heavily influenced by questions of identity, as well as the various linkages with the erstwhile colonial powers. Overall, while regional organizations have assumed or consciously sought to promote a collective identity, this has not meant institutional design features that are singular or highly distinctive.

Systemic and subsystemic power distribution The importance of systemic and subsystemic power distribution in institutional design varies considerably. Throughout the Third World superpower retrenchment

[19] See Amitav Acharya, *The Quest for Identity: International Relations of Southeast Asia* (Singapore: Oxford University Press, 2000).

might have opened more space for regional institution-building. But the major powers were especially important in the case of Asia, particularly in creating the impetus toward the founding of the ASEAN Regional Forum. They were less important in Latin America. In general, the role of external powers has not been important in promoting regional integration or shaping institutional design. Subsystemic power distributions, including country size and power, are perhaps more important in shaping institutional design. As the leading Southeast Asian power, Indonesia was instrumental in shaping ASEAN's consensus-based framework and now the role of China and increasingly India is a major factor in shaping the ARF. But the role of big regional players does not seem to count in Latin America, where the "participation of large countries in an integration scheme does not ensure its success, or their absence doom such a scheme to failure."[20] Moreover, this variable has not been important in the Middle East, where no single state has been able to impress its blueprint for the Arab League, not even Egypt.[21]

Domestic politics The most important common factor shaping institutional design in all cases was domestic politics. "Domestic politics" can have different components. In the case of the EU, domestic variables that have been critical to institutional design include "the match between the structure of domestic and regional institutions," and "the embeddedness of agents in pre-existing national norms and values."[22] In Asia, and in much of the Third World, the primary domestic issue is one of regime legitimacy and survival. This has led to a tendency among actors to be highly protective of their sovereignty, which in turn creates the basis for consensus-based institutional designs, and the acceptance of a great deal of diversity in political systems. Khong and Nesadurai argue that in Southeast Asia, the *type* of institutional arrangement entered into was predicated on domestic regimes and the level of political legitimacy that they enjoyed. The Arab League too shows the extreme salience of the domestic survival of ruling coalitions. In Africa, as Herbst notes, "leaders are, in fact, quite attentive to the rational design of institutions but their focus, more often than not, is to protect and extend their domestic standing rather than strengthen their states' standing on international issues."[23] Generalizing from Africa, Herbst offers a critique of the Rational Design of International Institutions project, which he accuses of

[20] Domínguez, this volume, p. 123. [21] Barnett and Solingen, this volume, p. 181.
[22] Checkel, this volume, p. 237. [23] Herbst, this volume, p. 130.

taking "seemingly as a given, that states are well-ordered enough that worries about international problems can be separated from domestic politics. That assumption needs to be questioned in some parts of the world."[24] It is only in the case of the OAS that the salience of domestic factors linked to regime type appear not to have been so pronounced in shaping the main features of institutional design, especially when it comes to trade promotion or dispute settlement. Democratic transitions did not specifically spur democracies to set up and/or join regional institutions.[25] But there is some evidence that once democratic transitions occurred, new democracies did attempt to increase the role of institutions in preserving democracy. In the one clear instance where an institution was used to help prevent a reversion to dictatorship – MERCOSUR's opposition to a coup attempt in Paraguay – the change in institutional rules (the addition of a democracy clause) came after the event. Prior to the coup there had been no specific demand for such a clause from other democracies.

Extra-regional institutions and non-state actors The sixth major variable, the role of extra-regional institutions and non-state actors, is most pronounced in Latin America, where international NGOs concerned with human rights and international political party federations, such as the Socialist International and the World Federation of Christian Democrats, helped significantly in promoting Latin America's democratization in the 1980s. Remarkably, this extra-regional participation was allowed by formalized mechanisms of institutional design. The OAS has since changed considerably to allow space to NGOs. But NGOs have not been important in other parts of the world. Non-state international actors have some influence in the EU, but again, not to the degree that might be expected in a league of liberal democratic states. NGOs have played a minimal role in regional institutional design and cooperation in Asia, Africa, and the Middle East.

Another aspect of the role of the external linkage of regional institutions concerns institutional borrowing and emulation. It has become increasingly part of the EU's game-plan to promote itself as a model elsewhere. Hence, inter-regional institutional borrowing was not only a function of emulation, but also dependent on how successfully the EU as "industry leader" promoted its model and how well it resonated in other

[24] Ibid.

[25] For these claims see Andrew Moravcsik. "The Origins of Human Rights Regimes: Democratic Delegation in Postwar Europe," *International Organization*, 54:2 (Spring 2000), pp. 217–52, and Edward D. Mansfield and Jon C. Pevehouse, "Democratization and International Organizations," *International Organization*, 60:1 (January 2006), pp. 137–67.

regions. The OSCE has been another source of emulation for regional organizations such as the ARF, the OAU/AU, and the OAS, but in most cases, institutional emulation has been subject to limitations, running into resistance from conservative regional leaders on grounds of geographic, cultural, and political differences between Europe and their respective regions.

History The seventh variable, history, does appear important in terms of the degree of path dependence it creates in shifts to initial institutional design. In ASEAN, being the first and only long-term regional organization in Asia during the Cold War, there was a historical basis to its claim of leadership of the ARF. Its previously developed practices, such as the "Dialogue Partner" meetings, provided the basis for the ARF's institutional design, making it "easy and natural for a new security forum to be 'grafted' onto these existing talk-shops."[26] History has been important to ASEAN in another sense; all its members share post-colonial identities, which creates a strong attachment to sovereignty and thus to "eschew sovereignty-pooling or integrationist projects" and embrace, with the limited exception of AFTA, "designs or modalities that are sovereignty-affirming."[27] Change has been slow and limited; while ASEAN has been somewhat prepared to develop measures in the face of external developments adversely affecting economic growth, this has so far entailed a limited dilution of the "ASEAN Way." The recent evolution of ASEAN and the ARF suggests a high degree of path dependence, whereby new institutional mechanisms developed in response to regional crises tend to be adaptive with only minor and gradual shift from existing processes.[28] Another case of path dependence highlighted in this volume is the Middle East, where new regional peace initiatives like the MMEPP were thwarted by "the resilience of decades-old path-dependent processes throughout the region that resisted the domestic and regional changes of the 1990s."[29]

Some propositions

The main conclusions of the first section, i.e. the nature and sources of regional institutional design, can be summed up in the following propositions. First:

[26] Khong and Nesadurai, this volume, p. 68. [27] Ibid.

[28] Amitav Acharya has drawn attention to this "localization" effect in his "How Ideas Spread: Whose Norms Matter? Norm Localization and Institutional Change in Asian Regionalism," *International Organization*, 58:2 (Spring 2004), pp. 239–75.

[29] Barnett and Solingen, this volume, p. 212.

the more insecure the regimes, the less intrusive are their regional institutions.

Regime insecurity and concern for survival is a stronger force than external threat in explaining regional institutional design in the developing world. It becomes more likely that regional institutions created by insecure regimes would see membership as a basis of strengthening regime survival. Democratic regimes are more likely to accept intrusive design features than authoritarian regimes, as evident in the case of the EU and the OAS, compared to ASEAN, the ARF, the AU, and the Arab League.

A second proposition is that:

the design of regional institutions in the developing world has been more consistently sovereignty-preserving than sovereignty-eroding.

Regional institutions in the developing world are more likely to possess design features that preserve sovereignty than challenge it. These design features are geared to upholding the core norms of sovereignty, especially non-intervention and territorial integrity (including its attendant principle of the sanctity of post-colonial boundaries). In no case were these norms significantly compromised, with the possible exception of Latin America, and even here, the shift away from non-intervention and toward democracy promotion is a fairly recent development. But there are questions as to whether this emphasis on sovereignty may be shifting in recent years in Asia, where notions such as "flexible engagement" have emerged as a way of coping with transnational challenges, such as the regional financial crisis of 1997, which require greater collective action.

Third:

functional imperatives are less important than ideational and normative considerations in shaping the design of regional institutions in the developing world.

The nature of the cooperation problem, such as responding to a common military threat, coping with transnational challenges, or promoting trade liberalization to cope with protectionism abroad has not been a decisive factor in designing regional institutions, or modifying the design in recent years. By contrast, sovereignty, regime survival, and the norm of non-intervention, as well as residual perceptions of subregional identity (as in the case of ASEAN), have played a more important role in the development of the initial institutional design and in resisting institutional innovation and change. Another ideational factor, history (defined here as perceptions of the authoritativeness of historical precedent), is also powerful in shaping institutional design functional imperatives. This is evident in the path dependency found in the responses of regional organizations in the developing world to changing functional pressures for institutional change.

Among regional organizations, Europe and NATO seem to be most functionally driven, at least in their origins. But even in the case of NATO, while the functional explanation of its institutional design is strong, it is also subject to limitations. The Arab League appears to be the most identity-driven organization. In Asia, the key variables are normative, especially sovereignty and non-intervention; there is much less evidence of a regional (pan-Asian) identity, except at the subregional level in Southeast Asia.

Finally:

> *the contrast between the design features of the European Union and regional institutions in the developing world can be overstated in relation to the commitment to supranationalism and the development of a regional identity.*

Checkel starts by noting that the EU is more advanced than other regional groupings. One indicator of this is that the EU uses persuasion, rather than material incentives or strategic calculation. Use of persuasion might be deemed to be an indicator of a higher form of cooperation. Other regional institutions were based more on strategic calculation. But a surprising finding of Checkel's chapter relating to the nature of cooperation is that the EU is less able to produce preference and identity change than commonly assumed. The EU's supranationalism and the sense of European regional identity fostered by it are overstated in the face of alternative explanations focusing on intergovernmentalism and resilient national identities and interests. Differences do remain between European and universal processes (as originally identified by Haas), especially in the type of mandate, formality of rules, and commitment to liberal norms, but the supranationalism of the EU is not what it is made out to be in popular and media accounts.

The nature of cooperation

As we have noted in the introduction to this volume, the Rational Design of International Institutions project did not try to measure how institutional design relates to effectiveness (although it did offer some tentative conclusions about effectiveness in the concluding chapter of the resulting volume). Indeed, a core member of the RDII project, Andrew Kydd, who also participated in our project as a discussant for the framework paper, began the discussion of an earlier version of the introduction to this volume by noting that, in addition to the questions of explaining the variations in institutional design and whether such variations lead to differences in the efficacy of these institutions, further research could focus on the nature of the cooperation. In this project, we asked contributors to see how design features of regional institutions may or may not affect the nature of cooperation. The purpose of the chapters is not to explain the nature of cooperation, but to see how institutional design illuminates cooperation. So, where institutional design does not appear to have much effect, we do not offer alternative explanations. Where design appears to matter, however, we offer some speculative ideas about how well it does as an independent variable vis-a-vis other plausible explanations. This effort constitutes an outline for further research, not a definitive test of alternative explanations.

This focus on the "nature" of cooperation is a shift from our initial efforts to develop a metric for "quality" of cooperation. As mentioned in the introduction, "quality" would have been measured by at least three dimensions: the degree of change that cooperation required in a state's original policies; the degree to which cooperation affected the relative power of the state; and whether the state's cooperation was elicited through either positive or negative economic and social sanctions, or through normative acceptance. But measuring "quality" in this way also posed the risk of allowing an implicit normative bias to affect the measurement of the dependent variable. High quality cooperation might be interpreted as inherently more desirable. In disaggregating the "nature" of cooperation, one might avoid this problem.

In the introduction, we had suggested to our chapter contributors several possible indicators of the nature of cooperation, including: (1) degree of institutionalization and legalization; (2) degree of normative and preference change; (3) degree of policy convergence across actors; (4) different routes to the above changes; (5) degree of adjustment of prior policies; and (6) degree to which the institution (or the agents active in the institution) has achieved set goals. The first major conclusion we would like to put forward is that institutional design does affect the nature of cooperation, especially when it comes to the realization of their initial goals, one of our main indicators of the nature of cooperation. One of the most important overall findings of the project is that the initial or "original" design features of institutions do set limits to change induced by functional imperatives or new normative goals adopted by regional institutions. As this volume shows, institutional design does not occur in a vacuum. Rather, it is a deliberate and complex process that reflects power realities, domestic politics, local circumstances, and normative pressures, among others. But once in place, the design features of institutions tend to linger and create a path dependency that shapes the response of institutions to future challenges. The path dependency remains even though the conditions and circumstances that gave rise to the institutional design have changed. In other words, the essays in this volume do suggest that the initial design features of regional institutions continue to exert a long-term impact beyond the time-frame and context in which they are first developed. In this crucial respect, the findings of this volume show that institutional design does affect the nature of cooperation in regional groups.

This is best reflected in the response of regional institutions to issues that have to do with the protection of sovereignty. In the introduction, we noted that one of the indicators of the nature of cooperation is the impact on original goals. In most cases, regional institutions outside Europe were designed to protect sovereignty. Hence, it is important not to be biased by the EU's model in judging the original goal of regional institutions. The EU was geared to suppressing nationalism and promoting supranationalism. By contrast, a primary goal of regional organizations in Africa was to promote national liberation and preserve the sovereignty and independence of the newly created states. Similarly, in Latin America and Asia, regional organization was meant to act as a bulwark of sovereignty and domestic order.

Going by their original goals, regional institutions geared to the "defense of sovereignty" have been "successful." Weak states in Asia, Africa, and the Middle East benefited from weak institutions because weak institutions legitimized their sovereignty. Weaker institutions are better able to meet their original goals of preserving state sovereignty and aiding the project of regime survival. This has been brought out most starkly by Barnett and Solingen, who argue that while the Arab League has achieved a relatively low level of cooperation, at the same time, "to the extent the League was *designed* to enhance state sovereignty, it has certainly succeeded in doing so."[30] With respect to Africa, one can view the "weakness" of African institutions in a similar light. It seems clear that African leaders desired weak institutions as a means of self-preservation. Regional institutions in Africa tended to focus on the promotion of sovereignty and the preservation of inherited boundaries, despite the fact that they had no means of enforcement. By contrast, projects that focused on economic integration have fared the worst.

But what happens when the goals of institutions change in response to new developments in the domestic and external environment of their members? Do design features also change or do they act as a brake on task expansion? Regional organizations in Asia, Africa, and Latin America have all faced pressures to adopt policies that require them to dilute the doctrine of non-interference. For example, both ASEAN and the AU

[30] Ibid., p. 180.

have had to deal with demands for humanitarian intervention, which goes against their traditionally conservative attitude toward state sovereignty. But initiatives to embrace this new role have been constrained by the original design features of these institutions. For example, when ASEAN debated in 1998 a proposal for "flexible engagement," which would require it to deal with the internal developments of member states, the more conservative members of the grouping fell back on the initial design principle of consensus to thwart the initiative. Similarly, sections within the AU membership have used traditional design features including consensus to slow down moves toward market-oriented economic integration in the continent. Even the EU's original design features, as Checkel notes, remain a threat to recent moves toward constitutionalism.

This does pose problems for judging institutional effectiveness. Might it not be said that while regional organizations in the Third World have been successful in one area, i.e. sovereignty preservation, this has come at a cost, including failure to achieve significant economic cooperation and regional order? Yet, sovereignty preservation is an important part of maintaining regional order. And at least in the case of Asian regional organizations, we have seen that they have contributed to regional peace through sovereignty preservation and by institutionalizing the rules of the Westphalian nation-state system.

Africa's boundary maintenance regime, which Herbst views as a success, should be seen in a similar light. Herbst points out that what is paramount in determining the success of regional cooperation in Africa is to discard the assumption that there is an inevitable conflict between sovereignty (or, more precisely, the prerogatives of individual leaders) and regional cooperation. African leaders usually seek to promote regional or continental agreements in order to enhance their own domestic standing and to cement state sovereignty. Hence, what constitutes the interest of African leaders must be carefully delineated. Often, leaders cannot divorce the pressures they feel from their domestic constituencies when making calculations about diplomatic efforts. And the actions of African leaders, predicated on their interests in survival, are the chief determinants of the fate of regional cooperation in this continent.

In this context, one of the project's findings is that an ideology of unification, far from inducing collective identity and problem-solving, is a force for division and consequently the ineffectiveness of regional institutions. The main contrast between Africa and the Middle East is that in the Middle East there has traditionally been a greater impetus for unification, whereas in Africa there is little desire for it. Yet, Africa has proven to be a more creative place for projects on regional institutions. Indeed, the case of the Middle East suggests that a strong cultural sense of regional identity can lead to weak institutions, especially if these are seen as a threat to sovereignty. The strongest sense of regional identity built around a common cultural pattern is found in the Arab League, but it is one of the weakest regional institutions. In contrast, in ASEAN greater cultural diversity has not precluded effectiveness in diffusing and managing regional conflicts. In Africa, the successes of regionalism are owed not to cultural factors but to a common predicament, such as their recent history of colonialism, arbitrarily marked post-colonial boundaries, weak political institutions, and frequency of external intervention. The unification ideology had less of an impact in Africa because, as Herbst noted at this project's Singapore workshop in 2004, in comparison with the Middle East, Pan-Africanism was generally an external phenomenon that united the African diasporas, but had little appeal to those within states in Africa. He also asked whether Middle Eastern states were born "illegitimate" and whether this is still the case. If this is not the case, this might be a source of success for the Arab League. Another case in point is Asia, where the most dramatic policy convergence has occurred in relation to market economics. Asia, as with Africa, has never accepted or seriously envisioned unification. A survey of other regions also reveals that projects such as federalism fail frequently. African initiatives, such as Senegambia, are prominent examples.

What is important is that the apparent salience of the "defense of sovereignty" is despite major changes in the circumstances within which the design features of institutions were initially framed. These changes include changes in functional imperatives (greater pressure toward marketization, especially relevant to Asia), changes in the systemic distribution of power (from bipolarity to unipolarity and/or multipolarity; this affects all regions), changes in domestic politics (increasing democratization, which is especially important in the case of the OAS), and changes in the global normative environment (from non-intervention to humanitarian intervention, salient in the case of Africa, a continent rife with internal conflicts).

Of course, evidence of path dependency and continued commitment to initial goals is but one indicator of the nature of cooperation. Moreover, it's a conservative indicator, where success is paradoxically measured in terms of resistance to change. This does not imply, however, that the nature and purpose of institutions remain fixed for ever or that they do not produce effective responses to emerging challenges that call for dilution of sovereignty and non-interference. What they do suggest, however, is that conservative factions within the membership who resist demands and pressures for change often use the initial design features of a regional institution. Second, and closely linked to the first, is the likelihood that any modification to these initial design features would have to be a gradual process, rather than a radical break.

Taking into account the possibility of such gradual shifts, the findings of this project point to several ways in which institutional design may affect the nature of cooperation. First, we notice that institutionalization and legalization (here used as indicators of the nature of cooperation) increase with expanding scope and mandate. This means that when important design features of regional institutions change – such as scope and mandate – they affect the nature of cooperation defined in terms of institutionalization and legalization. In ASEAN, the advent of AFTA, and the inclusion of environmental issues in the agenda, have led to greater institutionalization and legalization.[31] A similar dynamic is evident in Africa, where the AU has developed new institutions and deepened existing ones. The OAS has also developed new mechanisms in response to an expanding scope that now includes the promotion of democracy. In some cases, new institutions have been created; in others existing institutional design features have been altered and new rules created. Of course, the complete story requires an explanation of why regional agenda issues change. Regional economic integration helps explain the inclusion of new mandates in ASEAN, which in turn help explain somewhat higher levels of institutionalization. Similarly, the "third wave" of democratization is a prior factor explaining the Latin American endorsement of democratic preservation. This, in turn, has expanded the intrusiveness of regional institutions. Other regions, notably the Arab world, have not faced this radical change in the norms of governance.

But a caveat is in order: new institutions created in response to a distributive mandate may not actually be used. Latin America is highly institutionalized, and its regional bodies have a more distributive mandate than their counterparts in the developing world. But Latin American states do not always make use of regional mechanisms to address their security and economic problems. The OAS has not been involved in the resolution of the most problematic and intractable of conflicts or civil/domestic disputes involving its members. By contrast, despite not having as wide a mandate and not using its formal institutions,[32] arguably ASEAN has been more successful in conflict resolution.

Another finding on the link between design features and the nature of cooperation is that more formally institutionalized regional groups do not necessarily produce more effective cooperation. At first glance, if ones goes by changing levels of formalization, then only the EU and NATO,

[31] On legalization see Miles Kahler, "Legalization as Strategy: The Asia-Pacific Case," *International Organization*, 54:3 (Summer 2000), pp. 549–71.

[32] For instance, ASEAN has avoided using its High Council for dispute settlement.

and to some degree the OAS, may be said to have been the most effective regional institutions in inducing normative and preference change. But beneath the surface, as Checkel's study of the EU suggests, national institutions and traditions remain a force in Europe despite its highly formalized setting. At the same time, less formalized regional institutions such as ASEAN have not been totally ineffectual in terms of producing preference change. Institutions can still help attain their original goals and induce preference change with informal rules and deliberative mandate. At the Singapore workshop for this project, participants agreed that NATO's effectiveness seemed to derive from having institutions such as ambassadors, the office of the Secretary-General, its brokerage role, and informal rules. More informal groups such as ASEAN have had a discernible impact in changing the preferences and norms of their members. For example, early on after its formation in 1967, ASEAN induced greater moderation in Indonesia when previously its nationalist outlook had threatened its neighbors in the 1960s. Unlike the EU, ASEAN started with a greater diversity in state preferences in the economic domain. While all the EU members were capitalist democracies, ASEAN's were marked by differing degrees of state managed economies. But over a period of interaction, ASEAN has produced a remarkable convergence among its members insofar as adherence to market economies is concerned. In addition, ASEAN institutions, such as the ARF, have had some effect in developing convergence around a common preference for cooperative security across divergent political systems. While the ARF has been criticized for lacking in institutionalization, and greater formalization and intrusiveness is deemed to be necessary for future success, Khong and Nesadurai still note a movement in the ARF toward three areas of cooperation: CBMs, extending the reach of the Treaty of Amity and Cooperation, and counter-terrorism.

Are there other possible explanations for this kind of evolution besides, or in addition to, socialization in the dominant norms of the institution? In the ASEAN marketization case, it seems plausible that an economic competition for openness is an alternative to the socialization argument. Still, there is a sense in ASEAN that this "rush to the bottom" to attract investments and markets needs to occur within limits that are established by the institution.

Changes in another design feature – inclusiveness – also produce changes in the nature of cooperation, although this can go in both directions. A tendency toward inclusive membership has been a common feature of regional institutions in Europe (EU, NATO) and Asia. While this has a discernible impact on the nature of cooperation in these institutions, this has not always been positive. Indeed, its impact on the effectiveness of regional institutions is uncertain in the short and medium term.

Regional institutions in Asia and Africa generally accept the expansion of membership as a desirable goal, but this comes at a price, in the form of new burdens. For example, the post-Cold War expansion of European (EU and NATO) and Asian (ASEAN and ARF) institutions have confronted these groupings with challenges, such as the need to meet the expectations of the newcomers about economic aid, socializing them with the norms and procedures of the institutions, and managing the transition of their economies (in many cases socialist) to market economies. These issues have challenged regional identity and the functioning of these institutions. This may be consistent with Karl Deutsch's observation, developed more fully by Acharya,[33] that membership expansion and increased socialization may create new burdens that could lead to the unraveling of security communities. These findings should be seen in the context of the earlier experience of the OAS, whose expansion of membership – predating the end of the Cold War – did not immediately lead to greater effectiveness.

To the extent that formalism in decision-making rules is an important design feature of regional institutions, it is important to ask whether this has an impact on the nature of cooperation. Again, a key question is whether shifts toward greater formalism (such as a shift from consensus to majority voting) indicate greater identity change (which we use as an indicator of nature of cooperation). Our conclusion is that greater formalism may actually affect cooperation negatively. Checkel observes that at the elite level, we see little evidence of bureaucrats and policymakers "going native" when working in EU institutions. The emergence of a distinctly European identity, spurred by regional institutions, is at best a distant prospect. At the same time, identity change can occur in less formal institutions. What is known as the ASEAN Way does capture a sense of group identity ("collective identity" might be too strong a term here), especially in relation to external major powers. Why this might be the case is a complex question. But it probably has to do with the extended and extensive interpersonal elite-level ties that ASEAN fosters.

Conclusion: agenda for further research on comparative regionalism

This collection of essays has only just begun to explore the similarities and differences in the design and efficacy of regional international institutions.

[33] Amitav Acharya, *Constructing a Security Community in Southeast Asia* (London: Routledge, 2001).

The research results here suggest a number of important questions worth following up.

The first is: why do institutions vary in the degree of domestic legitimacy that they bestow on leaders? Africa is a case in point. As Herbst notes, African leaders support sovereignty-reinforcing institutions because: (1) they do not challenge the power of individual leaders; and (2) they help enhance the domestic legitimacy of these leaders. In other regions, however, membership in a regional institution does not have the latter type of payoff, or at least not to the same degree.

Why this difference? It is unclear why domestic constituencies would care whether their leaders were members of an international institution. One explanation is that the institution polishes a country's international image. This speaks to the question of international image and why sensitivity to it varies across states. International image and reputation are two different concepts. The latter refers to the reputation gained in the eyes of others from a cooperative act at time t, a reputation that enhances the credibility of a state's commitment to cooperation at time $t + 1$. In other words, reputation affects the probability of a concrete exchange of benefits. Image, on the other hand, is the public manifestation of status. Actors desire to maximize status for its own sake, not for the purposes of some future exchange of concrete benefits with another actor. This much is clear. There is tremendous variation in the degree to which leaders respond to international opprobrium or back-patting. If one looks at United Nations General Assembly (UNGA) voting, for example, there is wide variation in the willingness of states to be left standing in a small "no" constituency on resolutions. Since 1989, for instance, China has been the least willing to do so, and has been more likely to abstain on resolutions it opposes if it appears that it will be in a small losing coalition than if the losing group is relatively large. Great Britain, on the other hand, has been happy to vote "no" regardless of the size of the "no" group. This variation in image sensitivity has not been explained in the literature; yet it appears relevant to understanding how regional institutions affect state behavior.

One direction for research might be to focus on the anthropomorphization of the state in international politics. Anthropomorphization is a key feature of religion and nationalism. It is a common response to use human-like metaphors to describe ambiguous non-human phenomena.[34] It enables people to attribute agency to phenomena that are, in reality,

[34] Stewart Guthrie, "A Cognitive Theory of Religion," *Current Anthropology*, 21:2 (April 1980), pp. 181–203; Katherine Verdery, "Whither 'Nation' and 'Nationalism'?" *Daedalus*, 122:3 (1993), p. 40

collections of agents. There is evidence that political leaders tend to anthropomorphize the state themselves (indeed the language of the state and its diplomacy has always been highly anthropomorphic, e.g. fatherlands, motherlands, prestige, dignity, honor, unitary national interests).[35] As O'Neill shows, much of the description and analysis of international diplomacy by leaders, pundits, and citizens alike relies on a "country-as-person" metaphor (sometimes as "country-as-specific-person," sometimes as "country-as-unspecified-person," sometimes as "country-as-its-leader") to describe interstate relations as social relationships.[36] This allows complex intergroup relations at the international level (where each group or state is in reality itself a function of complex intragroup relations) to be simplified, understood, and identified with emotionally.

It should not be surprising, then, that leaders and their attentive publics tend to isomorphize criticism or praise of the state with criticisms and praise of the national ingroup, and of each individual in the ingroup.[37] Consistent with O'Neill's analysis, even among those who are critical of the Chinese government's repressiveness, one hears a common argument that the leaders and the state are isomorphized especially when Chinese leaders interact with the external world. How Jiang Zemin is personally treated, for instance, is seen as a direct indicator of how China the collective is treated.[38] Recent research on the role of ethical and normative discourses in Chinese foreign relations suggests that one element of leadership legitimacy in the eyes of relevant publics in China is the degree to which the leadership appears to uphold and bolster China's international image.[39]

The process might go in the other direction as well: criticism of the collective is personalized by decision-makers. To give one example from China's environmental diplomacy, Qu Geping, at the time the head of China's National Environment Protection Agency, argued in internal

[35] Alexander Wendt, *Social Theory of International Politics* (Cambridge: Cambridge University Press 1999), pp. 195 and 219.

[36] Barry O'Neill, *Honor, Symbols, and War* (Ann Arbor: University of Michigan Press, 1999), pp. 11–16.

[37] On the question of aggregation see Martha Finnemore and Kathryn Sikkink, "International Norm Dynamics and Political Change," *International Organization*, 52:4 (Autumn 1998), p. 904.

[38] This effect could be reinforced by the relationship between self-esteem and perceived esteem bestowed on the social group, a relationship at the heart of social identity theory. See Daniel Druckman, "Nationalism, Patriotism, and Group Loyalty: A Social-Psychology Perspective," *Merson International Studies Review*, 38:1 (April 1994), pp. 48–9.

[39] Lucy M. Cummings, *PRC Foreign Policy Responsiveness to Domestic Ethical Sentiment: Understanding the Link Between Ethics and Regime Legitimacy* (Baltimore: Johns Hopkins University, Ph.D. dissertation, 2000), p. 62.

discussions in the State Council that China would have to participate in efforts to protect endangered species because otherwise China would be criticized as "stupid, backward and savage," harming the "Chinese people's image." He expressed personal frustration with the "pressure" he felt whenever he attended international conferences because of the stories about Chinese people eating wild animals.[40]

Diffuse image concerns among state leaders probably derive from both a top-down and a bottom-up anthropomorphization of leaders and national image on the international stage. The top-down process plays on individual leaders' sensitivities to an anthropomorphized state's status markers. At this stage psychological variables – the desire for positive self-image, self-esteem, self-efficacy, and the desire for social approval and liking – probably kick in. The bottom-up process plays on individual leaders' sensitivities to domestic legitimacy derived, in part, from status markers valued by relevant publics. The precise mix will depend on the issue, and the degree to which the relevant publics consider the issue salient.

If this is the case – if the anthropomorphization of the state is the basis for how external events and actors affect the legitimacy of the state in the eyes of relevant publics – then one still needs to ask why international institutions per se are important external factors in estimating the legitimacy of the leadership. There are a number of possibilities. Two will suffice. One is that post-colonial ideology in ex-colonies embodies a strong desire to be seen as a sovereign equal to more powerful states. The place where this equality is most on display is inside international institutions. The more salient the post-colonial ideology, the more important domestic legitimation through participation as equals in sovereignty-preserving institutions will be. Another similar, though more general, hypothesis might be that weak states are the ones where domestic legitimation rests more heavily on participation in international institutions. Participation in high-profile institutions is an important symbol of status that resonates domestically, especially for states that have little else in terms of soft or hard power.

[40] Qu Geping "Guowuyuan huanjing baohu weiyuanhui fu zhuren, guojia huanjing baohu ju juzhang Qu Geping zai guowuyuan huanjing baohu weiyuanhui di shi jiu ci huiyi shang de jianghua" [State Council environmental protection committee deputy director, National Environmental Protection Agency director, Qu Geping's speech to the 19th meeting of the State Council environmental protection committee], 18 December 1990, in State Council Environmental Protection Committee Secretariat (eds.), *Guowuyuan huanjing baohu weiyuanhui wenjian huibian* [Collected documents of the State Council environmental protection committee], vol. 2 (Beijing), p. 195.

A second question that follows from the collective findings in this book is why democratization is apparently so important for the efficacy of many institutions. As the Latin American case suggests, regional institutions did not really become more intrusive or proactive until the wave of democratization in the 1980s and 1990s. The European case certainly seems to confirm that political democracies are more willing to push their institutions toward higher levels of efficacy in almost all the senses of the term that we outlined above. Even in ASEAN it appears that the hesitant moves toward "flexible engagement" – ever so gingerly bringing domestic governance issues to the table – occurred after the overall level of democracy across ASEAN increased somewhat from the end of the 1990s on. In the African case, one might argue that regardless of practice, the norm of liberal democracy has won the intellectual battle and that this has enabled African states to be more experimental in moving African institutions in more intrusive directions.[41]

There are a number of hypotheses that might explain the relationship between democracy and the demand for and efficacy of regional institutions. First, the relationship might be spurious; it is levels of economic development that matter, and it just so happens that democracies are more developed and more marketized. This explains the demand for regional institutions, especially economic ones.

A second might be that it is an accident of history that the institutions which a lot of countries want into are controlled by democracies. Membership in the European Union and access to all the political, economic, and legitimacy benefits thereof requires democratization.

A third possibility draws from median voter arguments: median voters prefer peaceful neighborhoods, therefore support efforts to reduce uncertain environments through institutionalized cooperation.

Fourth, stable democracies do not need to rely on hyper-sovereignty discourses in "normal" times and places; their leaderships are more legitimate and therefore, in "normal" times there is less opposition to sovereignty-restraining institutions.

Fifth, new democracies want to join powerful and legitimate institutions in order to protect democracy at home. Institutions can provide material assistance, political assistance, and legitimacy. They can help "tie the hands" of democratic reformers at home as a leverage against anti-reform forces.[42]

[41] This is a point that Etel Solingen made at the Singapore conference, May 2004.

[42] Jon C. Pevehouse, "Democratization, Credible Commitments, and International Organizations," in Daniel Drezner (ed.), *Locating the Proper Authorities: The Interaction of Domestic and International Institutions* (Ann Arbor: University of Michigan Press, 2002).

Sixth, relative to non-democracies, democracies practice norms of transparency in domestic politics, and expect that transparency will also reduce interstate conflicts. Institutions are providers of interstate transparency.[43]

Seventh, a critical mass of democracies in the region creates credible restraint when it comes to institutional intervention in the internal affairs of states. Institutions will do so in defense of democracy, but will be restrained from intervening for other purposes by the transparency of the institution, the relative transparency of the democratic members of the institution, and by the self-interested restraint of median voters in democracies. Thus, in a predominantly democratic region states will coordinate around intrusive, but credibly restrained institutions.[44]

In addition to these hypotheses about why democracies in particular are more likely to demand and supply more intrusive institutions than non-democracies, there may be some critical scope conditions worth investigating. For instance, democracies will have preferences for these kinds of institutions only insofar as they perceive the dominant norm and dominant form of governance in their region to be democracy.[45] Relatedly, democracies will have preferences for these kinds of institutions only insofar as they perceive that the dominant powers in the region are democracies. In this regard, the existence of a democratic hegemon or hegemonic coalition may provide the power conditions necessary for democracies to take the lead in setting up functionally more demanding regional institutions. It would be interesting, for example, to compare further the changes in design and efficacy of Latin American and East Asian institutions. In both cases the 1980s and 1990s have seen the emergence and/or consolidation of new democracies. Yet there appears to be considerable variation in the willingness of regional institutions to take on, say, democratic defense roles, with East Asian democracies more reluctant than Latin American democracies. It therefore may not be irrelevant that democracies are still a minority in East Asia, whereas in Latin America they are not.[46] Is this difference mainly a function of numbers and

[43] None of these arguments can account for the fact that in the Middle East the proponents of regional cooperative liberalization have tended to be monarchies. Thanks to Michael Barnett and Etel Solingen for pointing this out at the Singapore conference, 2004.

[44] Thanks to Andy Kydd for raising this argument at the Singapore conference, 2004.

[45] Thanks to Andy Kydd for raising this possibility at the Harvard conference, 2002.

[46] According to the Polity IV dataset, in 2003, only five out of fourteen East Asian states (ASEAN, China, Japan, Taiwan, and the two Koreas) had polity scores above 6, the standard threshold used to delineate a mature democracy. In South America all twelve states were classified as democracies. Of the ten central and north American countries (excluding the US and Canada), eight were classified as democracies in 2003. See the Polity IV Country Reports, 2003, www.cidcm.umd.edu/inscr/polity/report.htm

perceived strength, or is there something about East Asian democracies where proactive democracy defense strategies are generally not central to the foreign policies of countries like Japan or South Korea?

A third area of future research concerns other kinds of institutions than those examined in this book. We have focused on intergovernmental regional institutions which vary in terms of complexity and purpose. But there are other kinds of institutions that operate independently of, even if complementary to, intergovernmental ones. In the Asia-Pacific, for instance, the Council for Security Cooperation in the Asia-Pacific (CSCAP) in the security field and the Pacific Economic Cooperation Council (PECC) in the economic field have been important Track II institutions that serve as ideas factories for the ARF and APEC respectively. Issues that are too controversial for Track I can be moved into Track II rather than being discarded entirely. This sustains the momentum behind issues that the intergovernmental institution might otherwise be reluctant to push. Given that many Track II participants are government officials who also participate in Track I activities, an issue is never really not within Track I's sphere of attention. This means that states are more likely to get used to an issue being part of their interaction than if the issues were initially considered illegitimate. Track II can also "filter" or sanitize proposals that would otherwise be deemed more controversial by dint of who made them.[47] *Who* makes a proposal can sometimes be more controversial than the *content* of the proposal itself.[48] Thus Track II can help define a Track I agenda that might not have otherwise appeared. There is, however, very little systematic cross-regional scholarly research on the design and efficacy of Track II institutions. And yet they exist in all the regions considered in this book. What we do know is that Track II institutions tend to be more informal, consensus driven, deliberative, and low-key, with a fair amount of continuity in participants, particularly if they are not government officials but academics or business people. In other words, their designs tend to present conditions that are ideal for normative or factual persuasion, and even the mutual constitution of new identities.[49]

[47] "Filter" is Paul Evans' term.

[48] Marie-France Desjardin, "Rethinking Confidence Building Measures: Obstacles to Agreement and the Risk of Overselling the Process," *Adelphi Papers*, 307 (1996).

[49] Dalia D. Kaye is one of the few to do comparative analyses of Track II processes. See her "Track Two Diplomacy and Regional Security in the Middle East," *International Negotiation: A Journal of Theory and Practice*, 6:1 (2001), pp. 49–77. For a discussion of the role of Track II in ASEAN politics, see Acharya, *Constructing a Security Community in Southeast Asia*, pp. 66–7.

A fourth area of future research suggested by this book has to do with the micro-processes by which institutions influence actors. As Checkel's chapter shows, a better test of the range of ways in which institutions matter – persuasion, social influence, material incentives, inducing preference change by influencing domestic political change, etc. – requires much more granularity than exists at the state or even the sub-state level of analysis. It requires looking at the individual and small-group level analysis as the representatives of states interact within the institution, as state representatives then interact with the policy process in their own state, as their own policy process affects leadership preferences and choices, and as leadership preferences and choices are turned into domestic and/or foreign policies in response. Checkel's chapter is about, in a sense, an ideal case – Europe – where researchers have relatively easy access to national and international leaders, bureaucrats, documents, public opinion polls, etc. His chapter sets up a model of sorts that researchers should try to replicate as best possible when working on the effects of other regional institutions.

This is not the place to provide a "how to" of micro-process analysis. Suffice it to say, it is not easy. For example, testing for the effects of persuasion ideally requires understanding the preferences of state diplomats prior to entry into an institution; understanding whether the social conditions inside the institution are conducive to persuasion;[50] understanding the preferences of the diplomats after exposure to these social conditions; understanding the ways in which these post-exposure preferences are communicated to the policy process – how they are sold if you will; and then how the policy process – itself a social environment in which similar persuasion processes might be taking place – translates these preferences into policy.

On top of this micro-focused analysis, one also would have to make comparisons concerning preference change with diplomats or policymakers who had not been exposed to these institutions. Testing for the effects of social influence requires understanding whether or not and how much political leaders care about the accumulation of status markers inside institutions; how messages about back-patting and/or opprobrium are communicated from the institution to the top leadership (e.g. why or how the state delegation, say, expresses the kind of opprobrium or back-patting they experience inside the institution). These kinds of tests would also have to take into account other plausible explanations

[50] Jeffrey Checkel, "Persuasion in International Institutions," *ARENA Working Papers*, 2:14 (2001), and Alastair Iain Johnston, "Treating International Institutions as Social Environments," *International Studies Quarterly*, 45:4 (December 2001), pp. 487–515.

either by explicitly testing for their empirical implications at the individual and small group level (for instance are leaders more responsive to offers of material side-payments than to social opprobrium?), or by research designs that control for the effects of these other explanations (e.g. looking at "hard cases" for persuasion and social influence where cooperation is unexpected given the high costs to material security or the absence of material side-payments and sanctions). Of course, the kind of access to decision-making processes that this kind of research requires is, as we noted, rare. But it is not impossible outside of Europe. It would most likely require the collaboration of local/regional partners to do the requisite interviewing, participant observation where possible, and document analysis. In cases where this kind of access is difficult, one might have to rely on the content analysis of writings of those exposed to these institutions and those who have not been to see whether exposure has the hypothesized effects.

This is not an exhaustive list of future research directions. But we believe that together they constitute the next step forward in more rigorous comparisons across regional institutions, and to answer more completely why it is that when facing common problems of cooperation different parts of the world seem to design institutions differently.

Bibliography

Abbott, Kenneth W. and Duncan Snidal "Why States Act Through Formal International Organizations," *Journal of Conflict Resolution*, 42:1 (1998) ,pp. 3–32.

Abdelal, Rawi, Yoshiko Herrera, Alastair Iain Johnston, and Rose McDermott, "Identity as a Variable," *Perspectives on Politics*, 4:4 (December 2006), pp. 695–711.

Abidi, Aqil Hyder Hasan, *Jordan, A Political Study* (New York: Asia Publishing House, 1965).

Acevedo, Domingo E. and Claudio Grossman, "The Organization of American States and the Protection of Democracy," in Tom J. Farer (ed.), *Beyond Sovereignty: Collectively Defending Democracy in the Americas* (Baltimore: Johns Hopkins University Press, 1996), pp. 132–49.

Acharya, Amitav, *Constructing a Security Community in Southeast Asia* (London: Routledge, 2001).

Acharya, Amitav, "Democracy in Burma: Does Anybody Really Care?" *YaleGlobal Online*, 1 September 2005. www.yaleglobal.yale.edu

Acharya, Amitav, "How Ideas Spread: Whose Norms Matter? Norm Localization and Institutional Change in Asian Regionalism," *International Organization*, 58:2 (Spring 2004), pp. 239–75.

Acharya, Amitav, "Ideas, Identity, and Institution-Building: From the 'ASEAN Way' to the 'Asia Pacific Way'?," *Pacific Review*, 10:3 (1997), pp. 319–46.

Acharya, Amitav, "Regional Approaches to Security in the Third World: Lessons and Prospects," in Larry A. Swatuk and Timothy M. Shaw (eds.), *The South at the End of the Twentieth Century* (London: Macmillan, 1994), pp. 79–94.

Acharya, Amitav, *The Quest for Identity: International Relations of Southeast Asia* (Singapore: Oxford University Press, 2000).

Adams, Francis, "The Emerging Hemispheric Democracy Regime," *FOCAL-Point*, 2:2 (February 2003), pp. 1–3.

Adler, Emanuel, "Constructivism and International Relations," in Walter Carlsnaes, Thomas Risse-Kappen, and Beth Simmons (eds.), *Handbook of International Relations* (London: Sage Publications, 2002), pp. 95–118.

Adler, Emanuel and Michael Barnett (eds.), *Security Communities* (Cambridge: Cambridge University Press, 1998).

Aggarwal, Vinod K., "Building International Institutions in Asia-Pacific," *Asian Survey*, 33:11 (November 1993), pp. 1029–42.

Aggarwal, Vinod K., "Comparing Regional Cooperation Efforts in the Asia-Pacific and North America," in Andrew Mack and John Ravenhill (eds.),

Pacific Cooperation: Building Economic and Security Regimes in the Asia-Pacific Region (St Leonards, NSW: Allen and Unwin, 1994), pp. 40–65.

Aggarwal, Vinod K., "Reconciling Multiple Institutions: Bargaining, Linkages and Nesting," in Vinod K. Aggarwal (ed.), *Institutional Designs for a Complex World: Bargaining, Linkages, and Nesting* (Ithaca, NY: Cornell University Press, 1998), pp. 1–31.

Akrasanee, Narongchai and David Stifel, "The Political Economy of the ASEAN Free Trade Area," in Pearl Imada and Seiji Naya (eds.), *AFTA: The Way Ahead* (Singapore: Institute of Southeast Asian Studies (ISEAS), 1992), pp. 27–47.

Allam, Abeer, "Influence in Iraq Emerges as Key Issue as Arab Conference Opens," *The New York Times*, 29 March 2006, p. A8.

Anderson, Lisa, "The State in the Middle East and North Africa," *Comparative Politics*, 20:1 (October 1987), pp. 1–18.

Ansari, Mohammad Iqbal, *The Arab League, 1945–1955* (Aligarh, India: Institute of Islamic Studies, Aligar Muslim University, 1968), p. 25.

Antolik, Michael, *ASEAN and the Diplomacy of Accommodation* (New York: M.E. Sharpe, 1990).

Antolik, Michael, *ASEAN: The Anatomy of a Security Entente*, Ph.D. dissertation (unpublished), Columbia University, 1986.

"ASEAN Regional Forum: *A Concept Paper," in ASEAN Regional Forum: Documents Series 1994–1998* (Jakarta, 1999).

ASEAN Secretariat, *ASEAN Annual Report 2003–4* (Jakarta: The ASEAN Secretariat, 2004).

ASEAN Secretariat, *ASEAN Investment Report 1999: Trends and Developments in Foreign Direct Investment* (Jakarta: The ASEAN Secretariat, 1999).

ASEAN Secretariat, *ASEAN Regional Forum: Document Series 1994–1998* (Jakarta: 1999).

ASEAN Secretariat, *Matrix of ASEAN Regional Forum Decisions and Status, 1994–2004*. www.aseansec.org/ARF/MatrixofARFDecsions.doc

ASEAN, *Declaration of ASEAN Concord II (Bali Concord II)*, Bali, Indonesia, 7 October 2003.

ASEAN, *Joint Communiqué of the 39th ASEAN Ministerial Meeting (AMM)*, Kuala Lumpur, 25 July 2006.

ASEAN, *Protocol on Dispute Settlement Mechanism*, Manila, 26 November 1996. www.aseansec.org/16654.htm

ASEAN, *Protocol on Enhanced Dispute Settlement Mechanism*, Vientiane, 29 November 2004.

ASEAN, *Protocol on Notification Procedures*, Makati City, Philippines, 7 October 1998. www.aseansec.org/712.htm

ASEAN, *Protocol on the Special Arrangement for Sensitive and Highly Sensitive Products*, Singapore, 30 September 1999. www.aseansec.org/1207.htm

ASEAN, *Protocol Regarding the Implementation of the CEPT Scheme Temporary Exclusion List*, Singapore, 23 November 2000. www.aseansec.org/609.htm

ASEAN, *The ASEAN Declaration (Bangkok Declaration)*, Thailand, 8 August 1967. www.aseansec.org/3640.htm

ASEAN, *36th ASEAN Economic Ministers Meeting: Joint Media Statement*, Jakarta, 3 September 2004.

ASEAN, *Treaty of Amity and Cooperation in Southeast Asia*, Indonesia, 24 February 1976. www.aseansec.org/1654.htm

Atkins, G. Pope, *Latin America in the International Political System*, 3rd edn. (Boulder, CO: Westview Press, 1995).

Awad, Ibrahim, "The Future of Regional and Subregional Organization in the Arab World," in Dan Tschirgi (ed.), *The Arab World Today* (Boulder, CO: Lynne Rienner, 1994), pp. 147–60.

Ayoob, Mohammed, "Regional Security and the Third World," in Mohammed Ayoob (ed.), *Regional Security in the Third World* (London: Croom Helm, 1986), pp. 3–23.

Ayoob, Mohammed, "Security in the Third World: The Worm About to Turn," *International Affairs*, 60:1 (1984), pp. 41–51.

Ayoob, Mohammed, "The Security Predicament of the Third World State," in Brian L. Job (ed.), *The (In)Security Dilemma: The National Security of Third World States* (Boulder, CO: Lynne Rienner, 1992), pp. 63–80.

Ayoob, Mohammed, "The Security Problematic of the Third World," *World Politics*, 43:2 (January 1991), pp. 257–83.

Ayoob, Mohammad, *The Third World Security Predicament* (Boulder, CO: Lynne Rienner, 1995).

Azar, Edward and Chung-in Moon, "Third World National Security: Towards a New Conceptual Framework," *International Interactions*, 11:2 (1984), pp. 103–35.

Banco Interamericano de Desarrollo, *Más Allá de las Fronteras: El Nuevo Regionalismo en América Latina. Progreso Económico y Social en América Latina. Informe 2002* (Washington, DC: Banco Interamericano de Desarrollo, 1982).

Barnett, Michael N., "Institutions, Roles, and Disorder: The Case of the Arab States System," *International Studies Quarterly*, 37:3 (September 1993), pp. 271–96.

Barnett, Michael N., *Confronting the Costs of War: Military Power, State, and Society in Egypt and Israel* (Princeton: Princeton University Press, 1992).

Barnett, Michael N., *Dialogues in Arab Politics: Negotiations in Regional Order* (New York: Columbia University Press, 1998).

Barnett, Michael N., *Rules for the World: International Organizations in Global Politics* (Ithaca, NY: Cornell University Press, 2004).

Barnett, Michael N. and Martha Finnemore, "The Politics, Power, and Pathologies of International Organizations," *International Organization*, 53:4 (1999), pp. 699–732.

Bernier, Ivan, and Martin Roy, "NAFTA and MERCOSUR: Two Competing Models?" in Gordon Mace and Louis Bélanger (eds.), *The Americas in Transition: The Contours of Regionalism* (Boulder, CO: Lynne Rienner, 1999), pp. 69–91.

Beyers, Jan, "Multiple Embeddedness and Socialization in Europe: The Case of Council Officials," *International Organization*, 59 (Fall 2005), pp. 899–936.

Bill, James A. and Robert Springborg, *Politics in the Middle East*, 3rd edn. (Glenview, IL: Scott, Foresman/Little, Brown Higher Education, 1990).

Blejer, Mario I., "Economic Integration: An Analytical Overview," in *Economic and Social Progress in Latin America: 1984 Report* (Washington, DC: Inter-American Development Bank, 1984).

Borrayo Reyes, Jorge Luis, "Aplicación de la Resolución 1080 del Compromiso de Santiago para la Democracia y la Renovación del Sistema Interamericano. El Caso de Guatemala," in Arlene Tickner (ed.), *Sistema Interamericano y Democracia: Antecedentes Históricos y Tendencias Futuras* (Bogotá: Ediciones Uniandes, 2000), pp. 227–30.

Botcheva, Liliana and Lisa L. Martin, "Institutional Effects on State Behavior: Convergence and Divergence," *International Studies Quarterly*, 45:1 (March 2001), pp. 1–26.

Breslin, Shaun, Richard Higgott, and Ben Rosamond, "Regions in Comparative Perspective," in Shaun Breslin, Christopher W. Hughes, Nicola Phillips, and Ben Rosamond (eds.), *New Regionalisms in the Global Political Economy* (London: Routledge, 2002), p. 13.

Britt, Joseph. "Deafening Arab Silence on Arab Genocide," *The Japan Times*, 16 July 2005, p. 16.

Brody, Richard, Diana Mutz, and Paul Sniderman (eds.), *Political Persuasion and Attitude Change* (Ann Arbor: University of Michigan Press, 1996).

Brownlie, Ian (ed.), *Basic Documents on African Affairs* (Oxford: Clarendon Press, 1971).

Burns, John F. and Edward Wong, "Death of Hussein Aide is Confirmed," *The New York Times*, 13 November 2005, p. A8.

Burr, Robert N., *By Reason or Force: Chile and the Balancing of Power in South America*, 1830–1905 (Berkeley: University of California Press, 1965).

Busse, Nikolas, "Constructivism and Southeast Asian Security," *The Pacific Review*, 12:1 (1999), pp. 39–60.

Buzan, Barry, "People, States and Fear: The National Security Problem in the Third World," in Edward Azar and Chung-in Moon (eds.), *National Security in the Third World* (Aldershot: Edward Elgar, 1988), pp. 14–43.

Byrnes, Timothy and Peter Katzenstein (eds.), *Religion in an Expanding Europe* (Cambridge: Cambridge University Press, 2006).

Caballero-Anthony, Mely, "Non-state Regional Governance Mechanisms for Economic Security: The Case of the ASEAN Peoples' Assembly," *The Pacific Review*, 17:4 (December 2004), pp. 567–85.

Caballero-Anthony, Mely, *Regional Security in Southeast Asia: Beyond the ASEAN Way* (Singapore: Institute of Southeast Asian Studies, 2005).

Centeno, Miguel Angel, *Blood and Debt: War and the Nation-State in Latin America* (University Park, PA: Pennsylvania State University Press, 2002).

Chayes, Abram and Antonia Handler Chayes, *The New Sovereignty: Compliance with International Regulatory Agreements* (Cambridge, MA: Harvard University Press, 1998).

Checkel, Jeffrey T., "*Compliance and Conditionality*," *ARENA Working Paper 00/18* (Oslo: ARENA Centre for European Studies, University of Oslo, September 2000).

Checkel, Jeffrey T., "Going Native in Europe? Theorizing Social Interaction in European Institutions," *Comparative Political Studies*, 36:1/2 (February/March 2003), pp. 209–31.

Checkel, Jeffrey T., "International Institutions and Socialization in Europe: Introduction and Framework," *International Organization*, 59 (Fall 2005), pp. 801–826.

Checkel, Jeffrey T. (ed.), "International Institutions and Socialization in Europe," a special issue of *International Organization*, 59 (Fall 2005).

Checkel, Jeffery T., "Persuasion in International Institutions," *ARENA Working Papers*, 12:14 (2001).

Checkel, Jeffrey T., "Why Comply? Social Learning and European Identity Change," *International Organization*, 55:3 (Summer 2001), pp. 553–88.

Checkel, Jeffrey T. and Andrew Moravcsik, "A Constructivist Research Program in EU Studies? (Forum Debate)," *European Union Politics*, 2 (June 2001), pp. 219–49.

Chejne, Anwar G., "Egyptian Attitudes on Pan-Arabism," *Middle East Journal*, 11.3 (Summer 1957), p. 253.

Clapham, Christopher, "The Changing World of Regional Integration in Africa," in Christopher Clapham *et al.* (eds.), *Regional Integration in Southern Africa: Comparative International Perspectives* (Johannesburg: South African Institute of International Affairs, 2001), pp. 59–60.

Clark, Wesley K., *Waging Modern War* (New York: B&T 2001).

Claude, Jr., Inis L., "Collective Legitimization as a Political Function of the United Nations," *International Organization*, 20 (Summer 1966), pp. 367–74.

Claude, Jr., Inis L., *Swords into Plowshares* (New York: Random House, 1964).

Cleary, Séan, "Variable Geometry and Varying Speed: An Operational Paradigm for SADC," in Christopher Clapham *et al.* (eds.), *Regional Integration in Southern Africa: Comparative International Perspectives* (Johannesburg: South African Institute of International Affairs, 2001), p. 87.

Clément, Jean A. P., *et al.*, *Aftermath of the CFA Franc Devaluation* (Washington, DC: International Monetary Fund, 1996).

Coleman, William D. and Geoffrey R. D. Underhill (eds.), *Regionalism and Global Economic Integration: Europe, Asia and the Americas* (London: Routledge, 1998).

Crum, David Leith, "Mali and the UMOA: A Case-Study of Economic Integration," *The Journal of Modern African Studies*, 22:3 (September 1984), pp. 469–86.

Cummings, Lucy M., *PRC Foreign Policy Responsiveness to Domestic Ethical Sentiment: Understanding the Link Between Ethics and Regime Legitimacy*, Ph.D dissertation, Johns Hopkins University, Baltimore, 2000.

Cuya, Esteban, "*La 'Operación Cóndor': El Terrorismo de Estado de Alcance Transnacional.*" www.derechos.org/koaga/vii/2/cuya.html

David, Steven R., "Explaining Third World Alignment," *World Politics*, 43:2 (January 1991), pp. 232–56.

Dawisha, Adeed, *Arab Nationalism in the Twentieth Century: From Triumph to Despair* (Princeton: Princeton University Press, 2003).

Desjardin, Marie-France, "Rethinking Confidence Building Measures: Obstacles to Agreement and the Risk of Overselling the Process," *Adelphi Papers*, 307 (1996).

Dessouki, Ali E. Hillal, "Nasser and the Struggle for Independence," in Roger Owen and Wm. Robert Louis (eds.), *Suez 1956: The Crisis and its Consequences* (New York: Oxford University Press, 1989).

Deutsch, Karl *et al.*, *Political Community in the North Atlantic Area* (Princeton: Princeton University Press, 1957).

Devarajan, Shantayanan and Dani Rodrik, "Do the Benefits of Fixed Exchange Rates Outweigh the Costs? The CFA Zone in Africa," in Ian Goldin and L. Alan Winters (eds.), *Open Economies: Structural Adjustment and Agriculture* (Cambridge: Cambridge University Press, 1992), pp. 66–85.

Devlin, Robert and Antoni Estevadeordal, "¿Qué Hay de Nuevo en el Nuevo Regionalismo de las Américas?" *Documento de Trabajo*, 7 (Buenos Aires: INTAL-ITD-STA, 2001).

Devlin, Robert, Antoni Estevadeordal, and Luis Jorge Garay, "Some Economic and Strategic Issues in the Face of the Emerging FTAA," in Jorge I. Domínguez (ed.), *The Future of Inter-American Relations* (New York: Routledge, 2000), pp. 153–96.

Diamint, Rut, "Evolución del Sistema Interamericano: Entre el Temor y la Armonía," in Arlene Tickner (ed.), *Sistema Interamericano y Democracia: Antecedentes Históricos y Tendencias Futuras* (Bogotá: Ediciones Uniandes, 2000), pp. 1–25.

Domínguez, Jorge I., *Boundary Disputes in Latin America, Peaceworks*, 50 (Washington, DC: United States Institute of Peace, 2003).

Domínguez, Jorge I., "Security, Peace, and Democracy in Latin America and the Caribbean: Challenges for the Post-Cold War Era," in Jorge I. Domínguez (ed.), *International Security and Democracy: Latin America and the Caribbean in the Post-Cold War Era* (Pittsburgh: University of Pittsburgh Press, 1998).

Downs, George W., David M. Rocke, and Peter N. Barsoom, "Is the Good News about Compliance Good News about Cooperation," *International Organization*, 50:3 (Summer 1996), pp. 379–406.

Downs, George W., David M. Rocke, and Peter. N. Barsoom, "Managing the Evolution of Multilateralism," *International Organization*, 52:2 (1998), pp. 397–419.

Druckman, Daniel, "Nationalism, Patriotism, and Group Loyalty: A Social-Psychology Perspective," *Merson International Studies Review*, 38:1 (April 1994), pp. 43–68.

Duffield, John S., "The Limits of 'Rational Design'," *International Organization*, 57:2 (Spring 2003), pp. 411–30.

Duffy, Charles A. and Werner J. Feld, "Whither Regional Integration Theory," in Gavin Boyd and Werner J. Feld (eds.), *Comparative Regional Systems* (New York: Pergamon Press, 1980).

Egeberg, Morten, "An Organizational Approach to European Integration: Outline of a Complementary Perspective," *European Journal of Political Research*, 43 (March 2004), pp. 199–219.

Egeberg, Morten, "Transcending Intergovernmentalism? Identity and Role Perceptions of National Officials in EU Decision-Making," *Journal of European Public Policy*, 6:3 (September 1999), pp. 456–74.

Eichengreen, Barry and T. J. Pempel, "Why Has There Been Less Financial Integration in East Asia Than in Europe?" A collaborative project of the Institute of East Asian Studies and the Institute of European Studies, submitted for funding under the umbrella of the "New Geographies, New Pedagogies" initiative of the Institute of International Studies (August 2002), available at: http://globetrotter.berkeley.edu/NewGeog/FinanInteg.pdf

Elbadawi, Ibrahim and Nader Majd, "Adjustment and Economic Performance under a Fixed Exchange Rate: A Comparative Analysis of the CFA Zone," *World Development*, 24:5 (May 1996), pp. 939–51.

Elliot, Lorraine, "ASEAN and Environmental Cooperation: Norms, Interests and Identity," *The Pacific Review*, 16:1 (2003), pp. 29–52.

Elster, Jon (ed.), *Deliberative Democracy* (New York: Cambridge University Press, 1998).

Escudé, Carlos and Andrés Fontana, "Argentina's Security Policies: Their Rationale and Regional Context", in Jorge I. Domínguez (ed.), *International Security and Democracy: Latin America and the Caribbean in the Post-Cold War Era* (Pittsburgh: University of Pittsburgh Press, 1998).

Eurobarometer, Public Opinion in the European Union, Report Number 51 (Brussels: European Commission, July 1999).

Eurobarometer, Public Opinion in the European Union: Autumn 2003, Report Number 60 (Brussels: European Commission, February 2004).

Evangelista, Matthew, "Norms, Heresthetics, and the End of the Cold War," *Journal of Cold War Studies*, 3:1 (Winter 2001), pp. 5–35.

Eyal, Jonathan, "NATO's Enlargement: Anatomy of a Decision," *International Affairs*, 73:4 (1997), pp. 695–719.

Farrell, Henry and Gregory Flynn, "Piecing Together the Democratic Peace: The CSCE and the 'Construction' of Security in Post-Cold War Europe," *International Organization*, 53 (Summer 1999), pp. 505–36.

Fattah, Hassan M., "Iraqi Factions Seek Timetable for US Pullout," *The New York Times*, 22 November 2005 p. A1.

Fattah, Hassan M., "Arab League Plan for Hussein Exile Went Sour, Arab Leader Says," *The New York Times*, 2 November 2005 p. A12.

Fattah, Hassan M., "Conference of Arab Leaders Yields Little of Significance," *The New York Times*, 24 March 2005 p. A3.

Fawcett, Louise and Andrew Hurrell (eds.), *Regionalism in World Politics: Regional Organization and International Order* (Oxford: Oxford University Press, 1995).

Fearon, James, "Deliberation as Discussion," in Jon Elster (ed.), *Deliberative Democracy* (New York: Cambridge University Press, 1998).

Fearon, James and Alexander Wendt, "Rationalism v Constructivism: A Skeptical View," in Walter Carlsnaes, Thomas Risse-Kappen, and Beth Simmons (eds.), *Handbook of International Relations* (London: Sage Publications, 2002), pp. 52–72.

Fernández de Castro, Rafael and Carlos Rosales, "Migration Issues: Raising the Stakes in US–Latin American Relations," in Jorge I. Domínguez (ed.), *The Future of Inter-American Relations* (New York: Routledge, 2000), pp. 237–59.

Finnemore, Martha and Kathryn Sikkink, "International Norm Dynamics and Political Change," *International Organization*, 52:4 (Autumn 1998), pp. 887–917.

Fischer, Stanley, "Prospects for Regional Integration in the Middle East," in Jaime de Melo and Arvind Panagariya (eds.), *New Dimensions in Regional Integration* (New York: Cambridge University Press, 1995).

Freedom House, *Freedom in the World, 1998–99: The Annual Survey of Political Rights and Civil Liberties* (Liscataway, NJ: Transaction, 1999).

Free Trade Area of the Americas, *Eighth Ministerial Meeting, Ministerial Declaration,* Miami, 20 November 2003. www.ftaa-alca.org/Ministerials/Miami/Miami_e.asp

Freund, C. and J. McLaren, "On the Dynamics of Trade Diversion: Evidence from Four Trade Blocks." (Washington, DC: Federal Reserve Board, 1999, mimeo).

Funston, John, "Challenges Facing ASEAN in a More Complex Age," *Contemporary Southeast Asia*, 21:2 (1999), pp. 205–19.

Gamble, Andrew and Anthony Payne (eds.), *Regionalism and World Order* (Basingstoke: Macmillan, 1996).

Geipel, Gary L., "The Cost of Enlarging NATO," in James Sperling, *Two Tiers or Two Speeds? The European Security Order and the Enlargement of the European Union and NATO* (Manchester: Manchester University Press, 1999), pp. 160–178.

Gerges, Fawaz A., *The Superpowers and the Middle East: Regional and International Politics* (Boulder, CO: Westview Press, 1994).

Ghali, Boutros Boutros, "The League of Arab States and the Organization of African Unity," in Yassin El-Ayouty (ed.), *The Organization of African Unity After Ten Years: Comparative Perspectives* (New York: Praeger, 1975), pp. 47–61.

Gheciu, Alexandra, *NATO in the "New Europe": The Politics of International Socialization after the Cold War* (Stanford: Stanford University Press, 2005).

Gheciu, Alexandra, "Security Institutions as Agents of Socialization? NATO and the 'New Europe'," *International Organisation*, 59: (Fall 2005), pp. 973–1012.

Goertz, Gary, and Paul F. Diehl, *Territorial Changes and International Conflict* (New York: Routledge, 1992).

Goldberg, Ellis, "Why Isn't There More Democracy in the Middle East?" *Contention*, 5:2 (Winter 1996), pp. 141–50.

Goldgeier, James M., *Not Whether but When: The US Decision to Enlarge NATO* (Washington, DC: The Brookings Institution, 1999).

Gomaa, Ahmed, *The Foundation of the League of Arab States* (London: Longman, 1977).

Gomez Mera, Laura, "Explaining Mercosur's Survival: Strategic Sources of Argentine-Brazilian Convergence," *Journal of Latin American Studies*, 37 (2005), pp. 109–40.

Gordon, Lincoln, "Economic Regionalism Reconsidered," *World Politics*, 13:2 (1961), pp. 231–53.

Gourevitch, Peter, "Domestic Politics and International Relations," in Walter Carlsnaes, Thomas Risse-Kappen, and Beth Simmons (eds.), *Handbook of International Relations* (London: Sage Publications, 2002).

Gourevitch, Peter A., "The Governance Problem in International Relations," in David A. Lake and Robert Powell (eds.), *Strategic Choice and International Relations* (Princeton: Princeton University Press, 1999), pp. 137–64.

Gourevitch, Peter, Peter Katzenstein, and Robert Keohane, "*Memo on Persuasion.*" Prepared for a workshop on "Arguing and Bargaining in European and International Affairs" (Florence: European University Institute, April 2002).

Grenville, Stephen, "Policy Dialogue in East Asia: Principles for Success," in Gordon de Brouwer and Yunjong Wang (eds.), *Financial Governance in East Asia: Policy Dialogue, Surveillance, and Cooperation* (London and New York: RoutledgeCurzon, 2004), pp. 16–37.

Grugel, Jean and Wil Hout (eds.), *Regionalism Across the North-South Divide* (London: Routledge, 1998).

Guthrie, Stewart, "A Cognitive Theory of Religion," *Current Anthropology*, 21:2 (April 1980), pp. 181–203.

Haas, Ernst B., *Beyond the Nation State* (Stanford: Stanford University Press, 1964).

Haas, Ernst B., "International Integration: The European and the Universal Process," in *International Political Communities: An Anthology* (Garden City, NY: Doubleday, Anchor Books, 1966), pp. 93–129.

Haas, Ernst B., "Regime Decay: Conflict Management and International Organizations," *International Organization*, 37 (Spring 1983), pp. 189–256.

Haas, Ernst B., "Regionalism, Functionalism and Universal Organization," *World Politics*, 8:2 (January 1956), pp. 238–63.

Haas, Ernst B., *The Obsolescence of Regional Integration Theory* (Berkeley: Institute of International Studies, 1975).

Haas, Ernst B., "The Study of Regional Integration: Reflections on the Joys and Anguish of Pretheorising," in Richard A. Falk and Saul H. Mendlovitz (eds.), *Regional Politics and World Order* (San Francisco: Institute of Contemporary Studies, 1972), pp. 103–31.

Haas, Ernst B., *The Uniting of Europe: Political, Economic and Social Forces, 1950–1957* (Stanford: Stanford University Press, 2nd edn., 1968).

Haas, Ernst B., *Why We Still Need the United Nations: The Collective Management of International Conflict* (Berkeley: University of California, Institute of International Relations, 1986).

Haas, Ernst B., Robert L. Butterworth and Joseph S. Nye, *Conflict Management by International Organizations* (Morristown, NJ: General Learning Press, 1972).

Haas, Michael, *The Asian Way to Peace: A Story of Regional Cooperation* (New York: Praeger, 1989).

Haas, Peter (ed.), "Knowledge, Power and International Policy Coordination." A special issue of *International Organization*, 46 (Winter 1992).

Haggard, Stephan, "Regionalism in Asia and the Americas," in Edward D. Mansfield and Helen V. Milner (eds.), *The Political Economy of Regionalism* (New York: Columbia University Press, 1997).

Haggard, Stephan, *The Political Economy of the Asian Financial Crisis* (Washington, DC: Institute for International Economics, 2000).

Hansen, Roger D., "Regional Integration: Reflections on a Decade of Theoretical Efforts," *World Politics*, 21:2 (January 1969), pp. 242–71.

Hasenclever, Andreas, *Die Macht der Moral in der internationalen Politik. Militärische Interventionen westlicher Staaten in Somalia, Ruanda und Bosnien-Herzegowina* (Frankfurt: Campus, 2001).

Hasou, Tawfig Y., *The Struggle for the Arab World: Egypt's Nasser and the Arab League* (Boston: Routledge and Kegan Paul, 1985).

Hassouna, Hussein A., *The League of Arab States and Regional Disputes: A Study of Middle East Conflicts* (Dobbs Ferry, NY: Oceana Publications, Inc, 1975).

Hedstroem, Peter and Richard Swedberg (eds.), *Social Mechanisms: An Analytical Approach to Social Theory* (Cambridge: Cambridge University Press, 1998).

Heikal, Mohamed H., *Cutting the Lion's Tail: Suez Through Egyptian Eyes* (New York: Arbor House, 1987).

Hemmer, Christopher and Peter J. Katzenstein, "Why is There no NATO in Asia? Collective Identity, Regionalism, and the Origins of Multilateralism" *International Organization*, 56:3 (2002), pp. 575–607.

Hensel, Paul, "One Thing Leads to Another: Recurrent Militarized Disputes in Latin America, 1816–1986," *Journal of Peace Research*, 31:3 (1994), pp. 281–97.

Herz, Mônica, "Límites y Posibilidades de la OEA en la Esfera de la Seguridad," in Wolf Grabendorff (ed.), *La Seguridad Nacional en las Américas* (Bogotá: Fondo Editorial CEREC, 2003), pp. 133–54.

Hettne, Björn, "Globalization and the New Regionalism: The Second Great Transformation," in Björn Hettne, András Inotai, and Osvaldo Sunkel (eds.), *Globalism and the New Regionalism* (New York: St. Martin's Press, 1999), pp. 1–24.

Hettne, Björn, "The New Regionalism: Implications for Development and Peace," in Björn Hettne and András Inotai, (eds.), *The New Regionalism: Implications for Global Development and International Security* (Helsinki:

United Nations University/World Institute for Development Economics Research, 1994).

Hettne, Björn and Fredrik Söderbaum, "Theorising the Rise of Regionness," in Shaun Breslin *et al.* (eds.), *New Regionalisms in the Global Political Economy – Theories and Cases* (London and New York: Routledge, 2002), p. 33.

Hilley, John, *Malaysia: Mahathirism, Hegemony and the New Opposition* (London and New York: Zed Books, 2001).

Hirst, Mônica, "Security Policies, Democratization, and Regional Integration in the Southern Cone," in Jorge I. Domínguez (ed.), *International Security and Democracy: Latin America and the Caribbean in the Post-Cold War Era* (Pittsburgh: University of Pittsburgh Press, 1998), pp. 299–322.

Hodges, Michael, "Integration Theory," in Trevor Taylor (ed.), *Approaches and Theory in International Relations* (New York: Longman, 1978).

Hooghe, Liesbet, "Several Roads Lead To International Norms, But Few Via International Socialization: A Case Study of the European Commission," *International Organization*, 59 (Fall 2005), pp. 861–98.

Hooghe, Liesbet, *The European Commission and the Integration of Europe: Images of Governance* (Cambridge: Cambridge University Press, 2002).

Hooghe, Liesbet, "Top Commission Officials on Capitalism: An Institutionalist Understanding of Preferences," in Mark Aspinwall and Gerald Schneider (eds.), *The Rules of Integration: Institutionalist Approaches to the Study of Europe* (Manchester: Manchester University Press, 2001), pp. 152–173.

Hooghe, Liesbet and Gary Marks, "*The Neo-functionalists Were (Almost) Right: Politicization and European Integration.*" Paper presented at the ARENA Research Seminar (Oslo: ARENA Centre for European Studies, University of Oslo, 5 October 2004).

Hopkins, Anthony G., *An Economic History of West Africa*, London: Longman (1973).

Hourani, Cecil, "The Arab League in Perspective," *Middle East Journal*, 1:2 (April 1947), pp. 125–36.

Hovi, Jon, "Causal Mechanisms and the Study of International Environmental Regimes," in Arild Underdal and Oran Young (eds.), *Regime Consequences: Methodological Challenges and Research Strategies* (Boston: Kluwer Academic Publishers, 2004), pp. 71–86.

Howland, Nina Davis (ed.), *Foreign Relations of the United States: Africa, 1961–1963* (Washington, DC: Government Printing Office, 1995).

Hudson, Michael C., *Arab Politics: The Search for Legitimacy* (New Haven: Yale University Press, 1977).

Hurd, Ian, "Legitimacy and Authority in International Politics," *International Organization*, 53 (Spring 1999), pp. 379–408.

Hurrell, Andrew, "An Emerging Security Community in South America?" in Emanuel Adler and Michael Barnett (eds.), *Security Communities*, (Cambridge: Cambridge University Press, 1998), pp. 228–64.

Hurrell, Andrew, "Regionalism in Theoretical Perspective," in Louise Fawcett and Andrew Hurrell (eds.), *Regionalism in World Politics: Regional Organization and International Order* (Oxford: Oxford University Press, 1995), pp. 37–73.

Hussein, King of Jordan. *Uneasy Lies the Head* (London: Heineman, 1962).

Huth, Paul, *Extended Deterrence and the Prevention of War* (New Haven: Yale University Press, 1988).

Huth, Paul, *Standing Your Ground: Territorial Disputes and International Conflict* (Ann Arbor: University of Michigan Press, 1996).

Huth, Paul and Todd Allee, "Domestic Political Accountability and the Escalation and Settlement of International Disputes," *Journal of Conflict Resolution*, 46:6 (December 2002), pp. 754–90.

Hymans, Jacques, "Of Gauchos and Gringos: Why Argentina Never Wanted the Bomb, and Why the United States Thought it Did," *Security Studies*, 10:3 (Spring 2001), pp. 153–85.

Inter-American Development Bank, *Integration and Trade in the Americas: A Preliminary Estimate of 2003 Trade* (Washington, DC: 2003).

Inter-American Development Bank, *Integration and Trade in the Americas: A Preliminary Estimate of 2004 Trade* (Washington, DC: 2004).

International Crisis Group, "Bolivia's Rocky Road to Reforms," *Latin America Report*, 18 (3 July 2006).

Jackson, Robert H., *The Global Covenant: Human Conduct in a World of States* (Oxford: Oxford University Press, 2000).

Jackson, Robert H., "The Weight of Ideas in Decolonization: Normative Change in International Relations," in Judith Goldstein and Robert Keohane (eds.), *Ideas and Foreign Policy* (Ithaca, NY: Cornell University Press, 1993), pp. 111–38.

Jayasuriya, Kanishka, "Introduction: The Vicissitudes of Asian Regional Governance," in Kanishka Jayasuriya (ed.), *Asian Regional Governance: Crisis and Change* (London: Routledge, 2004), pp. 1–18.

Jentleson, Bruce and Dalia Kaye, "Explaining the Limits of Regional Security Cooperation: The Middle East ACRS Case." Paper presented at the Annual Conference of the American Political Science Association, Washington, DC, 28–31 August 1997.

Jentleson, Bruce and Dalia Kaye, "Symptomatic Arab Silence on Darfur," *The International Herald Tribune*, 13 August 2004, p. 6.

Job, Brian, "ASEAN Stalled: Dilemmas and Tensions Over Conflicting Norms." Paper presented to the 1999 Annual Meeting of the American Political Science Association, Atlanta, USA, 2–5 September, 1999.

Job, Brian, "Track 2 Diplomacy: Ideational Contribution to the Evolving Asian Security Order," in Muthiah Alagappa, *Asian Security Order: Instrumental and Normative Features* (Stanford: Stanford University Press, 2003), pp. 241–79.

Joergensen, Knud Erik, Mark Pollack, and Ben Rosamond (eds.), *Handbook of European Union Politics* (London: Sage Publications, 2006).

Joerges, Christian and Juergen Neyer, "From Intergovernmental Bargaining to Deliberative Political Processes: The Constitutionalisation of Comitology," *European Law Journal*, 3:3 (September 1997), pp. 273–99.

Joerges, Christian and Juergen Neyer, "Transforming Strategic Interaction into Deliberative Problem-Solving: European Comitology in the Foodstuffs Sector," *Journal of European Public Policy*, 4:4 (December 1997), pp. 609–25.

Johnson, R. W., "Guinea," in John Dunn (ed.), *West African States: Failure and Promise* (Cambridge: Cambridge University Press, 1978), p. 48.

Johnston, Alastair Iain, "Conclusions and Extensions – Toward Mid-Range Theorizing and Beyond Europe," *International Organization*, 59 (Fall 2005), pp. 1013–44.

Johnston, Alastair Iain, *Social States: China in International Institutions* (Princeton: Princeton University Press, forthcoming).

Johnston, Alastair Iain, "The Myth of the ASEAN Way? Explaining the Evolution of the ASEAN Regional Forum," in Helga Haftendorn, Robert Keohane, and Celeste Wallander (eds.), *Imperfect Unions: Security Institutions in Time and Space* (London: Oxford University Press, 1999), pp. 287–324.

Johnston, Alastair Iain, "Treating International Institutions as Social Environments," *International Studies Quarterly*, 45:4 (December 2001), pp. 487–515.

Jorgensen-Dahl, Arnfinn, *Regional Organization and Order in Southeast Asia* (London: Macmillan, 1982).

Kacowicz, Arie M., *Zones of Peace in the Third World: South America and West Africa in Comparative Perspective* (Albany, NY: State University of New York Press, 1998).

Kadi, Leila S., *Arab Summit Conferences and the Palestine Problem* (Beirut: Research Centre, Palestine Liberation Organization, 1966).

Kagan, Robert, *Of Paradise and Power. America and Europe in the New World Order* (New York: Knopf, 2003).

Kahler, Miles, "Institution-Building in the Pacific," in Andrew Mack and John Ravenhill (eds.), *Pacific Cooperation: Building Economic and Security Regimes in the Asia-Pacific Region* (St Leonards, NSW: Allen and Unwin, 1994), pp. 16–39.

Kahler, Miles, "Legalization as Strategy: The Asia-Pacific Case," *International Organization*, 54:3 (Summer 2000), pp. 549–71.

Katsumata, Hiro, "Why is ASEAN Diplomacy Changing?," *Asian Survey*, 44:2 (2004), pp. 237–54.

Katzenstein, Peter J., "Introduction: Asian Regionalism in Comparative Perspective," in Peter J. Katzenstein and Takashi Shiraishi (eds.), *Network Power: Japan and Asia* (Ithaca, NY: Cornell University Press, 1997), pp. 1–46.

Katzenstein, Peter J. (ed.), *Tamed Power: Germany in Europe* (Ithaca, NY: Cornell University Press, 1997).

Kay, Sean, *NATO and the Future of European Security* (Oxford: Rowman & Littlefield, 1998).

Kaye, Dalia, *Beyond the Handshake: Multilateral Cooperation in the Arab–Israeli Peace Process, 1991–1996* (New York: Columbia University Press, 2001).

Kaye, Dalia, "Track Two Diplomacy and Regional Security in the Middle East," *International Negotiation: A Journal of Theory and Practice*, 6:1 (2001), pp. 49–77.

Kelley, Judith, *Ethnic Politics in Europe: The Power of Norms and Incentives* (Princeton: Princeton University Press, 2004).

Keohane, Robert, *After Hegemony: Cooperation and Discord in the World Political Economy* (Princeton: Princeton University Press, 1984).

Keohane, Robert, "Governance in a Partially Globalized World," *American Political Science Review*, 95 (March 2001), pp. 1–13.

Keohane, Robert, Gary King, and Sidney Verba, *Designing Social Inquiry: Scientific Inference in Qualitative Research* (Princeton: Princeton University Press, 1994).

Kerr, Malcom H., *The Arab Cold War, 1958–1964: A Study of Ideology in Politics* (New York: Oxford University Press, 1965).

Khadduri, Majjid, "Towards an Arab Union: The League of Arab States," *American Political Science Review*, 40:1 (February 1946), pp. 90–100.

Khalil, Muhammad, *The Arab States and the Arab League: A Documentary Record*, vols.1 and 2. (Beirut: Khayat's, 1962).

Khong, Yuen Foong, "ASEAN's Post-Ministerial Conference and Regional Forum: A Convergence of Post-Cold War Security Strategies," in Peter Gourevitch, Takashi Inoguchi, and Courtney Purrington (eds.), *United States-Japan Relations and International Institutions After the Cold War* (La Jolla: University of California Graduate School of International Relations and Pacific Studies, 1995), pp. 37–58.

Khong, Yuen Foong, "Coping with Strategic Uncertainty: The Role of Institutions and Soft Balancing in Southeast Asia's Post-Cold War Strategy," in Allen Carlson, Peter Katzenstein, and J. J. Suh (eds.), *Rethinking Security in East Asia: Identity, Power, and Efficiency* (Stanford: Stanford University Press, 2004), pp. 172–208.

Khong, Yuen Foong, "Making Bricks without Straw in the Asia Pacific?" *The Pacific Review*, 10:2 (1997), pp. 289–300.

Kindleberger, Charles P., "Dominance and Leadership in the International Economy. Exploitation, Public Goods, and Free Rides," *International Studies Quarterly*, 25:2 (1981), pp. 242–54.

Koh, Harold Hongju, "Review Essay: Why Do Nations Obey International Law?," *The Yale Law Journal*, 106 (June 1997), pp. 2599–659.

Korany, Baghat, "The Dialectics of Inter-Arab Relations, 1967–87," in Yehuda Lukacs and Abdalla Battah (eds.), *The Arab-Israeli Conflict: Two Decades of Change* (Boulder, CO: Westview Press, 1988).

Korany, Baghat and Ali Hillal Dessouki, "The Global System and Arab Foreign Policies, in B. Korany and A. Dessouki (eds.), *The Foreign Policies of the Arab States*: *The Challenge of Change* (Boulder, CO: Westview, 1991), pp. 19–40.

Koremenos, Barbara, Charles Lipson, and Duncan Snidal (eds.), "Rational Design: Looking Back to Move Forward," *International Organization*, 55:4 (Autumn 2001), pp. 1051–82.

Koremenos, Barbara, Charles Lipson, and Duncan Snidal, *The Rational Design of International Institutions* (Cambridge: Cambridge University Press, 2004).

Koremenos, Barbara, Charles Lipson, and Duncan Snidal, "The Rational Design of International Institutions," *International Organization*, 55:4 (Autumn 2001), pp. 761–800.

Kurth, James, "The Pacific Basin versus the Atlantic Alliance: Two Paradigms of International Relations," *The Annals of the American Academy of Political and Social Science*, 505 (September 1989), pp. 34–45.

Kydd, Andrew, "Trust Building, Trust Breaking: The Dilemma of NATO Enlargement," *International Organization*, 55:4 (2001), pp. 801–828.

Laffan, Brigid, "The European Union: A Distinctive Model of Internationalization," *Journal of European Public Policy*, 5:2 (1998), pp. 235–53.

Lagos, Marta, "Public Opinion," in Jorge I. Domínguez and Michael Shifter (eds.), *Constructing Democratic Governance in Latin America*, 2nd edn. (Baltimore: Johns Hopkins University Press, 2003), pp. 137–61.

Lawson, Fred H., "Theories of Integration in a New Context: The Gulf Cooperation Council," in Kenneth P. Thomas and Mary Ann Tefreault (eds.), *Racing to Regionalize: Democracy, Capitalism, and Regional Political Economy* (Boulder, CO: Lynne Rienner, 1999).

Lebow, Richard Ned and Janice Gross Stein, "Deterrence: The Elusive Dependent Variable," *World Politics* 42:3 (April 1990), pp. 336–69.

Leifer, Michael, *ASEAN and the Security of Southeast Asia* (London: Routledge, 1989).

Leifer, Michael, *The ASEAN Regional Forum: Extending ASEAN's Model of Regional Security*. IISS Adelphi Paper 302 (Oxford: Oxford University Press, 1996).

Lerman, Eran, "A Revolution Prefigured: Foreign Policy Orientation in the Postwar Years," in Shimon Shamir (ed.), *Egypt: From Monarchy to Republic* (Boulder, CO: Westview Press, 1995), pp. 291–2.

Lewis, Jeffery, "Institutional Environments and Everyday Decision Making: Rationalist or Constructivist?" *Comparative Political Studies*, 36:1/2 (February/March 2003), pp. 97–124.

Lewis, Jeffery, "The Janus Face of Brussels: Socialization and Everyday Decision-Making in the European Union," *International Organization*, 59 (Fall 2005), pp. 937–71.

Lim, Robyn, "The ASEAN Regional Forum: Building on Sand," *Contemporary Southeast Asia*, 20:2 (1998), pp. 115–36.

Lindberg, Leon N., "Decision Making and Integration in the European Community," in *International Political Communities: An Anthology* (Garden City, NY: Anchor Books, 1966).

Lindberg, Leon N. and Stuart A. Scheingold, *Regional Integration: Theory and Research* (Cambridge, MA: Harvard University Press, 1971).

Lipson, Charles, *Standing Guard: Protecting Foreign Capital in the Nineteenth and Twentieth Centuries* (Berkeley: University of California Press, 1985).

Lipson, Charles, "Why Are Some International Agreements Informal?" *International Organisation*, 45:4 (1992), pp. 495–538.

Little, T. R., "The Arab League: A Reassessment," *The Middle East Journal*, 10 (Spring 1957), pp. 138–50.

Lizano, Eduardo, and José M. Salazar-Xirinachs, "The Central American Common Market and Hemispheric Free Trade," in Ana Julia Jatar and Sidney Weintraub (eds.), *Integrating the Hemisphere: Perspective from Latin America and the Caribbean* (Washington, DC: Inter-American Dialogue, 1997), pp. 111–35.

Lynch, Marc, *State Interests and Public Spheres: The International Politics of Jordan's Identity* (New York: Columbia University Press, 1999).

Macdonald, Robert, *The League of Arab States: A Study in the Dynamics of Regional Organization* (Princeton: Princeton University Press, 1965).

MacFarquhar, Neil, "Arab Summit Meeting Collapses Over Reforms," *The New York Times* 28 March 2004, p. 10.

Maddy-Weitzman, Bruce, *The Crystallization of the Arab States System* (Syracuse: Syracuse University Press, 1993).

Magnette, Paul, "Coping with Constitutional Incompatibilities: Bargains and Rhetoric in the Convention on the Future of Europe." Paper presented at the ARENA Research Seminar (Oslo: ARENA Centre for European Studies, 2 March 2004).

Maksoud, Clovis, "Diminished Sovereignty, Enhanced Sovereignty: United Nations-Arab League Relations at 50," *The Middle East Journal*, 49:4 (Autumn 1995), pp. 582–94.

Malamud, Andrés, "Presidential Diplomacy and the Institutional Underpinnings of MERCOSUR: An Empirical Examination," *Latin American Research Review*, 40:1 (February 2005), pp. 138–64.

Mansfield, Edward D. and Helen D. Milner (eds.), *The Political Economy of Regionalism* (New York: Columbia University Press, 1997).

Mansfield, Edward D. and Jack Snyder, "Democratic Transitions, Institutional Strength, and War," *International Organization*, 56:2 (Spring 2002), pp. 297–337.

Mansfield, Edward D. and Jon C. Pevehouse, "Democratization and International Organizations," *International Organization*, 60:1 (January 2006), pp. 137–67.

Manzetti, Luigi, "The Political Economy of MERCOSUR," *Journal of Inter-American Studies and World Affairs*, 35:4 (Winter 1993–1994), pp. 101–141.

March, James and Herbert Simon, "Decision-Making Theory," in O. Grusky and G. A. Miller (eds.), *The Sociology of Organizations: Basic Studies*, 2nd edn. (New York: The Free Press, 1981), pp. 93–102.

Mares, David R., "Boundary disputes in the western Hemisphere," *Pensamiento Propio*, 14 (July–December 2001), pp. 31–59.

Mares, David R., *Violent Peace: Militarized Interstate Bargaining in Latin America* (New York: Columbia University Press, 2001).

Mares, David R. and Francisco Rojas Aravena, *The United States and Chile: Coming in From the Cold* (New York: Routledge, 2001).

Martin, Lisa L., "The Rational State Choice of Multilateralism," in John Gerard Ruggie (ed.), *Multilateralism Matters: The Theory and Praxis of an Institutional Form* (New York: Columbia University Press, 1993), pp. 91–121.

Martin, Lisa and Beth Simmons, "Theories and Empirical Studies of International Institutions," *International Organization*, 52 (Autumn 1998), pp. 729–57.

Mattli, Walter, *The Logic of Regional Integration: Europe and Beyond* (Cambridge: Cambridge University Press, 1999).

Maull, Hans, Gerald Segal and Josef Wanandi (eds.), *Europe and the Asia Pacific* (London: Routledge, 1998).

McDougal, Derek, "Regional Institutions and Security: Implications of the 1999 East Timor Lipson Crisis," in Andrew Tan and Kenneth Boutin (eds.),

Non-Traditional Security Issues in Southeast Asia (Singapore: Institute of Defence and Strategic Studies, 2001), pp. 166–89.

McNamara, Kathleen, *The Currency of Ideas: Monetary Politics in the European Union* (Ithaca, NY: Cornell University Press, 1998).

McSherry, J. Patrice, "Operation Condor: Clandestine Inter-American System," *Social Justice*, 26 (Winter 1999), pp. 144–74.

Means, Gordon, "ASEAN Policy Responses to North American and European Trading Agreements," in Amitav Acharya and Richard Stubbs (eds.), *New Challenges for ASEAN: Emerging Policy Issues* (Vancouver: University of British Columbia Press, 1995), pp. 146–81.

Mecham, J. Lloyd, *A Survey of United States-Latin American Relations* (Boston: Houghton Mifflin, 1965).

Meyer, John and David Strang, "Institutional Conditions for Diffusion," *Theory and Society*, 22:4 (August 1993), pp. 487–511.

Mitchell, Christopher, "The Future of Migration as an Issue in Inter-American Relations," in Jorge I. Domínguez (ed.), *The Future of Inter-American Relations* (New York: Routledge, 2000), pp. 217–36.

Mittelman, James H., *The Globalization Syndrome: Transformation and Resistance* (Princeton: Princeton University Press, 2000).

Mora, Frank O., "Paraguay y el Sistema Interamericano: Del Autoritarismo y la Parálisis a la Democracia y la Aplicación de la Resolución 1080," in Arlene Tickner (ed.), *Sistema Interamericano y Democracia: Antecedentes Históricos y Tendencias Futuras* (Bogotá: Ediciones Uniandes, 2000), pp. 235–57.

Moravcsik, Andrew, "Constructivism and European Integration: A Critique," in Thomas Christiansen, Knud Erik Joergensen, and Antje Wiener (eds.), *The Social Construction of Europe* (London: Sage Publications, 2001), pp. 176–88.

Moravcsik, Andrew, "Explaining International Human Rights Regimes: Liberal Theory and Western Europe," *European Journal of International Relations*, 1:2 (June 1995), pp. 157–89.

Moravcsik, Andrew, *The Choice for Europe: Social Purpose and State Power from Messina to Maastricht* (Ithaca, NY: Cornell University Press, 1998).

Moravcsik, Andrew, "The Origins of Human Rights Regimes: Democratic Delegation in Postwar Europe," *International Organization*, 54 (Spring 2000), pp. 217–52.

Mufti, Malik, *Sovereign Creations: Pan-Arabism and Political Order in Syria and Iraq* (Ithaca, NY: Cornell University Press, 1996), pp. 51–2.

Munro, Dana G., *Intervention and Dollar Diplomacy in the Caribbean, 1900–1921* (Princeton: Princeton University Press, 1964).

Nesadurai, Helen E. S., *Globalisation, Domestic Politics and Regionalism: The ASEAN Free Trade Area* (London and New York: Routledge, 2003).

Nesadurai, Helen E. S., "Networking their Way to Cooperation: Finance Ministers and Central Bankers in East Asian Financial Cooperation," *Project on Developing Country Finance Networks* (Global Economic Governance Programme, Oxford University, March 2006).

Noble, Paul C., "The Arab System: Pressures, Constraints and Opportunities," in Bahgat Korany and Ali E. Hillal Dessouki (eds.), *The Foreign Policies of Arab States: The Challenge of Change* (Boulder, CO: Westview, 1991), pp. 49–102.

Nye, Joseph S., "Central American Regional Integration", in Nye (ed.), *International Regionalism* (Boston: Little, Brown, 1968).

Nye, Joseph S., *International Regionalism* (Boston: Little Brown, 1968).

Nye, Joseph S., "Neorealism and Neoliberalism," *World Politics*, 40:2 (January 1988), pp. 235–51.

Nye, Joseph S., *Peace in Parts: Integration and Conflict in Regional Organization* (Lanham: University Press of America, 1987).

Okolo, Julius Emeka, "Integrative and Cooperative Regionalism: The Economic Community of West African States," *International Organization*, 39:1 (Winter 1985), pp. 121–53.

Olsen, Johan P., "The Many Faces of Europeanization," *Journal of Common Market Studies*, 40:5 (December 2002), pp. 921–52.

Olson, Mancur, *The Logic of Collective Action: Public Goods and the Theory of Groups* (Cambridge, MA: Harvard University Press, 1965).

O'Neill, Barry, *Honor, Symbols, and War* (Ann Arbor: University of Michigan Press, 1999).

Orbell, John M., Robyn M. Dawes, and Alphons van de Kragt, "Explaining Discussion-Induced Cooperation," *Journal of Personality and Social Psychology*, 54:5 (1988), pp. 811–19.

Orozco, Manuel, "Boundary Disputes in Central America: Past Trends and Present Developments," *Pensamiento Propio*, 14 (July–December 2001), pp. 99–134.

Owen, Roger and Sevket Pamuk, *A History of Middle East Economies in the Twentieth Century* (Cambridge, MA: Harvard University Press, 1999).

Padelford, Norman J., "Regional Organizations and the United Nations," *International Organization*, 8:2 (1954), pp. 203–16.

Palmer, N. D., *The New Regionalism in Asia and the Pacific* (Lexington, MA: Lexington Books, 1991).

Parkinson, Fred, "Latin America," in Robert H. Jackson and Alan James (eds.), *States in a Changing World: A Contemporary Analysis* (Oxford: Clarendon Press, 1993), pp. 240–61.

Payne, Rodger, "Persuasion, Frames, and Norm Construction," *European Journal of International Relations*, 7:1 (March 2001), pp. 37–61.

Pena, Celina, and Ricardo Rozemberg, "MERCOSUR: A Different Approach to Institutional Development," FOCAL FPP-05-06 (Ottawa: 2006), pp. 1–14.

Peña, Félix, *Concertación de Intereses. Efectividad de las Reglas del Juego y Calidad Institucional en el MERCOSUR*, www.fundacionbankboston.org.ar

Perloff, Richard, *The Dynamics of Persuasion* (Hillsdale, NJ: Erlbaum Associates, 1993).

Peters, Joel, *Building Bridges: The Arab-Israeli Multilateral Talks* (London: Royal Institute of International Affairs, 1994).

Peters, Joel, *Pathways to Peace: The Multilateral Arab-Israeli Peace Talks* (London: Royal Institute of International Affairs, 1996).

Pevehouse, Jon C., "Democratization, Credible Commitments and International Organizations," in Daniel Drezner (ed.), *Locating the Proper Authorities: The Interaction of Domestic and International Institutions* (Ann Arbor: University of Michigan Press, 2002).

Pevehouse, Jon C., *Democracy From Above: Regional Organizations and Democratization* (Cambridge: Cambridge University Press, 2005).

Phillips, Nicola, "Moulding Economic Governance in the Americas: US Power and the New Regional Political Economy," in Michèle Rioux (ed.), *Building the Americas* (Bruyland, 2005).

Phillips, Nicola, *The Southern Cone Model: The Political Economy of Regional Capitalist Development in Latin America* (London: Routledge, 2004).

Pierson, Paul, "The Path to European Integration – A Historical Institutionalist Analysis," *Comparative Political Studies*, 29:2 (April 1996), pp. 123–63.

Pion-Berlin, David. "Will Soldiers Follow? Economic Integration and Regional Security in the Southern Cone," *Journal of Interamerican Studies and World Affairs*, 42:1 (Spring 2000), pp. 43–69.

Pipes, Daniel, *Greater Syria: History of an Ambition* (New York: Oxford University Press, 1990).

Plummer, Michael, "ASEAN and Institutional Nesting in the Asia-Pacific: Leading from Behind in APEC," in Vinod K. Aggarwal and Charles E. Morrison (eds.), *Asia-Pacific Crossroads: Regime Creation and the Future of APEC* (London: Macmillan, 1998), pp. 279–314.

Podeh, Elie, *The Quest for Hegemony in the Arab World: The Struggle over the Baghdad Pact* (New York: E.J. Brill, 1995).

Poku, Nana, *Regionalization and Security in Southern Africa* (Basingstoke: Palgrave, 2001).

Porath, Yehoshua, *In Search of Arab Unity, 1930–1945* (London: Cass, 1986).

Poynton, Sir H., "The Currency System in West Africa: Memorandum," reprinted in Richard Rathbone (ed.), *British Documents on the End of Empire: Ghana, series B,* vol.1 (London: Her Majesty's Stationary Office, 1992), p. 56.

Premdas, Ralph, "Identity and Secession in a Small Island State: Nevis," *Canadian Review of Studies in Nationalism*, 28 (2001), pp. 27–44.

Puchala, Donald J., "The Integration Theorists and the Study of International Relations," in Charles Kegley and Eugene Wittkopf (eds.), *The Global Agenda: Issues and Perspectives* (New York: Random House, 1984).

Pundik, Ron, *The Struggle for Sovereignty: Relations Between Great Britain and Jordan, 1946–1951* (Oxford: Basil Blackwell, 1994).

Qu Geping, "Guowuyuan huanjing baohu weiyuanhui fu zhuren, guojia huanjing baohu ju juzhang Qu Geping zai guowuyuan huanjing baohu weiyuanhui di shi jiu ci huiyi shang de jianghua," [State Council environmental protection committee deputy director, National Environmental Protection Agency director, Qu Geping's speech to the 19th meeting of the State Council environmental protection committee], December 18, 1990, in State Council Environmental Protection Committee Secretariat (eds.), *Guowuyuan huanjing baohu weiyuanhui wenjian huibian* [Collected documents of the State Council environmental protection committee] (vol.2, Beijing), p. 195.

Rabinovich, Itamar, *The Road Not Taken: Early Arab-Israeli Negotiations* (New York: Oxford University Press, 1991).

Ravenhill, John, "Economic Cooperation in Southeast Asia," *Asian Survey*, 35:9 (1995), pp. 850–66.

Ravenhill, John, *APEC and the Construction of Pacific Rim Regionalism* (Cambridge: Cambridge University Press, 2001).

Reus-Smit, Christian, "The Constitutional Structure of International Society and the Nature of Fundamental Institutions," *International Organization*, 51:4 (1997), pp. 555–89.

Richards, A. and J. Waterbury, *A Political Economy of the Middle East – State, Class, and Economic Development* (Boulder: Westview, 1990).

Riker, William, *The Art of Political Manipulation* (New Haven, CT: Yale University Press, 1986).

Riker, William, *The Strategy of Rhetoric* (New Haven, CT: Yale University Press, 1996).

Rimmer, Douglas, *The Economies of West Africa* (New York: St. Martin's Press, 1984).

Risse-Kappen, Thomas, *Cooperation Among Democracies: The European Influence on US Foreign Policy* (Princeton: Princeton University Press, 1995).

Risse-Kappen, Thomas, "Let's Argue! Communicative Action in World Politics," *International Organization*, 54, (Winter 2000), pp. 1–39.

Risse-Kappen, Thomas and Matthias Maier (eds.), *Europeanization, Collective Identities, and Public Discourses. Draft Final Report submitted to the European Commission* (Florence: European University Institute and Robert Schuman Centre for Advanced Studies, 2003).

Rochester, J. Martin, "The Rise and Fall of International Organization as a Field of Study," *International Organization*, 40:4 (1986), pp. 777–814.

Rodan, Garry, "Reconstructing Divisions of Labour: Singapore's New Regional Emphasis," in R. Higgott, R. Leaver, and J. Ravenhill (eds.), *Pacific Economic Relations in the 1990s: Cooperation or Conflict?* (Boulder, CO: Lynne Rienner, 1993), pp. 223–49.

Rodríguez, Ennio "Central America: Common Market, Trade Liberalization, and Trade Agreements", in Roberto Bouzas and Jaime Ross (eds.), *Economic Integration in the Western Hemisphere* (Notre Dame: University of Notre Dame Press, 1994), pp. 146–70.

Rogowski, Ronald, "Institutions as Constraints on Strategic Choice," in David Lake and Robert Powell (eds.), *Strategic Choice and International Relations* (Princeton: Princeton University Press, 1999), pp. 115–36.

Rojas Aravena, Francisco. "Transition and Civil-Military Relations in Chile: Contributions in a New International Framework", in Jorge I. Domínguez (ed.), *International Security and Democracy: Latin America and the Caribbean in the Post-Cold War Era* (Pittsburgh: University of Pittsburgh Press, 1998), pp. 80–101.

Rojas Aravena, Francisco, "Building a Strategic Alliance: The Case of Chile and Argentina," *Pensamiento Propio*, 14 (July-December 2002), pp. 61–97.

Ronning, C. Neale, *Law and Politics in Inter-American Diplomacy* (New York: Wiley, 1963).

Rosenberg, Christopher P. "Fiscal Policy Coordination in the WAEMU after the Devaluation," International Monetary Fund Working Paper, WP/95/25 (February, 1995).

Rousseau, Jean-Jacques, *The Social Contract*, trans. G. D. H. Cole (New York: E.P. Dutton, 1950).

Ruggie, John G., "Multilateralism: The Anatomy of an Institution," in John G. Ruggie (ed.), *Multilateralism Matters* (New York: Columbia University Press, 1993), pp. 3–50.

Sachs, Susan, "Internal Rift Dooms Arab League Plan to Help Avert a War by Pressing Iraq," *The New York Times*, 14 March 2003, p. A11.

Sadowski, Yahya M., *Scuds or Butter? The Political Economy of Arms Control in the Middle East* (Washington, DC: Brookings Institution, 1993).

Safran, Nadav, *Saudi Arabia: The Ceaseless Quest for Security* (Ithaca, NY: Cornell University Press, 1988).

Salamé, Ghassan, "Integration in the Arab World: The Institutional Framework," in G. Luciani and G. Salamé (eds.), *The Politics of Arab Integration* (New York: Croom Helm, 1988), pp. 256–79.

Salamé, Ghassan, "Inter-Arab Politics: The Return to Geography," in W. Quandt (ed.), *The Middle East: Ten Years After Camp David* (Washington, DC: Brookings Institution, 1988), pp. 319–56.

Sayigh, Yezid, *Confronting the 1990s: Security in the Developing Countries*, Adelphi Papers, 251 (London: International Institute for Strategic Studies, 1990).

Schimmelfennig, Frank, "International Socialization in the New Europe: Rational Action in an Institutional Environment," *European Journal of International Relations*, 6:1 (March 2000), pp. 109–39.

Schimmelfennig, Frank, "NATO Enlargement: A Constructivist Explanation," *Security Studies*, 8:2 (1999), pp. 198–234.

Schimmelfennig, Frank, "Strategic Calculation and International Socialization: Membership Incentives, Party Constellations, and Sustained Compliance in Central and Eastern Europe," *International Organization*, 59 (Fall 2005), pp. 827–60.

Schimmelfennig, Frank, "The Community Trap: Liberal Norms, Rhetorical Action, and the Eastern Enlargement of the European Union," *International Organization*, 55 (Winter 2001), pp. 47–80.

Schimmelfennig, Frank, *The EU, NATO, and the Integration of Europe: Rules and Rhetoric* (Cambridge: Cambridge University Press, 2003).

Scott, James, *Weapons of the Weak: Everyday Forms of Peasant Resistance* (New Haven: Yale University Press, 1985).

Seale, Patrick, *The Struggle for Syria: A Study of Post-War Arab Politics, 1945–1958*, new edn., with a foreword by Albert Hourani (London: I.B. Tauris, 1986).

Sela, Avraham, *The Decline of the Arab-Israeli Conflict: Middle Eastern Politics and the Quest for Regional Order* (Albany: SUNY Press, 1997).

Shaw, Carolyn M., *Cooperation, Conflict, and Consensus in the Organization of American States* (New York: Palgrave MacMillan, 2004).

Shlaim, Avi, *Collusion Across the Jordan: King Abdullah, the Zionist Movement, and the Partition of Palestine* (New York: Columbia University Press, 1988), pp. 359–60.

Sicker, Martin, *Between Hashemites and Zionists: The Struggle for Palestine, 1908–1988* (New York: Holmes and Meier, 1989).

Snyder, Glenn H., "The Security Dilemma in Alliance Politics," *World Politics*, 36:4 (1984), pp. 461–95.

Snyder, Jack, *Myths of Empire: Domestic Politics and International Ambition* (Ithaca, NY: Cornell University Press, 1991).

Söderbaum, Fredrik and Timothy M. Shaw (eds.), *Theories of New Regionalism: A Palgrave Reader* (New York: Palgrave Macmillan, 2003).

Solingen, Etel, "Mapping Internationalization: Domestic and Regional impacts," *International Studies Quarterly*, 45:4 (2001), pp. 517–56.

Solingen, Etel, *Regional Orders at Century's Dawn: Global and Domestic Influences on Grand Strategy* (Princeton: Princeton University Press, 1998).

Solingen, Etel, "The Multilateral Arab-Israeli Negotiations: Genesis, Institutionalization, Pause, Future," *Journal of Peace Research*, 37:2 (March 2000), pp. 167–87.

Solingen, Etel, "The Triple Logic of the European-Mediterranean Partnership: Hindsight and International Politics," *International Politics*, 40:2 (June 2003), pp. 179–94.

Solingen, Etel "Pax Asiatica versus Belli Levantini: The Foundations of War and Peace in East Asia and the Middle East," *American Political Science Review* 101:4 (November, 2007).

Solís, Luis Guillermo, "Collective Mediations in the Caribbean Basin," in Carl Kaysen, Robert Pastor, and Laura Reed (eds.), *Collective Responses to Regional Problems: The Case of Latin America and the Caribbean* (Cambridge, MA: American Academy of Arts and Sciences, 1994), pp. 95–125.

Sotomayor Velázquez, Arturo C., "Civil-Military Affairs and Security Institutions in the Southern Cone: The Sources of Argentine-Brazilian nuclear cooperation," *Latin American Politics and Society* 46:4 (Winter 2004), pp. 29–60.

St. John, Ronald Bruce, "Ecuador-Peru Endgame," *Boundary and Security Bulletin*, 6:4 (Winter 1998–1999), pp. 79–85.

St. John, Ronald Bruce, "Chile, Peru and the Treaty of 1929: The Final Settlement," *Boundary and Security Bulletin*, 8:1 (Spring 2000), pp. 91– 100.

Stasvage, David, "The CFA Franc Zone and Fiscal Discipline," *Journal of African Economies*, 6 (1996), p. 134.

Stevens, Georgiana, "Arab Neutralism and Bandung," *Middle East Journal*, 11:2 (1957), pp. 139–52.

Stryker, Sheldon, *Symbolic Interactionism: A Social Structural Perspective* (Reading, MA: Benjamin-Cummings, 1980).

Stubbs, Richard, "Performance Legitimacy and Soft Authoritarianism," in Amitav Acharya, Michel Frolic, and Richard Stubbs (eds.), *Democracy, Human Rights and Civil Society in Southeast Asia* (Toronto: Joint Centre for Asia-Pacific Studies, York University, 2001), pp. 37–54.

Syed Hamid Albar, *Keynote Speech at the 5th Workshop on an ASEAN Regional Mechanism on Human Rights*, Kuala Lumpur, 29 June 2006.

Takirambudde, Peter, "The Rival Strategies of SADC and PTA/COMESA in Southern Africa," in Daniel C. Bach (ed.), *Regionalisation in Africa: Integration and Disintegration* (Oxford: James Currey, 1999).

Tan, See Seng *et al.*, *A New Agenda for the ASEAN Regional Forum*, Monograph, 4 (Singapore: Institute of Defense and Strategic Studies, 2002).

Taylor, Alan B., *The Arab Balance of Power* (Syracuse: Syracuse University Press, 1982).

Tilly, Charles, "Reflections on the History of European State-Making," in Charles Tilly (ed.), *The Formation of National States in Western Europe* (Princeton: Princeton University Press, 1975).

Tongzon, Jose, "Role of AFTA in an ASEAN Economic Community," in Denis Hew (ed.), *Roadmap to an ASEAN Economic Community* (Singapore: Institute of Southeast Asian Studies, 2005), pp. 127–47.

Torrey, Gordon H., *Syrian Politics and the Military, 1945–1958* (Columbus: Ohio State University Press, 1964).

Tripp, Charles, "Regional Organizations in the Arab Middle East," in Louise Fawcett and Andrew Hurrell (eds.), *Regionalism in World Politics: Regional Organization and International Order* (New York: Oxford University Press, 1995), pp. 283–308.

US–ASEAN Business Council, *Special Report Update on AFTA and Regional Economic Integration* (PricewaterhouseCoopers, August 2000).

Vaky, Viron P. and Heraldo Muñoz, *The Future of the Organization of American States* (New York: Twentieth Century Fund, 1993).

Valenzuela, Arturo, "Paraguay: The Coup That Didn't Happen," *Journal of Democracy*, 8:1 (January 1997), pp. 43–55.

Van Evera, Stephen, "Hypotheses on Nationalism and War," *International Security*, 18:4 (Spring 1994), pp. 5–39.

Van Oudenaren, John, "The Limits of Conditionality: Nuclear Reactor Safety in Central and Eastern Europe, 1991–2001," *International Politics*, 38 (December 2001).

Verdery, Katherine, "Whither 'Nation' and 'Nationalism'?" *Daedalus*, 122:3 (1993), p. 40.

Wallander, Celeste A., "Institutional Assets and Adaptability: NATO After the Cold War," *International Organization*, 54:4 (2000), pp. 705– 35.

Wallander, Celeste A. and Robert Keohane, "Risk, Threat, and Security Institutions," in Helga Haftendorn, Robert Keohane, and Celeste A. Wallander, *Imperfect Unions: Security Institutions over Time and Space* (Oxford: Oxford University Press, 1999), pp. 21–47.

Walt, Stephen M., *The Origins of Alliances* (Ithaca, NY: Cornell University Press, 1987).

Waltz, Kenneth N., "The Emerging Structure of International Politics," *International Security*, 18:2 (1993), pp. 44–79.

Weber, Steven, "Origins of the European Bank for Reconstruction and Development," *International Organization*, 48:1 (1994), pp. 1–38.

Weber, Steven, "Shaping the Postwar Balance of Power: Multilateralism in NATO," in John Gerard Ruggie (ed.), *Multilateralism Matters. The Theory and Praxis of an Institutional Form* (New York: Columbia University Press, 1993), pp. 233–92.

Welch Jr., Claude E., *Dream of Unity: Pan-Africanism and Political Unification in West Africa* (Ithaca, NY: Cornell University Press, 1966).

Wendt, Alexander, *Social Theory of International Politics* (Cambridge: Cambridge University Press 1999).

Wendt, Alexander, "Driving with the Rearview Mirror: On the Rational Science of Institutional Design," in Barbara Koremenos, Charles Lipson, and Duncan Snidal (eds.), *The Rational Design of International Institutions* (Cambridge: Cambridge University Press, 2004), pp. 1019–49.

Wessels, Wolfgang, "Comitology: Fusion in Action – Politico-Administrative Trends in the EU System," *Journal of European Public Policy*, 5 (1998), pp. 209–34.

Whitaker, Arthur P, *The Western Hemisphere Idea: Its Rise and Decline* (Ithaca, NY: Cornell University Press, 1954).

Whitehead, Laurence, "International Aspects of Democratization," in Guillermo O'Donnell, Philippe Schmitter, and Laurence Whitehead (eds.), *Transitions from Authoritarian Rule: Comparative Perspectives* (Baltimore: Johns Hopkins University Press, 1986), pp. 3–47.

Whitfield, Teresa, "The Role of the United Nations in El Salvador and Guatemala: A Preliminary Comparison," in Cynthia Aronson (ed.), *Comparative Peace Processes in Latin America* (Stanford: Stanford University Press, 1999), pp. 257–90.

Wilcox, Francis W., "Regionalism and the United Nations," *International Organization*, 19:3 (1965), pp. 789–811.

Williams, Rocky, "From Collective Security to Peace-building? The Challenges of Managing Regional Security in Southern Africa," in Christopher Clapham *et al.* (eds.), *Regional Integration in Southern Africa: Comparative International Perspectives* (Johannesburg: South African Institute of International Affairs, 2001).

Wilson, Mary C., *King Abdullah, Britain, and the Making of Jordan* (New York: Cambridge University Press, 1987).

Wolfers, Arnold, *Discord and Collaboration: Essays on International Politics* (Baltimore: Johns Hopkins University Press, 1962).

Worth, Robert F., "Leader Says Other Arabs are Insensitive to Iraq's Plight," *The New York Times*, 6 September 2005, p. A9.

Yalem, Ronald J., "Regional Security Communities," in George W. Keeton and George Scharzenberger (eds.), *The Year Book of International Affairs 1979* (London: Stevens and Sons, 1979).

Yoshimatsu, Hidetaka, "Collective Action and Regional Integration in ASEAN," *CSGR Working Paper No. 198/06* (Centre for the Study of Globalisation and Regionalisation, University of Warwick, March 2006).

Zacher, Mark W., *International Conflicts and Collective Security, 1946–77: The United Nations, Organization of American States, Organization of African Unity, and Arab League* (New York: Praeger, 1979).

Zacher, Mark W., "The Territorial Integrity Norm: International Boundaries and the Use of Force," *International Organization*, 55:2 (Spring 2001), pp. 215–50.

Zaid Ibrahim, "ASEAN Can Do More For Change in Myanmar," *New Straits Times*, 31 July 2006.

Zimbardo, Philip and Michael Leippe, *The Psychology of Attitude Change and Social Influence* (New York: McGraw Hill, 1991).

Zürn, Michael and Jeffrey T. Checkel, "Getting Socialized to Build Bridges: Constructivism and Rationalism, Europe and the Nation State," *International Organization*, 59 (Fall 2005), pp. 1045–79.

Index